Library Wars

10

Love & War

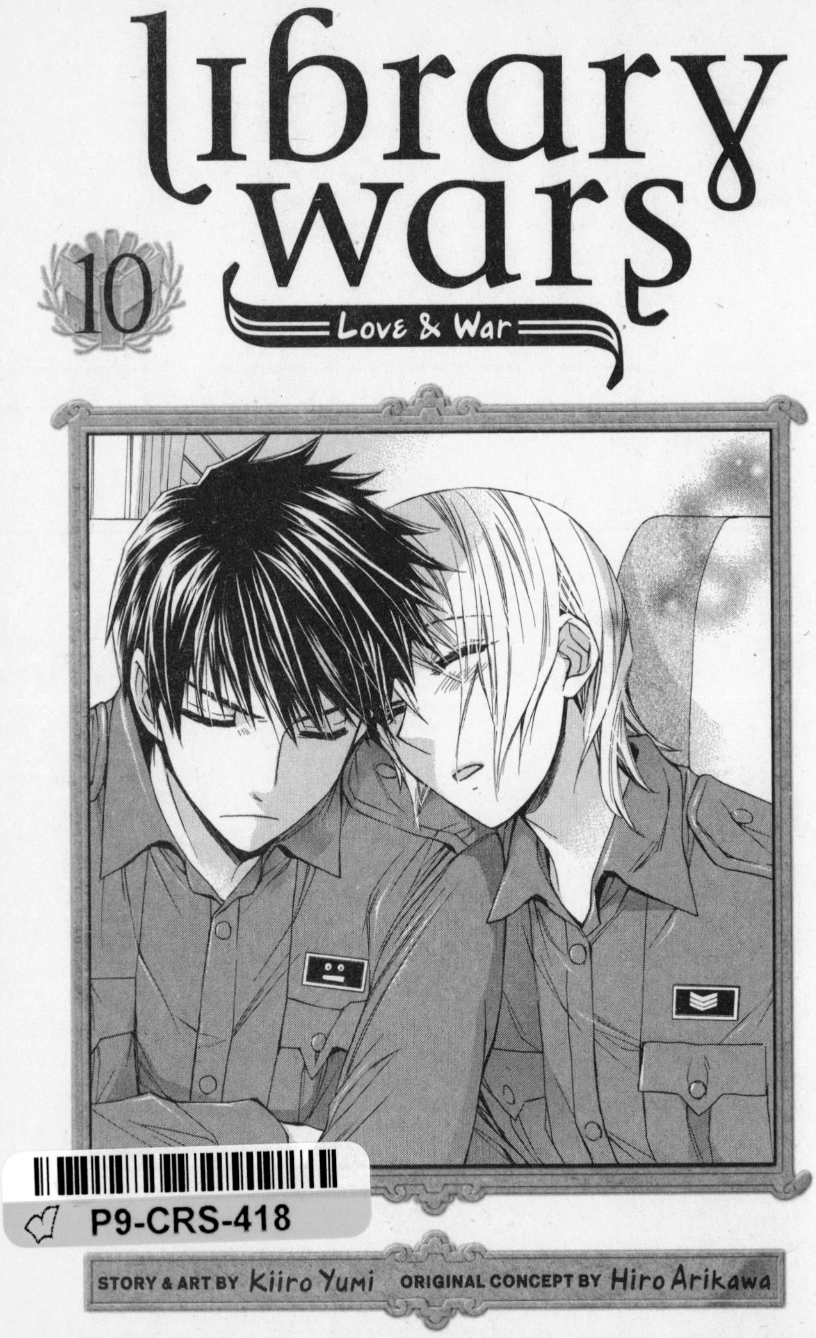

STORY & ART BY Kiiro Yumi ORIGINAL CONCEPT BY Hiro Arikawa

Library Wars

Love & War

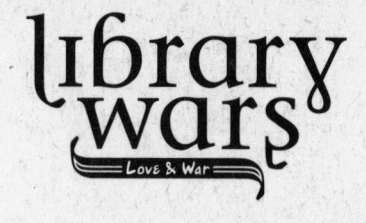

Contents

The Library Freedom Act

Libraries have the freedom to acquire their collections.

Libraries have the freedom to circulate
materials in their collections.

Libraries guarantee the privacy of their patrons.

Libraries oppose any type of censorship.

When libraries are imperiled,
librarians will join together
to secure their freedom.

library wars

Love & War

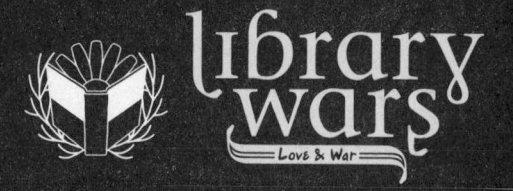

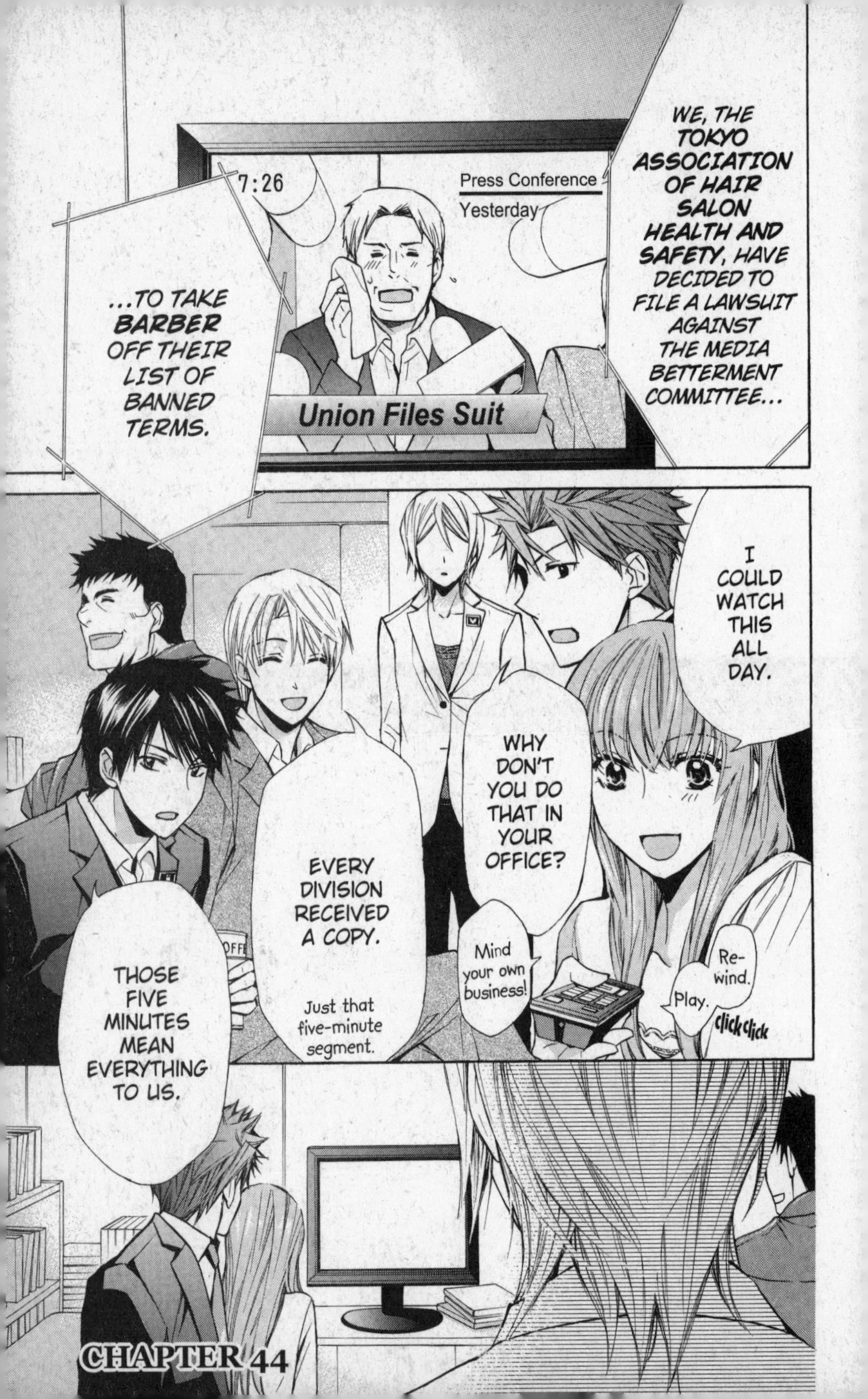
WE, THE TOKYO ASSOCIATION OF HAIR SALON HEALTH AND SAFETY, HAVE DECIDED TO FILE A LAWSUIT AGAINST THE MEDIA BETTERMENT COMMITTEE...
Press Conference
Yesterday
7:26
Union Files Suit
...TO TAKE BARBER OFF THEIR LIST OF BANNED TERMS.
I COULD WATCH THIS ALL DAY.
WHY DON'T YOU DO THAT IN YOUR OFFICE?
Re-wind.
Play.
click click
Mind your own business!
EVERY DIVISION RECEIVED A COPY.
Just that five-minute segment.
THOSE FIVE MINUTES MEAN EVERYTHING TO US.
CHAPTER 44

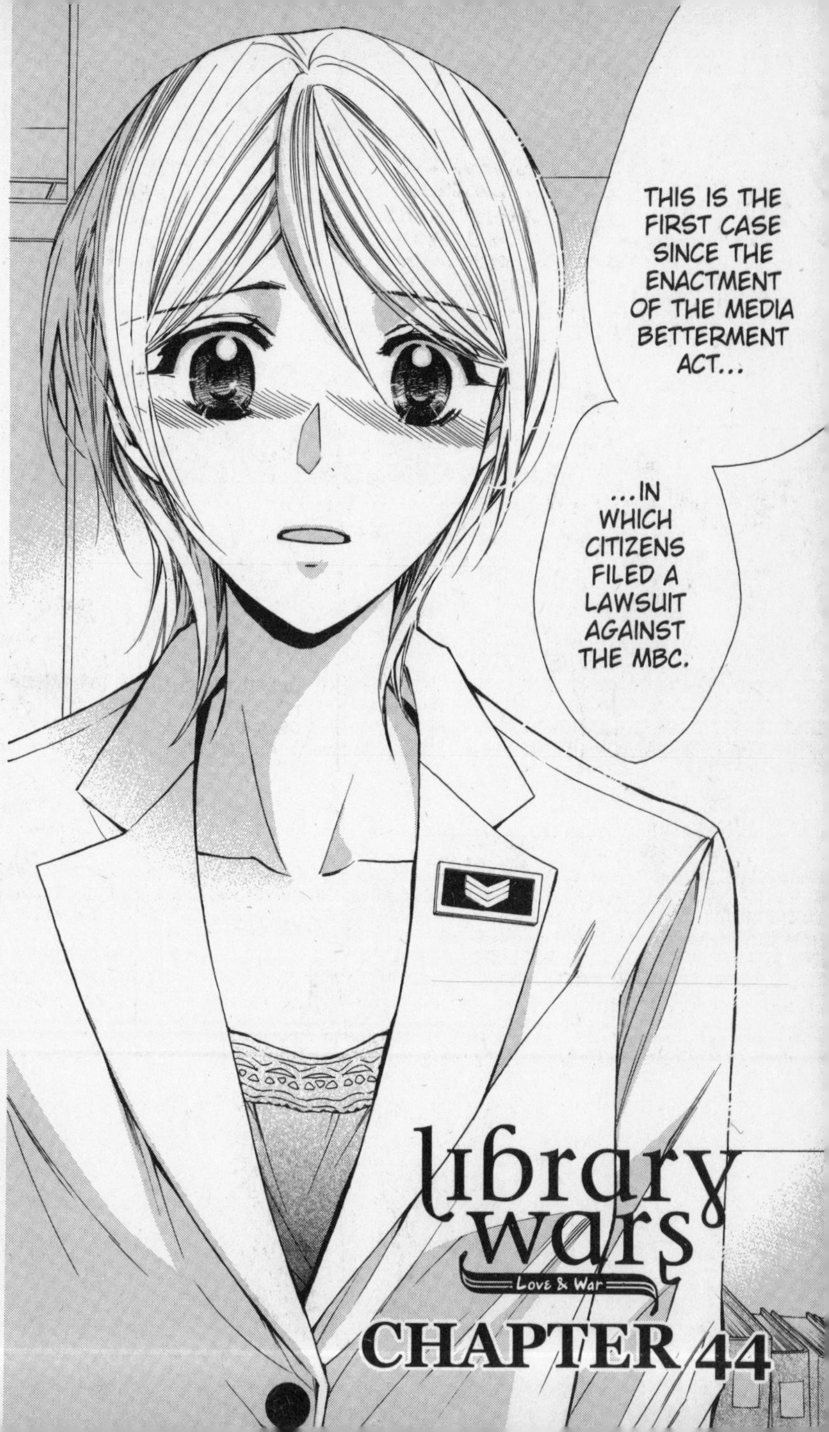
THIS IS THE FIRST CASE SINCE THE ENACTMENT OF THE MEDIA BETTERMENT ACT...
...IN WHICH CITIZENS FILED A LAWSUIT AGAINST THE MBC.
Library Wars
Love & War
CHAPTER 44

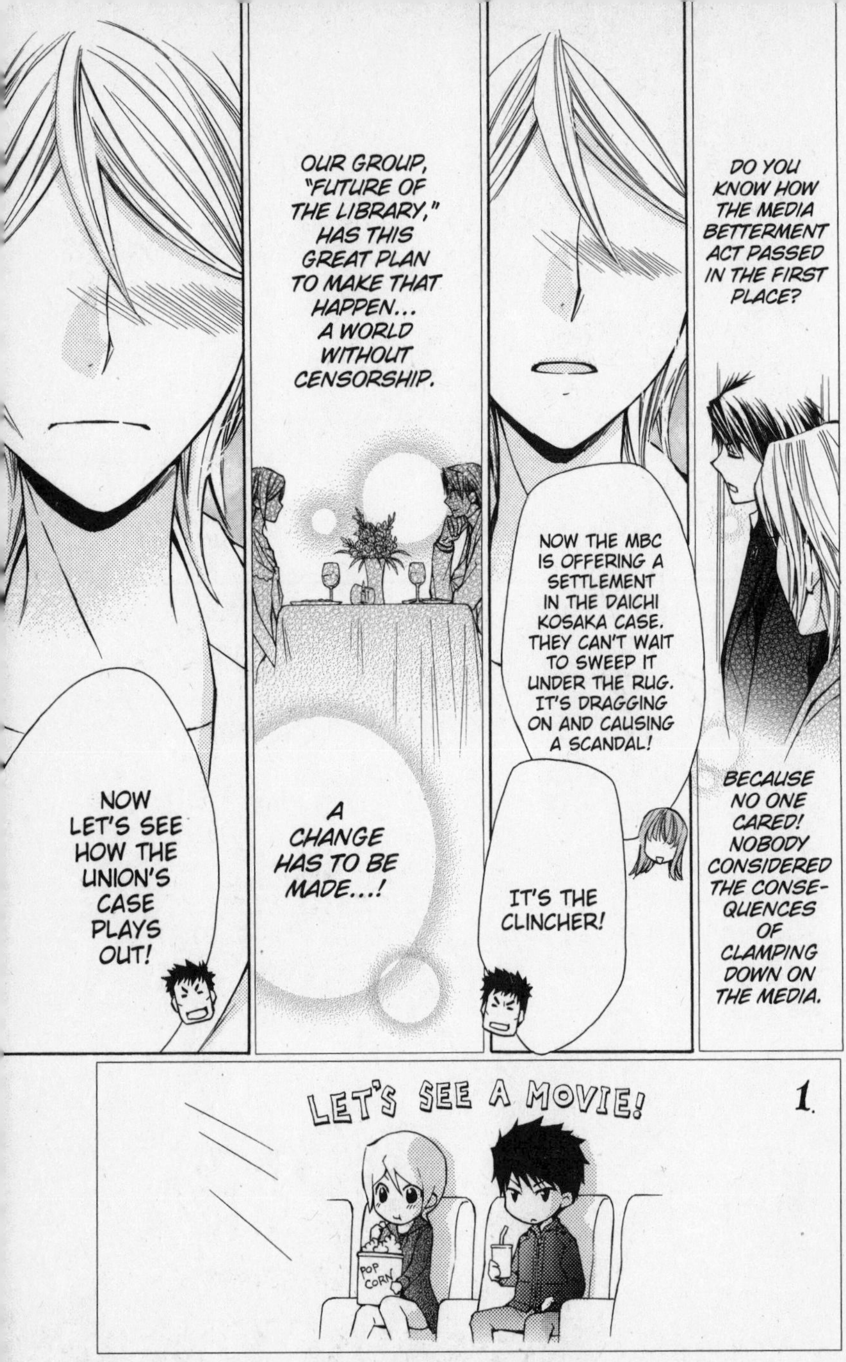
DO YOU KNOW HOW THE MEDIA BETTERMENT ACT PASSED IN THE FIRST PLACE?
BECAUSE NO ONE CARED! NOBODY CONSIDERED THE CONSE-QUENCES OF CLAMPING DOWN ON THE MEDIA.
NOW THE MBC IS OFFERING A SETTLEMENT IN THE DAICHI KOSAKA CASE. THEY CAN'T WAIT TO SWEEP IT UNDER THE RUG. IT'S DRAGGING ON AND CAUSING A SCANDAL!
IT'S THE CLINCHER!
OUR GROUP, "FUTURE OF THE LIBRARY," HAS THIS GREAT PLAN TO MAKE THAT HAPPEN... A WORLD WITHOUT CENSORSHIP.
A CHANGE HAS TO BE MADE...!
NOW LET'S SEE HOW THE UNION'S CASE PLAYS OUT!
LET'S SEE A MOVIE!
1.
POP CORN

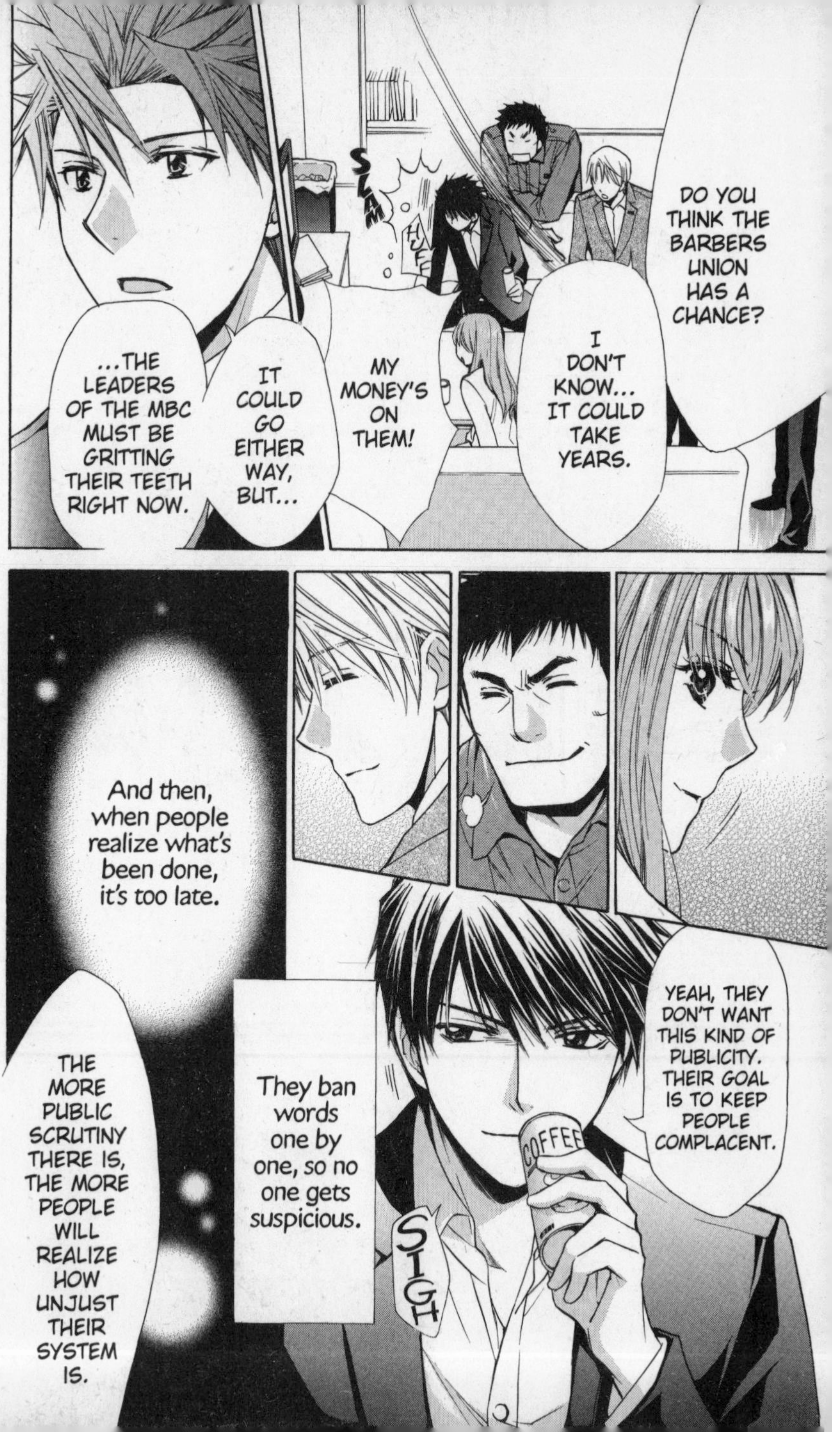

DO YOU THINK THE BARBERS UNION HAS A CHANCE?
I DON'T KNOW... IT COULD TAKE YEARS.
SLAM
HUFF
MY MONEY'S ON THEM!
IT COULD GO EITHER WAY, BUT...
...THE LEADERS OF THE MBC MUST BE GRITTING THEIR TEETH RIGHT NOW.
YEAH, THEY DON'T WANT THIS KIND OF PUBLICITY. THEIR GOAL IS TO KEEP PEOPLE COMPLACENT.
COFFEE
SIGH
They ban words one by one, so no one gets suspicious.
And then, when people realize what's been done, it's too late.
THE MORE PUBLIC SCRUTINY THERE IS, THE MORE PEOPLE WILL REALIZE HOW UNJUST THEIR SYSTEM IS.

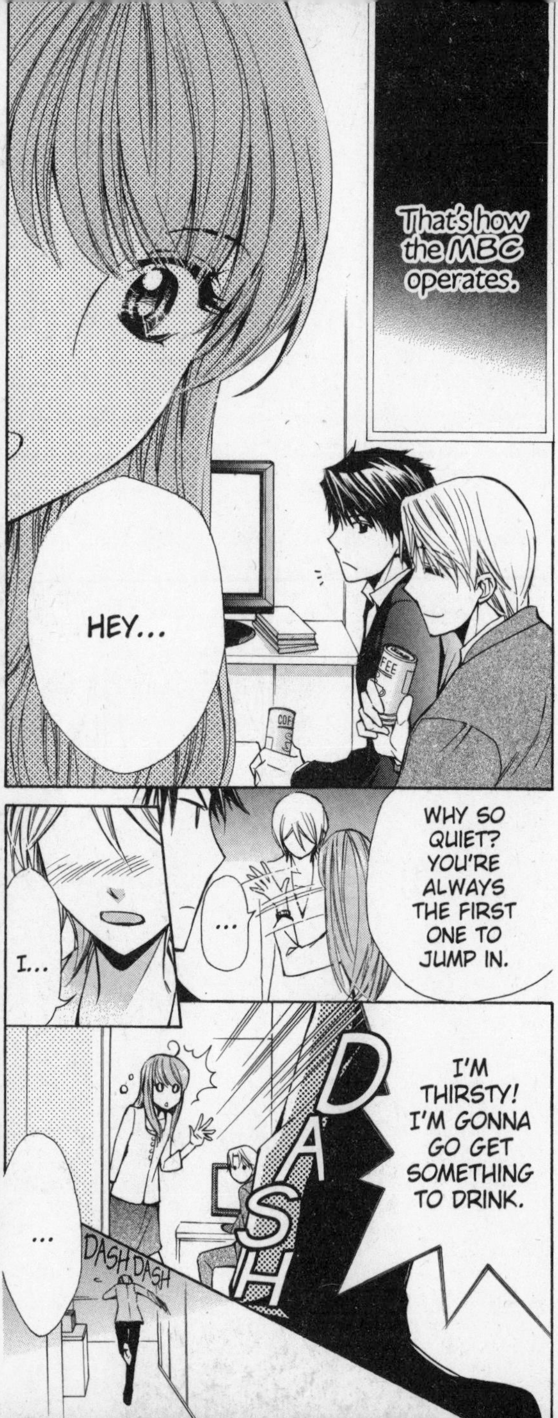
That's how the MBC operates.
HEY...
WHY SO QUIET? YOU'RE ALWAYS THE FIRST ONE TO JUMP IN.
...
I...
I'M THIRSTY! I'M GONNA GO GET SOMETHING TO DRINK.
DASH
DASH DASH
...

1

*

Hello, this is Kiiro Yumi. Welcome to *Library Wars* volume 10.

Yes, it's in double figures now...! Somebody pinch me! I am sincerely grateful for your support, and the support of everyone involved in this series. Is this really happening...? Thank you so, so much!

It might not be perfect, but I hope you enjoy this volume from cover to cover.

*

*

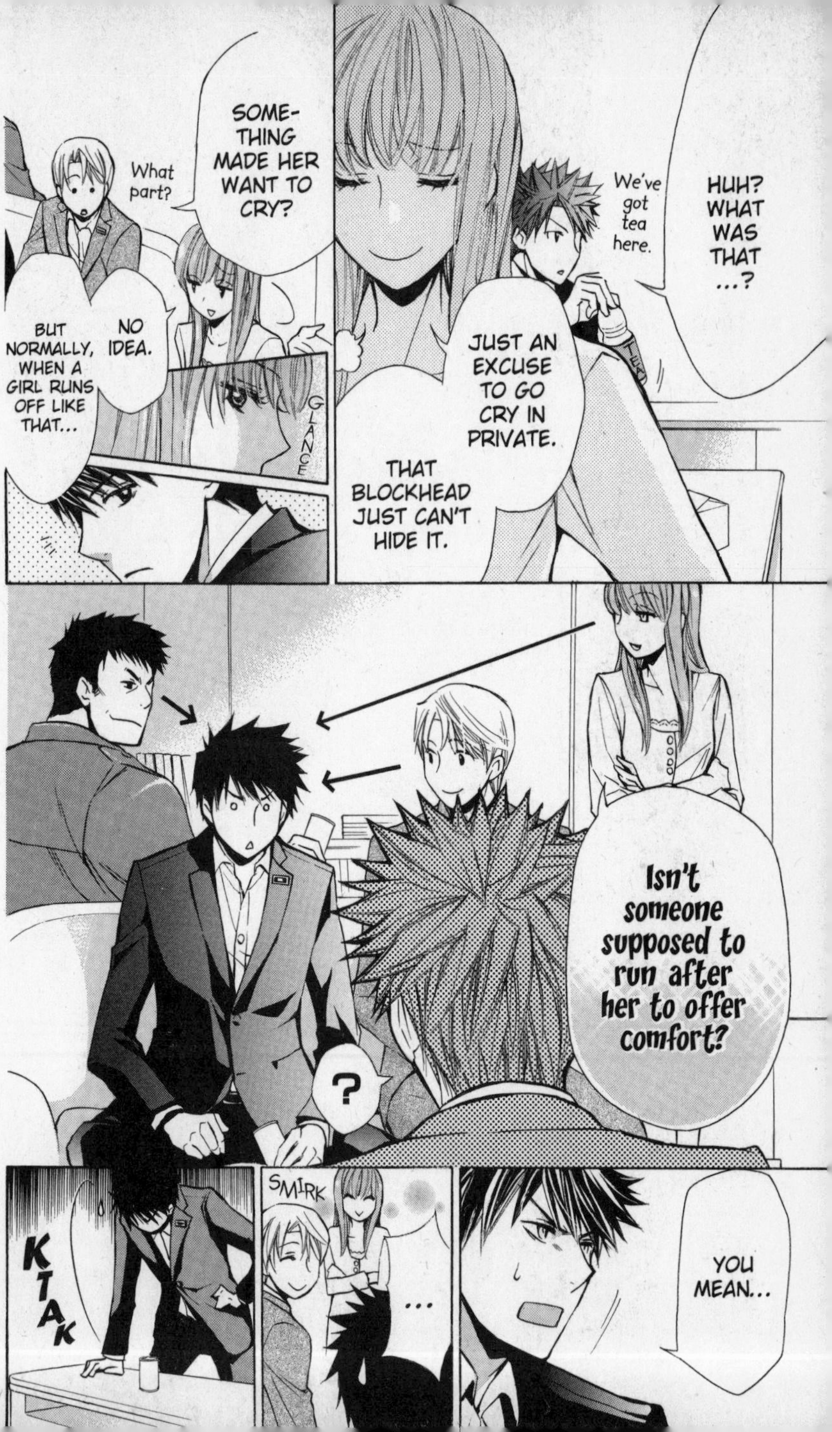
HUH? WHAT WAS THAT ...?
We've got tea here.
TEA
JUST AN EXCUSE TO GO CRY IN PRIVATE.
THAT BLOCKHEAD JUST CAN'T HIDE IT.
SOME-THING MADE HER WANT TO CRY?
What part?
NO IDEA.
BUT NORMALLY, WHEN A GIRL RUNS OFF LIKE THAT...
GLANCE
Isn't someone supposed to run after her to offer comfort?
?
YOU MEAN...
SMIRK
...
KTAK

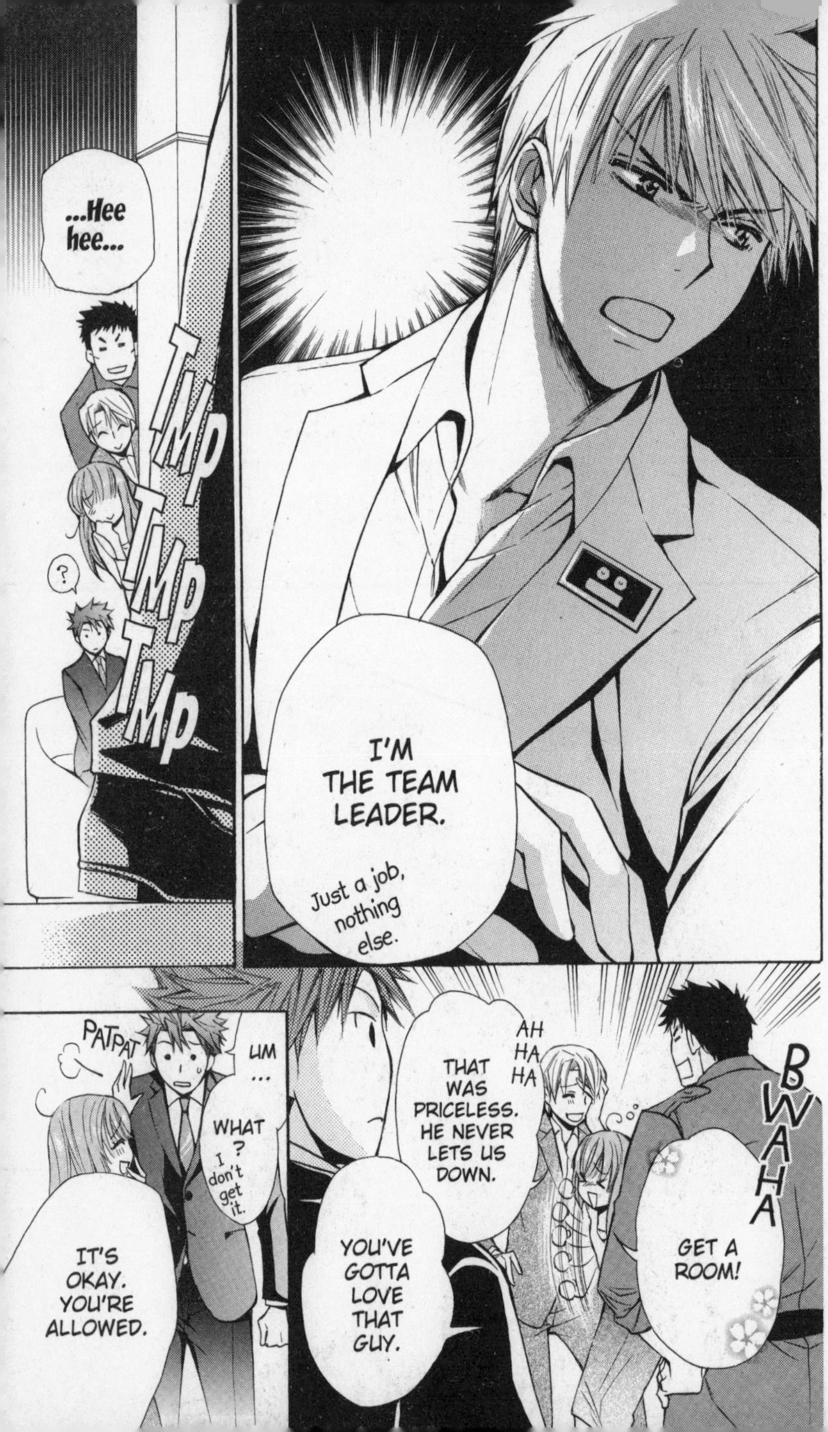
I'M THE TEAM LEADER.
Just a job, nothing else.
TMP TMP TMP TMP
?
...Hee hee...
BWAHA
GET A ROOM!
AH HA HA
THAT WAS PRICELESS. HE NEVER LETS US DOWN.
YOU'VE GOTTA LOVE THAT GUY.
PATPAT
UM ...
WHAT ?
I don't get it.
IT'S OKAY. YOU'RE ALLOWED.

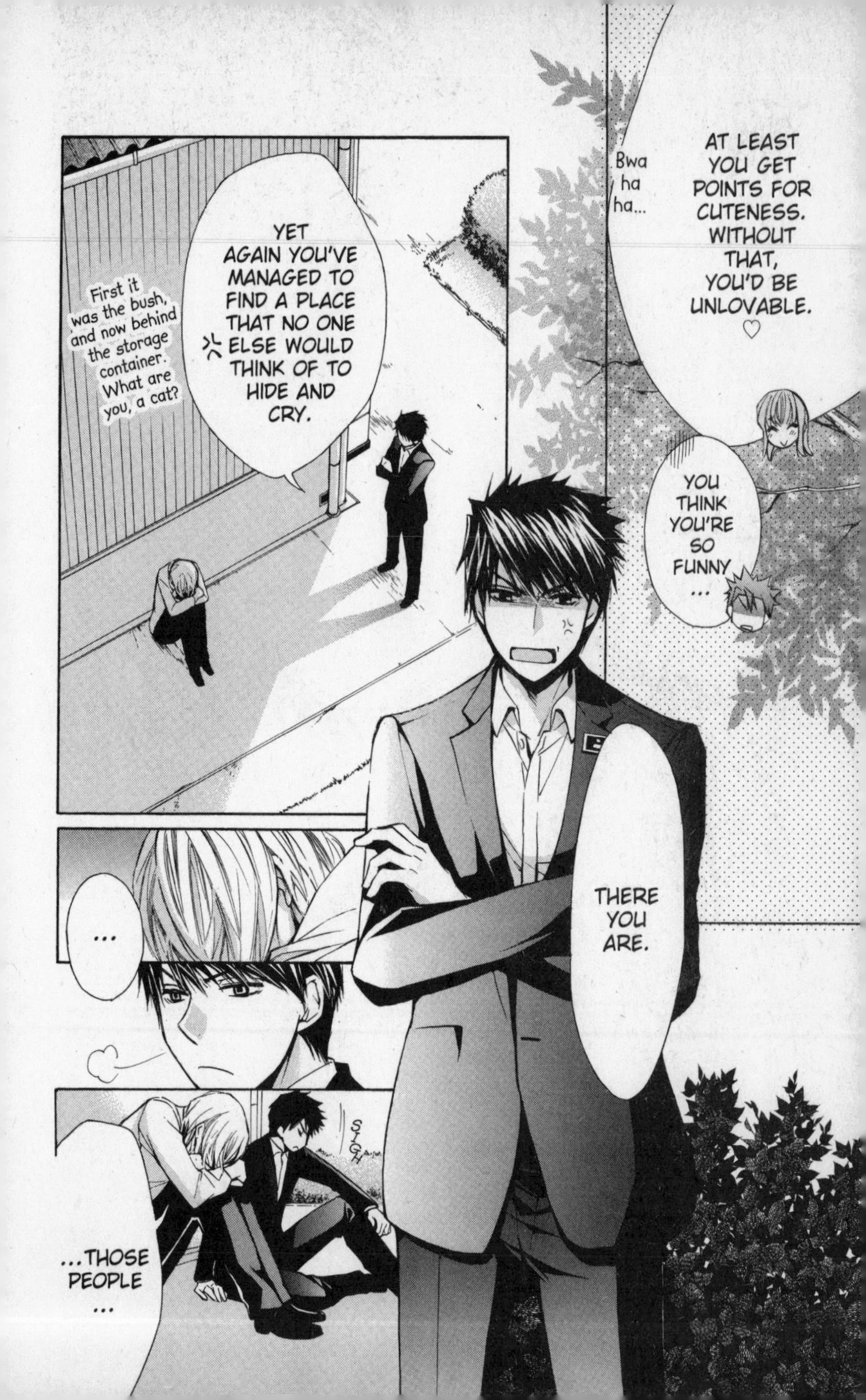
AT LEAST YOU GET POINTS FOR CUTENESS. WITHOUT THAT, YOU'D BE UNLOVABLE. ♡
Bwa ha ha...
YOU THINK YOU'RE SO FUNNY...
THERE YOU ARE.
YET AGAIN YOU'VE MANAGED TO FIND A PLACE THAT NO ONE ELSE WOULD THINK OF TO HIDE AND CRY.
First it was the bush, and now behind the storage container. What are you, a cat?
...
SIGH
...THOSE PEOPLE...

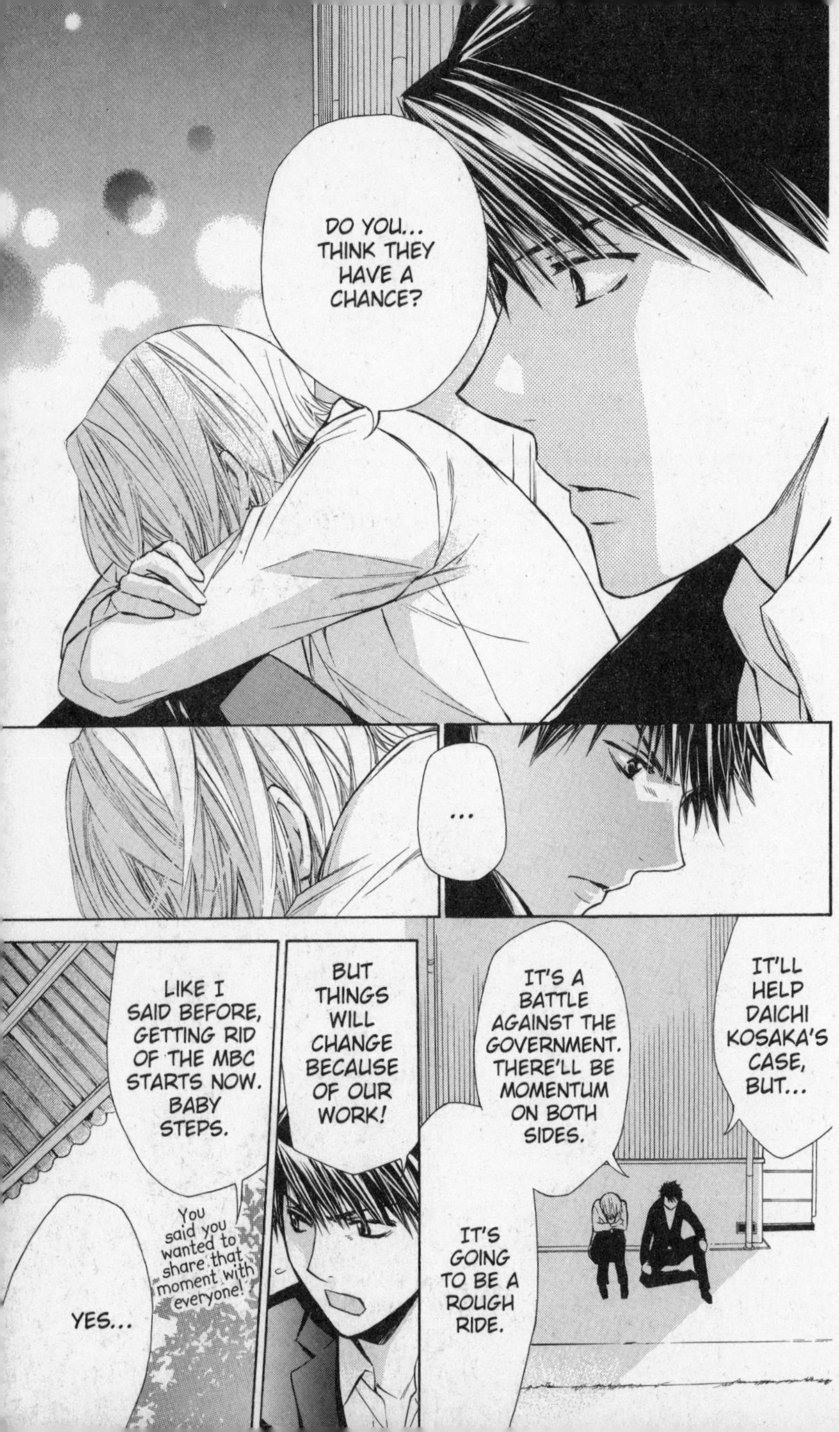
DO YOU... THINK THEY HAVE A CHANCE?
...
IT'LL HELP DAICHI KOSAKA'S CASE, BUT...
IT'S A BATTLE AGAINST THE GOVERNMENT. THERE'LL BE MOMENTUM ON BOTH SIDES.
IT'S GOING TO BE A ROUGH RIDE.
BUT THINGS WILL CHANGE BECAUSE OF OUR WORK!
LIKE I SAID BEFORE, GETTING RID OF THE MBC STARTS NOW. BABY STEPS.
You said you wanted to share that moment with everyone!
YES...

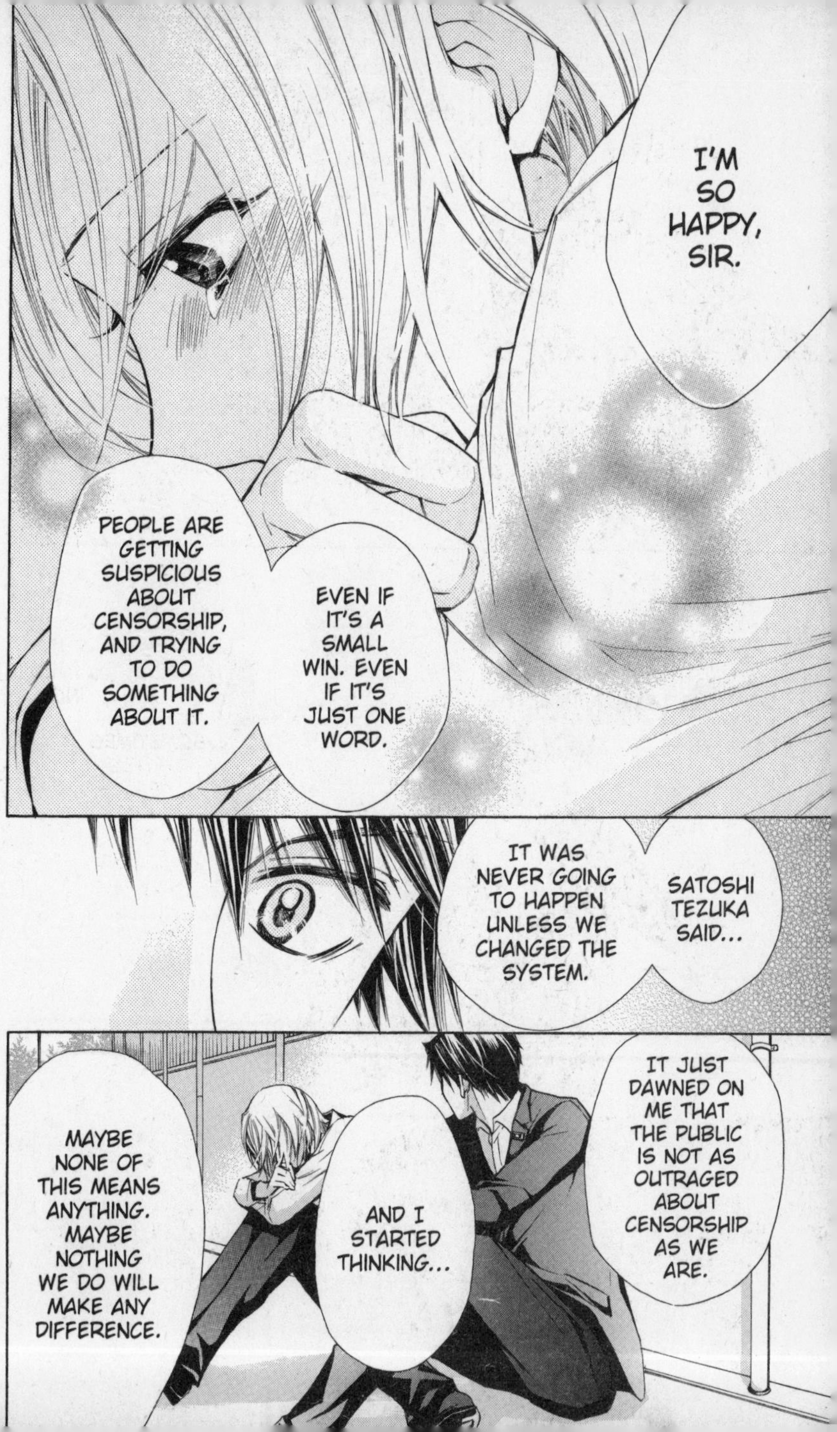
I'M SO HAPPY, SIR.
PEOPLE ARE GETTING SUSPICIOUS ABOUT CENSORSHIP, AND TRYING TO DO SOMETHING ABOUT IT.
EVEN IF IT'S A SMALL WIN. EVEN IF IT'S JUST ONE WORD.
SATOSHI TEZUKA SAID...
IT WAS NEVER GOING TO HAPPEN UNLESS WE CHANGED THE SYSTEM.
IT JUST DAWNED ON ME THAT THE PUBLIC IS NOT AS OUTRAGED ABOUT CENSORSHIP AS WE ARE.
AND I STARTED THINKING...
MAYBE NONE OF THIS MEANS ANYTHING. MAYBE NOTHING WE DO WILL MAKE ANY DIFFERENCE.

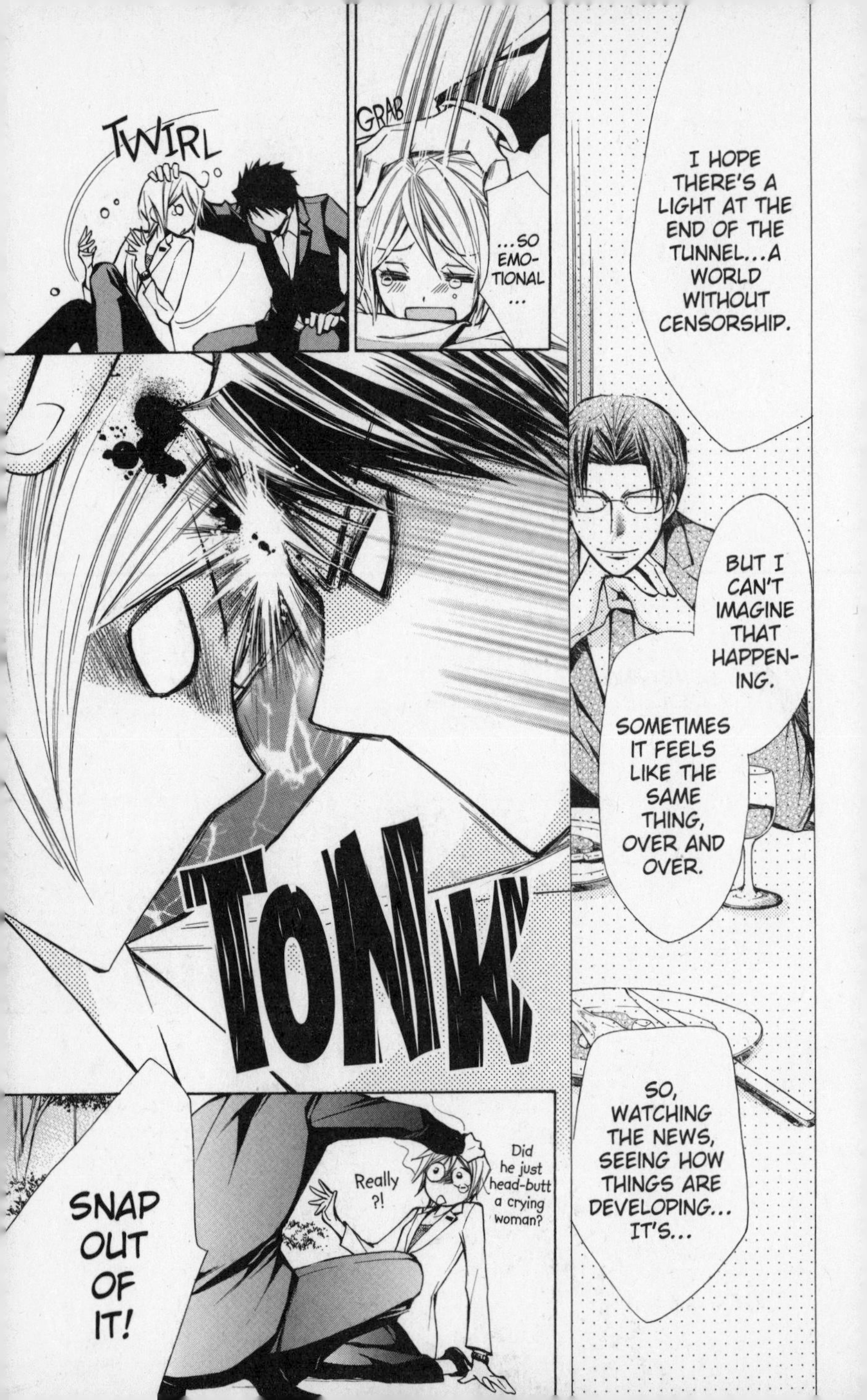
I HOPE THERE'S A LIGHT AT THE END OF THE TUNNEL...A WORLD WITHOUT CENSORSHIP.
BUT I CAN'T IMAGINE THAT HAPPEN-ING.
SOMETIMES IT FEELS LIKE THE SAME THING, OVER AND OVER.
SO, WATCHING THE NEWS, SEEING HOW THINGS ARE DEVELOPING... IT'S...
GRAB
...SO EMO-TIONAL ...
TWIRL
TONK
Did he just head-butt a crying woman?
Really ?!
SNAP OUT OF IT!

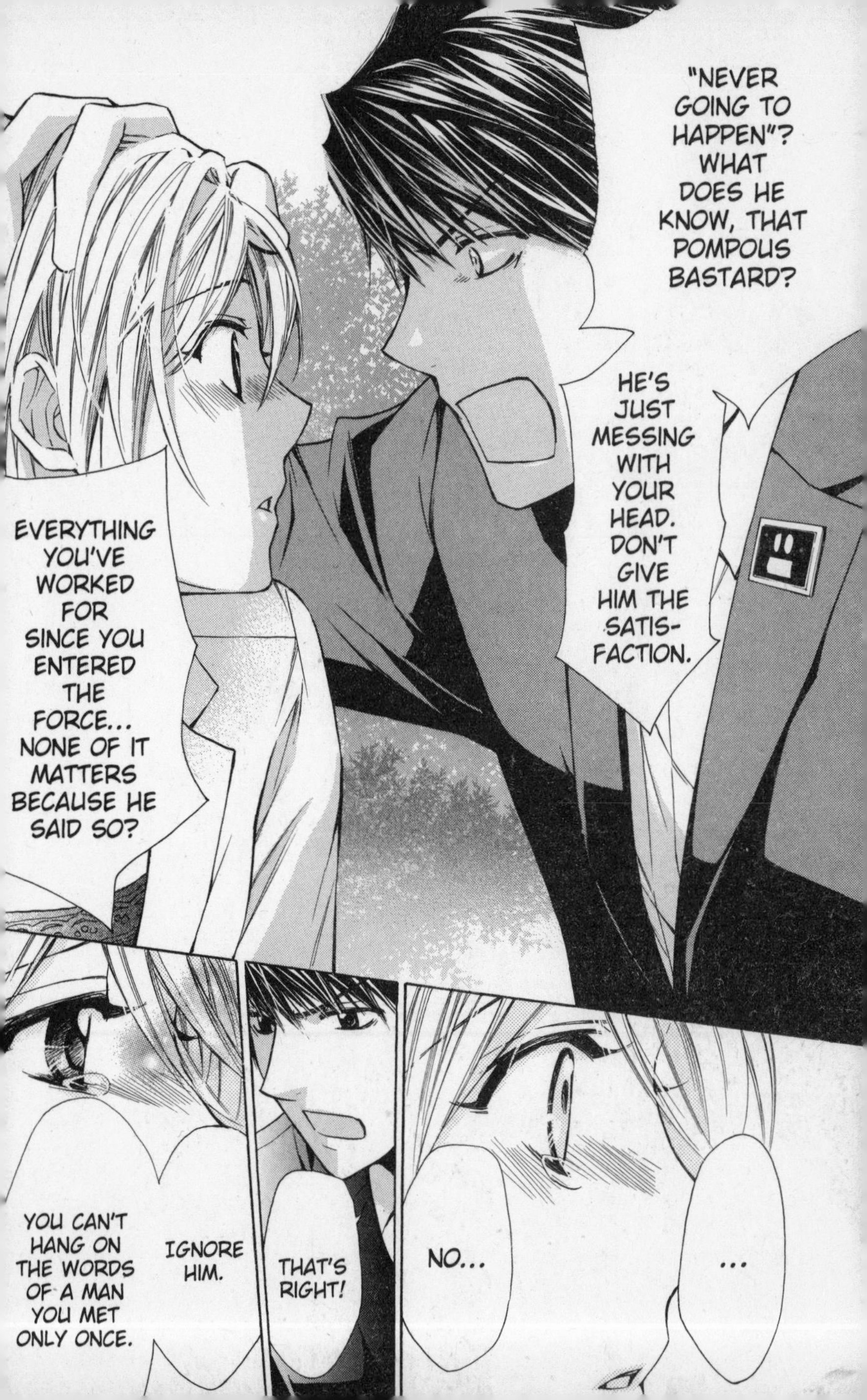
"NEVER GOING TO HAPPEN"? WHAT DOES HE KNOW, THAT POMPOUS BASTARD?
HE'S JUST MESSING WITH YOUR HEAD. DON'T GIVE HIM THE SATIS-FACTION.
EVERYTHING YOU'VE WORKED FOR SINCE YOU ENTERED THE FORCE... NONE OF IT MATTERS BECAUSE HE SAID SO?
...
NO...
THAT'S RIGHT!
IGNORE HIM.
YOU CAN'T HANG ON THE WORDS OF A MAN YOU MET ONLY ONCE.

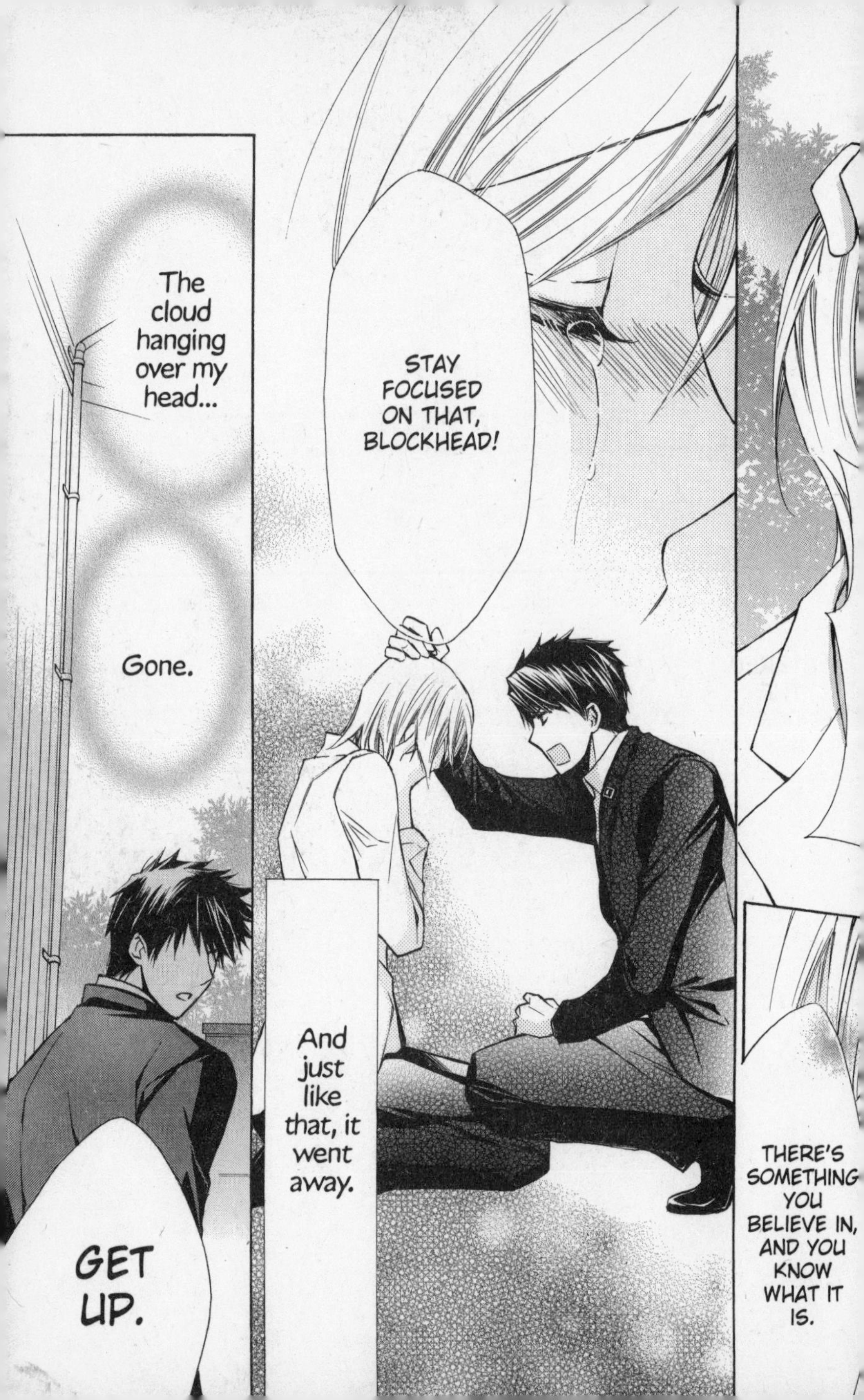
THERE'S SOMETHING YOU BELIEVE IN, AND YOU KNOW WHAT IT IS.
STAY FOCUSED ON THAT, BLOCKHEAD!
And just like that, it went away.
The cloud hanging over my head...
Gone.
GET UP.

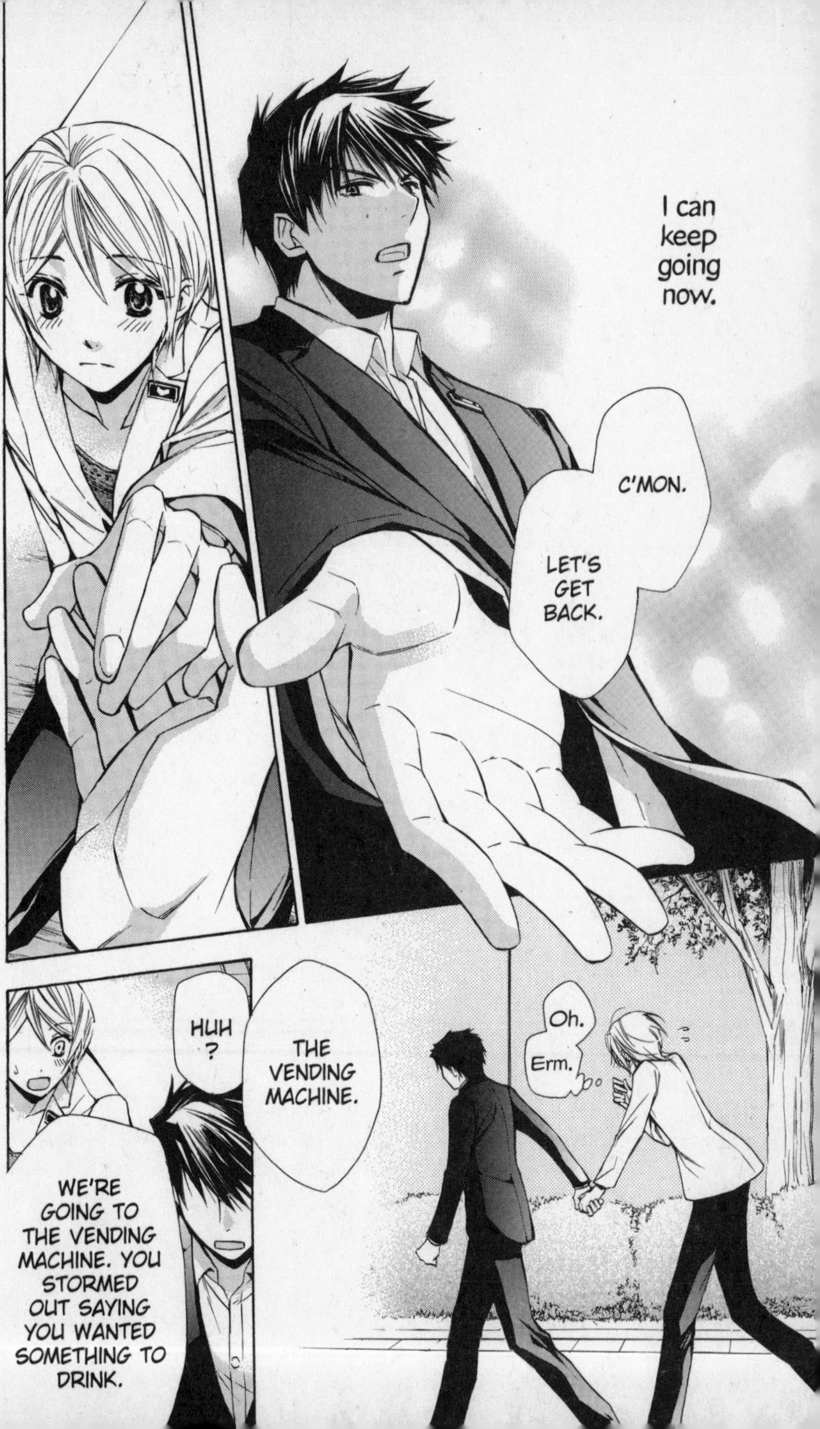
I can keep going now.
C'MON.
LET'S GET BACK.
Oh.
Erm.
THE VENDING MACHINE.
HUH?
WE'RE GOING TO THE VENDING MACHINE. YOU STORMED OUT SAYING YOU WANTED SOMETHING TO DRINK.

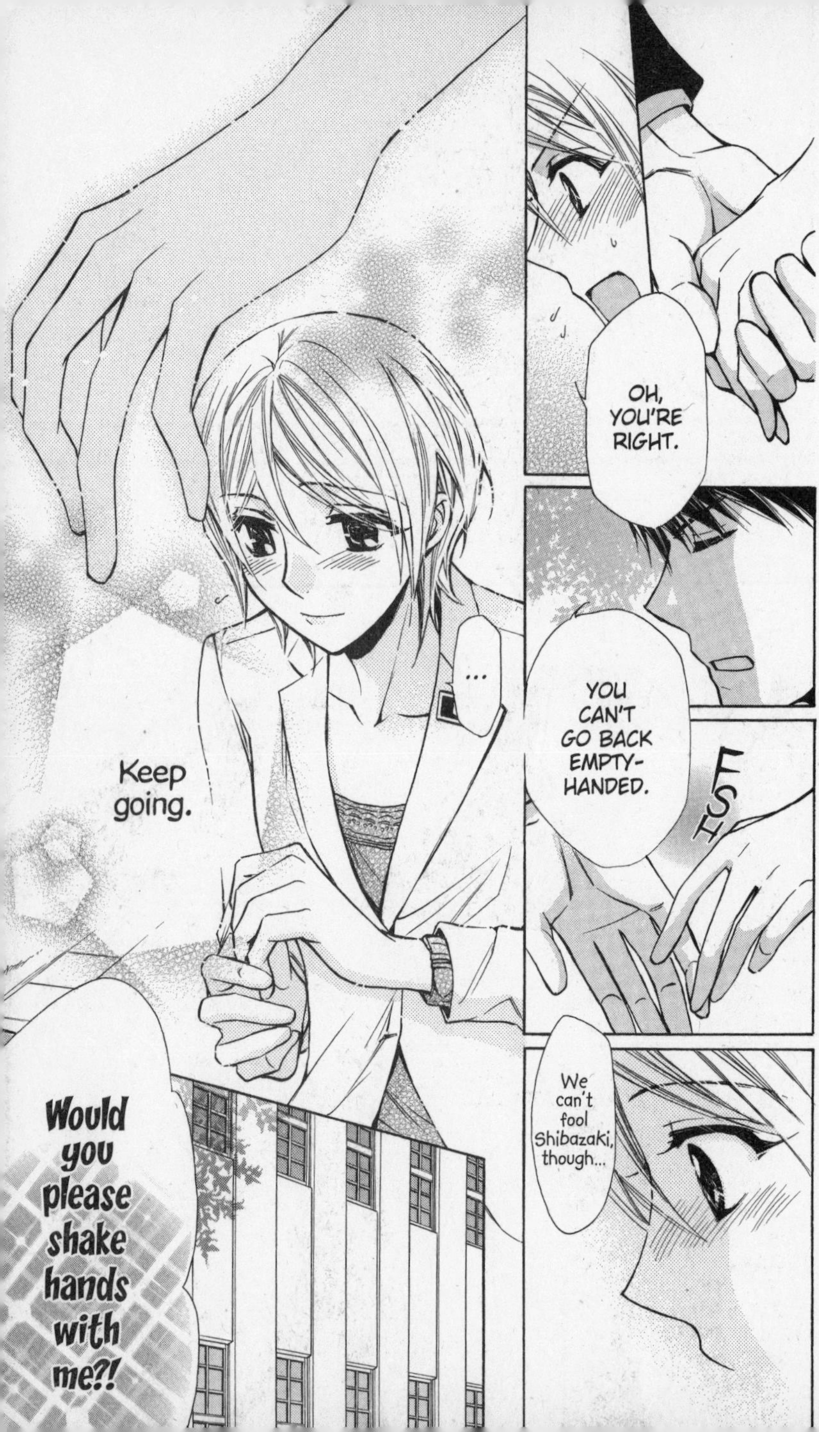
OH, YOU'RE RIGHT.
YOU CAN'T GO BACK EMPTY-HANDED.
FSH
We can't fool Shibazaki, though...
...
Keep going.
Would you please shake hands with me?!

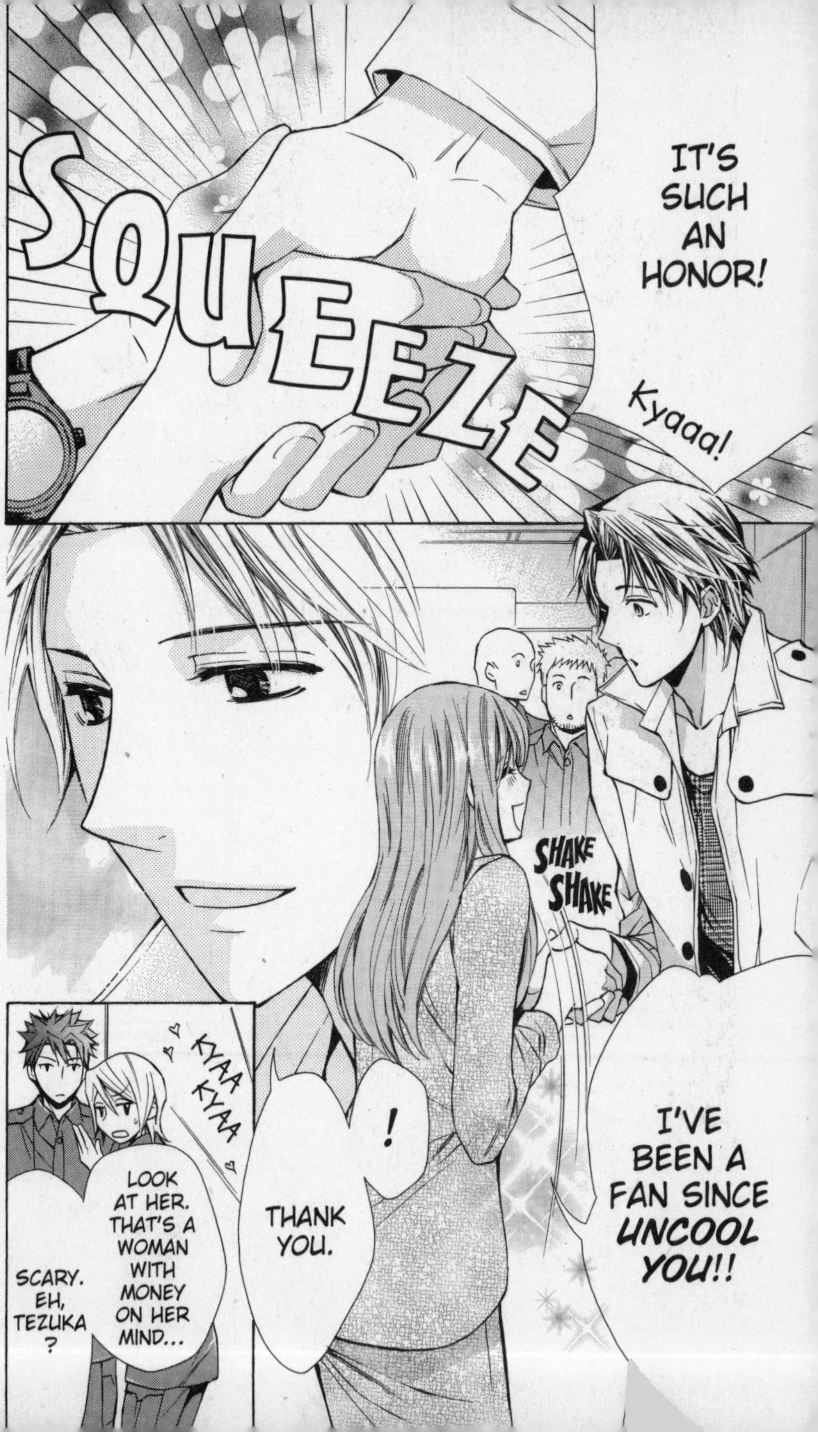
IT'S SUCH AN HONOR!
SQUEEZE
Kyaaa!
I'VE BEEN A FAN SINCE UNCOOL YOU!!
SHAKE SHAKE
!
THANK YOU.
KYAA KYAA
LOOK AT HER. THAT'S A WOMAN WITH MONEY ON HER MIND...
SCARY. EH, TEZUKA?

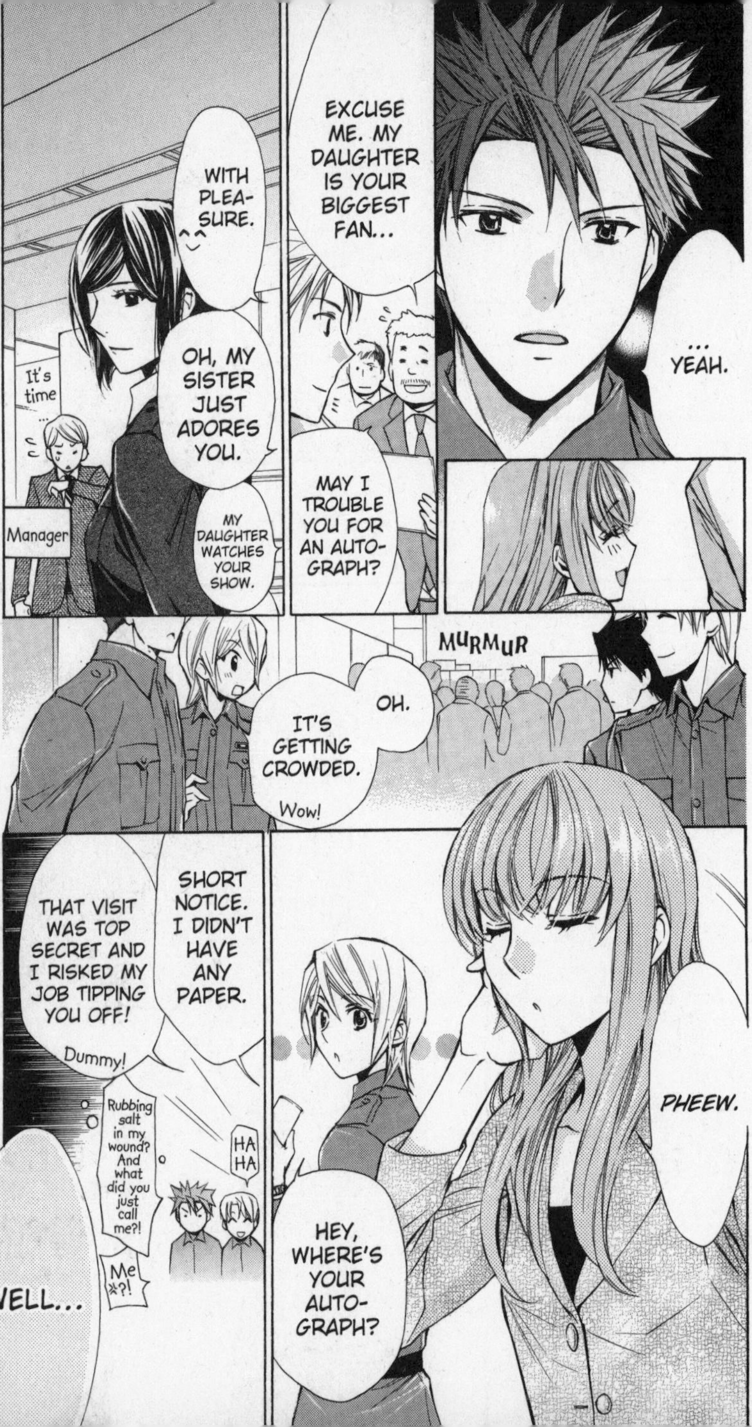
...YEAH.
EXCUSE ME. MY DAUGHTER IS YOUR BIGGEST FAN...
MAY I TROUBLE YOU FOR AN AUTO-GRAPH?
WITH PLEA-SURE.
^^
OH, MY SISTER JUST ADORES YOU.
MY DAUGHTER WATCHES YOUR SHOW.
It's time...
Manager
MURMUR
OH.
IT'S GETTING CROWDED.
Wow!
PHEEW.
HEY, WHERE'S YOUR AUTO-GRAPH?
WELL...
SHORT NOTICE. I DIDN'T HAVE ANY PAPER.
THAT VISIT WAS TOP SECRET AND I RISKED MY JOB TIPPING YOU OFF!
Dummy!
HA HA
Rubbing salt in my wound? And what did you just call me?!
Me*?!

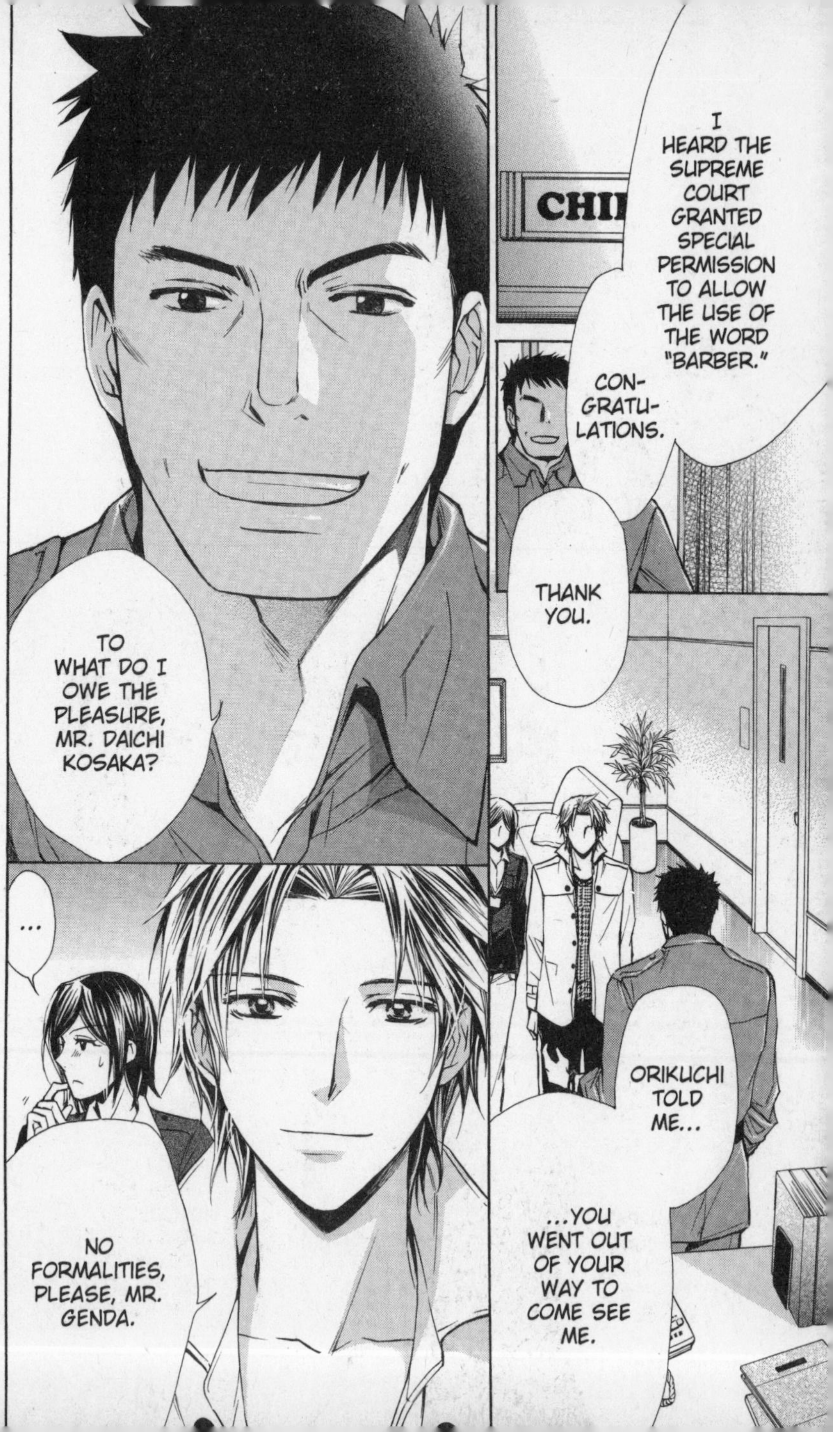
I HEARD THE SUPREME COURT GRANTED SPECIAL PERMISSION TO ALLOW THE USE OF THE WORD "BARBER."
CON-GRATU-LATIONS.
THANK YOU.
ORIKUCHI TOLD ME...
...YOU WENT OUT OF YOUR WAY TO COME SEE ME.
TO WHAT DO I OWE THE PLEASURE, MR. DAICHI KOSAKA?
...
NO FORMALITIES, PLEASE, MR. GENDA.

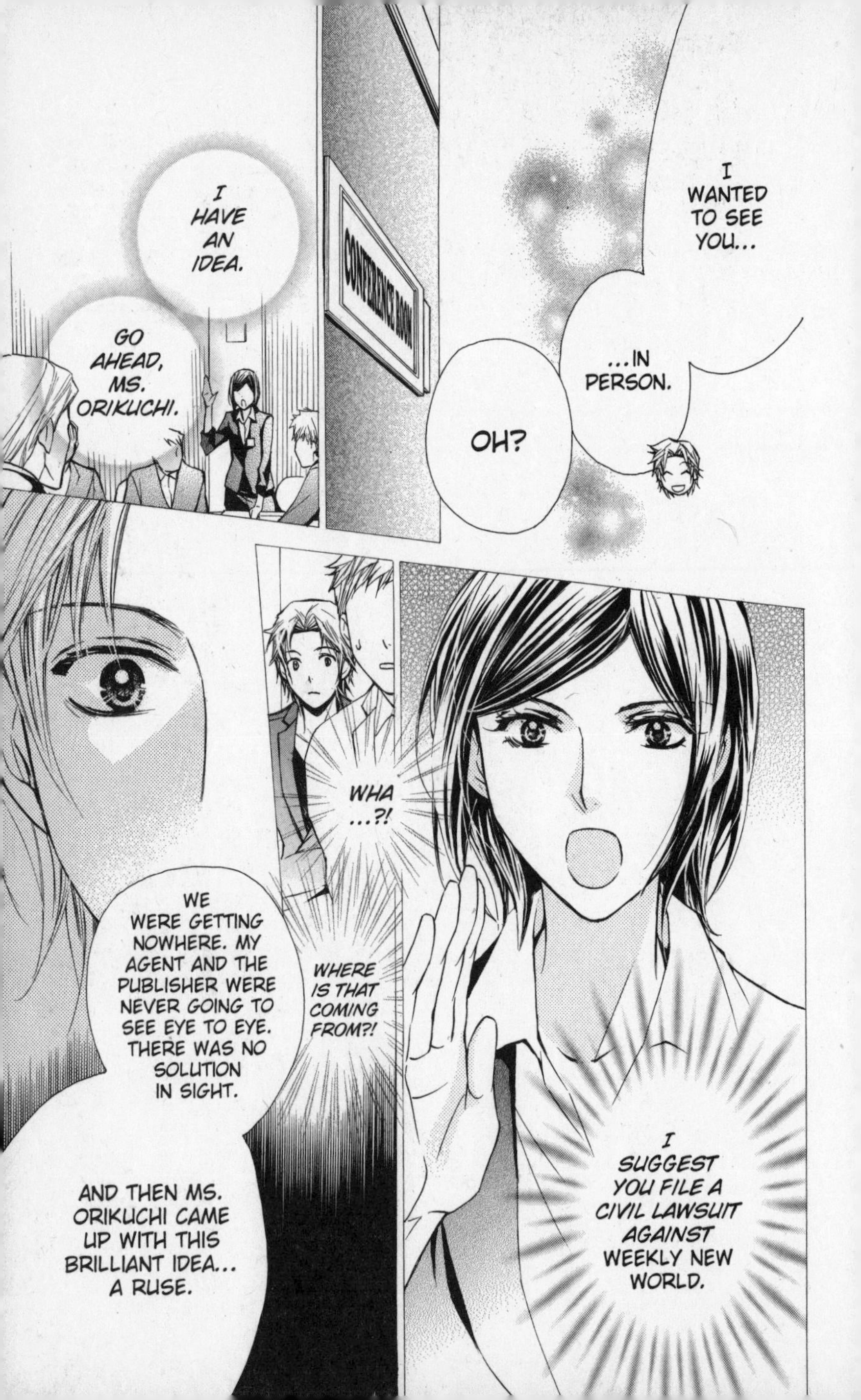
I WANTED TO SEE YOU...
...IN PERSON.
OH?
CONFERENCE ROOM
I HAVE AN IDEA.
GO AHEAD, MS. ORIKUCHI.
I SUGGEST YOU FILE A CIVIL LAWSUIT AGAINST WEEKLY NEW WORLD.
WHA ...?!
WHERE IS THAT COMING FROM?!
WE WERE GETTING NOWHERE. MY AGENT AND THE PUBLISHER WERE NEVER GOING TO SEE EYE TO EYE. THERE WAS NO SOLUTION IN SIGHT.
AND THEN MS. ORIKUCHI CAME UP WITH THIS BRILLIANT IDEA... A RUSE.

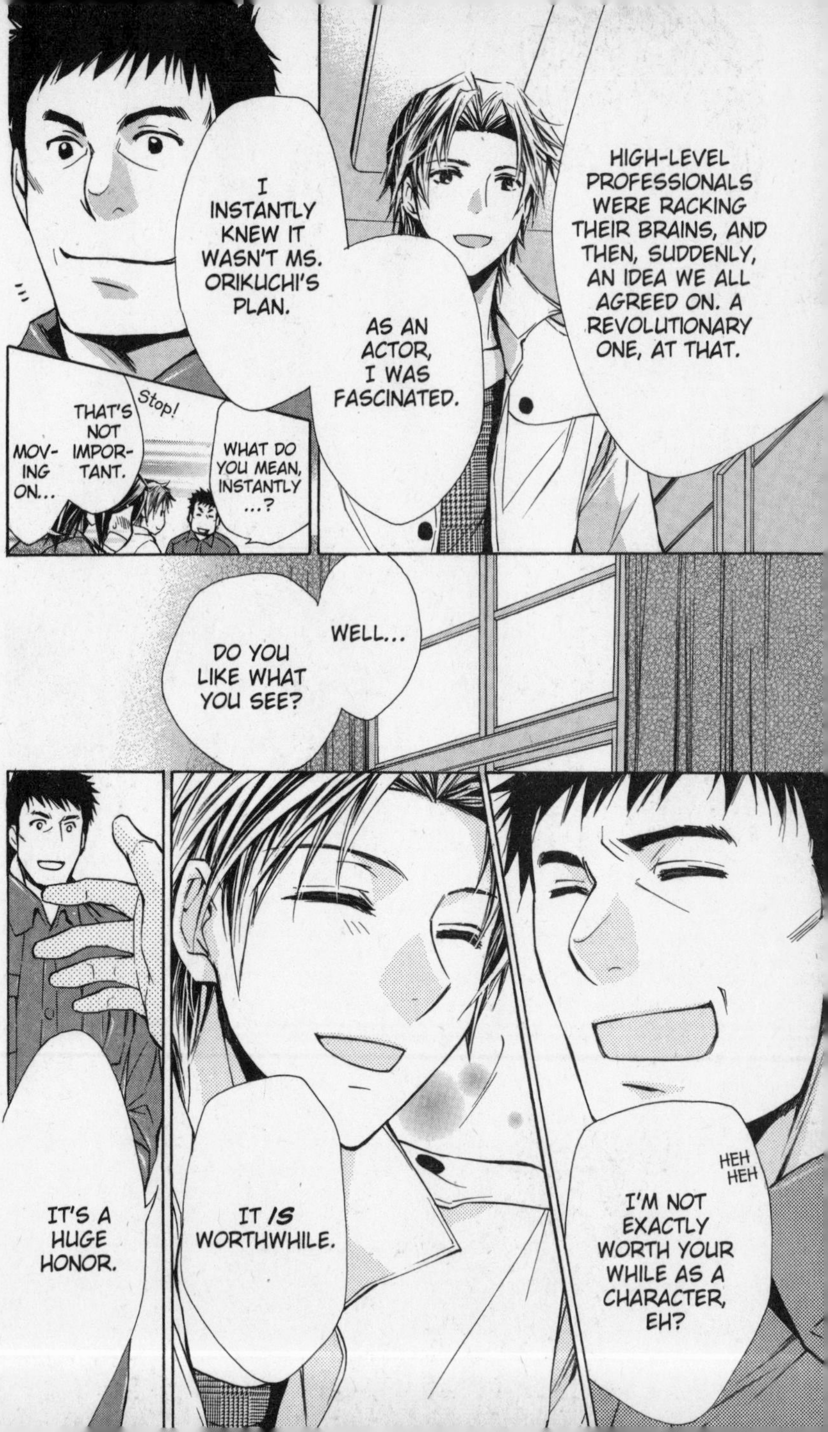
HIGH-LEVEL PROFESSIONALS WERE RACKING THEIR BRAINS, AND THEN, SUDDENLY, AN IDEA WE ALL AGREED ON. A REVOLUTIONARY ONE, AT THAT.
AS AN ACTOR, I WAS FASCINATED.
I INSTANTLY KNEW IT WASN'T MS. ORIKUCHI'S PLAN.
WHAT DO YOU MEAN, INSTANTLY ...?
Stop!
THAT'S NOT IMPORTANT.
MOVING ON...
WELL...
DO YOU LIKE WHAT YOU SEE?
HEH HEH
I'M NOT EXACTLY WORTH YOUR WHILE AS A CHARACTER, EH?
IT *IS* WORTHWHILE.
IT'S A HUGE HONOR.

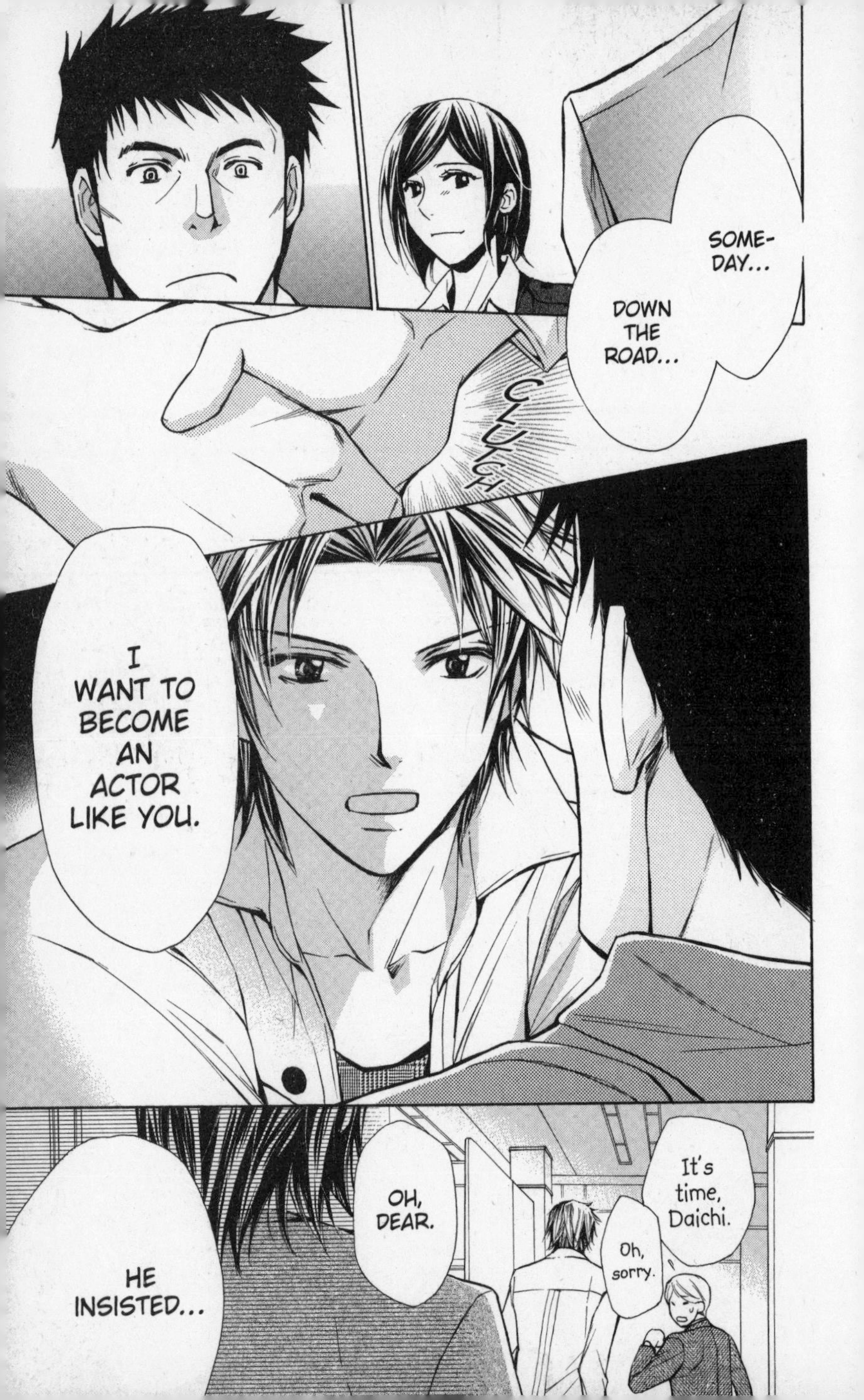
SOME-DAY...
DOWN THE ROAD...
CLUTCH
I WANT TO BECOME AN ACTOR LIKE YOU.
It's time, Daichi.
Oh, sorry.
OH, DEAR.
HE INSISTED...

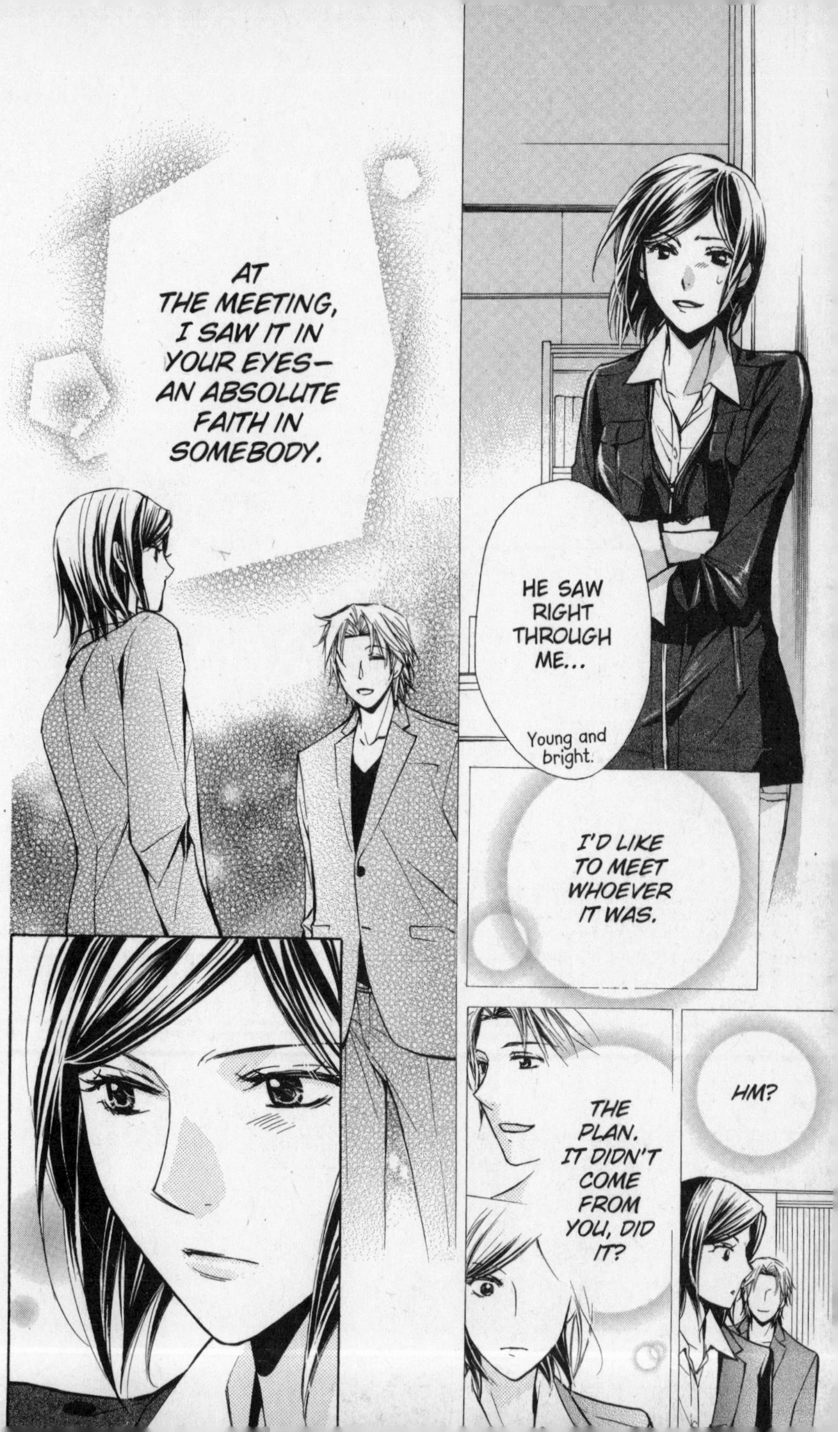
HE SAW RIGHT THROUGH ME...
Young and bright.
I'D LIKE TO MEET WHOEVER IT WAS.
HM?
THE PLAN. IT DIDN'T COME FROM YOU, DID IT?
AT THE MEETING, I SAW IT IN YOUR EYES— AN ABSOLUTE FAITH IN SOMEBODY.

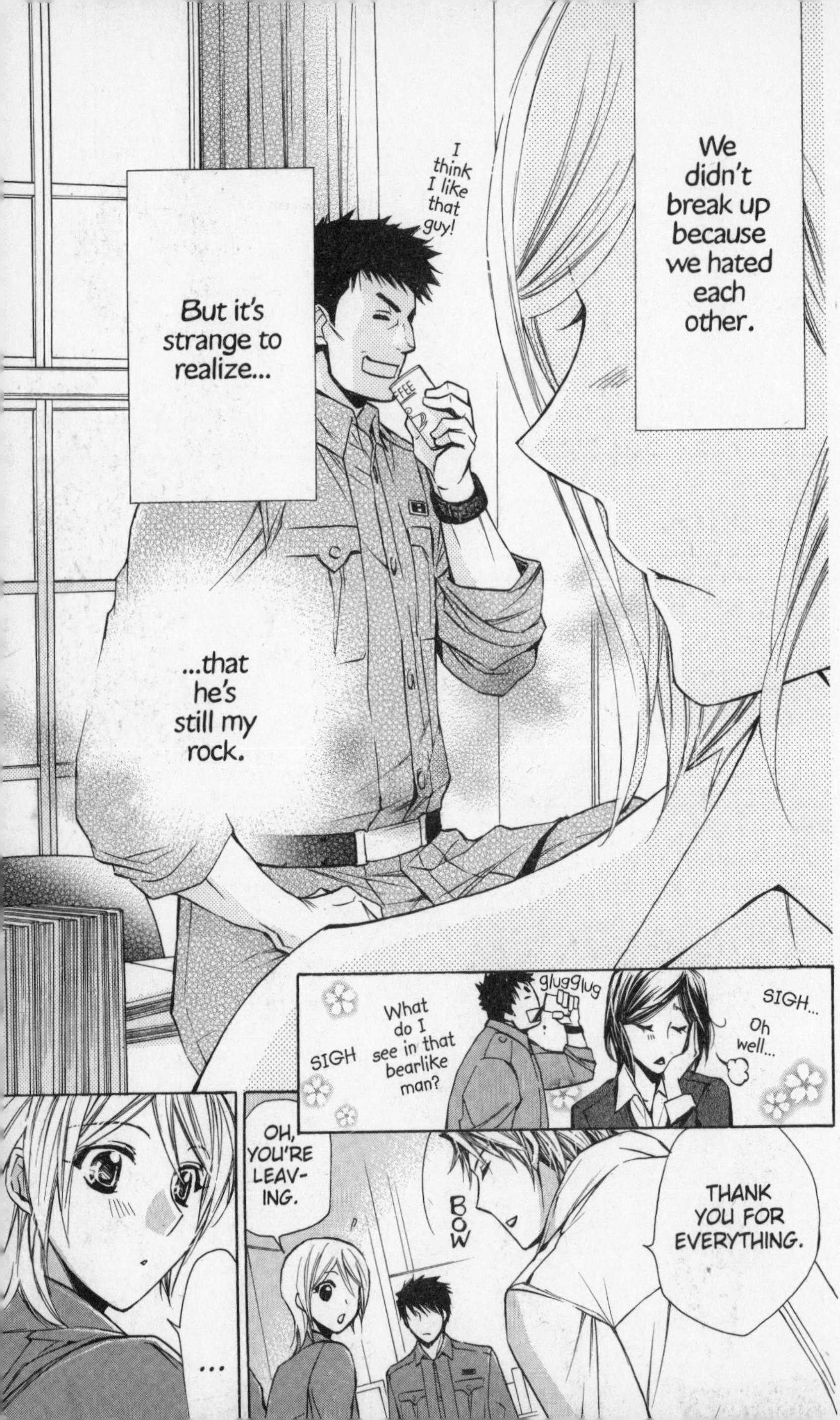
We didn't break up because we hated each other.
I think I like that guy!
But it's strange to realize...
...that he's still my rock.
SIGH... Oh well...
glugglug
What do I see in that bearlike man?
SIGH
THANK YOU FOR EVERYTHING.
BOW
OH, YOU'RE LEAVING.
...

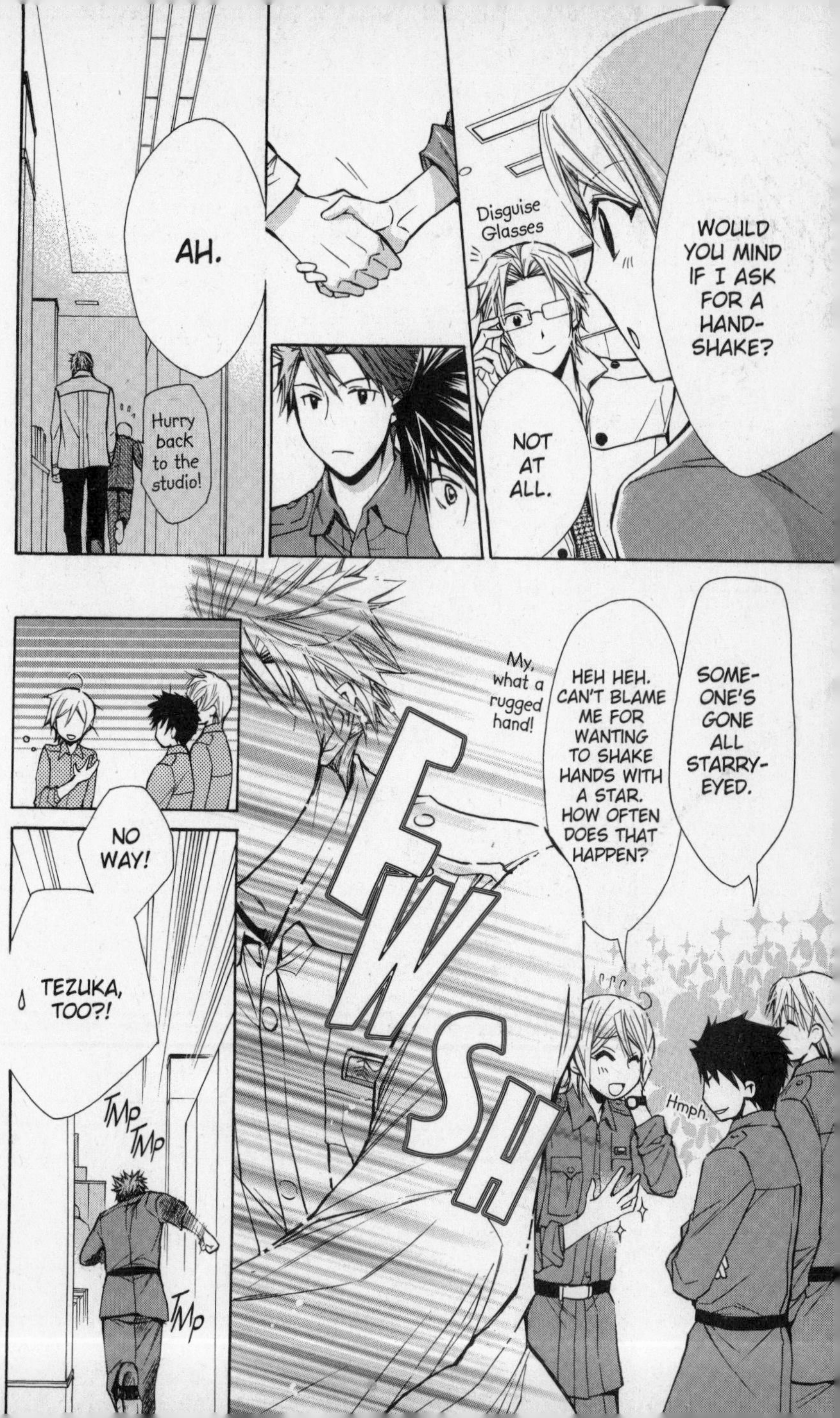
WOULD YOU MIND IF I ASK FOR A HAND-SHAKE?
Disguise Glasses
NOT AT ALL.
AH.
Hurry back to the studio!
SOME-ONE'S GONE ALL STARRY-EYED.
HEH HEH. CAN'T BLAME ME FOR WANTING TO SHAKE HANDS WITH A STAR. HOW OFTEN DOES THAT HAPPEN?
My, what a rugged hand!
Hmph.
FWSH
NO WAY!
TEZUKA, TOO?!
TMP TMP
TMP

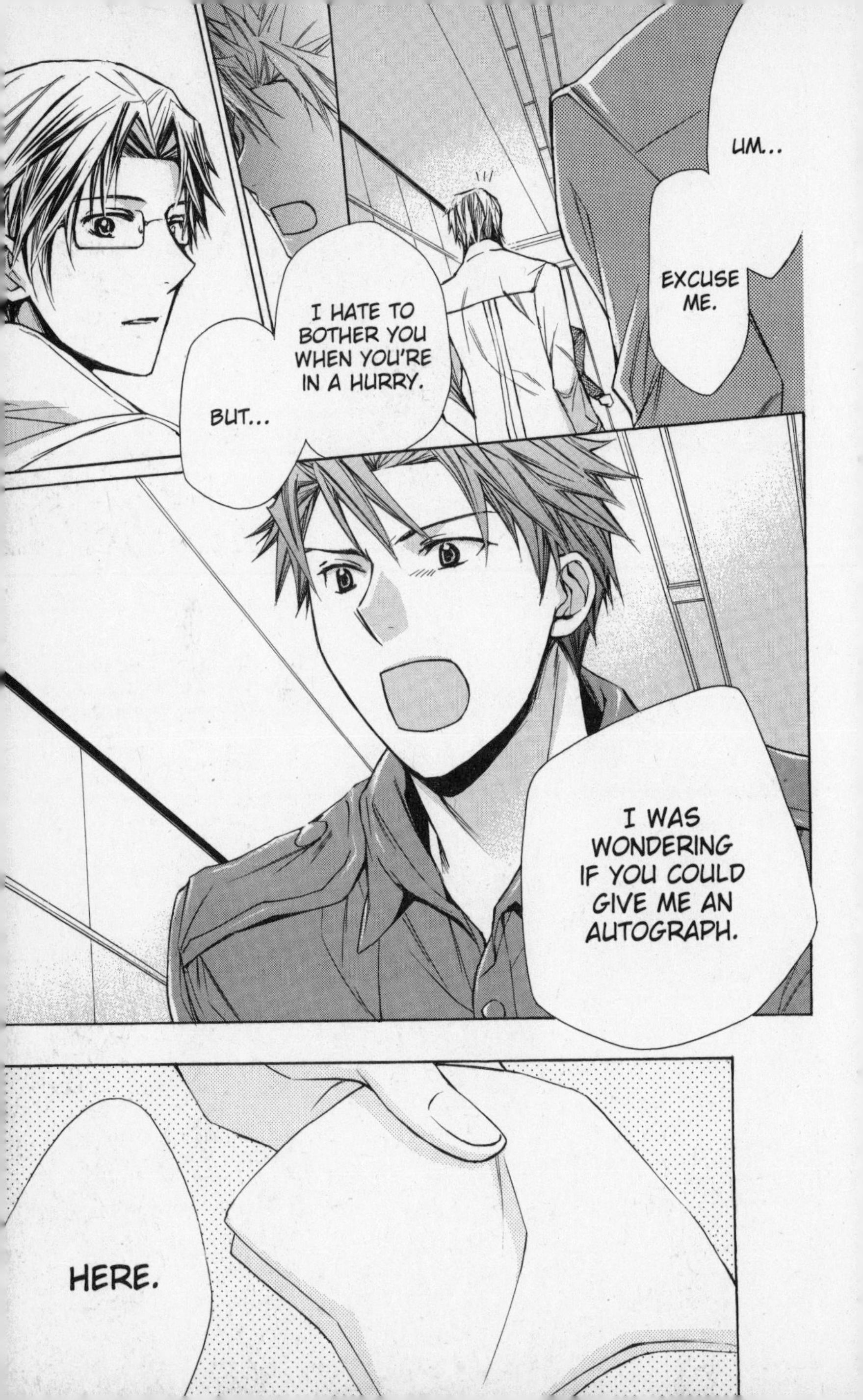
UM...
EXCUSE ME.
I HATE TO BOTHER YOU WHEN YOU'RE IN A HURRY.
BUT...
I WAS WONDERING IF YOU COULD GIVE ME AN AUTOGRAPH.
HERE.

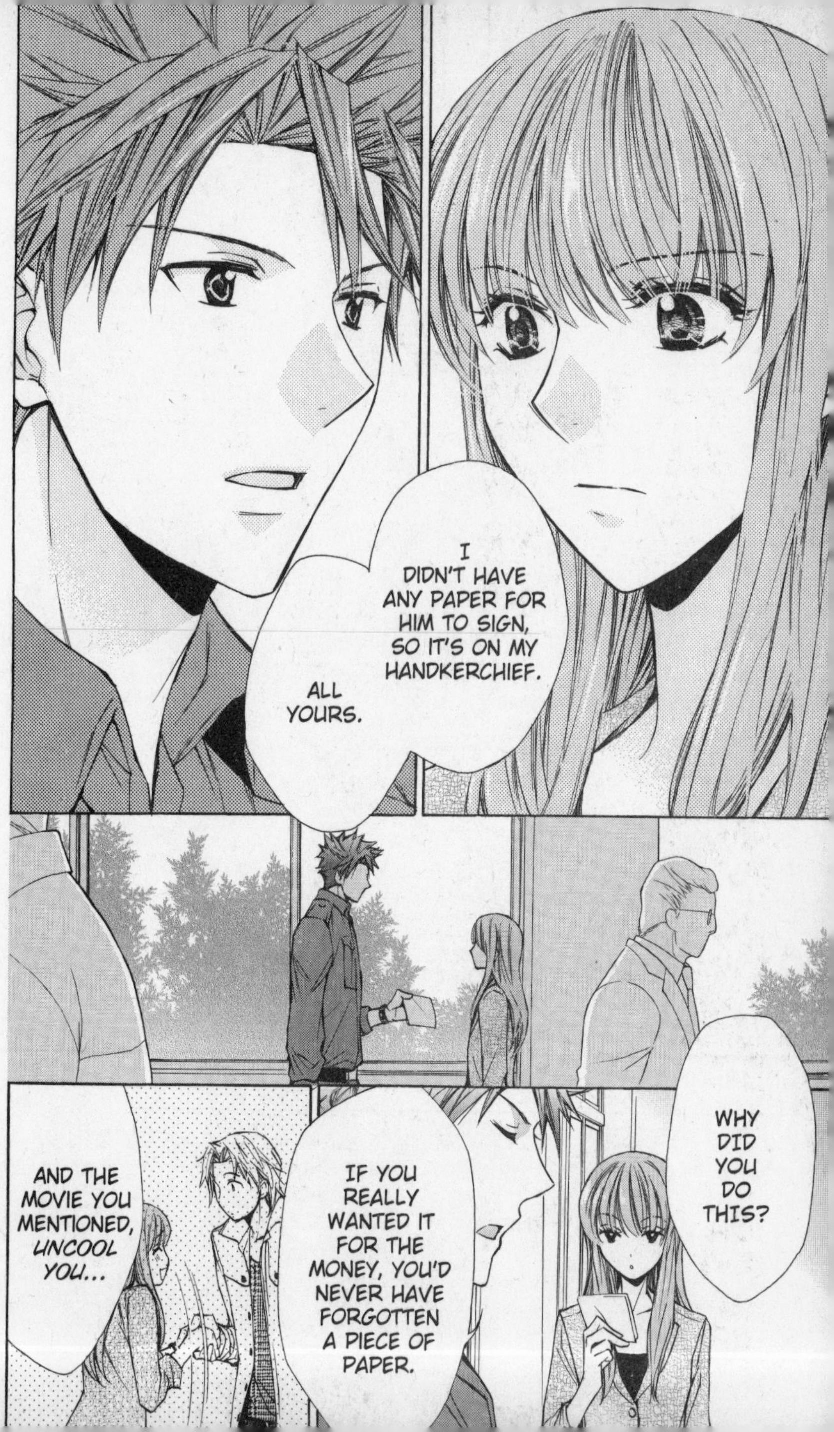
I DIDN'T HAVE ANY PAPER FOR HIM TO SIGN, SO IT'S ON MY HANDKERCHIEF.
ALL YOURS.
WHY DID YOU DO THIS?
IF YOU REALLY WANTED IT FOR THE MONEY, YOU'D NEVER HAVE FORGOTTEN A PIECE OF PAPER.
AND THE MOVIE YOU MENTIONED, UNCOOL YOU...

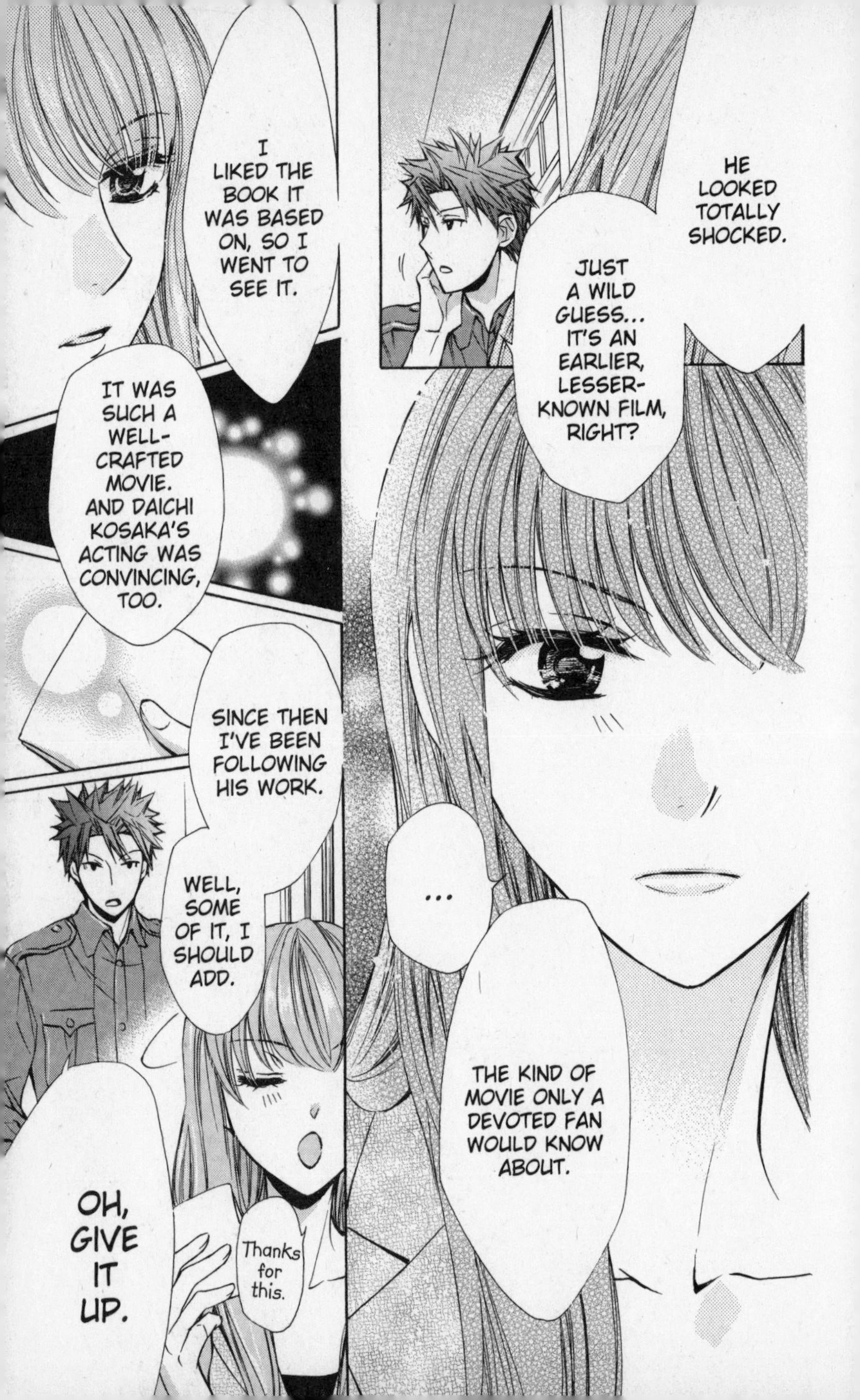
HE LOOKED TOTALLY SHOCKED.
JUST A WILD GUESS... IT'S AN EARLIER, LESSER-KNOWN FILM, RIGHT?
...
THE KIND OF MOVIE ONLY A DEVOTED FAN WOULD KNOW ABOUT.
I LIKED THE BOOK IT WAS BASED ON, SO I WENT TO SEE IT.
IT WAS SUCH A WELL-CRAFTED MOVIE. AND DAICHI KOSAKA'S ACTING WAS CONVINCING, TOO.
SINCE THEN I'VE BEEN FOLLOWING HIS WORK.
WELL, SOME OF IT, I SHOULD ADD.
OH, GIVE IT UP.
Thanks for this.

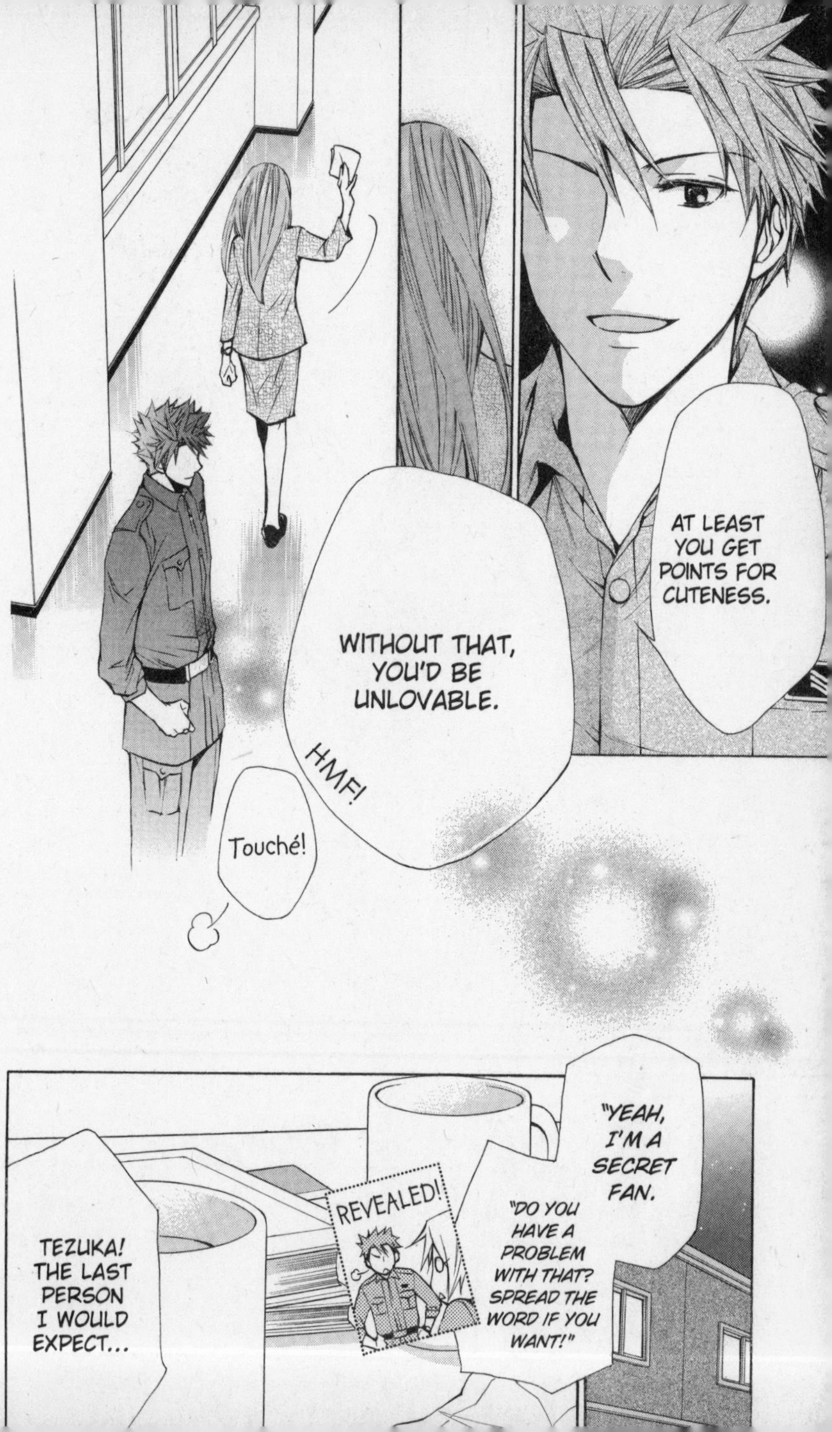
AT LEAST YOU GET POINTS FOR CUTENESS.
WITHOUT THAT, YOU'D BE UNLOVABLE.
HMF!
Touché!
"YEAH, I'M A SECRET FAN.
"DO YOU HAVE A PROBLEM WITH THAT? SPREAD THE WORD IF YOU WANT!"
REVEALED!
TEZUKA! THE LAST PERSON I WOULD EXPECT...

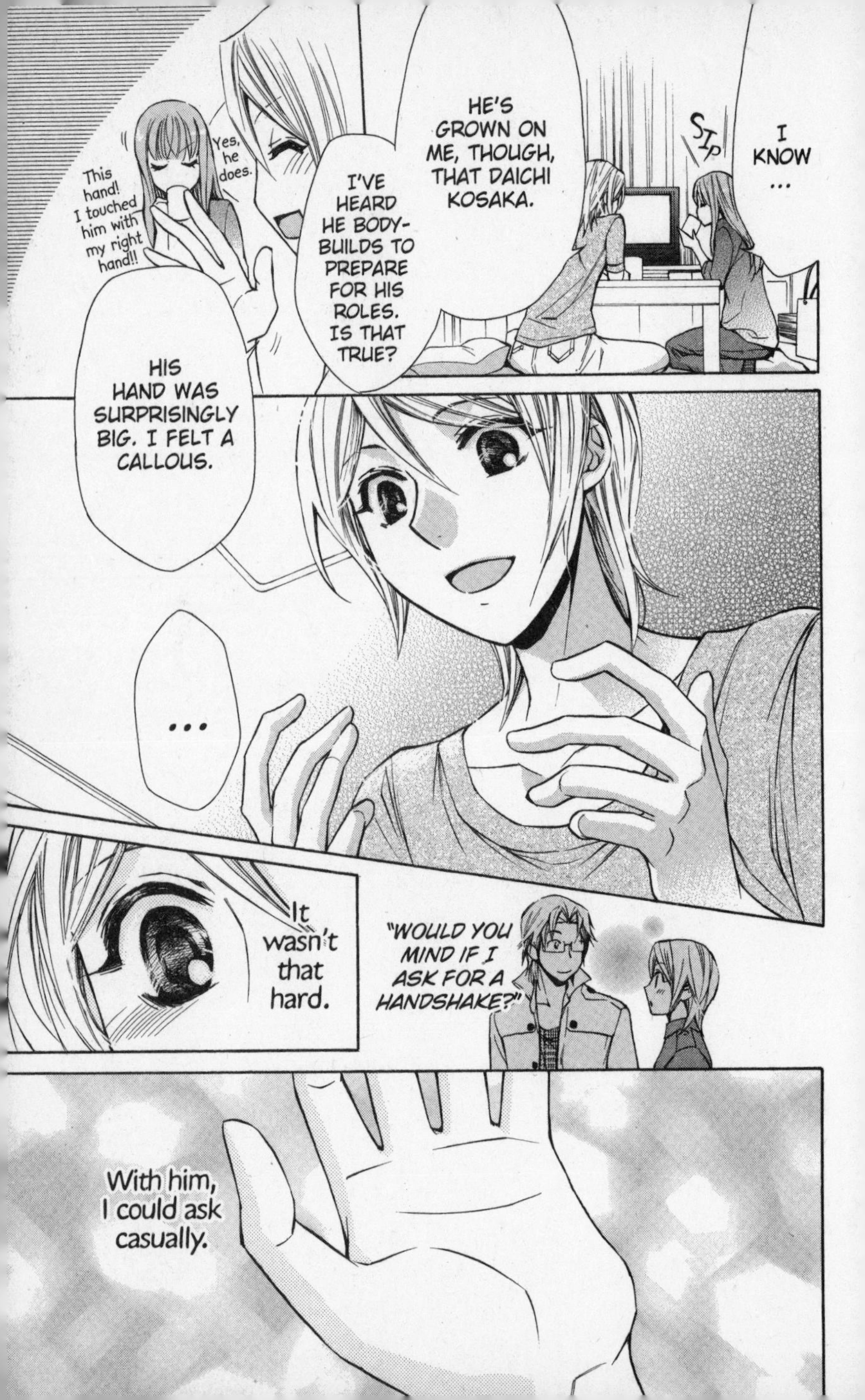
I KNOW ...
STIP
HE'S GROWN ON ME, THOUGH, THAT DAICHI KOSAKA.
I'VE HEARD HE BODY-BUILDS TO PREPARE FOR HIS ROLES. IS THAT TRUE?
Yes, he does.
This hand! I touched him with my right hand!!
HIS HAND WAS SURPRISINGLY BIG. I FELT A CALLOUS.
...
"WOULD YOU MIND IF I ASK FOR A HANDSHAKE?"
It wasn't that hard.
With him, I could ask casually.

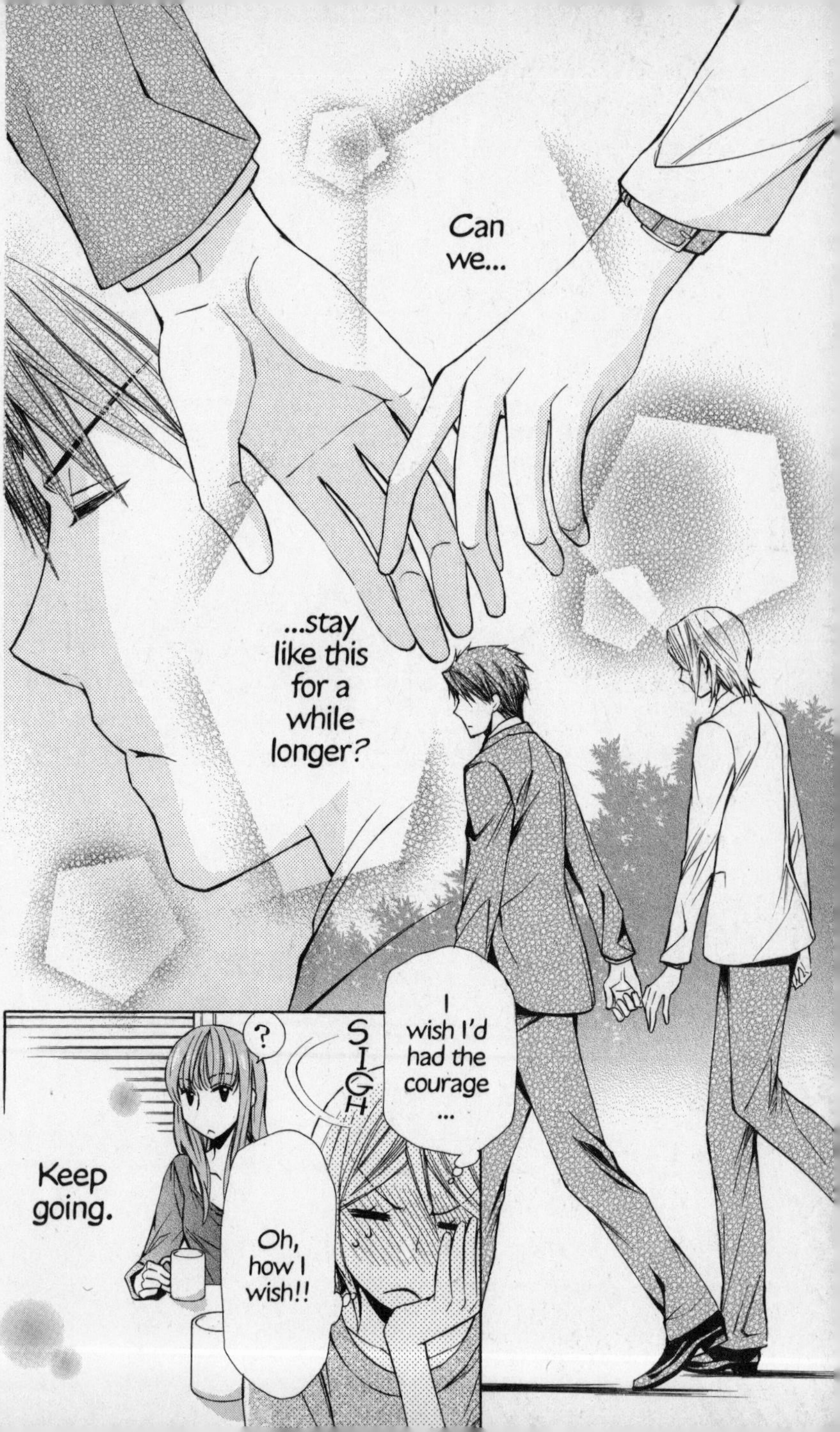
Can we...
...stay like this for a while longer?
I wish I'd had the courage ...
SIGH
?
Oh, how I wish!!
Keep going.

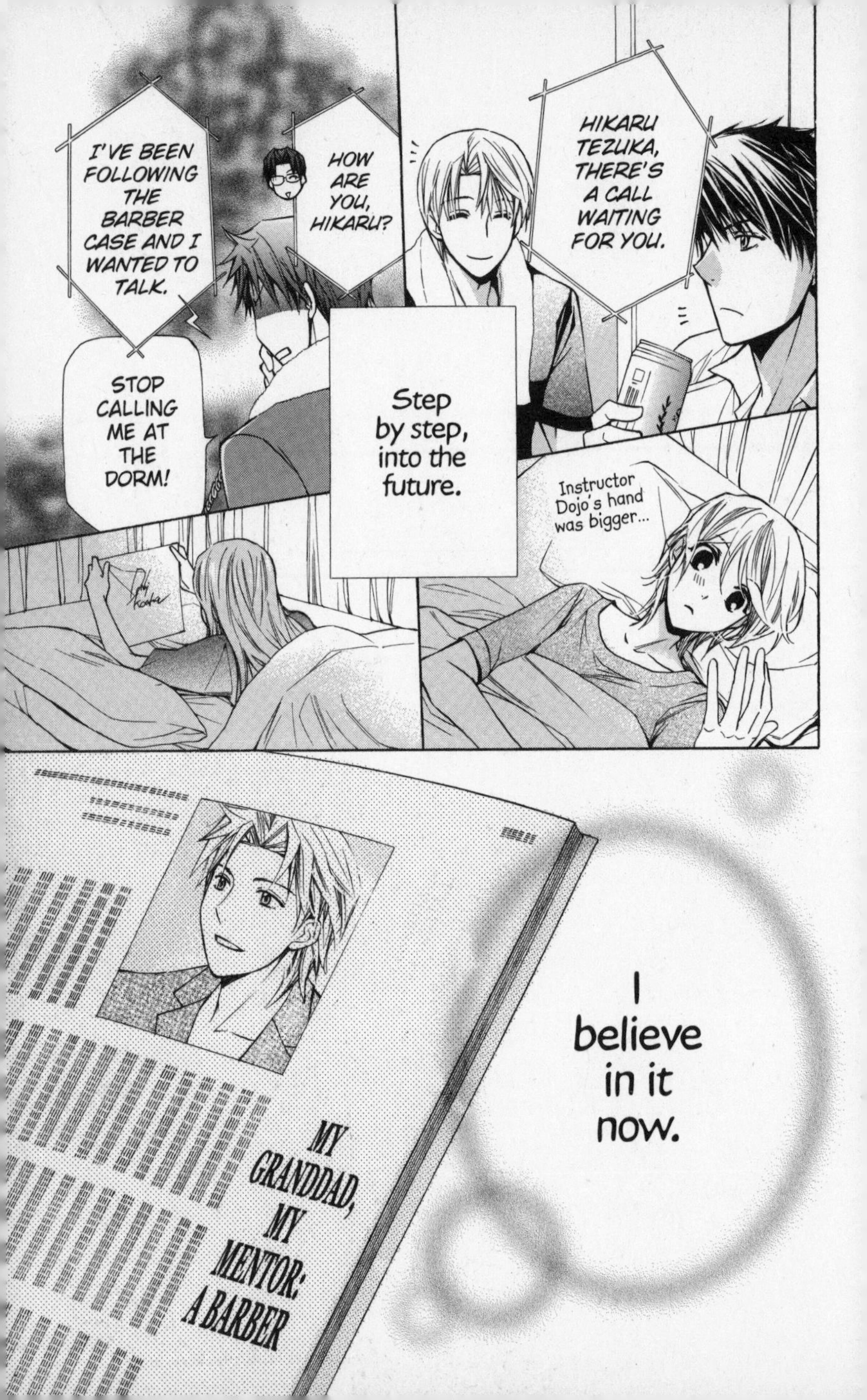
HIKARU TEZUKA, THERE'S A CALL WAITING FOR YOU.
HOW ARE YOU, HIKARU?
I'VE BEEN FOLLOWING THE BARBER CASE AND I WANTED TO TALK.
STOP CALLING ME AT THE DORM!
Step by step, into the future.
Instructor Dojo's hand was bigger...
MY GRANDDAD, MY MENTOR: A BARBER
I believe in it now.

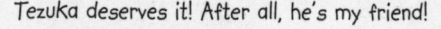

Tezuka deserves it! After all, he's my friend!

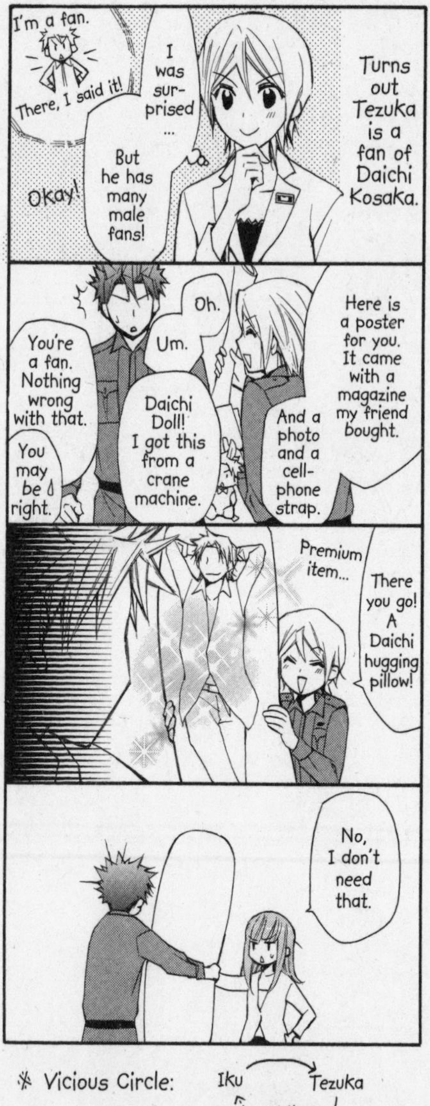

Turns out Tezuka is a fan of Daichi Kosaka.
I was surprised ...
But he has many male fans!
I'm a fan.
There, I said it!
Okay!
Here is a poster for you. It came with a magazine my friend bought.
And a photo and a cell-phone strap.
Oh.
Um.
Daichi Doll! I got this from a crane machine.
You're a fan. Nothing wrong with that.
You may be right.
There you go! A Daichi hugging pillow!
Premium item...
No, I don't need that.

※ Vicious Circle: Iku → Tezuka → Shiba-zaki → Iku

Will Iku find out?

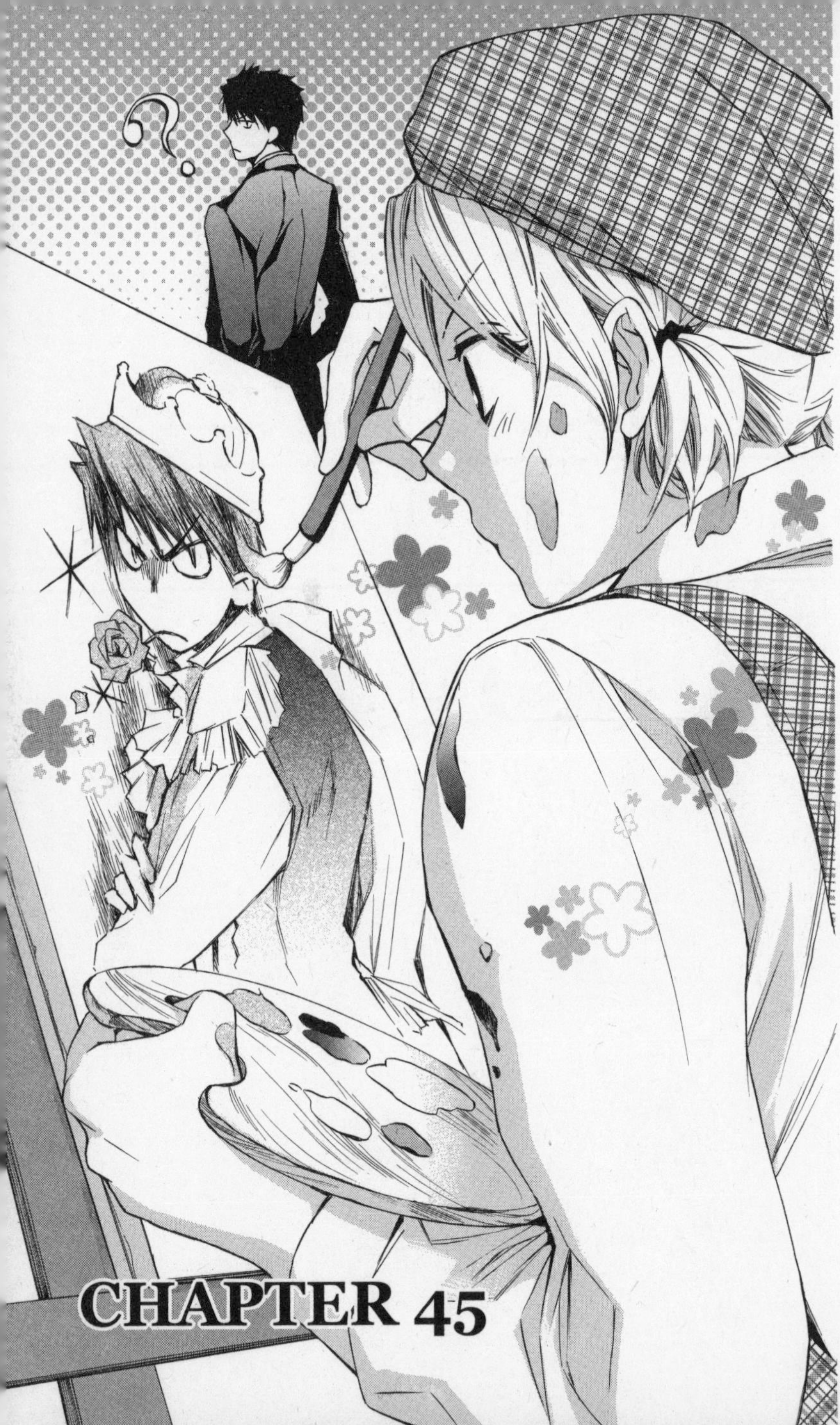
CHAPTER 45

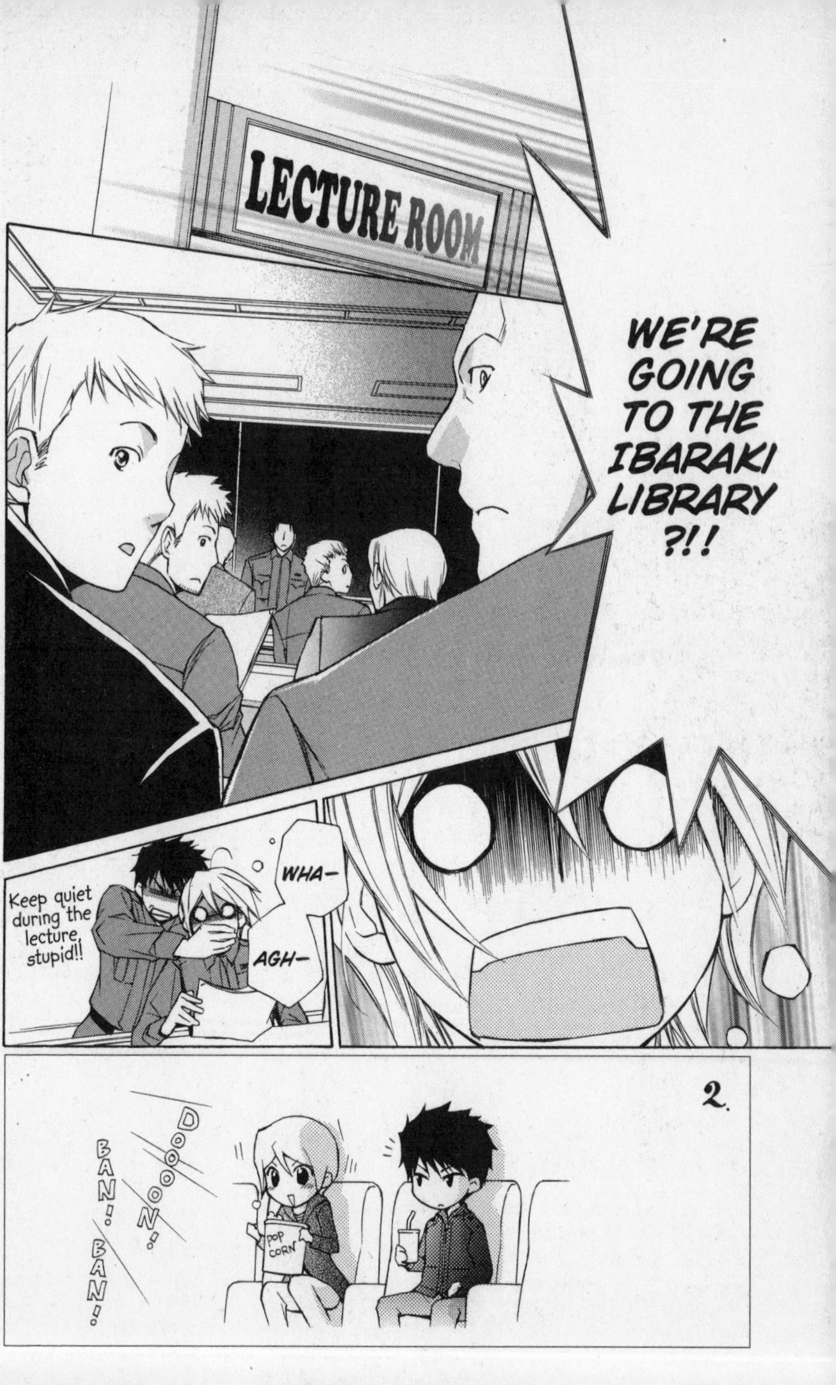
LECTURE ROOM
WE'RE GOING TO THE IBARAKI LIBRARY ?!!
WHA-
AGH-
Keep quiet during the lecture, stupid!!
2.
DOOOON!
BAN! BAN!
POP CORN

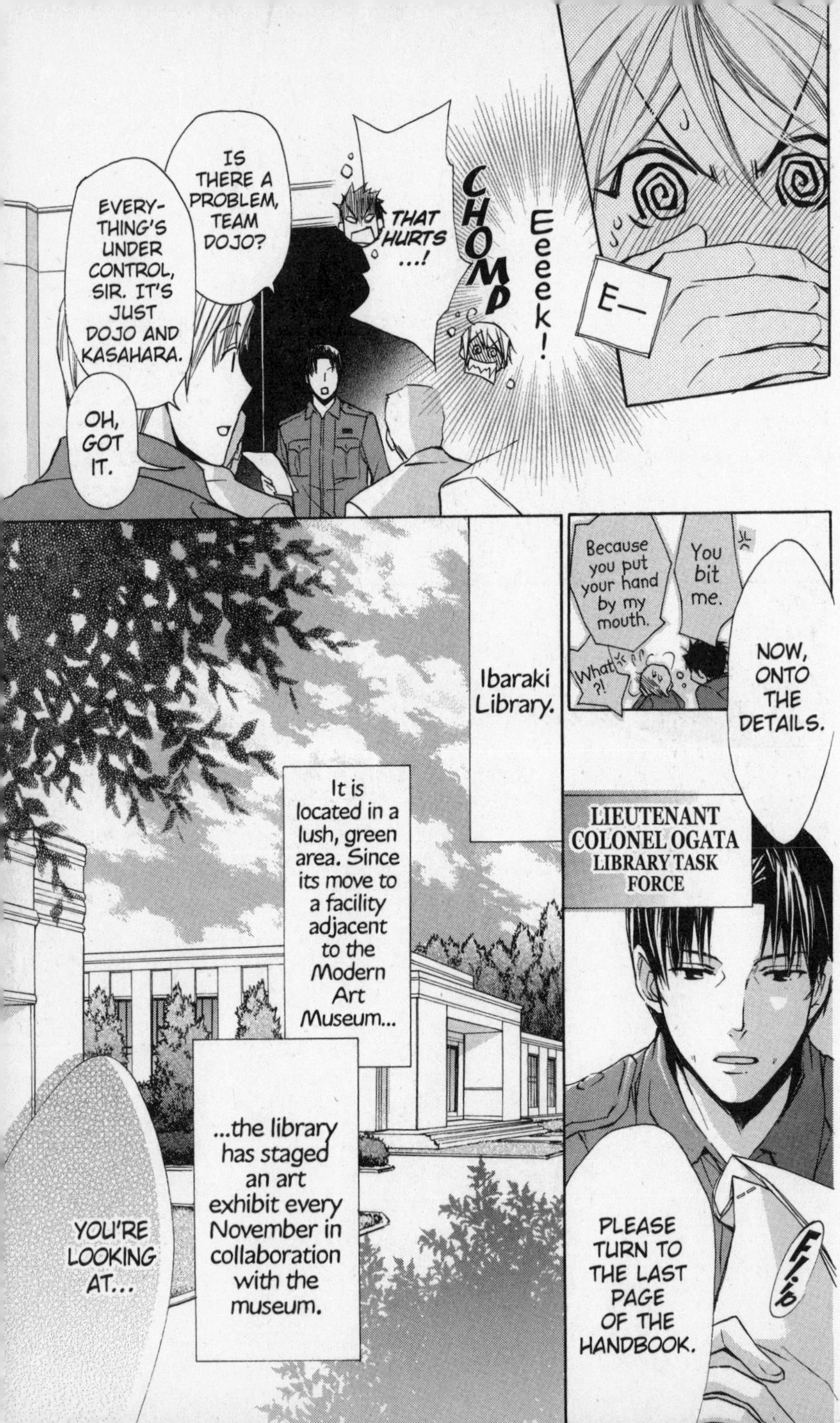
E—
Eeeek!
CHOMP
THAT HURTS ...!
IS THERE A PROBLEM, TEAM DOJO?
EVERY-THING'S UNDER CONTROL, SIR. IT'S JUST DOJO AND KASAHARA.
OH, GOT IT.
You bit me.
Because you put your hand by my mouth.
What?!
NOW, ONTO THE DETAILS.
LIEUTENANT COLONEL OGATA LIBRARY TASK FORCE
PLEASE TURN TO THE LAST PAGE OF THE HANDBOOK.
Ibaraki Library.
It is located in a lush, green area. Since its move to a facility adjacent to the Modern Art Museum...
...the library has staged an art exhibit every November in collaboration with the museum.
YOU'RE LOOKING AT...

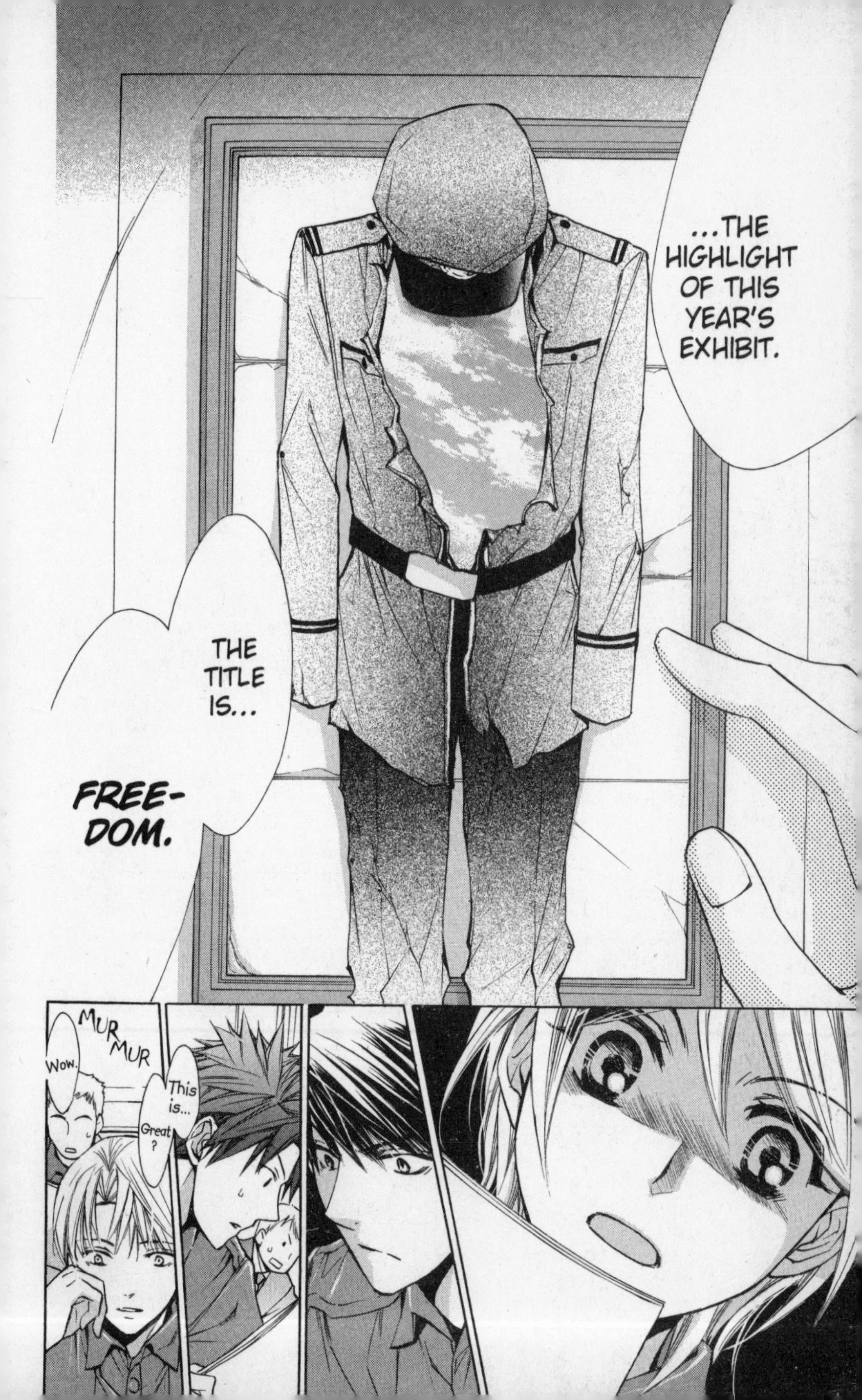
...THE HIGHLIGHT OF THIS YEAR'S EXHIBIT.
THE TITLE IS...
FREE-DOM.
This is...
Great?
MUR MUR
Wow.

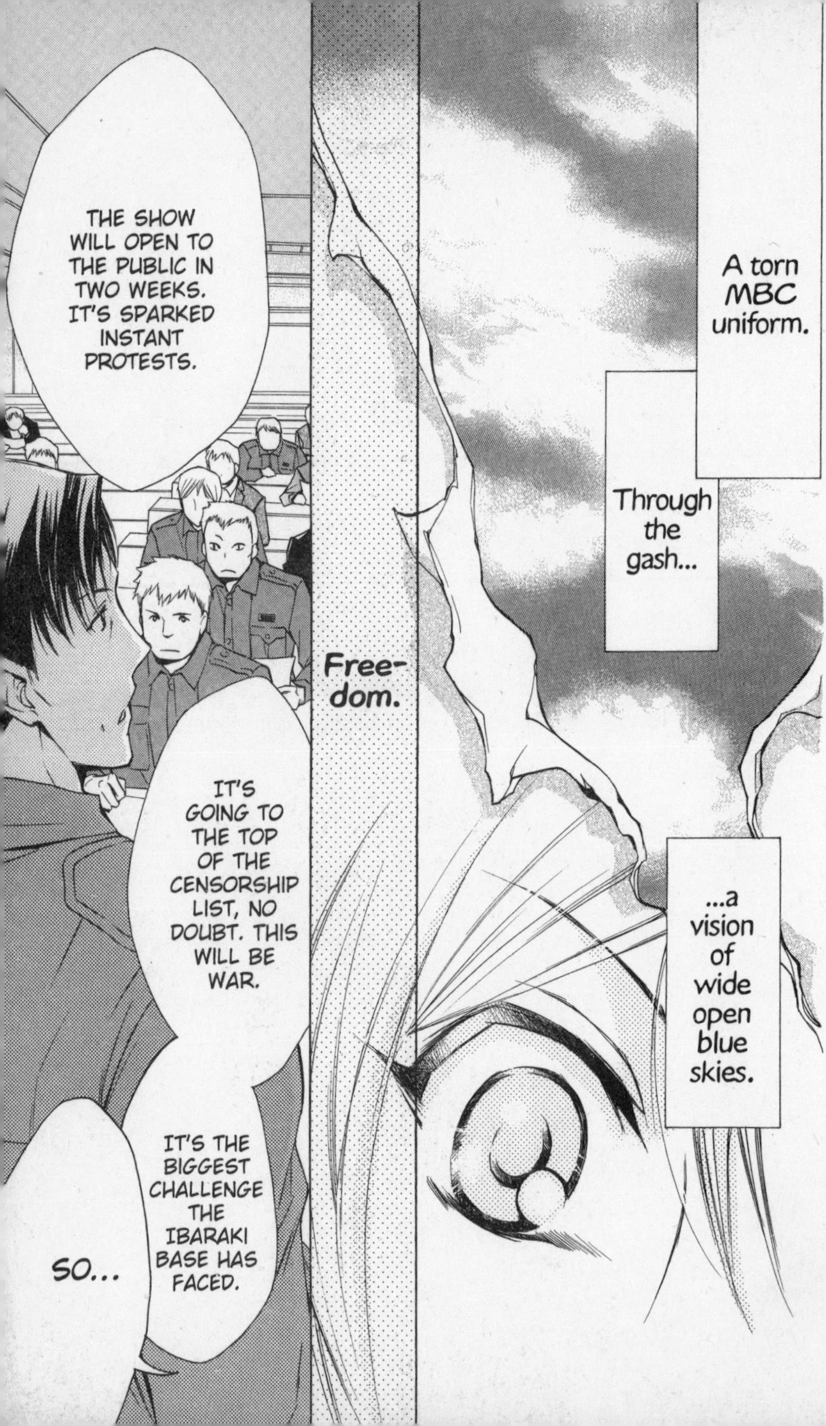
A torn MBC uniform.
Through the gash...
...a vision of wide open blue skies.
Free-dom.
THE SHOW WILL OPEN TO THE PUBLIC IN TWO WEEKS. IT'S SPARKED INSTANT PROTESTS.
IT'S GOING TO THE TOP OF THE CENSORSHIP LIST, NO DOUBT. THIS WILL BE WAR.
IT'S THE BIGGEST CHALLENGE THE IBARAKI BASE HAS FACED.
SO...

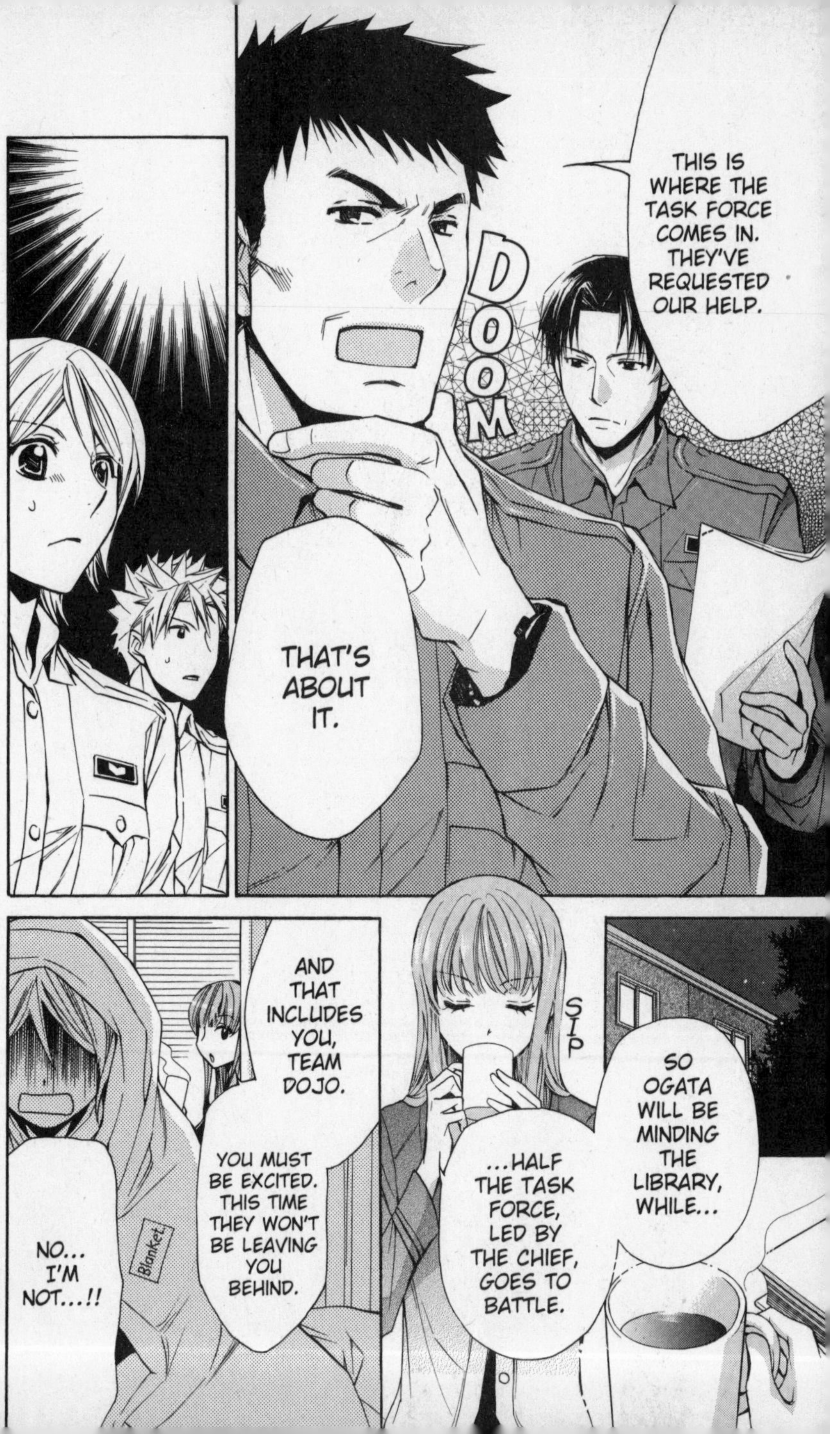
THIS IS WHERE THE TASK FORCE COMES IN. THEY'VE REQUESTED OUR HELP.
DOOM
THAT'S ABOUT IT.
SO OGATA WILL BE MINDING THE LIBRARY, WHILE...
...HALF THE TASK FORCE, LED BY THE CHIEF, GOES TO BATTLE.
SIP
AND THAT INCLUDES YOU, TEAM DOJO.
YOU MUST BE EXCITED. THIS TIME THEY WON'T BE LEAVING YOU BEHIND.
Blanket.
NO... I'M NOT...!!

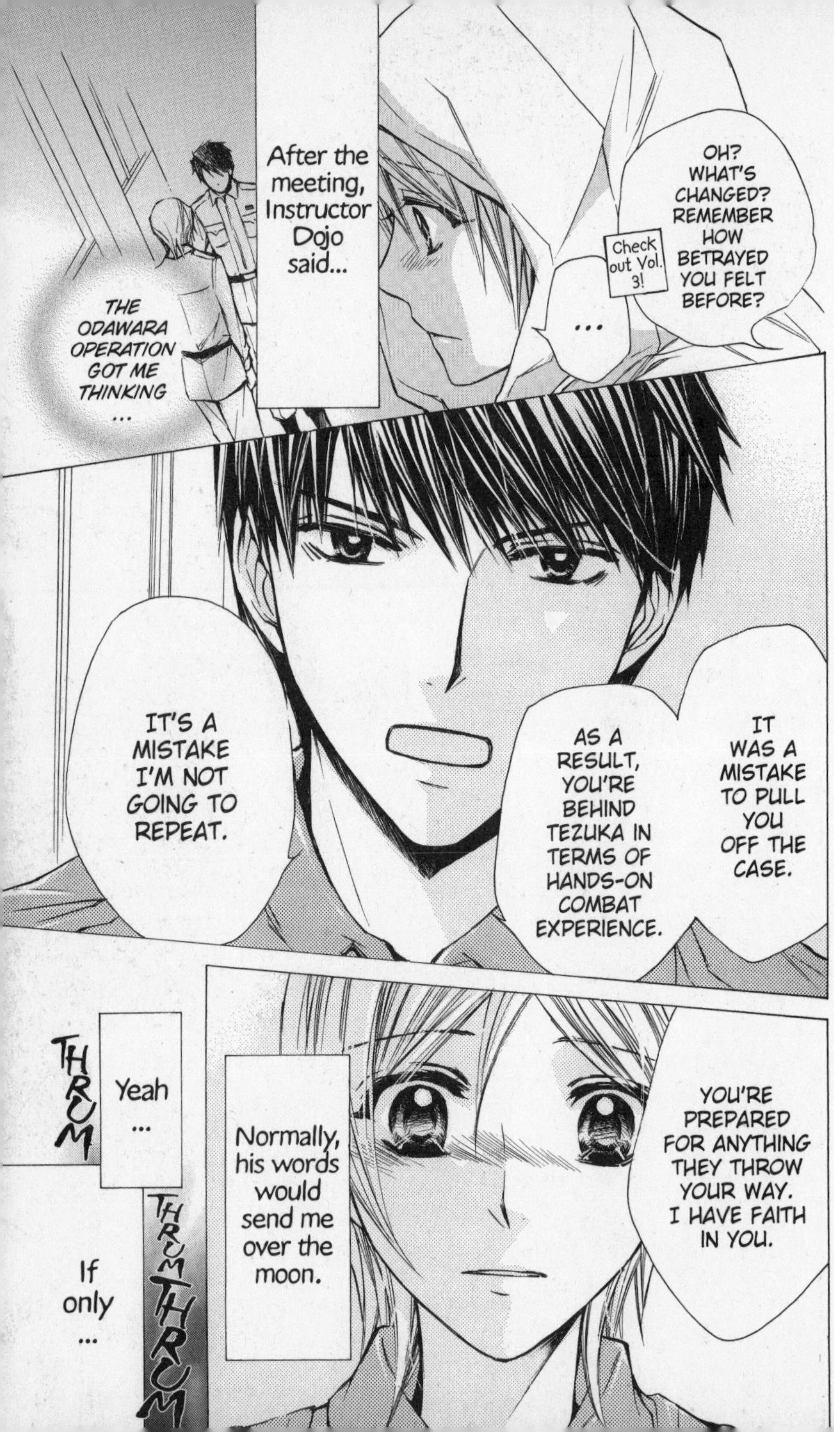
OH? WHAT'S CHANGED? REMEMBER HOW BETRAYED YOU FELT BEFORE?
Check out Vol. 3!
...
After the meeting, Instructor Dojo said...
THE ODAWARA OPERATION GOT ME THINKING ...
IT WAS A MISTAKE TO PULL YOU OFF THE CASE.
AS A RESULT, YOU'RE BEHIND TEZUKA IN TERMS OF HANDS-ON COMBAT EXPERIENCE.
IT'S A MISTAKE I'M NOT GOING TO REPEAT.
YOU'RE PREPARED FOR ANYTHING THEY THROW YOUR WAY. I HAVE FAITH IN YOU.
Normally, his words would send me over the moon.
THRUM
Yeah ...
THRUM THRUM
If only ...

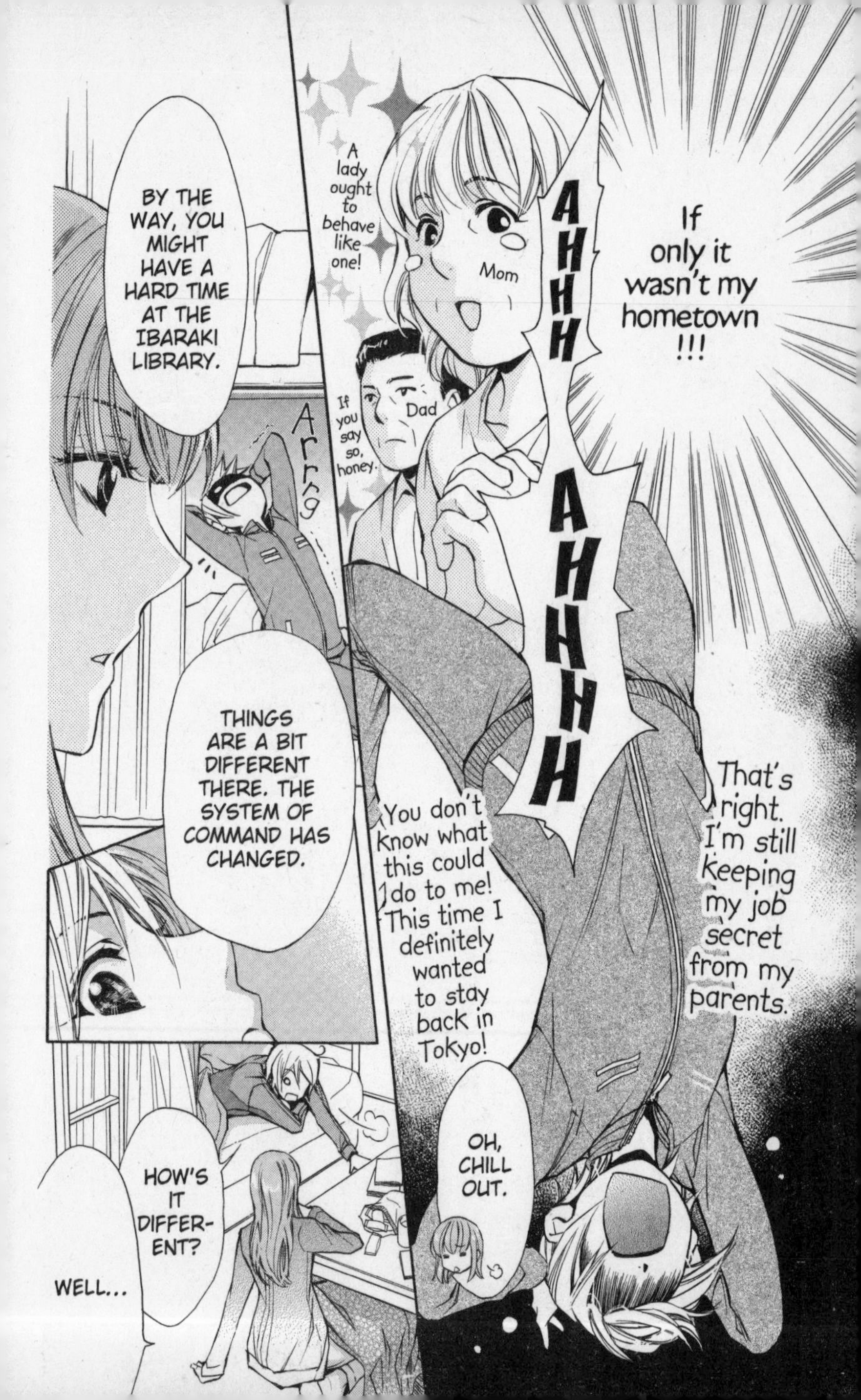
If only it wasn't my hometown !!!
AHHH AHHHHH
Mom
A lady ought to behave like one!
Dad
If you say so, honey.
That's right. I'm still keeping my job secret from my parents.
You don't know what this could do to me! This time I definitely wanted to stay back in Tokyo!
OH, CHILL OUT.
BY THE WAY, YOU MIGHT HAVE A HARD TIME AT THE IBARAKI LIBRARY.
Arrrg
THINGS ARE A BIT DIFFERENT THERE. THE SYSTEM OF COMMAND HAS CHANGED.
HOW'S IT DIFFER-ENT?
WELL...

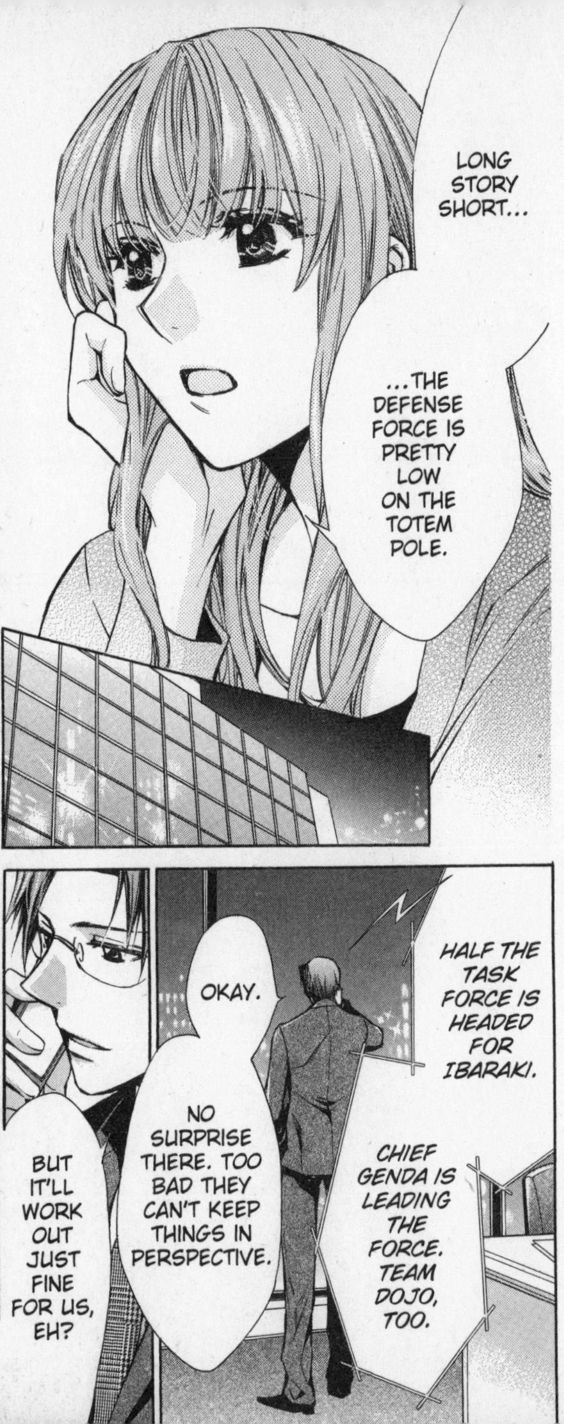
LONG STORY SHORT...
...THE DEFENSE FORCE IS PRETTY LOW ON THE TOTEM POLE.
HALF THE TASK FORCE IS HEADED FOR IBARAKI.
CHIEF GENDA IS LEADING THE FORCE. TEAM DOJO, TOO.
OKAY.
NO SURPRISE THERE. TOO BAD THEY CAN'T KEEP THINGS IN PERSPECTIVE.
BUT IT'LL WORK OUT JUST FINE FOR US, EH?

2

This volume was so full there was no space left for a bonus manga. It's not up to me to decide—if there's enough space for extra episodes, I'll gladly oblige. The volume covers a whole story arc from cover to cover. But would the readers of *LaLa* magazine prefer a few extra short stories at the end? I don't know which is better...

Anyway, I look forward to making more bonus manga.

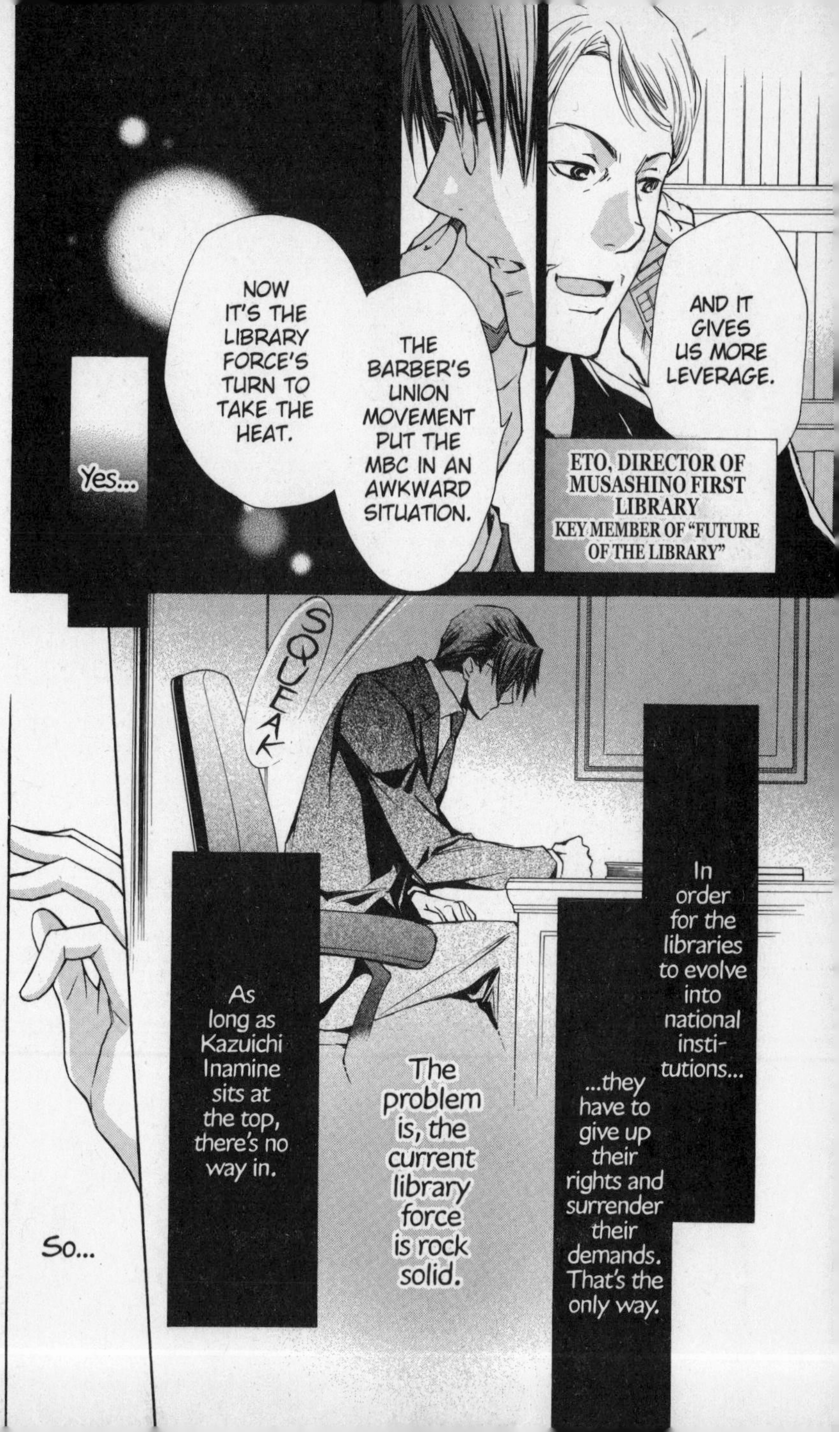
AND IT GIVES US MORE LEVERAGE.
ETO, DIRECTOR OF MUSASHINO FIRST LIBRARY
KEY MEMBER OF "FUTURE OF THE LIBRARY"
THE BARBER'S UNION MOVEMENT PUT THE MBC IN AN AWKWARD SITUATION.
NOW IT'S THE LIBRARY FORCE'S TURN TO TAKE THE HEAT.
Yes...
SQUEAK
In order for the libraries to evolve into national institutions...
...they have to give up their rights and surrender their demands. That's the only way.
The problem is, the current library force is rock solid.
As long as Kazuichi Inamine sits at the top, there's no way in.
So...

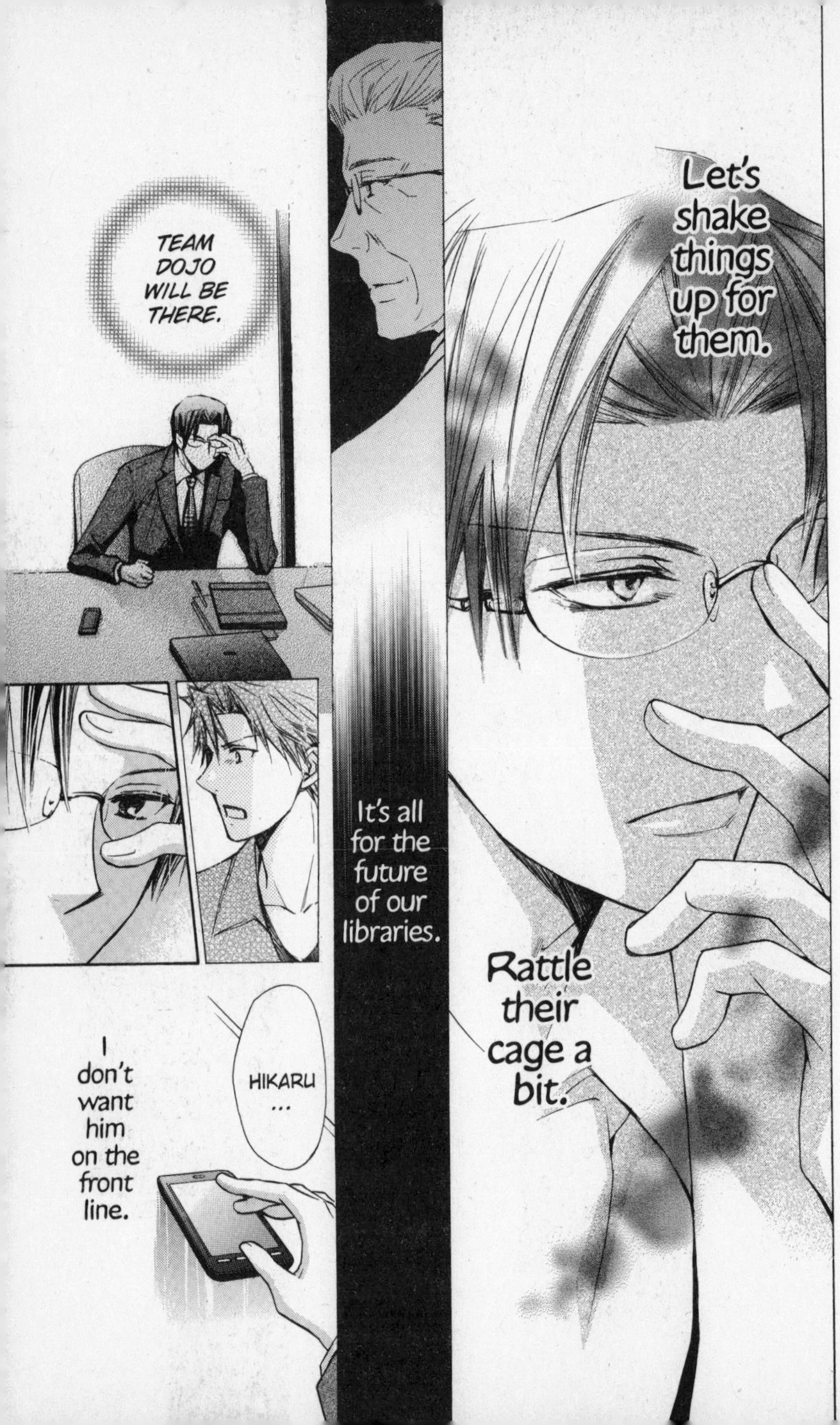
Let's shake things up for them.
Rattle their cage a bit.
It's all for the future of our libraries.
TEAM DOJO WILL BE THERE.
HIKARU ...
I don't want him on the front line.

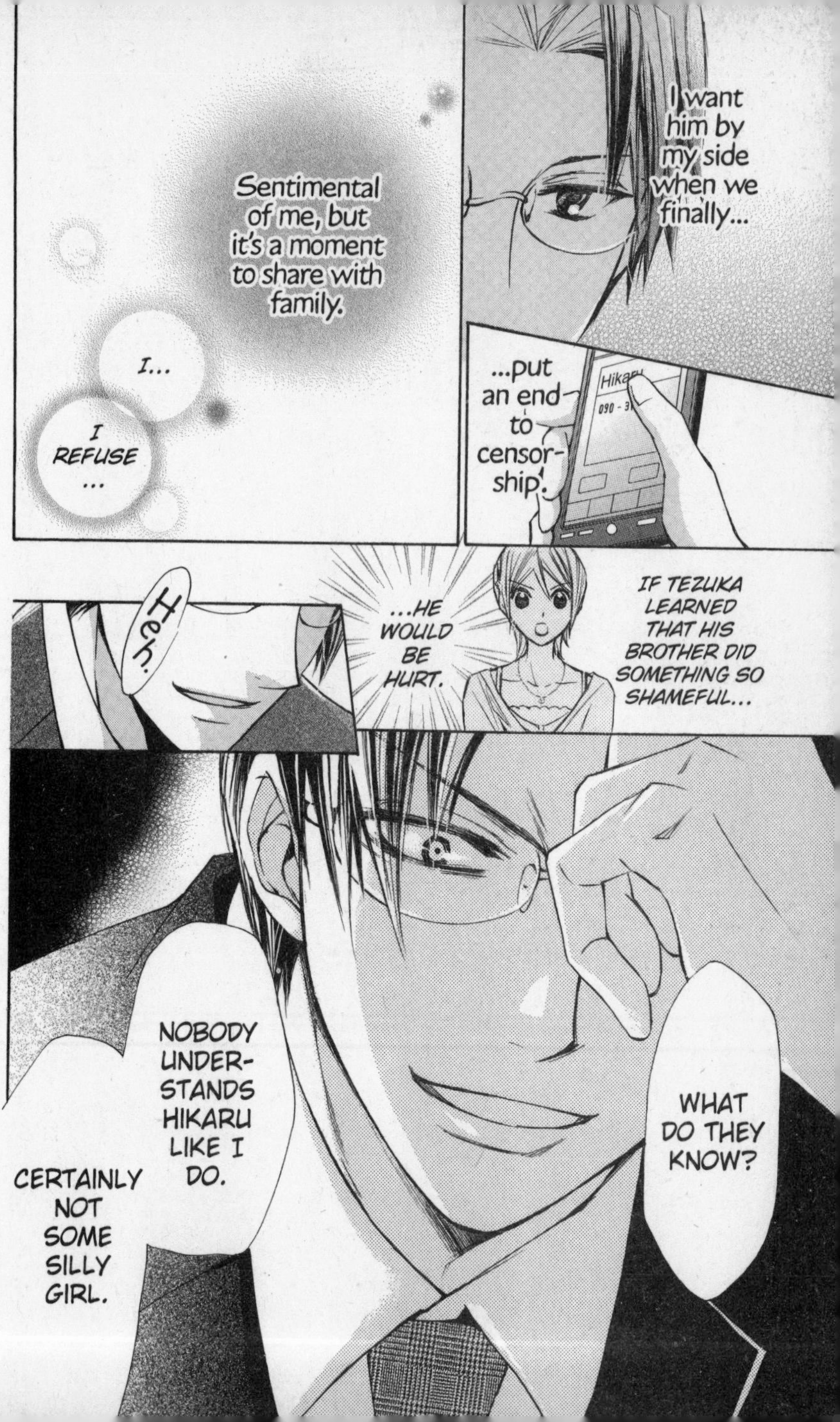
I want him by my side when we finally...
...put an end to censorship.
Sentimental of me, but it's a moment to share with family.
I...
I REFUSE ...
IF TEZUKA LEARNED THAT HIS BROTHER DID SOMETHING SO SHAMEFUL...
...HE WOULD BE HURT.
Heh.
WHAT DO THEY KNOW?
NOBODY UNDER-STANDS HIKARU LIKE I DO.
CERTAINLY NOT SOME SILLY GIRL.

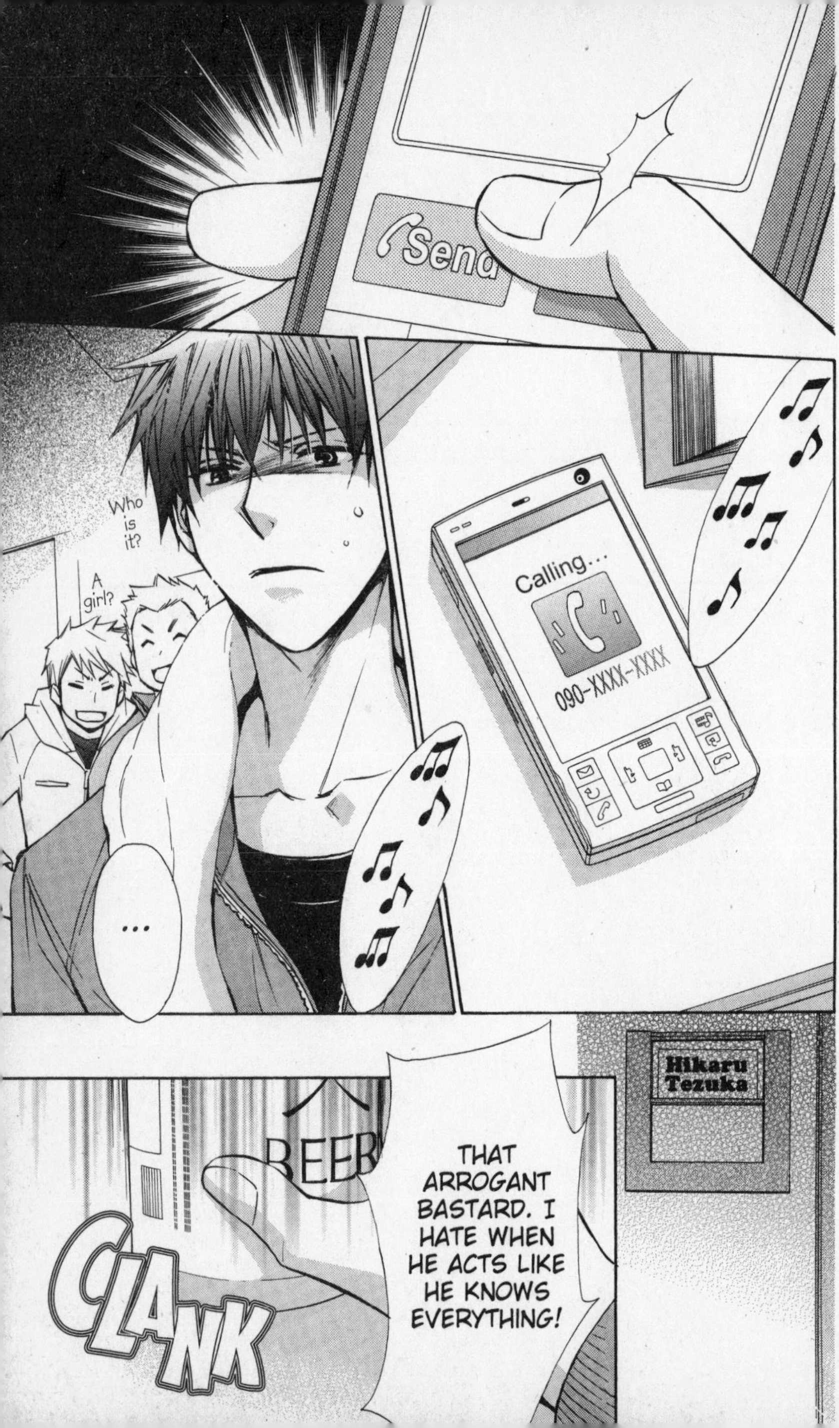
Send
Calling...
090-XXXX-XXXX
Who is it?
A girl?
...
Hikaru Tezuka
THAT ARROGANT BASTARD. I HATE WHEN HE ACTS LIKE HE KNOWS EVERYTHING!
BEER
CLANK

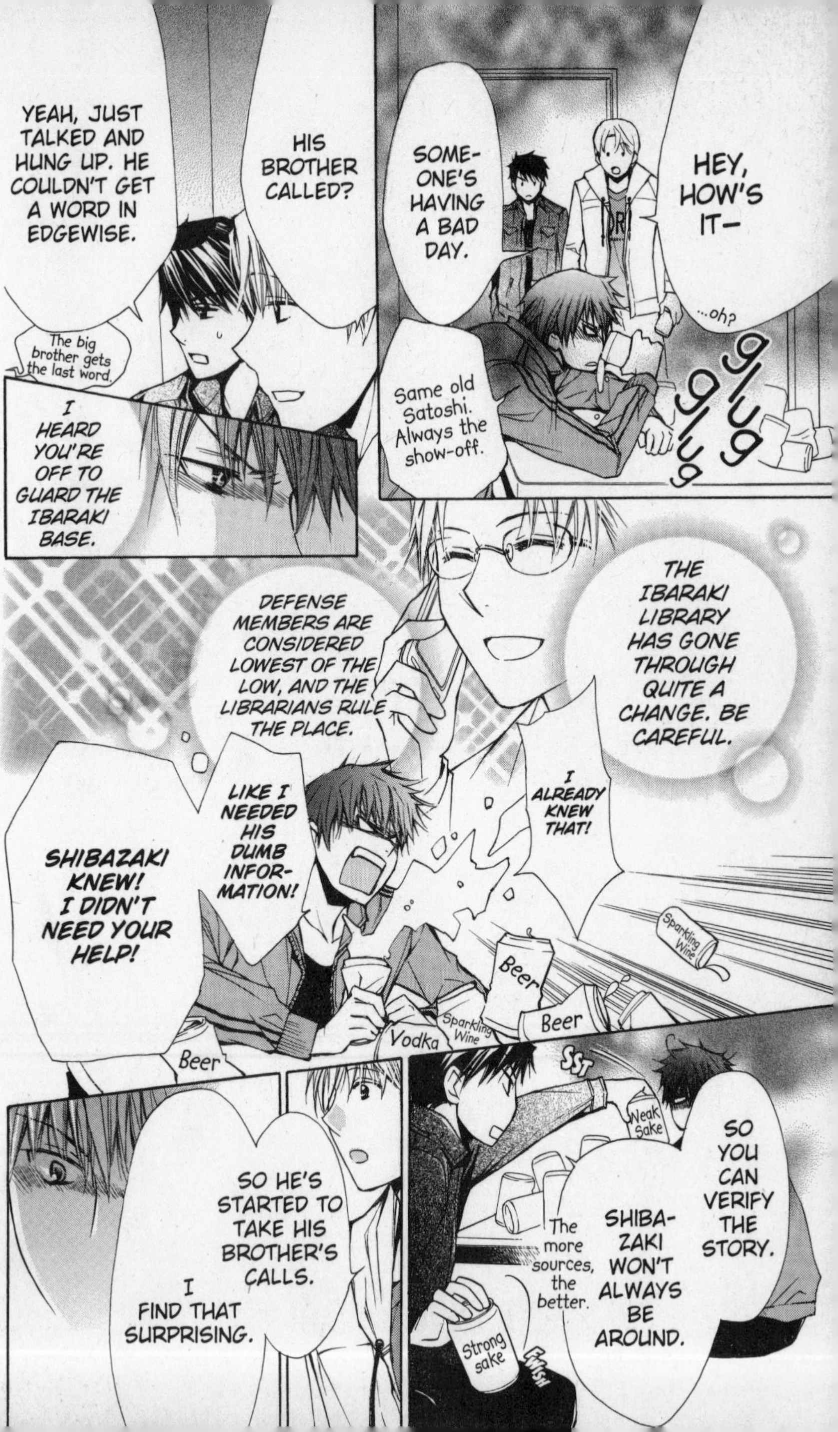
HEY, HOW'S IT—
...oh?
glug glug glug
SOME-ONE'S HAVING A BAD DAY.
Same old Satoshi. Always the show-off.
HIS BROTHER CALLED?
YEAH, JUST TALKED AND HUNG UP. HE COULDN'T GET A WORD IN EDGEWISE.
The big brother gets the last word.
I HEARD YOU'RE OFF TO GUARD THE IBARAKI BASE.
THE IBARAKI LIBRARY HAS GONE THROUGH QUITE A CHANGE. BE CAREFUL.
DEFENSE MEMBERS ARE CONSIDERED LOWEST OF THE LOW, AND THE LIBRARIANS RULE THE PLACE.
I ALREADY KNEW THAT!
LIKE I NEEDED HIS DUMB INFORMATION!
SHIBAZAKI KNEW! I DIDN'T NEED YOUR HELP!
Sparkling Wine
Beer
Beer
Sparkling Wine
Vodka
Beer
SST
Weak Sake
SO YOU CAN VERIFY THE STORY.
SHIBA-ZAKI WON'T ALWAYS BE AROUND.
The more sources, the better.
Strong sake
SO HE'S STARTED TO TAKE HIS BROTHER'S CALLS.
I FIND THAT SURPRISING.

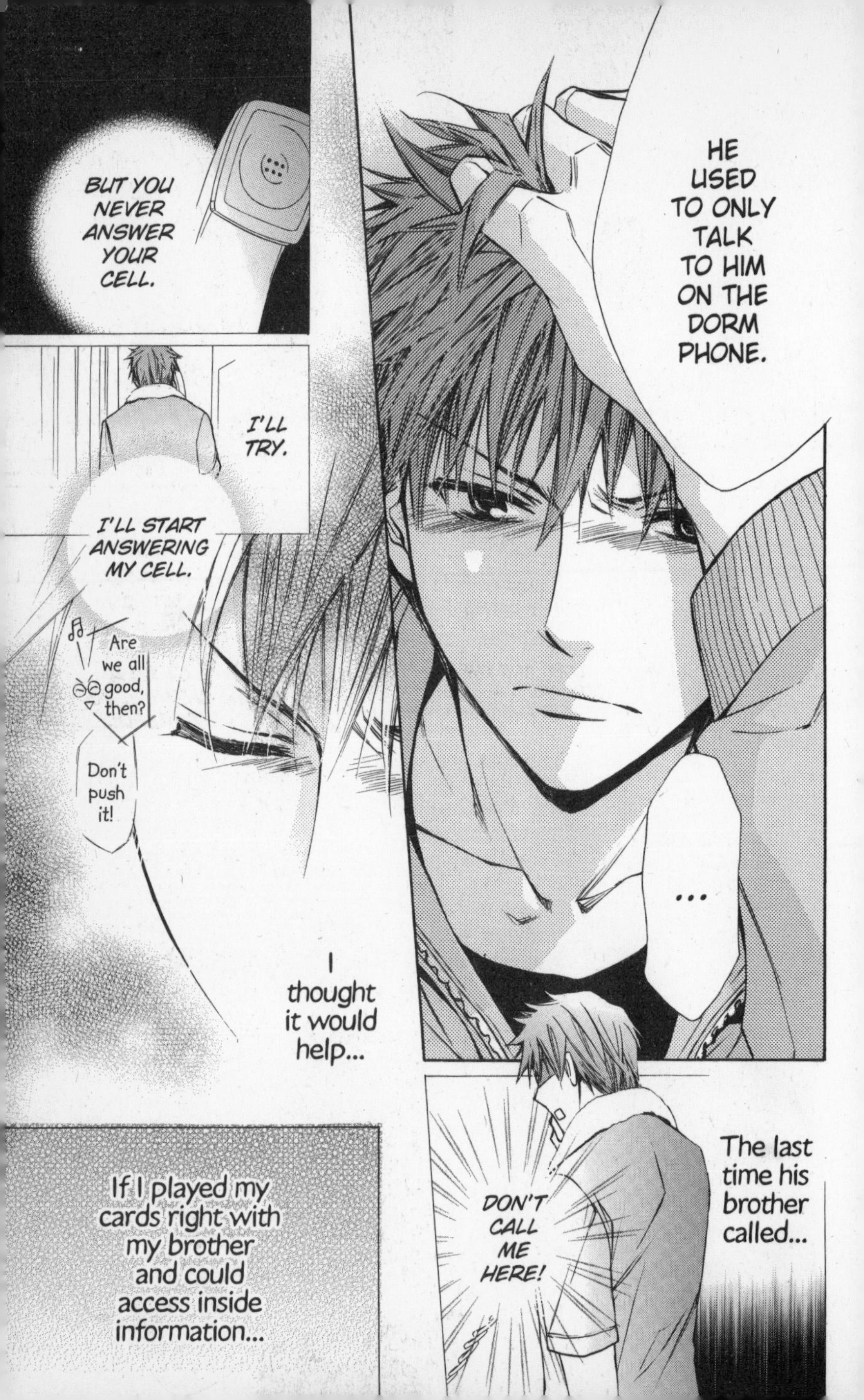
HE USED TO ONLY TALK TO HIM ON THE DORM PHONE.
...
The last time his brother called...
DON'T CALL ME HERE!
BUT YOU NEVER ANSWER YOUR CELL.
I'LL TRY.
I'LL START ANSWERING MY CELL.
Are we all good, then?
Don't push it!
I thought it would help...
If I played my cards right with my brother and could access inside information...

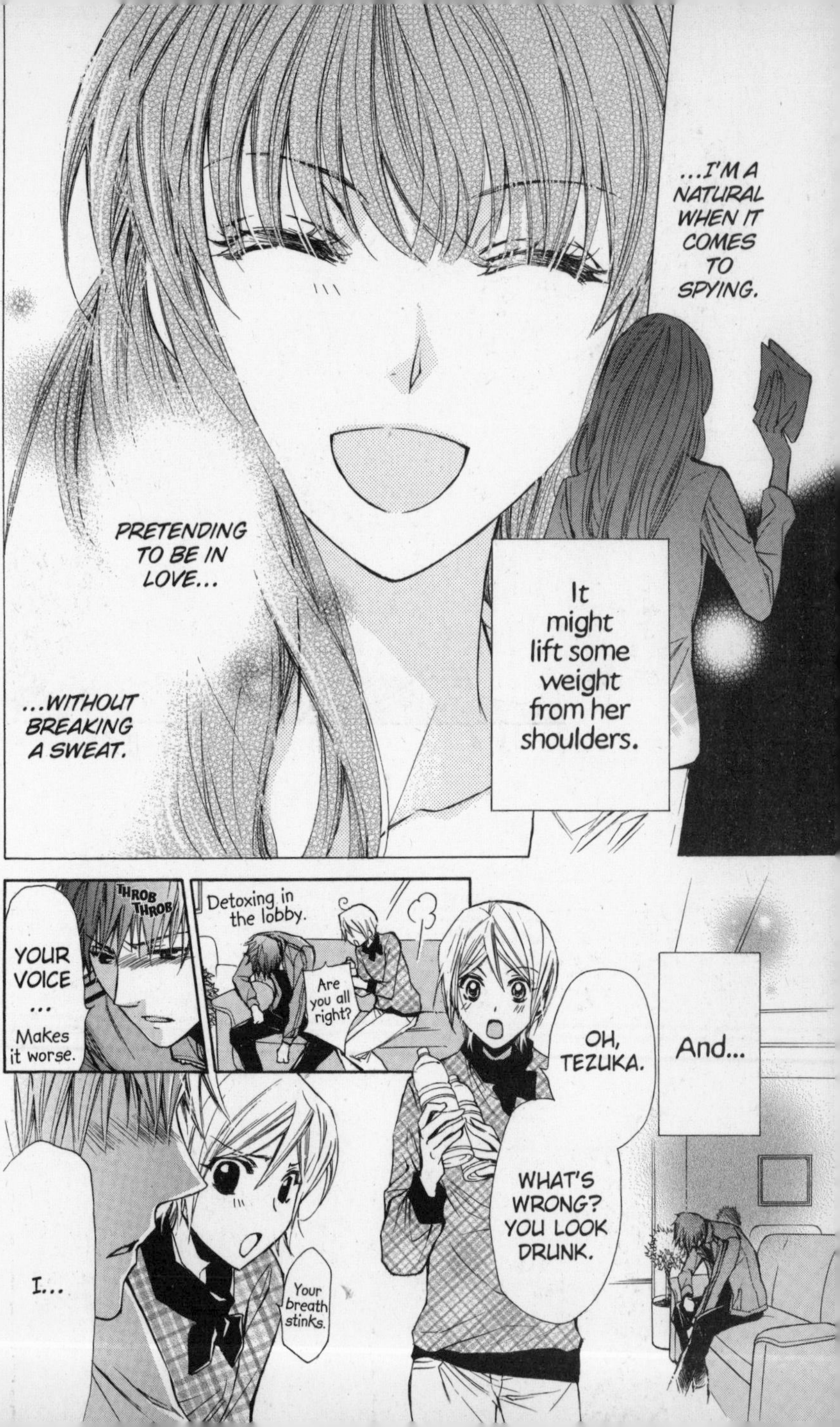
...I'M A NATURAL WHEN IT COMES TO SPYING.
PRETENDING TO BE IN LOVE...
...WITHOUT BREAKING A SWEAT.
It might lift some weight from her shoulders.
And...
Detoxing in the lobby.
Are you all right?
THROB THROB
YOUR VOICE ... Makes it worse.
OH, TEZUKA.
WHAT'S WRONG? YOU LOOK DRUNK.
Your breath stinks.
I...

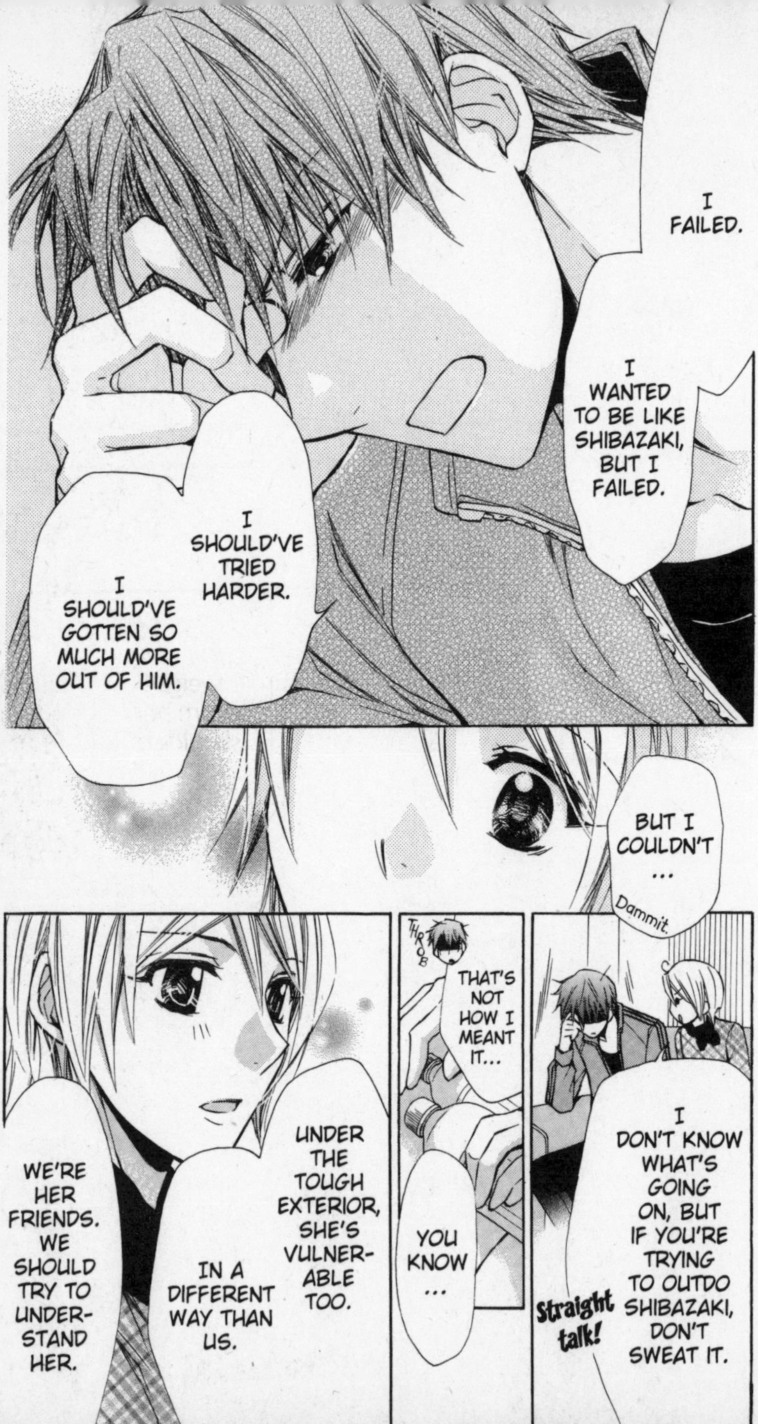
I FAILED.
I WANTED TO BE LIKE SHIBAZAKI, BUT I FAILED.
I SHOULD'VE TRIED HARDER.
I SHOULD'VE GOTTEN SO MUCH MORE OUT OF HIM.
BUT I COULDN'T ...
Dammit.
I DON'T KNOW WHAT'S GOING ON, BUT IF YOU'RE TRYING TO OUTDO SHIBAZAKI, DON'T SWEAT IT.
Straight talk!
THROB
THAT'S NOT HOW I MEANT IT...
YOU KNOW ...
UNDER THE TOUGH EXTERIOR, SHE'S VULNER-ABLE TOO.
IN A DIFFERENT WAY THAN US.
WE'RE HER FRIENDS. WE SHOULD TRY TO UNDER-STAND HER.

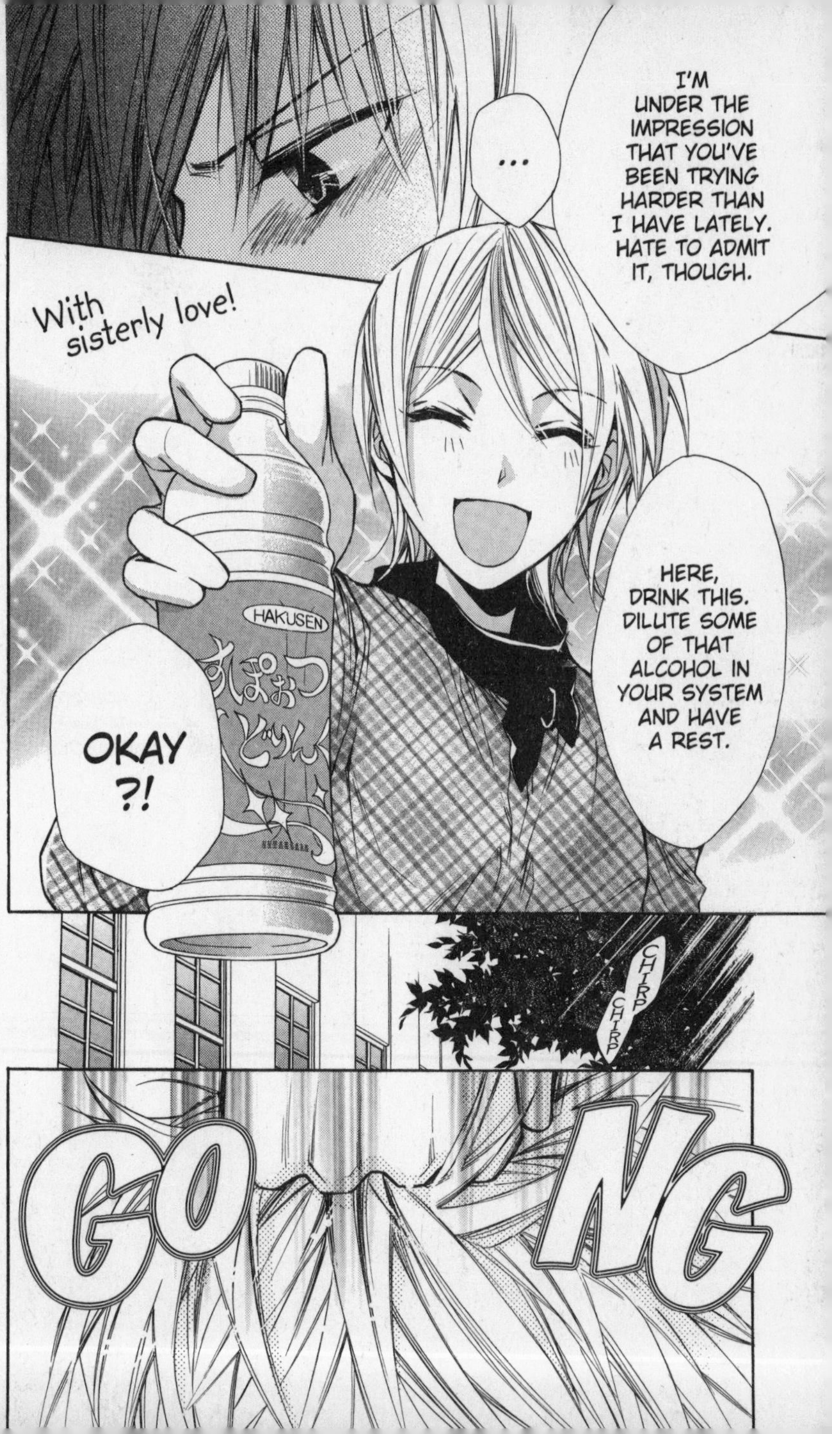
I'M UNDER THE IMPRESSION THAT YOU'VE BEEN TRYING HARDER THAN I HAVE LATELY. HATE TO ADMIT IT, THOUGH.
...
HERE, DRINK THIS. DILUTE SOME OF THAT ALCOHOL IN YOUR SYSTEM AND HAVE A REST.
With sisterly love!
OKAY ?!
HAKUSEN
CHIRP CHIRP
GO NG

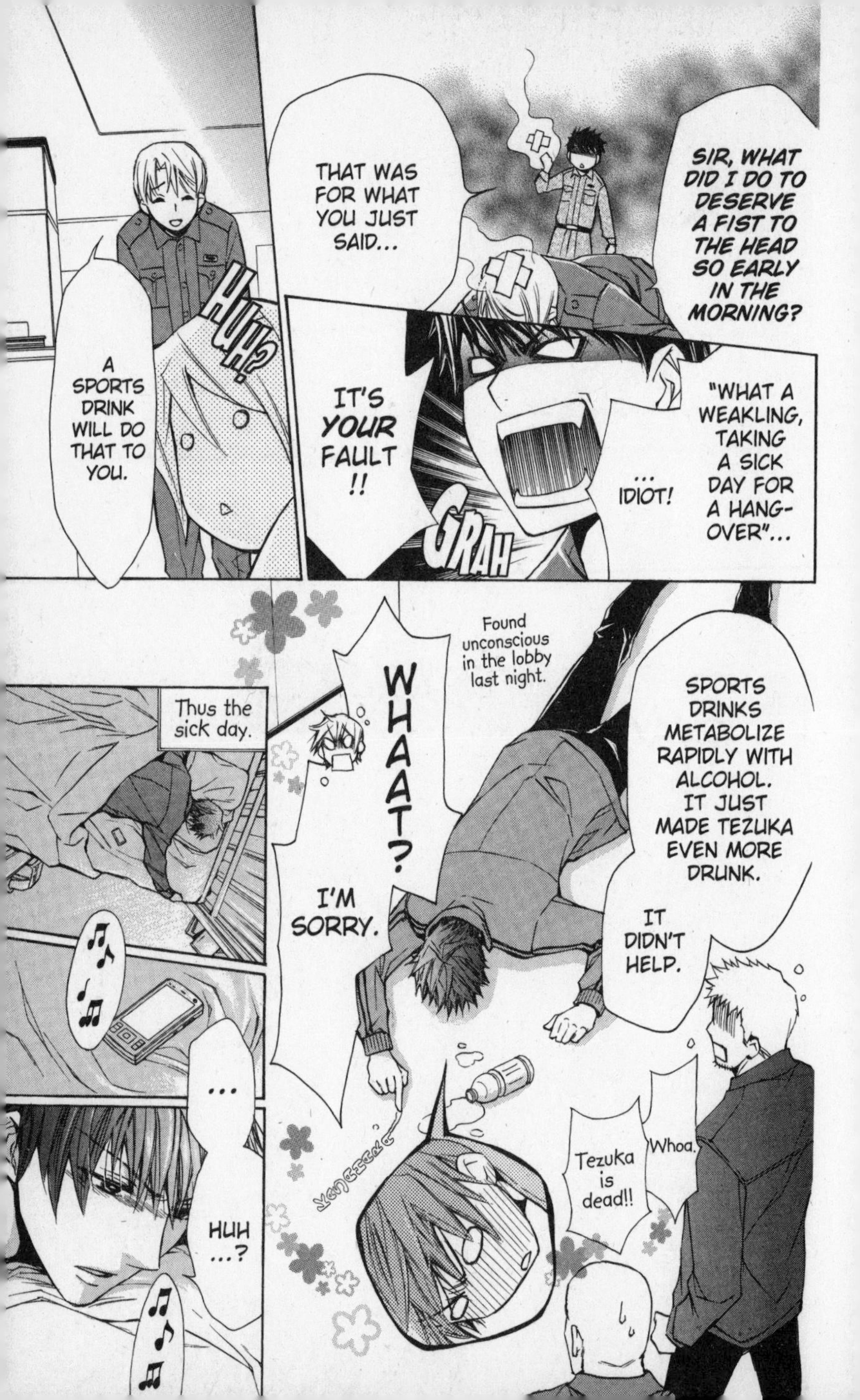
SIR, WHAT DID I DO TO DESERVE A FIST TO THE HEAD SO EARLY IN THE MORNING?
THAT WAS FOR WHAT YOU JUST SAID...
"WHAT A WEAKLING, TAKING A SICK DAY FOR A HANG-OVER"...
...IDIOT!
IT'S YOUR FAULT!!
GRAH
HUH?
A SPORTS DRINK WILL DO THAT TO YOU.
SPORTS DRINKS METABOLIZE RAPIDLY WITH ALCOHOL. IT JUST MADE TEZUKA EVEN MORE DRUNK.
IT DIDN'T HELP.
Found unconscious in the lobby last night.
WHAAT?
I'M SORRY.
Whoa.
Tezuka is dead!!
Thus the sick day.
...
HUH...?

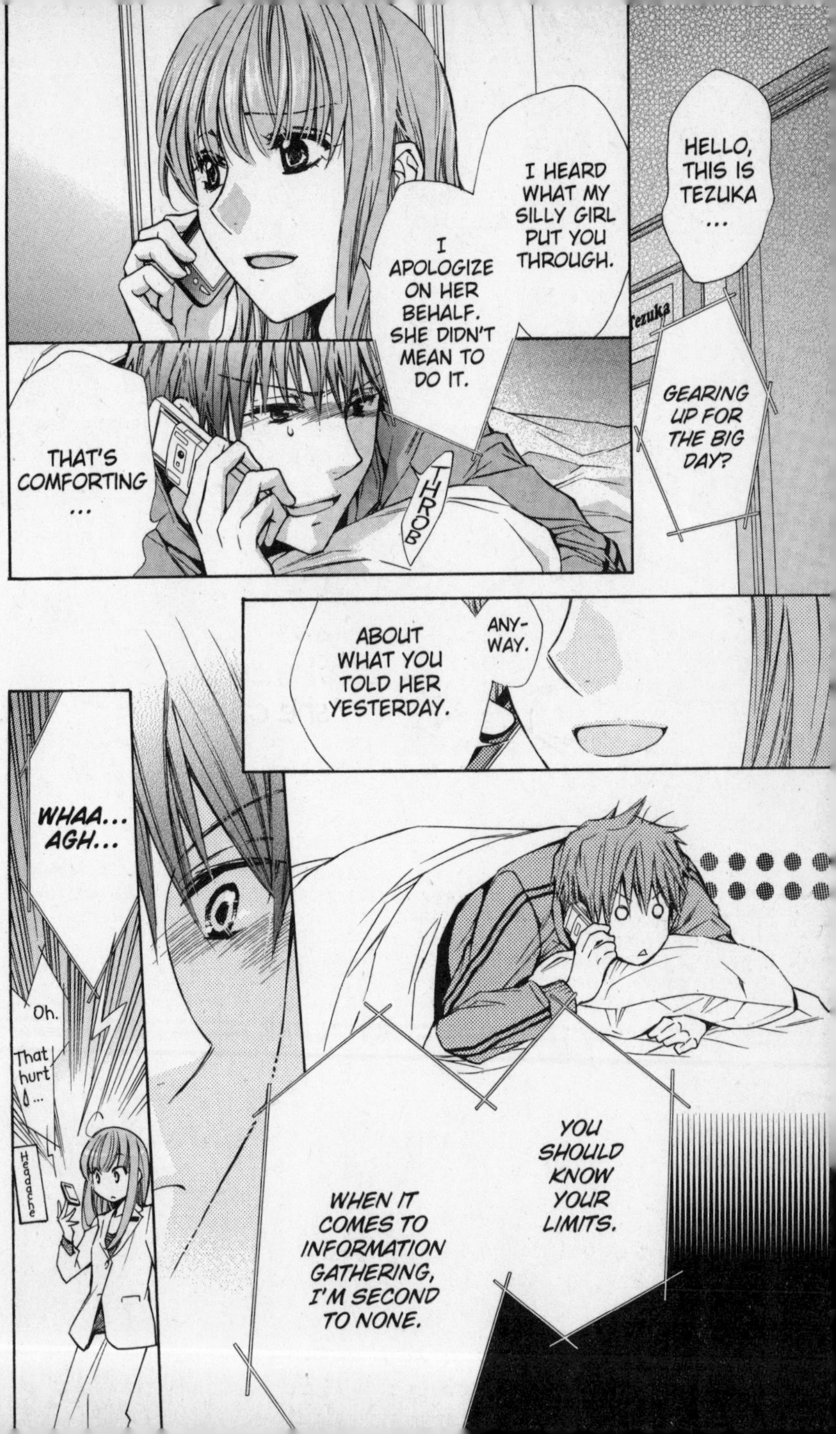
HELLO, THIS IS TEZUKA ...
GEARING UP FOR THE BIG DAY?
Tezuka
I HEARD WHAT MY SILLY GIRL PUT YOU THROUGH.
I APOLOGIZE ON HER BEHALF. SHE DIDN'T MEAN TO DO IT.
THROB
THAT'S COMFORTING ...
ANY-WAY.
ABOUT WHAT YOU TOLD HER YESTERDAY.
YOU SHOULD KNOW YOUR LIMITS.
WHEN IT COMES TO INFORMATION GATHERING, I'M SECOND TO NONE.
WHAA... AGH...
Oh.
That hurt ...
Headache

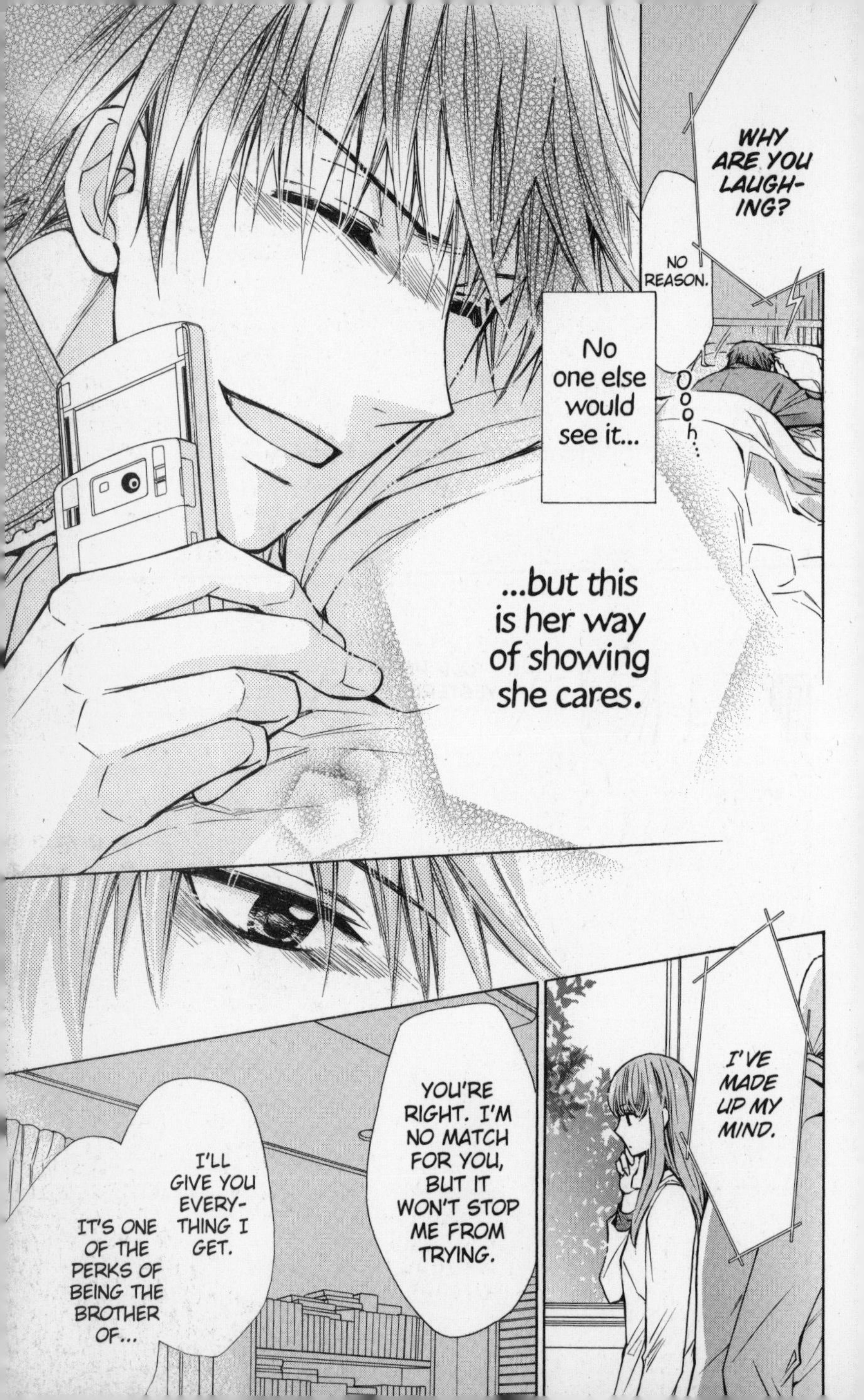
WHY ARE YOU LAUGHING?
NO REASON.
Oooh...
No one else would see it...
...but this is her way of showing she cares.
I'VE MADE UP MY MIND.
YOU'RE RIGHT. I'M NO MATCH FOR YOU, BUT IT WON'T STOP ME FROM TRYING.
I'LL GIVE YOU EVERYTHING I GET.
IT'S ONE OF THE PERKS OF BEING THE BROTHER OF...

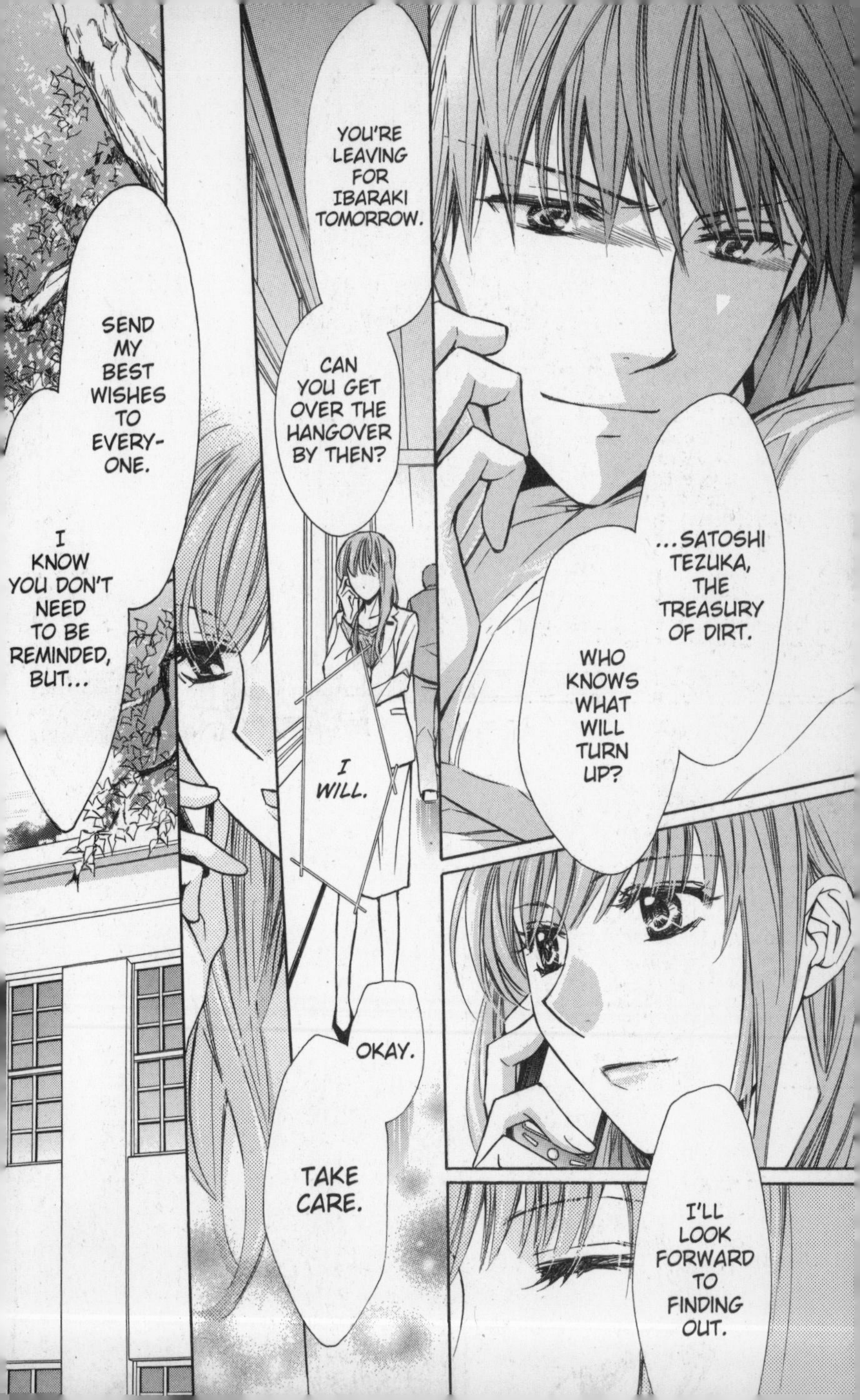
YOU'RE LEAVING FOR IBARAKI TOMORROW.
CAN YOU GET OVER THE HANGOVER BY THEN?
I WILL.
OKAY.
TAKE CARE.
SEND MY BEST WISHES TO EVERY-ONE.
I KNOW YOU DON'T NEED TO BE REMINDED, BUT...
...SATOSHI TEZUKA, THE TREASURY OF DIRT.
WHO KNOWS WHAT WILL TURN UP?
I'LL LOOK FORWARD TO FINDING OUT.

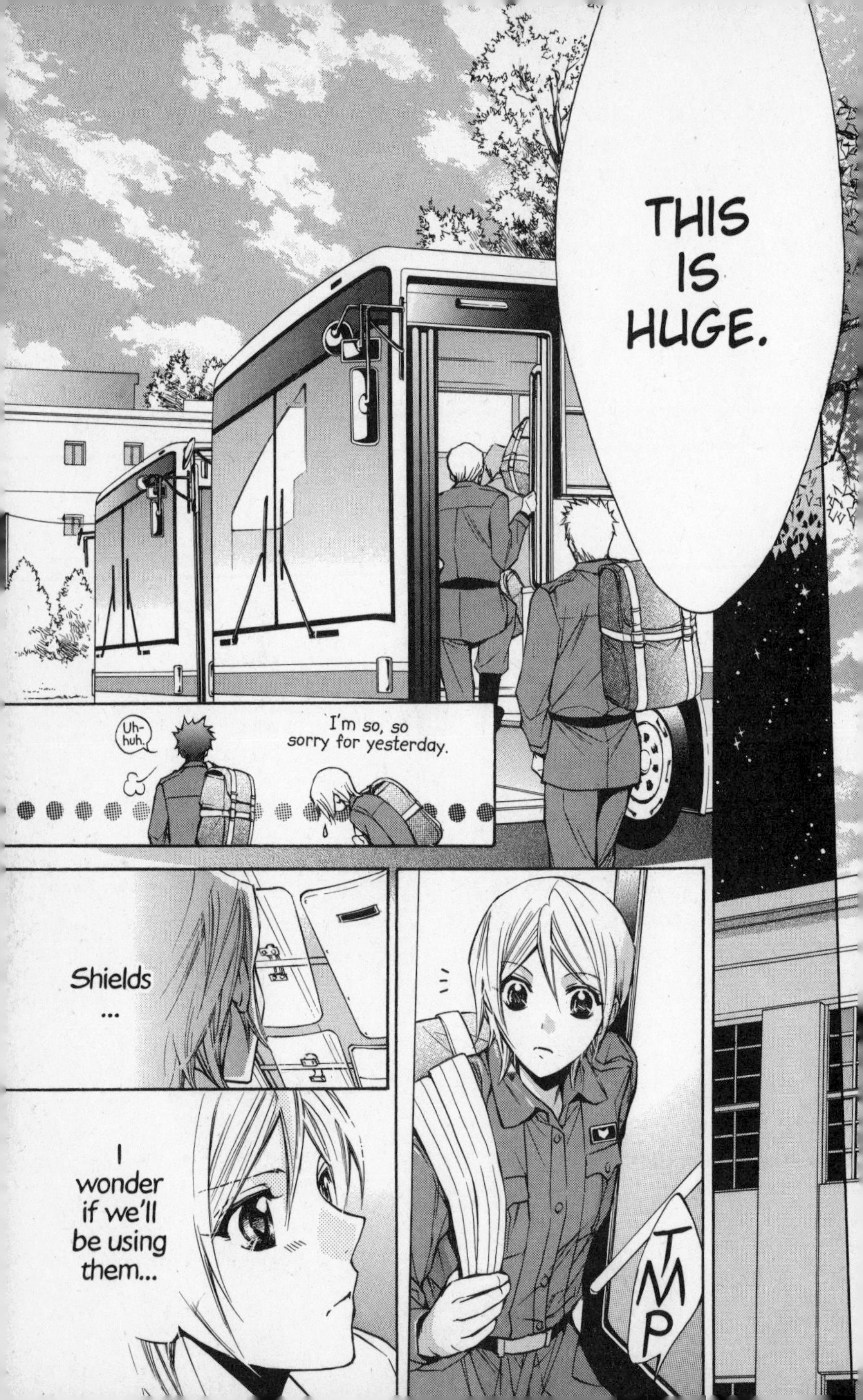
THIS IS HUGE.
I'm so, so sorry for yesterday.
Uh-huh.
TMP
Shields ...
I wonder if we'll be using them...

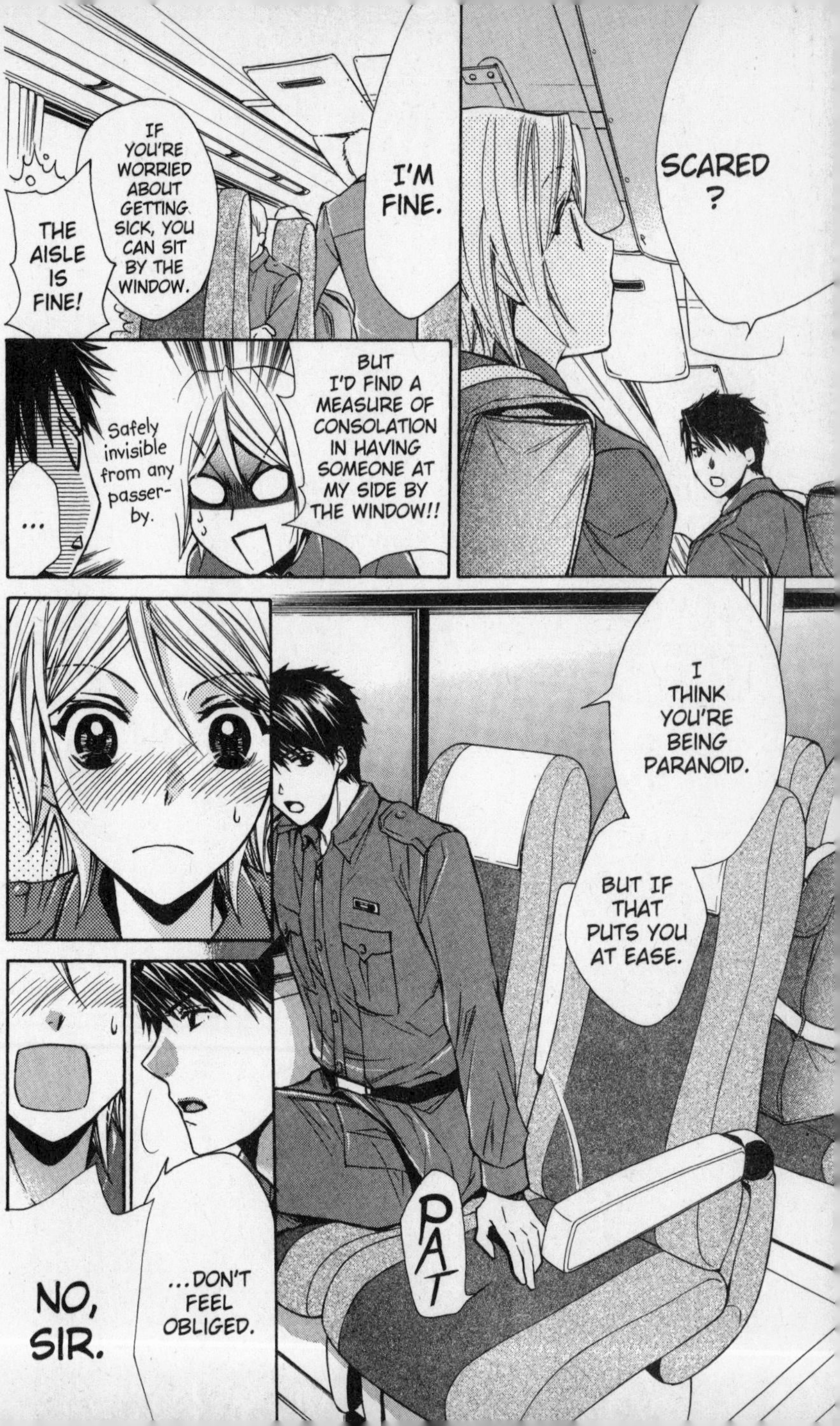
SCARED ?
I'M FINE.
IF YOU'RE WORRIED ABOUT GETTING SICK, YOU CAN SIT BY THE WINDOW.
THE AISLE IS FINE!
BUT I'D FIND A MEASURE OF CONSOLATION IN HAVING SOMEONE AT MY SIDE BY THE WINDOW!!
Safely invisible from any passer-by.
...
I THINK YOU'RE BEING PARANOID.
BUT IF THAT PUTS YOU AT EASE.
PAT
...DON'T FEEL OBLIGED.
NO, SIR.

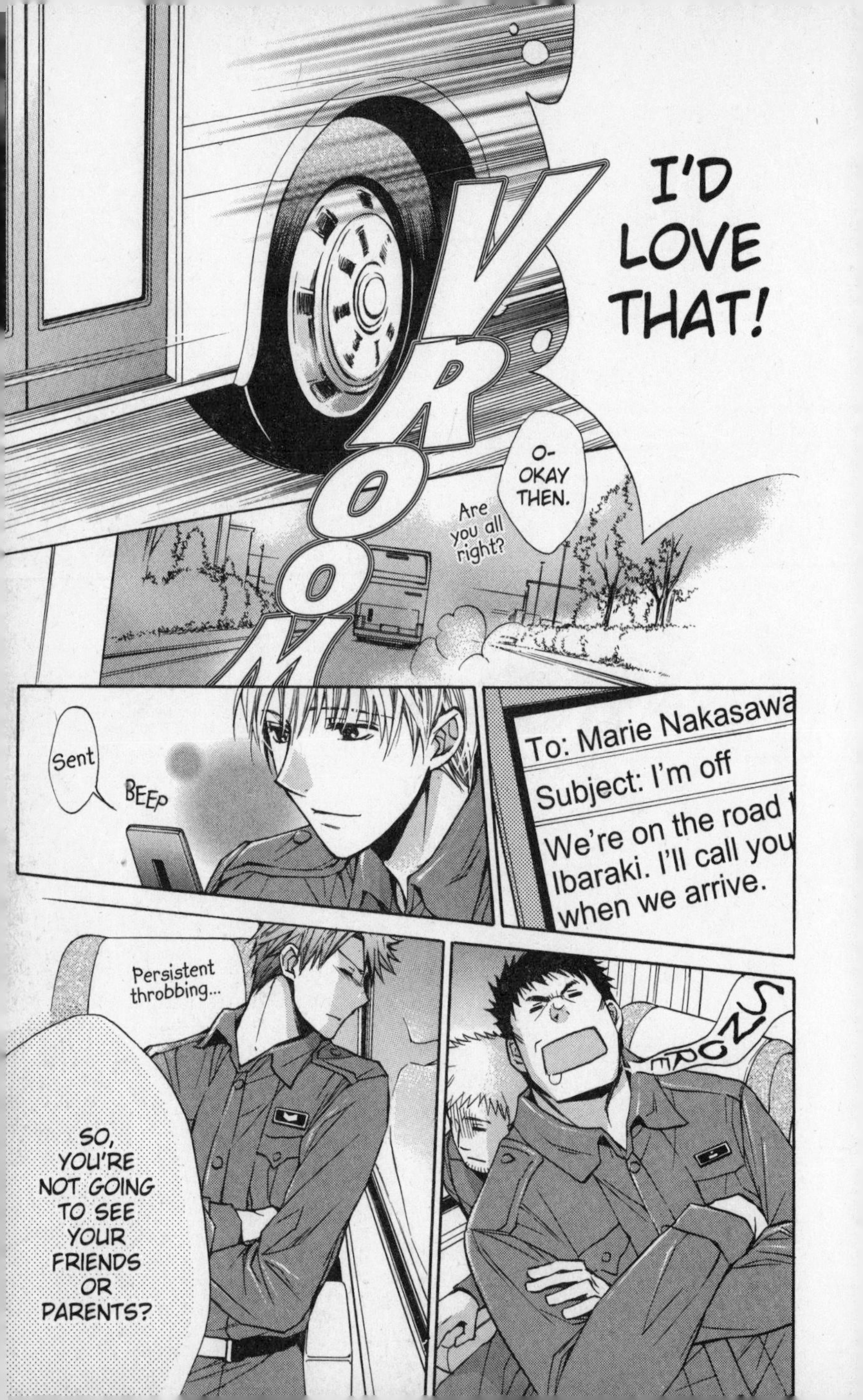
I'D LOVE THAT!
VROOM
O-OKAY THEN.
Are you all right?
To: Marie Nakasawa
Subject: I'm off
We're on the road
Ibaraki. I'll call you
when we arrive.
Sent
BEEP
SNORE
Persistent throbbing...
SO, YOU'RE NOT GOING TO SEE YOUR FRIENDS OR PARENTS?

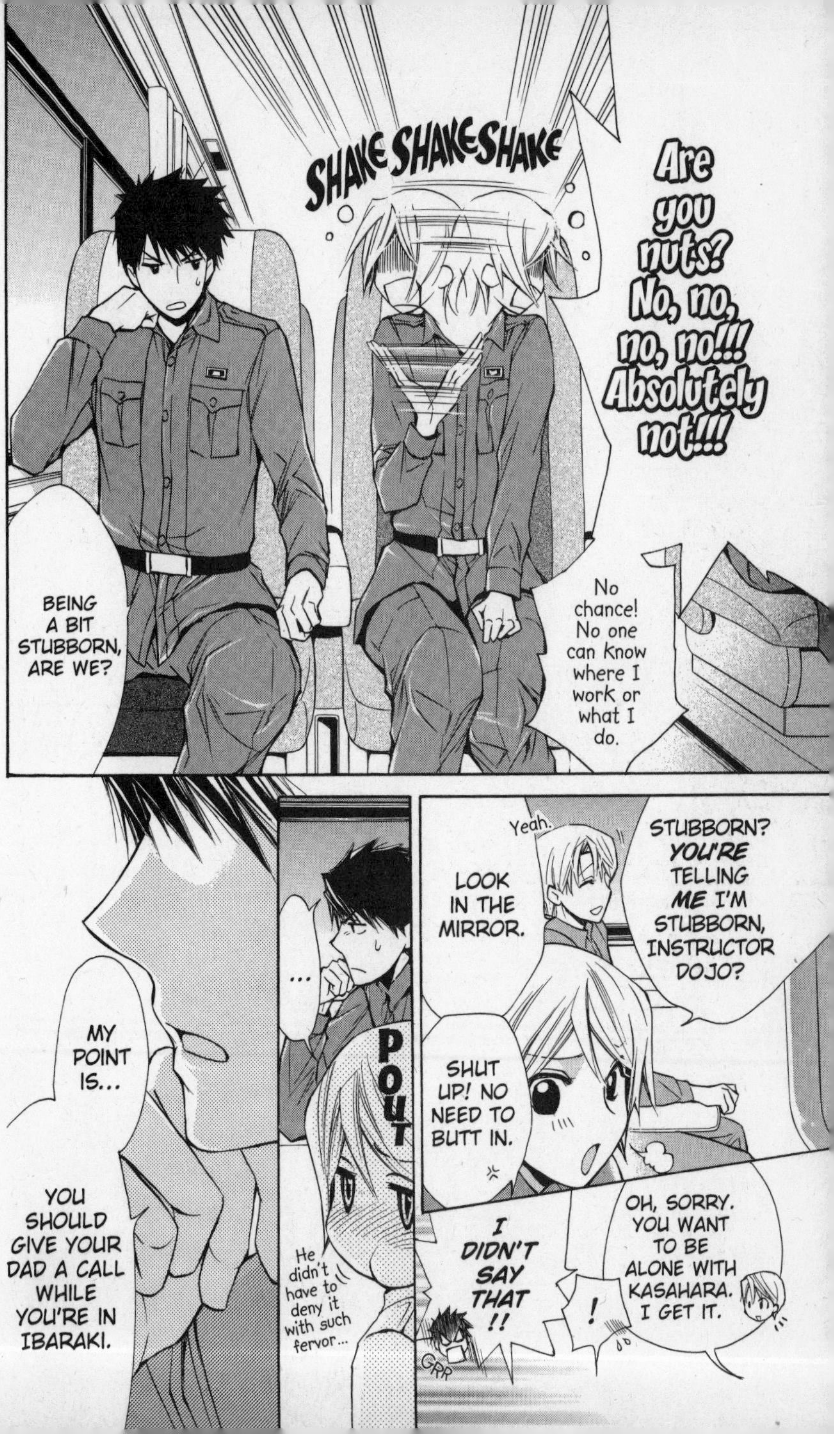
Are you nuts? No, no, no, no!!! Absolutely not!!!
SHAKE SHAKE SHAKE
No chance! No one can know where I work or what I do.
BEING A BIT STUBBORN, ARE WE?
STUBBORN? YOU'RE TELLING ME I'M STUBBORN, INSTRUCTOR DOJO?
Yeah.
LOOK IN THE MIRROR.
...
SHUT UP! NO NEED TO BUTT IN.
POUT
OH, SORRY. YOU WANT TO BE ALONE WITH KASAHARA. I GET IT.
!
I DIDN'T SAY THAT !!
GRR
He didn't have to deny it with such fervor...
MY POINT IS...
YOU SHOULD GIVE YOUR DAD A CALL WHILE YOU'RE IN IBARAKI.

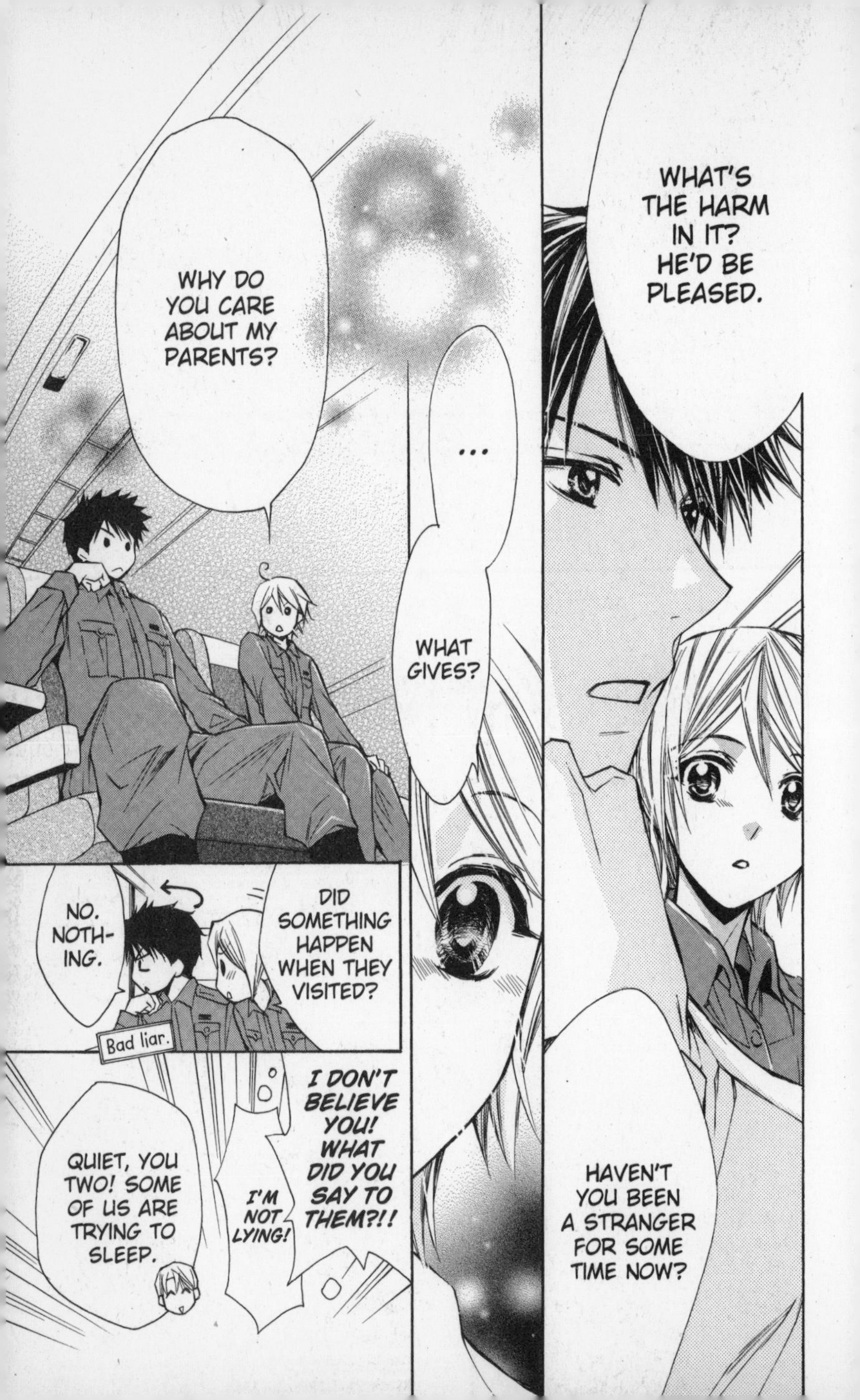
WHAT'S THE HARM IN IT? HE'D BE PLEASED.
HAVEN'T YOU BEEN A STRANGER FOR SOME TIME NOW?
...
WHAT GIVES?
WHY DO YOU CARE ABOUT MY PARENTS?
DID SOMETHING HAPPEN WHEN THEY VISITED?
NO. NOTH-ING.
Bad liar.
I DON'T BELIEVE YOU! WHAT DID YOU SAY TO THEM?!!
I'M NOT LYING!
QUIET, YOU TWO! SOME OF US ARE TRYING TO SLEEP.

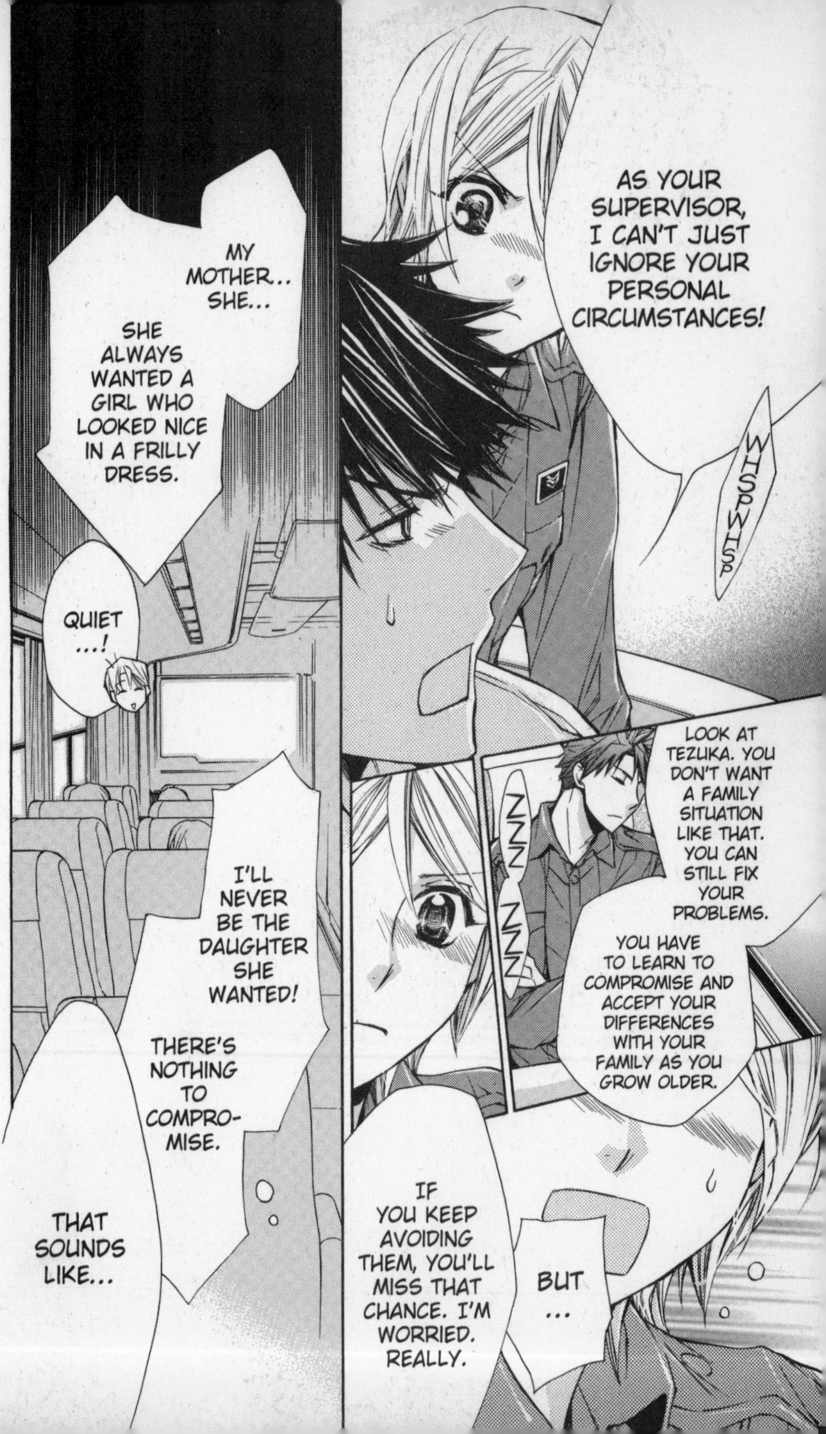
AS YOUR SUPERVISOR, I CAN'T JUST IGNORE YOUR PERSONAL CIRCUMSTANCES!
WHSP WHSP
LOOK AT TEZUKA. YOU DON'T WANT A FAMILY SITUATION LIKE THAT. YOU CAN STILL FIX YOUR PROBLEMS.
ZZZ ZZZ
YOU HAVE TO LEARN TO COMPROMISE AND ACCEPT YOUR DIFFERENCES WITH YOUR FAMILY AS YOU GROW OLDER.
BUT ...
IF YOU KEEP AVOIDING THEM, YOU'LL MISS THAT CHANCE. I'M WORRIED. REALLY.
MY MOTHER... SHE...
SHE ALWAYS WANTED A GIRL WHO LOOKED NICE IN A FRILLY DRESS.
QUIET ...!
I'LL NEVER BE THE DAUGHTER SHE WANTED!
THERE'S NOTHING TO COMPRO-MISE.
THAT SOUNDS LIKE...

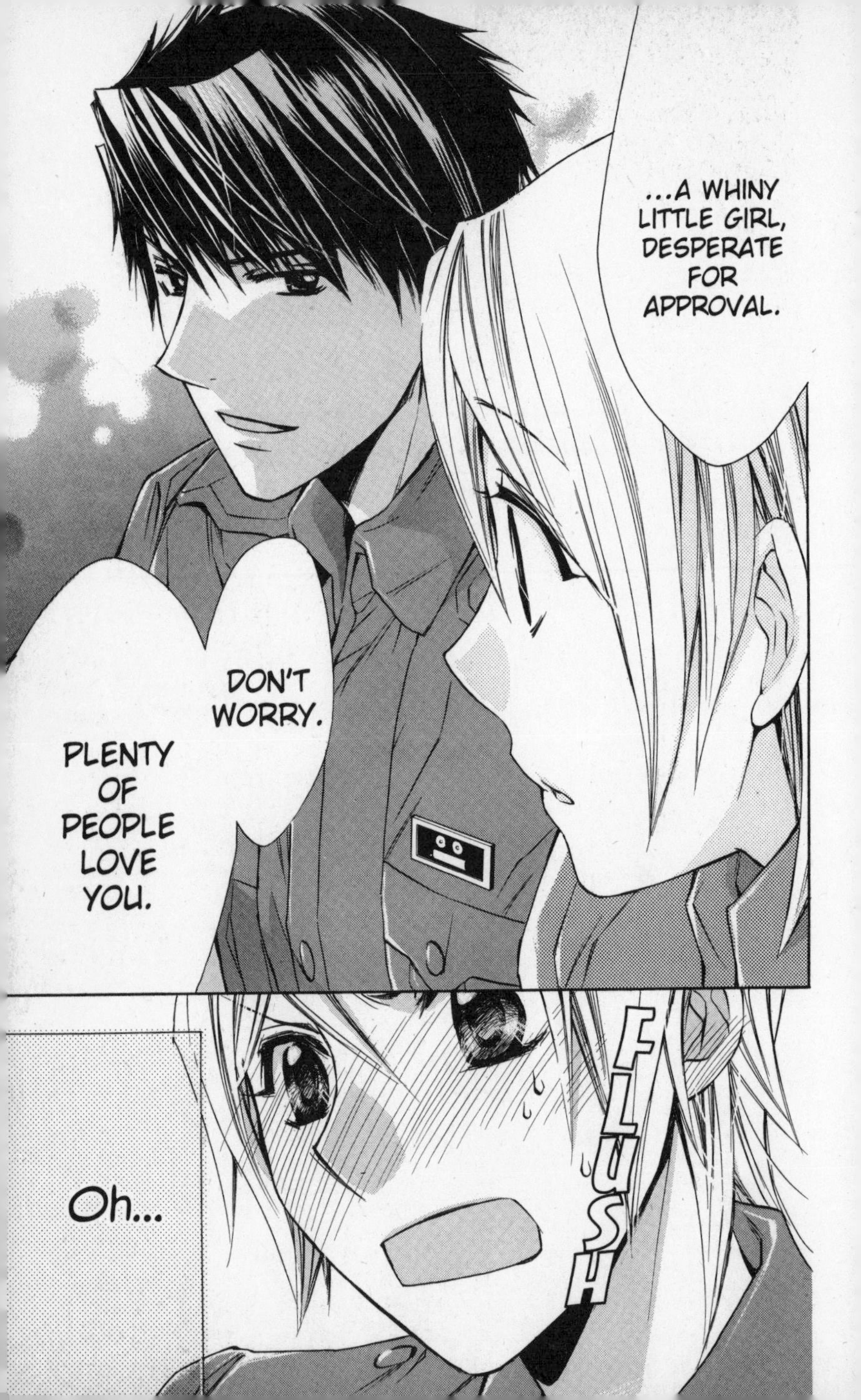
...A WHINY LITTLE GIRL, DESPERATE FOR APPROVAL.
DON'T WORRY.
PLENTY OF PEOPLE LOVE YOU.
FLUSH
Oh...

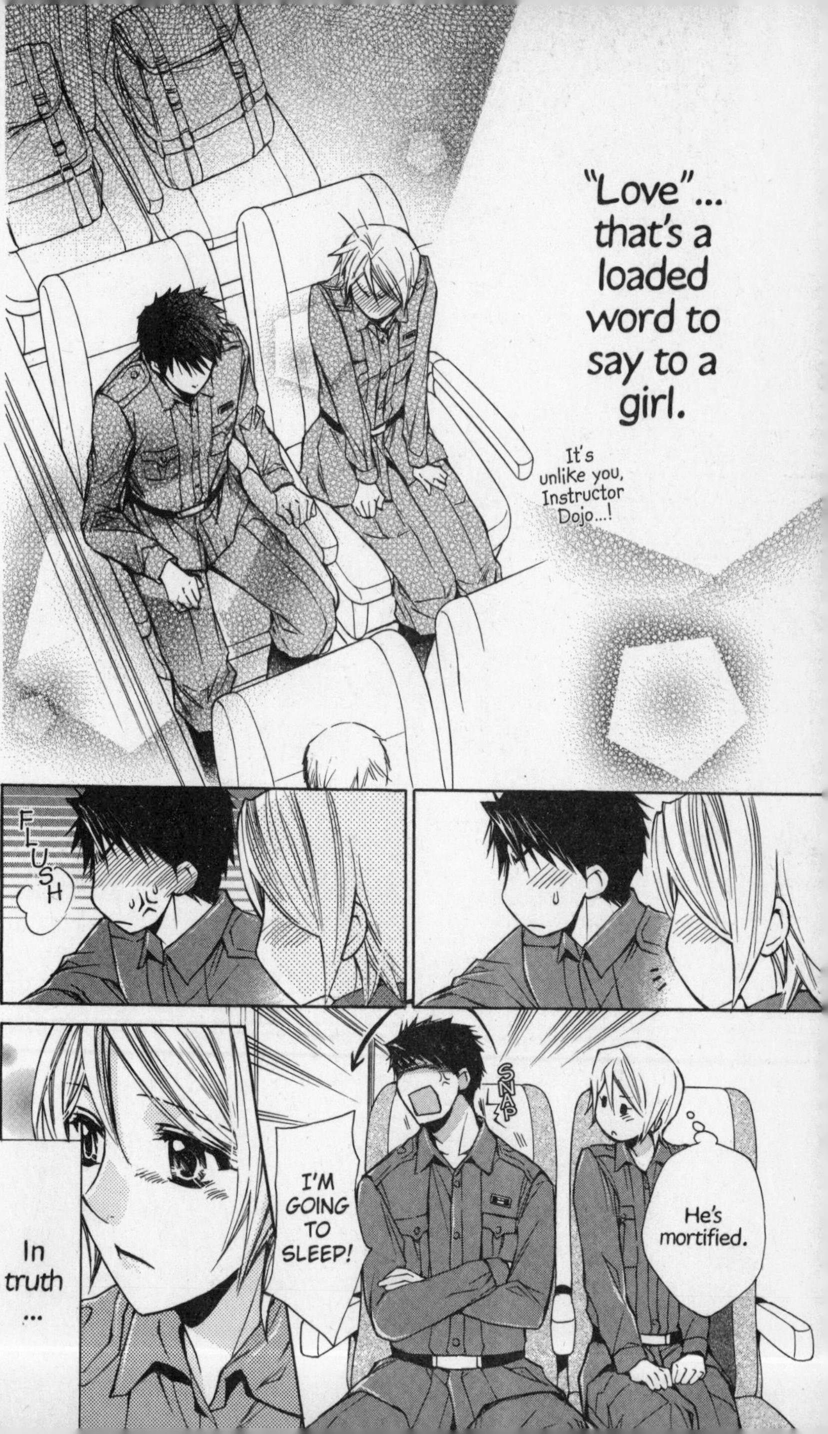
"Love"... that's a loaded word to say to a girl.
It's unlike you, Instructor Dojo...!
FLUSH
He's mortified.
SNAP
I'M GOING TO SLEEP!
In truth...

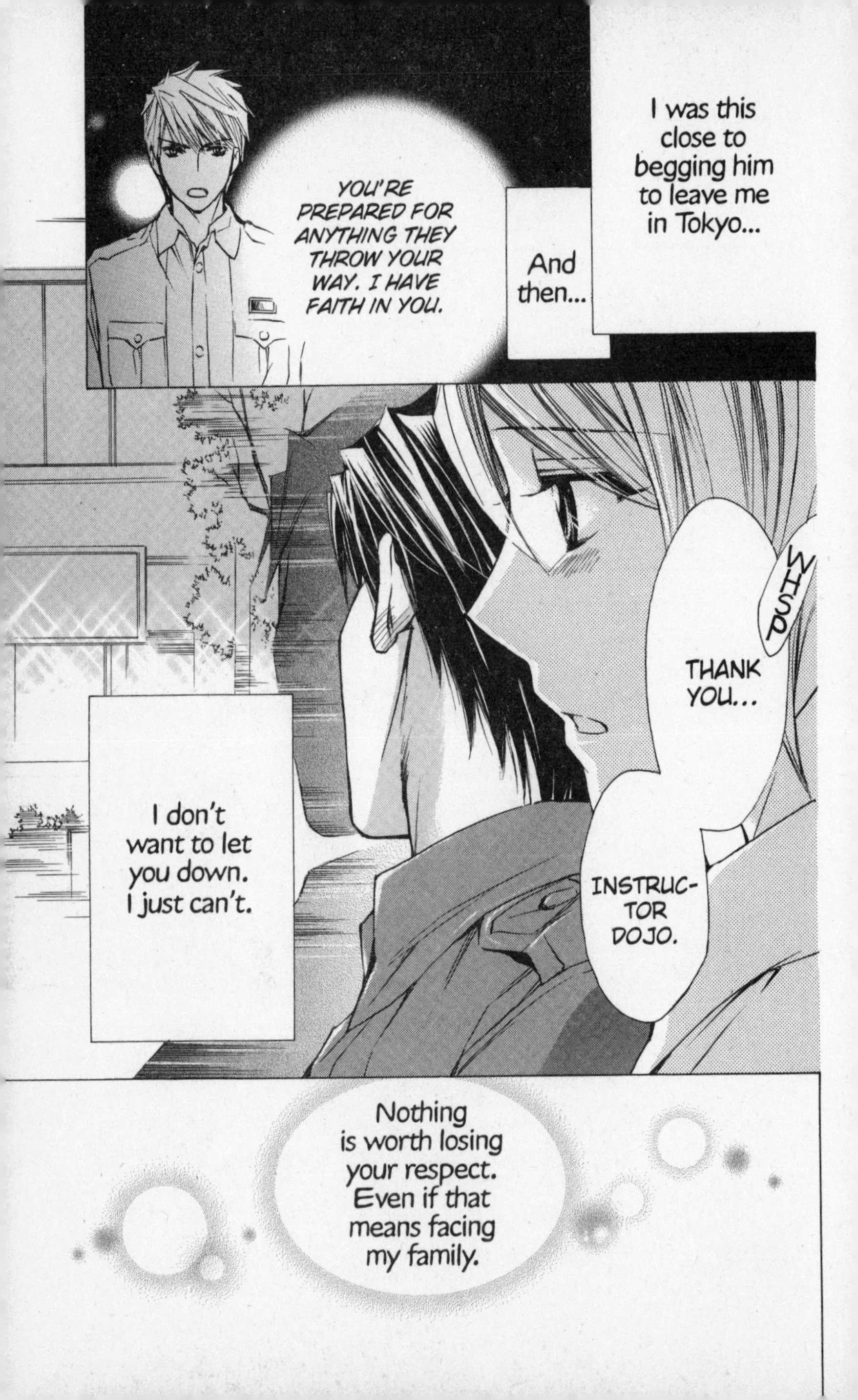
I was this close to begging him to leave me in Tokyo...
And then...
YOU'RE PREPARED FOR ANYTHING THEY THROW YOUR WAY. I HAVE FAITH IN YOU.
WHSP
THANK YOU...
INSTRUC-TOR DOJO.
I don't want to let you down. I just can't.
Nothing is worth losing your respect. Even if that means facing my family.

Drama Face.

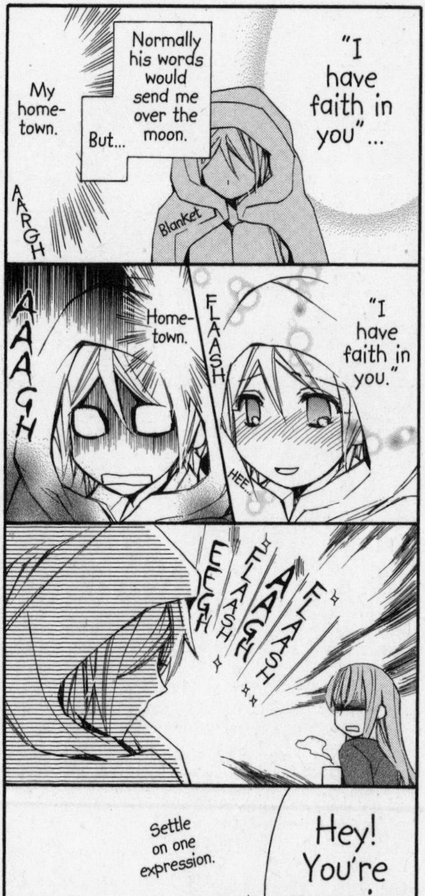
"I have faith in you"...
Normally his words would send me over the moon.
But...
My home-town.
Blanket
AARGH
"I have faith in you."
FLAASH
HEE...
Home-town.
AAAGH
FLAASH
AAAGH
FLAASH
EEEGH
Hey! You're creeping me out.
Settle on one expression.

CHAPTER 46

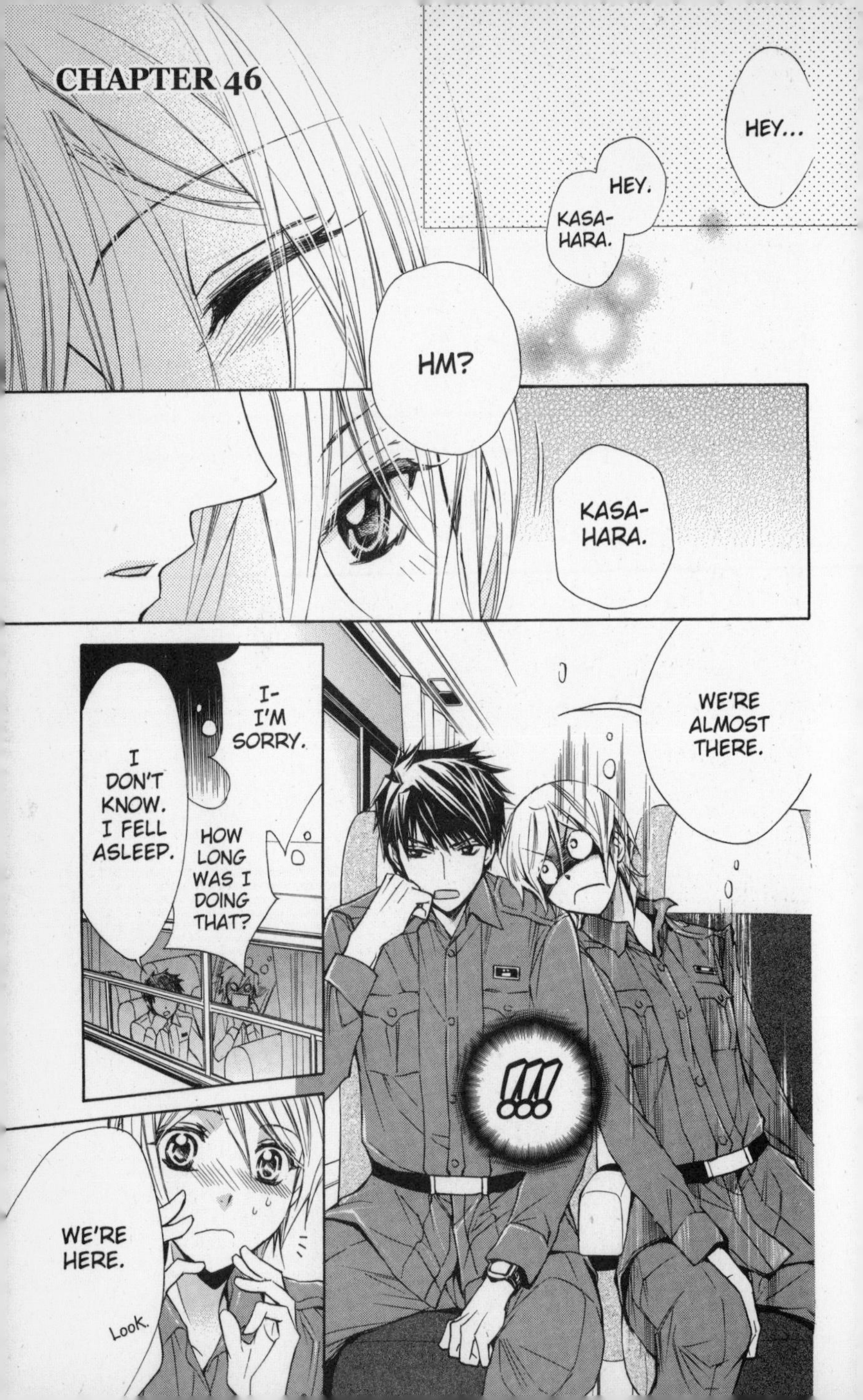
HEY...
HEY. KASA-HARA.
HM?
KASA-HARA.
WE'RE ALMOST THERE.
!!!
I- I'M SORRY.
I DON'T KNOW. I FELL ASLEEP.
HOW LONG WAS I DOING THAT?
WE'RE HERE.
Look.

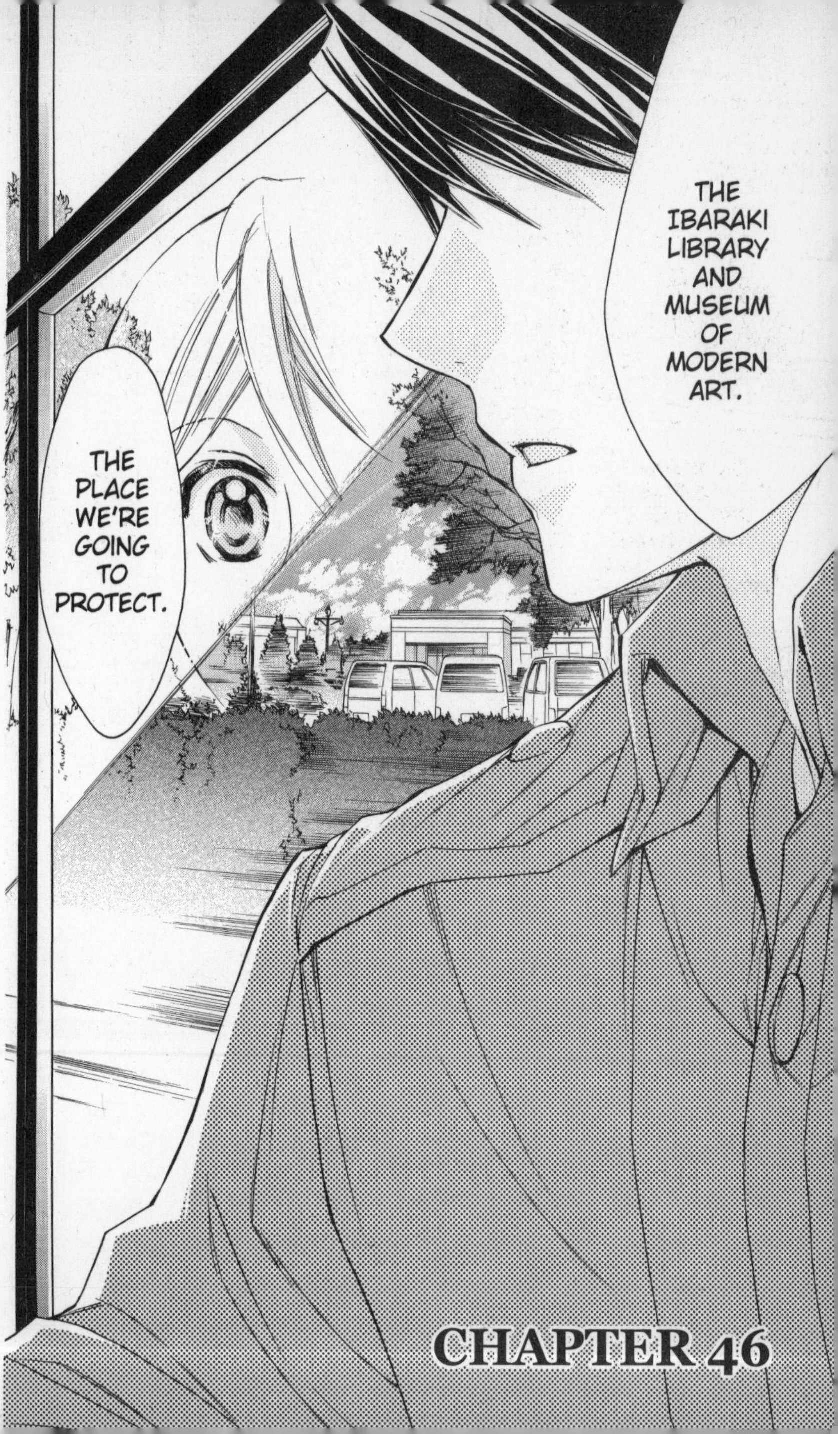
THE IBARAKI LIBRARY AND MUSEUM OF MODERN ART.
THE PLACE WE'RE GOING TO PROTECT.
CHAPTER 46

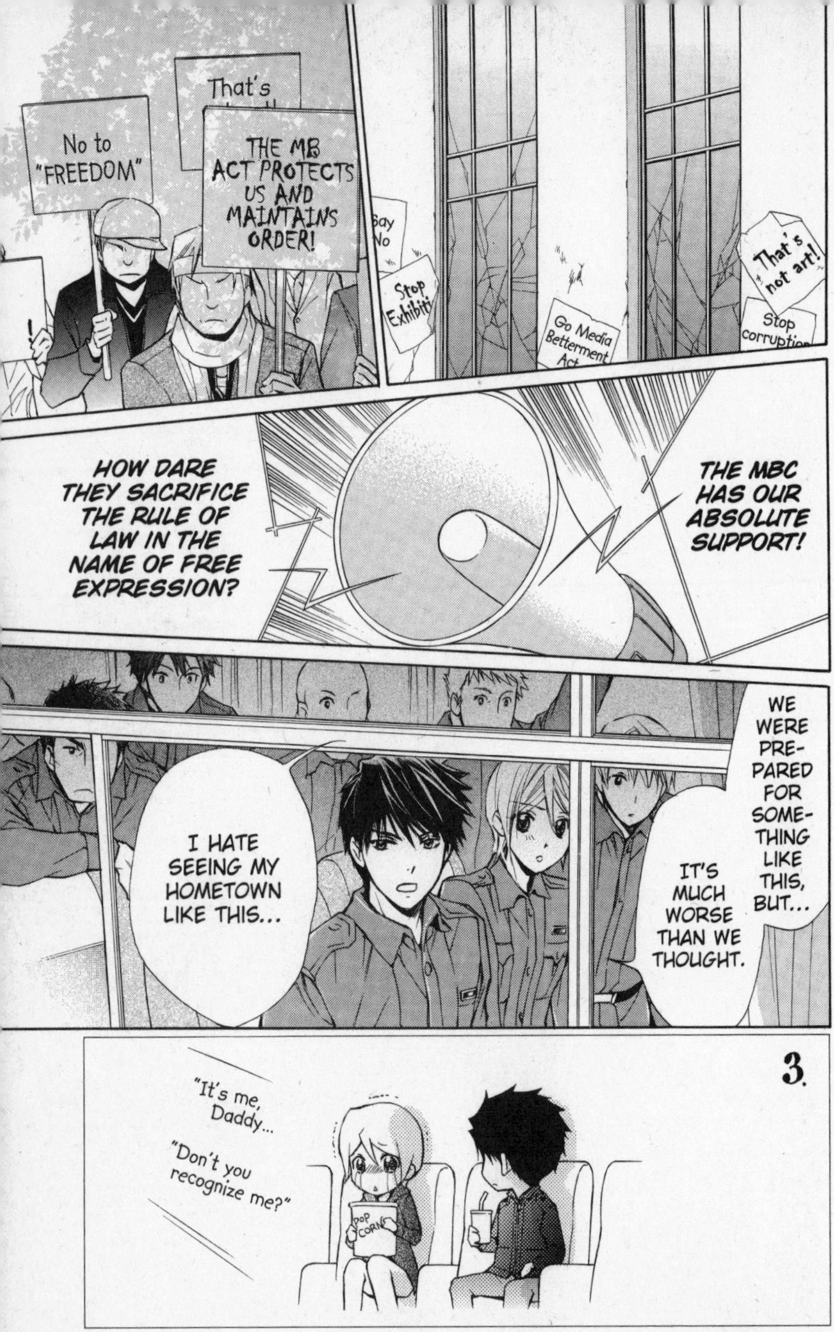
That's not art!
Stop corruption
Go Media Betterment Act
Stop
Say No
THE MB ACT PROTECTS US AND MAINTAINS ORDER!
That's
No to "FREEDOM"
THE MBC HAS OUR ABSOLUTE SUPPORT!
HOW DARE THEY SACRIFICE THE RULE OF LAW IN THE NAME OF FREE EXPRESSION?
WE WERE PRE-PARED FOR SOME-THING LIKE THIS, BUT...
IT'S MUCH WORSE THAN WE THOUGHT.
I HATE SEEING MY HOMETOWN LIKE THIS...
3.
"It's me, Daddy...
"Don't you recognize me?"
POP CORN

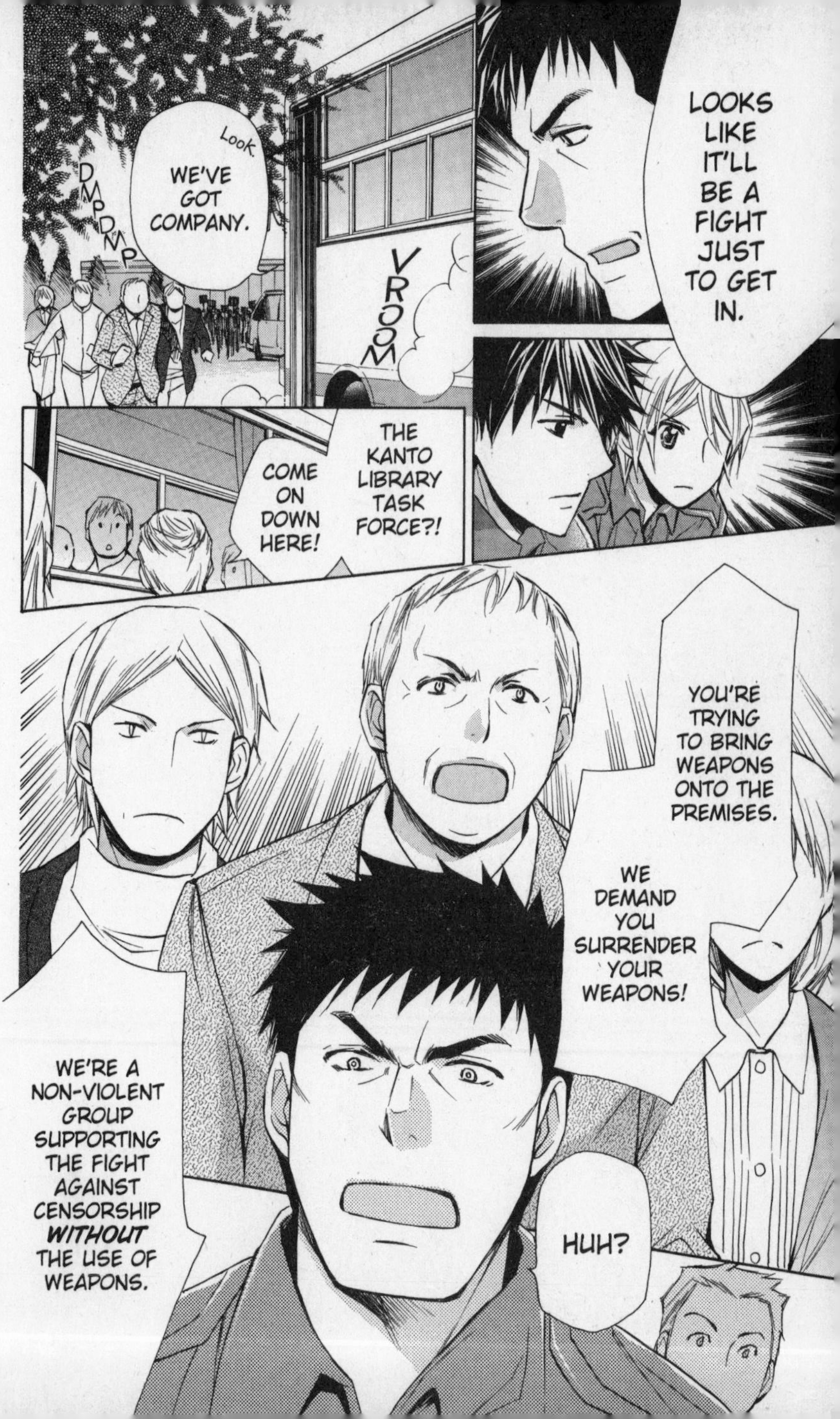
LOOKS LIKE IT'LL BE A FIGHT JUST TO GET IN.
Look.
WE'VE GOT COMPANY.
DMPDMP
VROOM
THE KANTO LIBRARY TASK FORCE?!
COME ON DOWN HERE!
YOU'RE TRYING TO BRING WEAPONS ONTO THE PREMISES.
WE DEMAND YOU SURRENDER YOUR WEAPONS!
HUH?
WE'RE A NON-VIOLENT GROUP SUPPORTING THE FIGHT AGAINST CENSORSHIP WITHOUT THE USE OF WEAPONS.

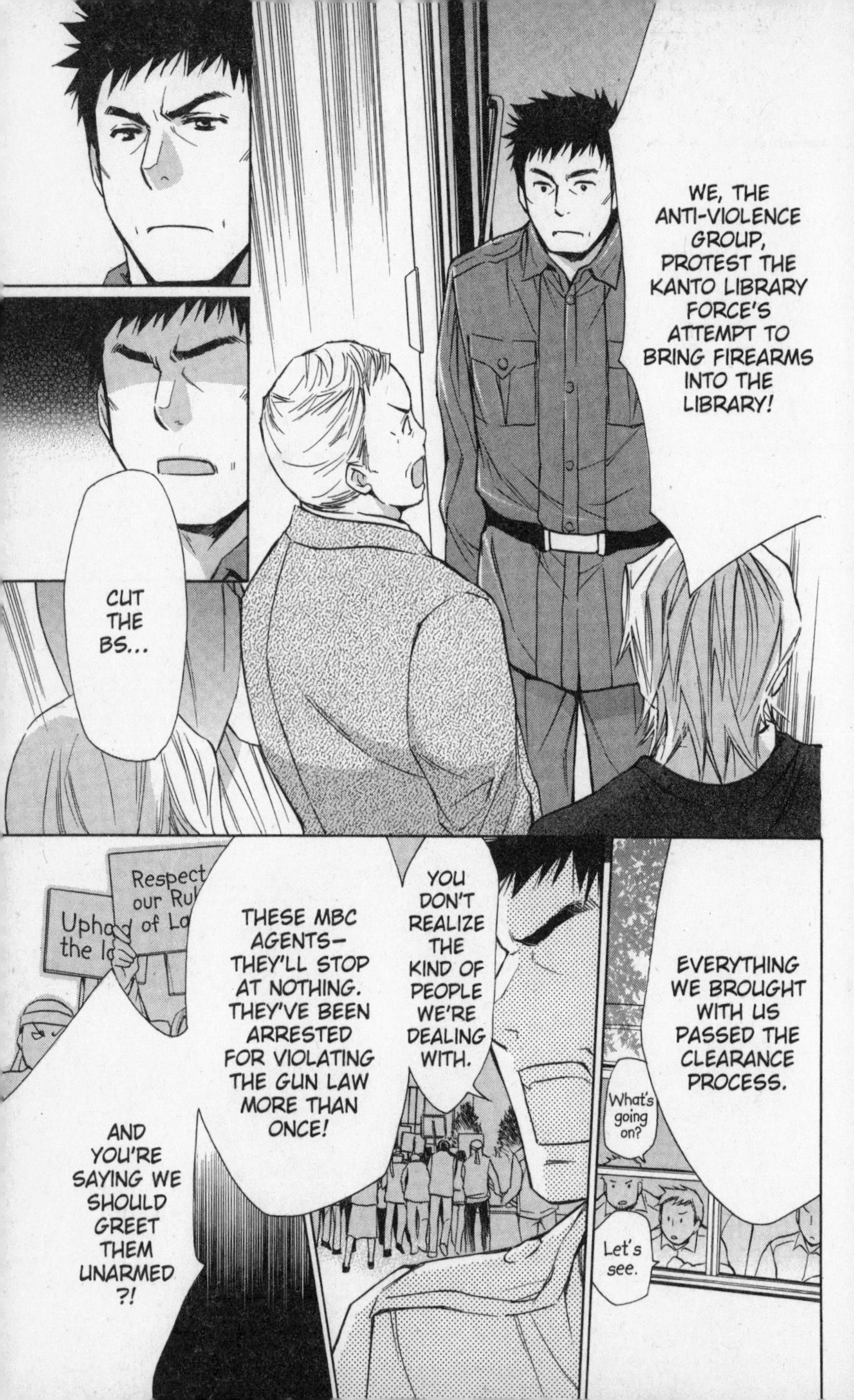
WE, THE ANTI-VIOLENCE GROUP, PROTEST THE KANTO LIBRARY FORCE'S ATTEMPT TO BRING FIREARMS INTO THE LIBRARY!
CUT THE BS...
EVERYTHING WE BROUGHT WITH US PASSED THE CLEARANCE PROCESS.
What's going on?
Let's see.
YOU DON'T REALIZE THE KIND OF PEOPLE WE'RE DEALING WITH.
THESE MBC AGENTS— THEY'LL STOP AT NOTHING. THEY'VE BEEN ARRESTED FOR VIOLATING THE GUN LAW MORE THAN ONCE!
Respect our Ru
Uphold of La
the la
AND YOU'RE SAYING WE SHOULD GREET THEM UNARMED ?!

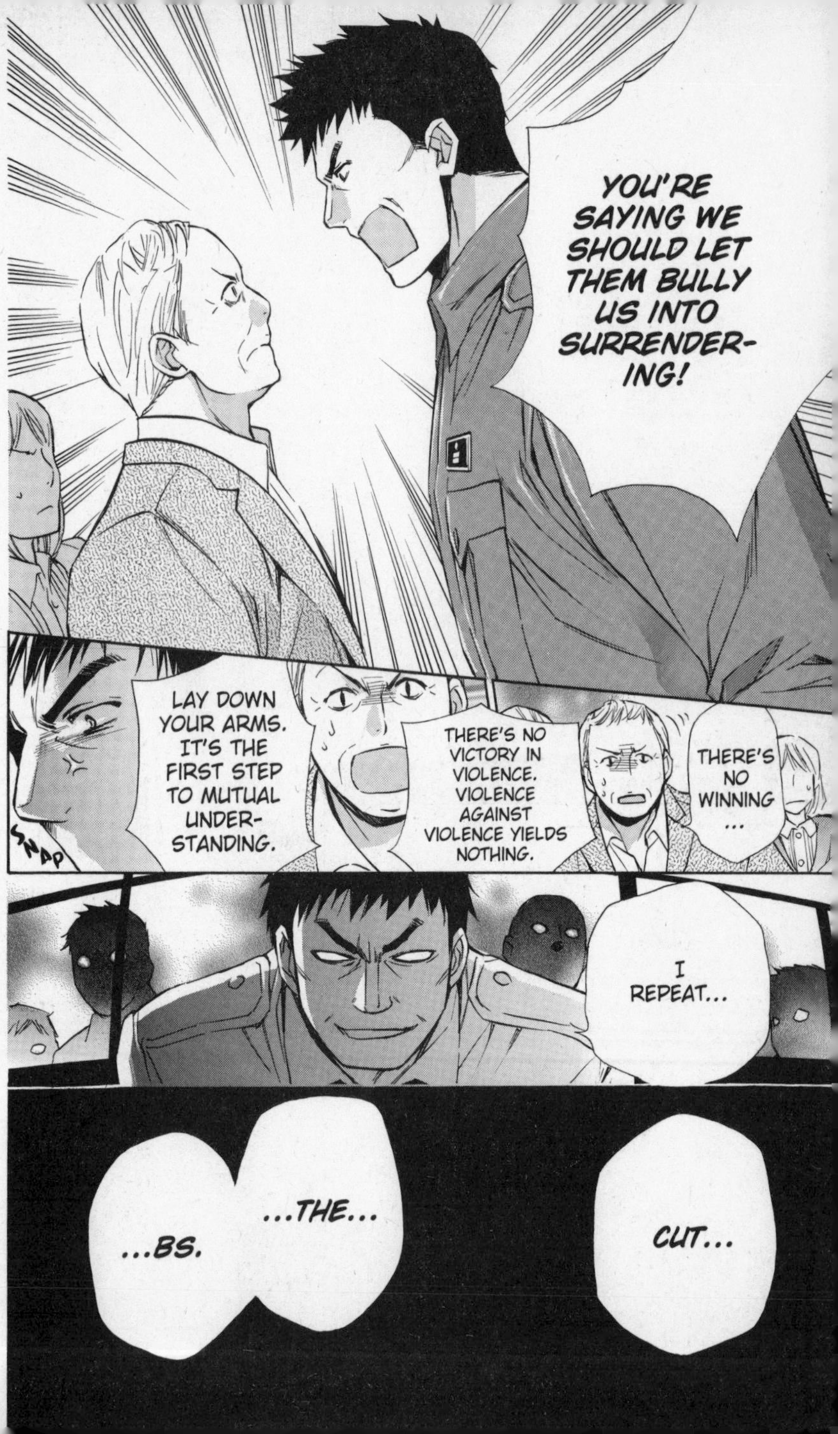
YOU'RE SAYING WE SHOULD LET THEM BULLY US INTO SURRENDER-ING!
THERE'S NO WINNING ...
THERE'S NO VICTORY IN VIOLENCE. VIOLENCE AGAINST VIOLENCE YIELDS NOTHING.
LAY DOWN YOUR ARMS. IT'S THE FIRST STEP TO MUTUAL UNDER-STANDING.
SNAP
I REPEAT...
CUT...
...THE...
...BS.

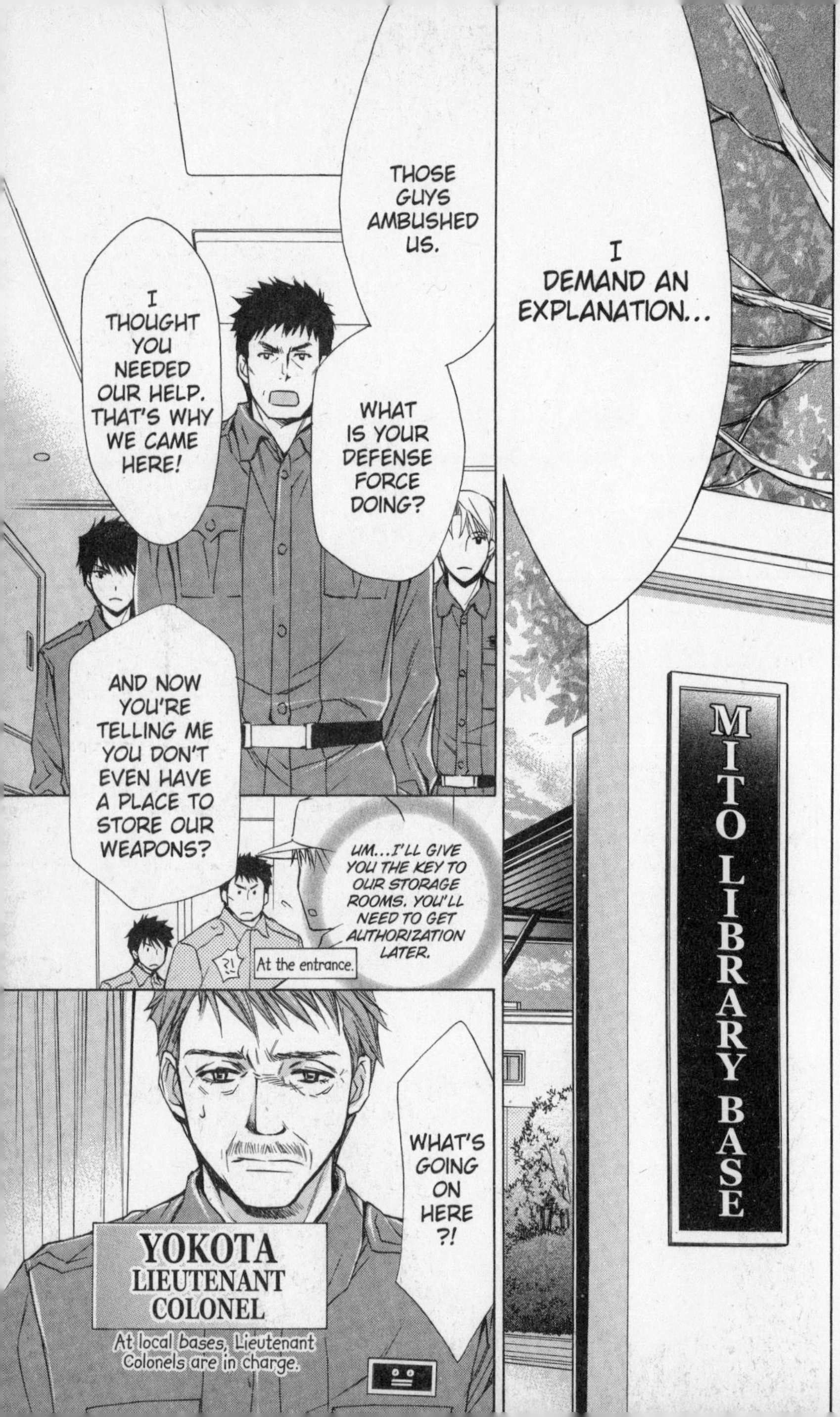
I DEMAND AN EXPLANATION...
MITO LIBRARY BASE
THOSE GUYS AMBUSHED US.
WHAT IS YOUR DEFENSE FORCE DOING?
I THOUGHT YOU NEEDED OUR HELP. THAT'S WHY WE CAME HERE!
AND NOW YOU'RE TELLING ME YOU DON'T EVEN HAVE A PLACE TO STORE OUR WEAPONS?
UM...I'LL GIVE YOU THE KEY TO OUR STORAGE ROOMS. YOU'LL NEED TO GET AUTHORIZATION LATER.
At the entrance.
?!
WHAT'S GOING ON HERE ?!
YOKOTA
LIEUTENANT COLONEL
At local bases, Lieutenant Colonels are in charge.

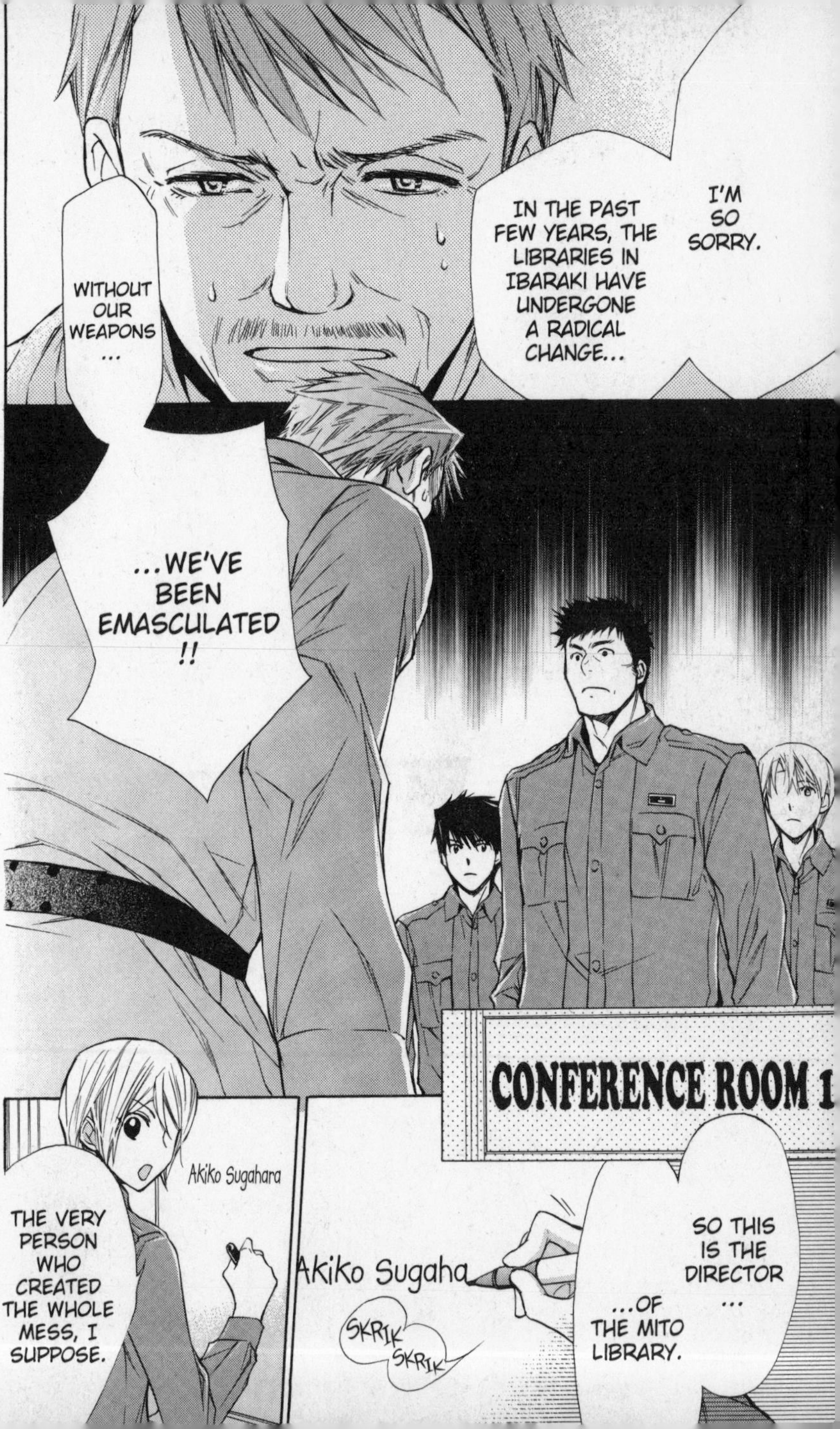
I'M SO SORRY.
IN THE PAST FEW YEARS, THE LIBRARIES IN IBARAKI HAVE UNDERGONE A RADICAL CHANGE...
WITHOUT OUR WEAPONS ...
...WE'VE BEEN EMASCULATED !!
CONFERENCE ROOM 1
SO THIS IS THE DIRECTOR ...
...OF THE MITO LIBRARY.
Akiko Sugaha
SKRIK SKRIK
Akiko Sugahara
THE VERY PERSON WHO CREATED THE WHOLE MESS, I SUPPOSE.

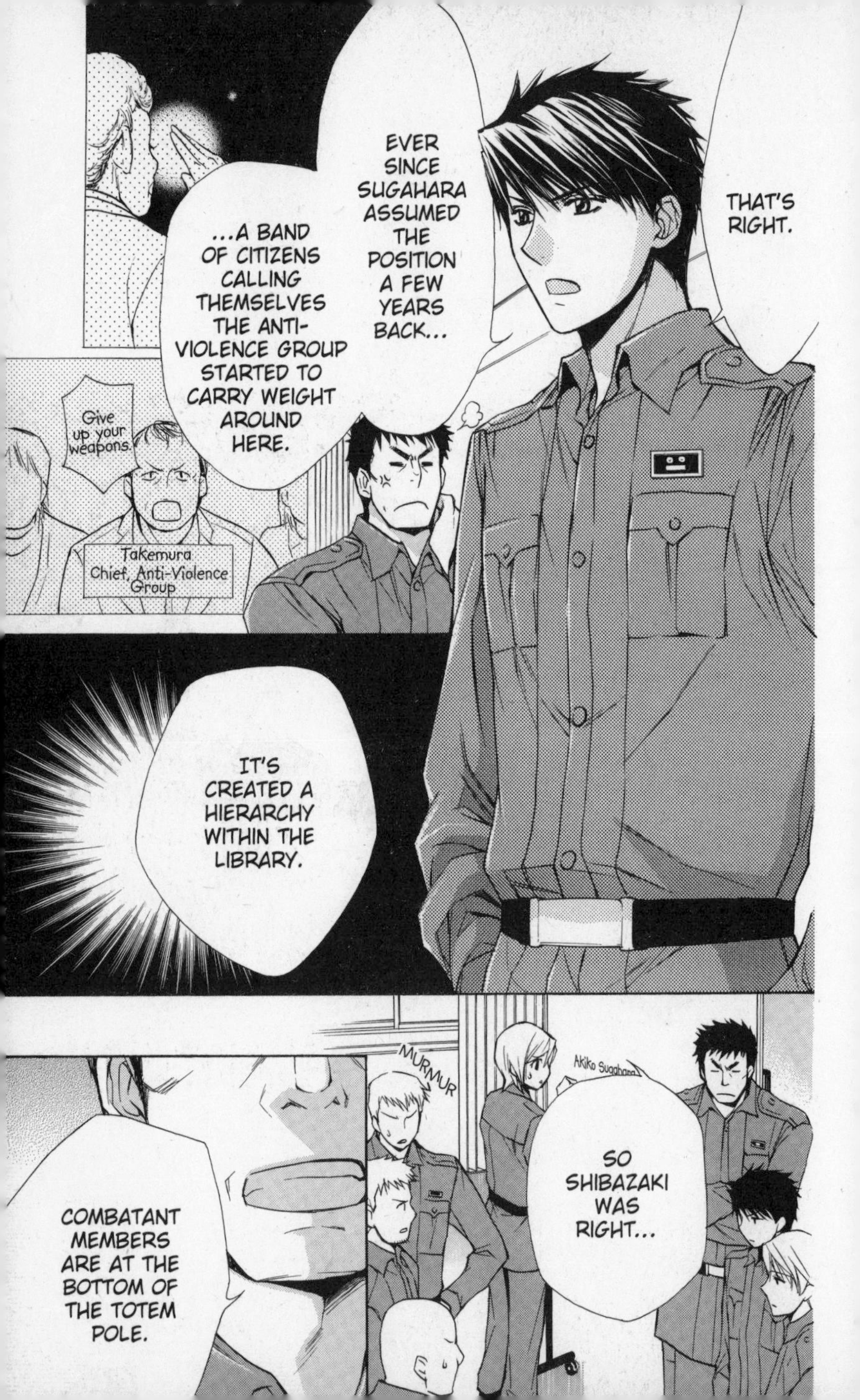
THAT'S RIGHT.
EVER SINCE SUGAHARA ASSUMED THE POSITION A FEW YEARS BACK...
...A BAND OF CITIZENS CALLING THEMSELVES THE ANTI-VIOLENCE GROUP STARTED TO CARRY WEIGHT AROUND HERE.
Give up your weapons.
Takemura Chief, Anti-Violence Group
IT'S CREATED A HIERARCHY WITHIN THE LIBRARY.
Akiko Sugahara
SO SHIBAZAKI WAS RIGHT...
MURMUR
COMBATANT MEMBERS ARE AT THE BOTTOM OF THE TOTEM POLE.

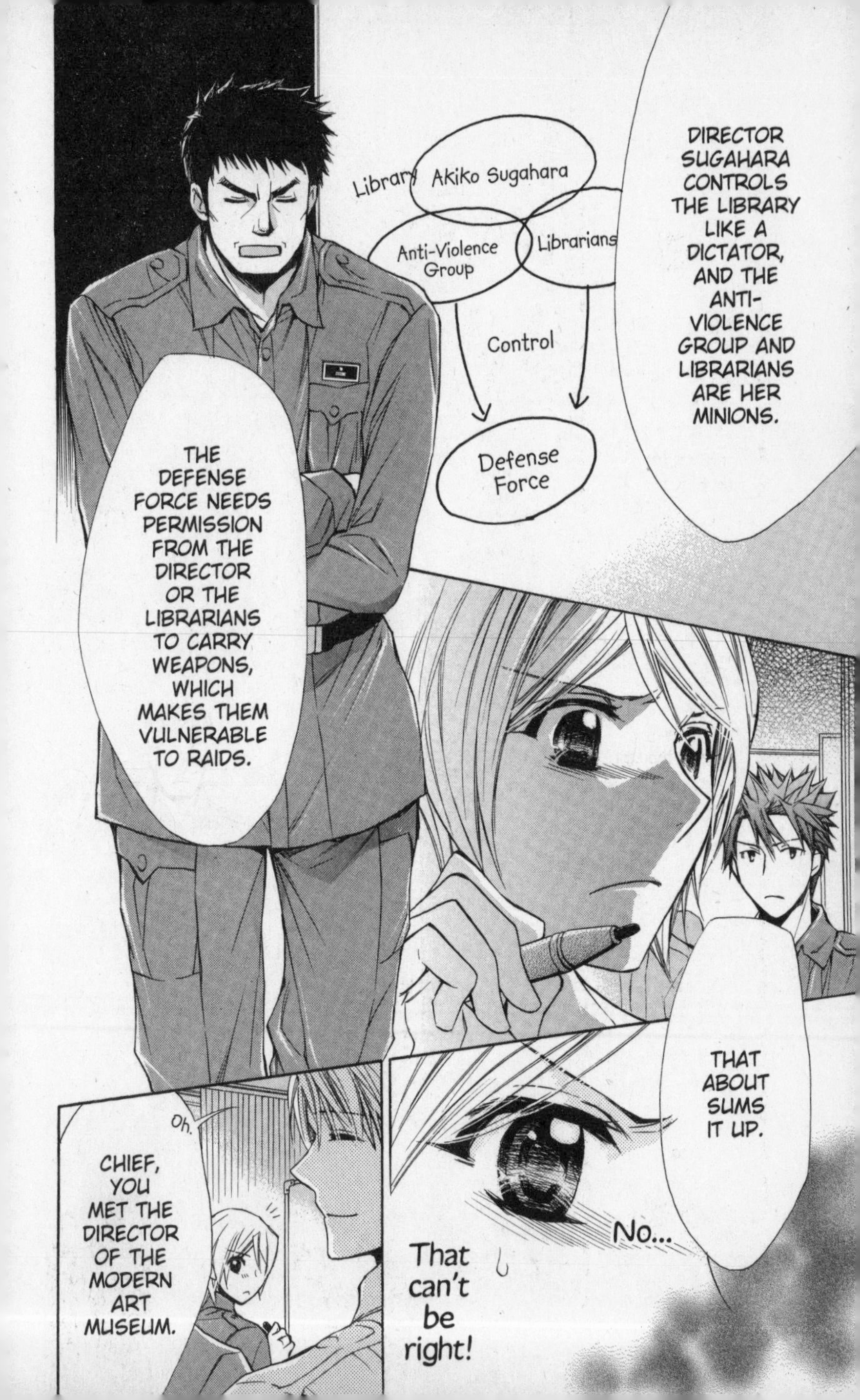
DIRECTOR SUGAHARA CONTROLS THE LIBRARY LIKE A DICTATOR, AND THE ANTI-VIOLENCE GROUP AND LIBRARIANS ARE HER MINIONS.
Library
Akiko Sugahara
Anti-Violence Group
Librarians
Control
Defense Force
THE DEFENSE FORCE NEEDS PERMISSION FROM THE DIRECTOR OR THE LIBRARIANS TO CARRY WEAPONS, WHICH MAKES THEM VULNERABLE TO RAIDS.
THAT ABOUT SUMS IT UP.
No...
That can't be right!
Oh.
CHIEF, YOU MET THE DIRECTOR OF THE MODERN ART MUSEUM.

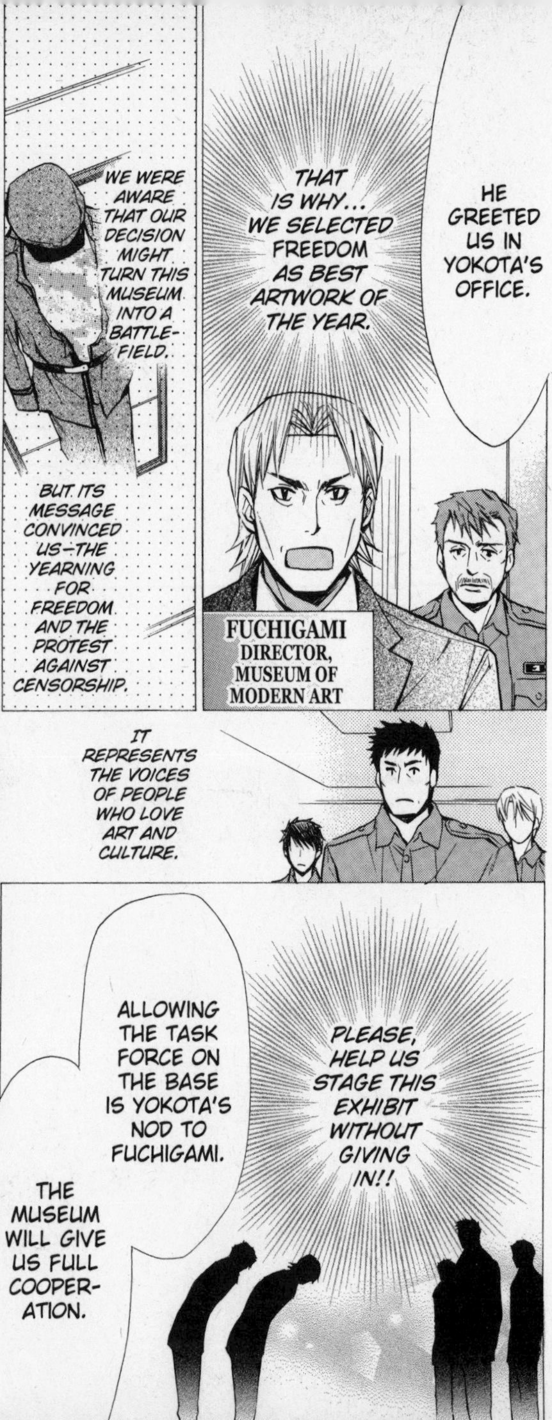
HE GREETED US IN YOKOTA'S OFFICE.
THAT IS WHY... WE SELECTED FREEDOM AS BEST ARTWORK OF THE YEAR.
FUCHIGAMI
DIRECTOR, MUSEUM OF MODERN ART
WE WERE AWARE THAT OUR DECISION MIGHT TURN THIS MUSEUM INTO A BATTLE-FIELD.
BUT ITS MESSAGE CONVINCED US—THE YEARNING FOR FREEDOM AND THE PROTEST AGAINST CENSORSHIP.
IT REPRESENTS THE VOICES OF PEOPLE WHO LOVE ART AND CULTURE.
PLEASE, HELP US STAGE THIS EXHIBIT WITHOUT GIVING IN!!
ALLOWING THE TASK FORCE ON THE BASE IS YOKOTA'S NOD TO FUCHIGAMI.
THE MUSEUM WILL GIVE US FULL COOPER-ATION.

3

Did you see the eclipse in May of 2012? I looked everywhere to find eclipse-viewing glasses the day before, and was up early that morning waiting for it to happen. There were clouds over my town, but the sun would peek through occasionally and I kept hoping. And when I thought "Finally, I can see it," as if on cue, the clouds got thicker...

Talk about bad timing (ha ha). But just for a second I caught sight of the beautiful ring between clouds! I was giddy! I'm glad I didn't give up.

*

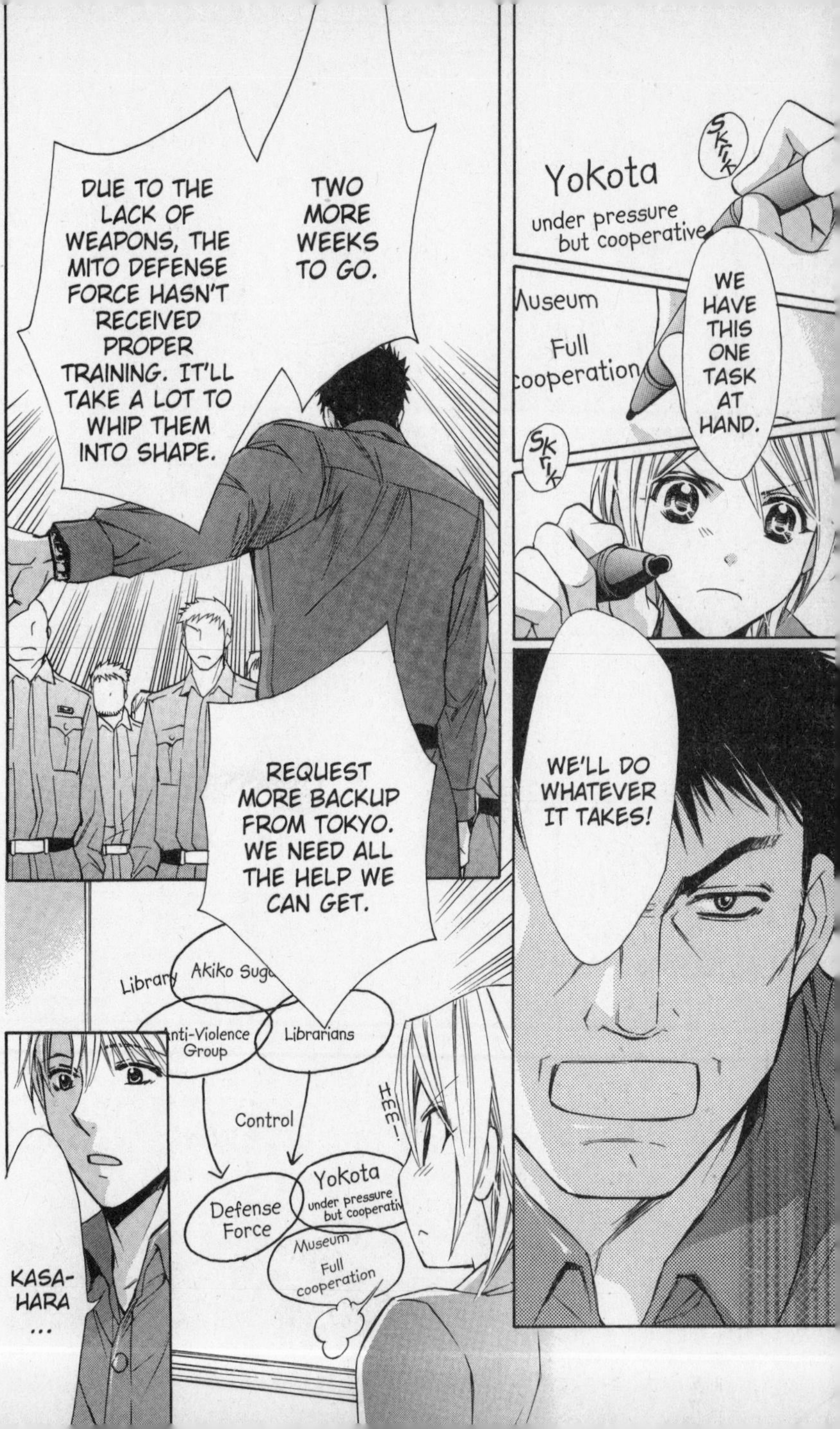
Skrik
Yokota
under pressure
but cooperative
Museum
Full
cooperation
WE HAVE THIS ONE TASK AT HAND.
Skrik
WE'LL DO WHATEVER IT TAKES!
TWO MORE WEEKS TO GO.
DUE TO THE LACK OF WEAPONS, THE MITO DEFENSE FORCE HASN'T RECEIVED PROPER TRAINING. IT'LL TAKE A LOT TO WHIP THEM INTO SHAPE.
REQUEST MORE BACKUP FROM TOKYO. WE NEED ALL THE HELP WE CAN GET.
Library
Akiko Sug
Anti-Violence Group
Librarians
Control
Yokota
under pressure
but cooperativ
Defense Force
Museum
Full cooperation
Hmm!
KASA-HARA ...

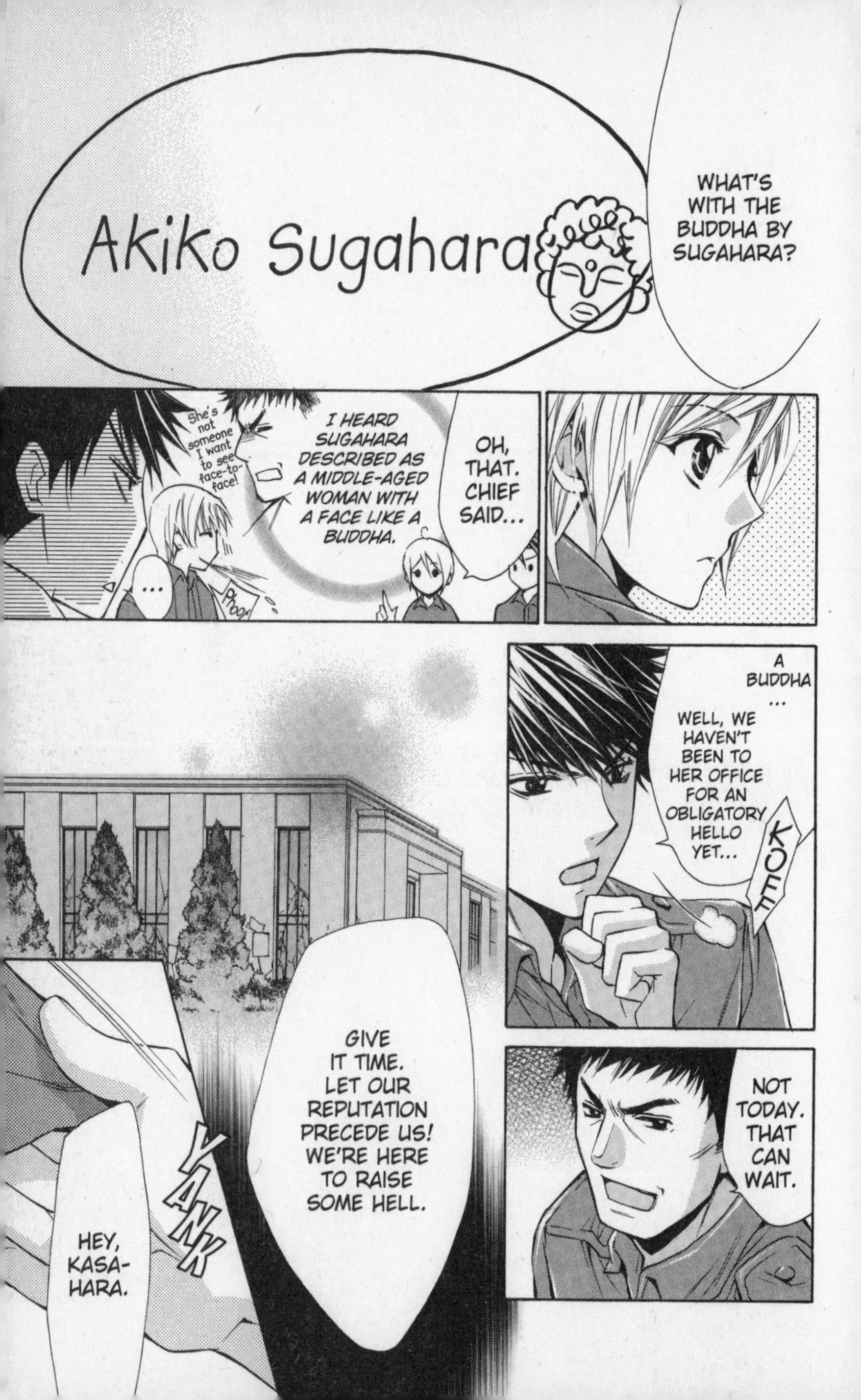
WHAT'S WITH THE BUDDHA BY SUGAHARA?
Akiko Sugahara
OH, THAT. CHIEF SAID...
I HEARD SUGAHARA DESCRIBED AS A MIDDLE-AGED WOMAN WITH A FACE LIKE A BUDDHA.
She's not someone I want to see face-to-face!
Phoo!
...
A BUDDHA ...
WELL, WE HAVEN'T BEEN TO HER OFFICE FOR AN OBLIGATORY HELLO YET...
KOFF
NOT TODAY. THAT CAN WAIT.
GIVE IT TIME. LET OUR REPUTATION PRECEDE US! WE'RE HERE TO RAISE SOME HELL.
YANK
HEY, KASA-HARA.

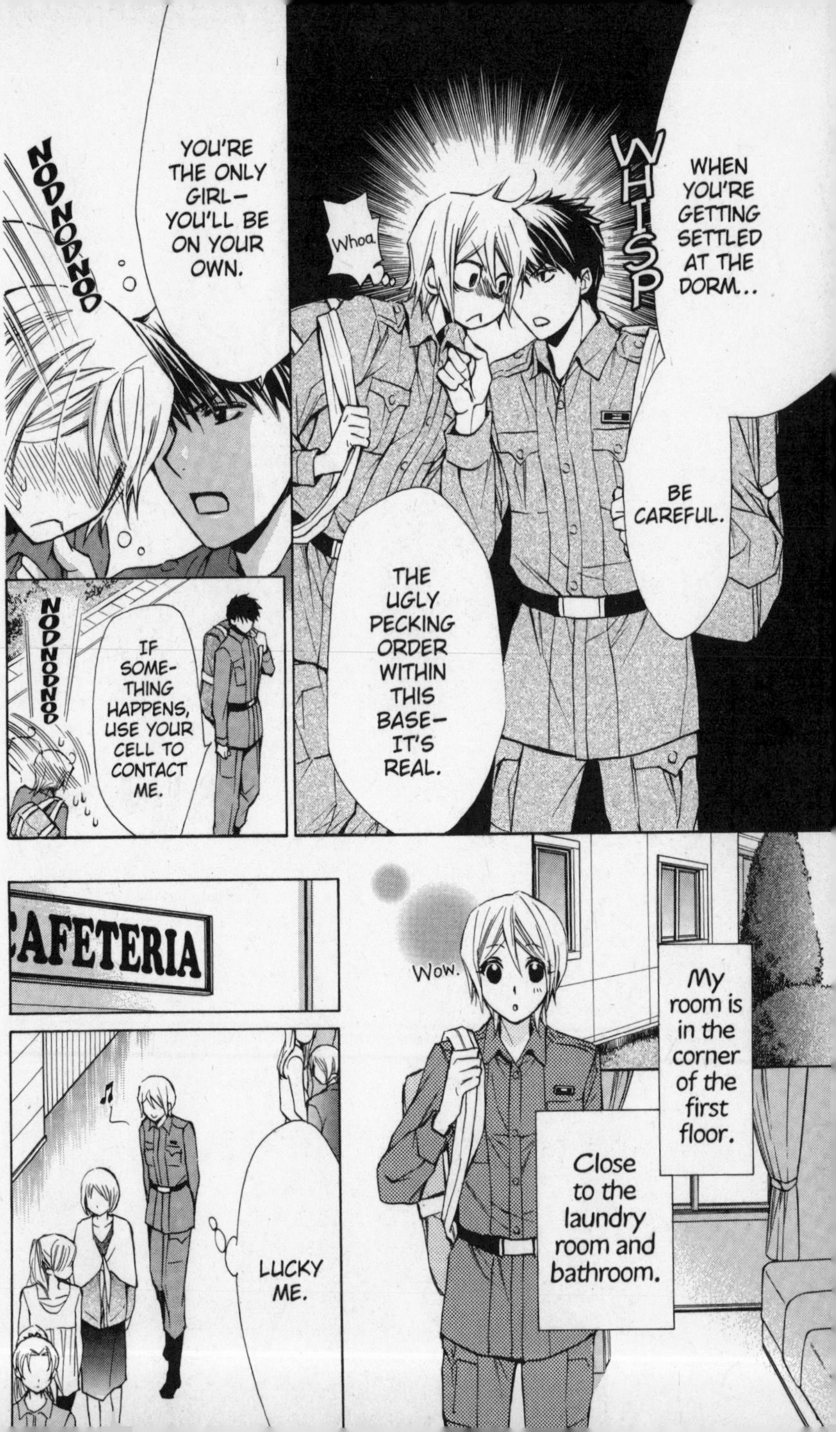
WHISP
WHEN YOU'RE GETTING SETTLED AT THE DORM...
BE CAREFUL.
Whoa.
THE UGLY PECKING ORDER WITHIN THIS BASE— IT'S REAL.
YOU'RE THE ONLY GIRL— YOU'LL BE ON YOUR OWN.
NODNODNODNOD
IF SOME-THING HAPPENS, USE YOUR CELL TO CONTACT ME.
NODNODNODNOD
My room is in the corner of the first floor.
Close to the laundry room and bathroom.
Wow.
CAFETERIA
LUCKY ME.

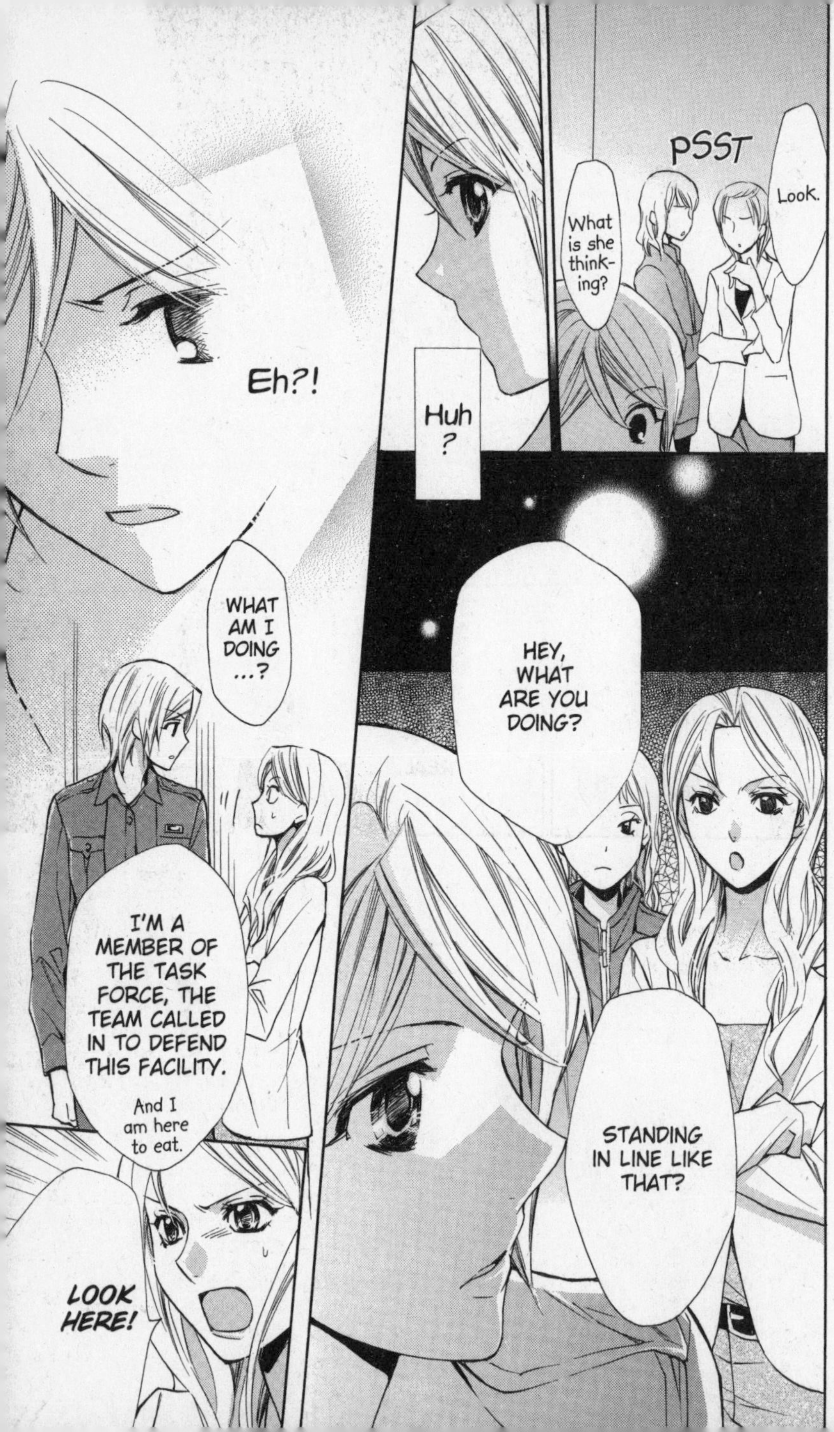
PSST
Look.
What is she think-ing?
Huh?
HEY, WHAT ARE YOU DOING?
STANDING IN LINE LIKE THAT?
Eh?!
WHAT AM I DOING ...?
I'M A MEMBER OF THE TASK FORCE, THE TEAM CALLED IN TO DEFEND THIS FACILITY.
And I am here to eat.
LOOK HERE!

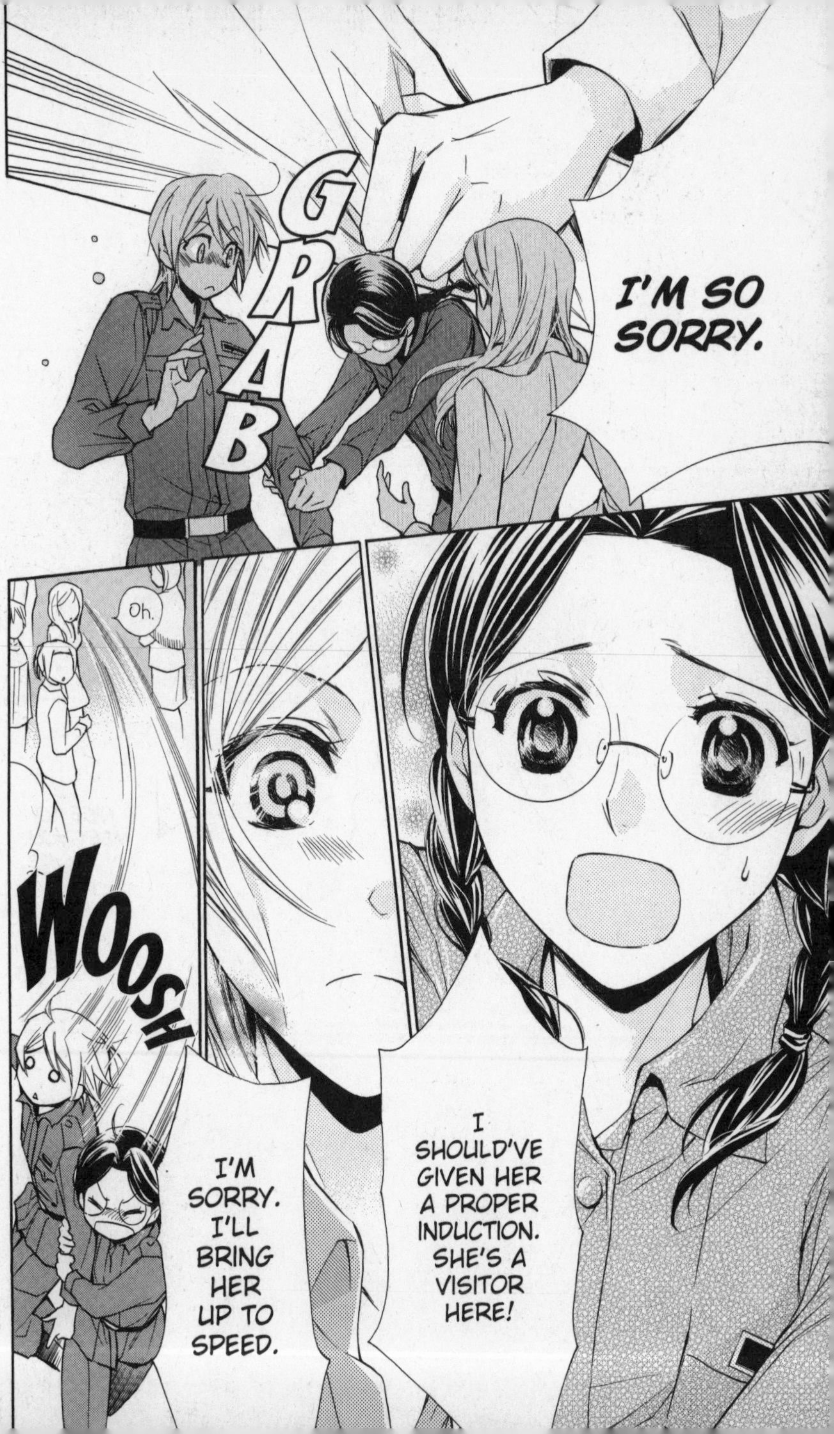
I'M SO SORRY.
GRAB
I SHOULD'VE GIVEN HER A PROPER INDUCTION. SHE'S A VISITOR HERE!
Oh.
WOOSH
I'M SORRY. I'LL BRING HER UP TO SPEED.

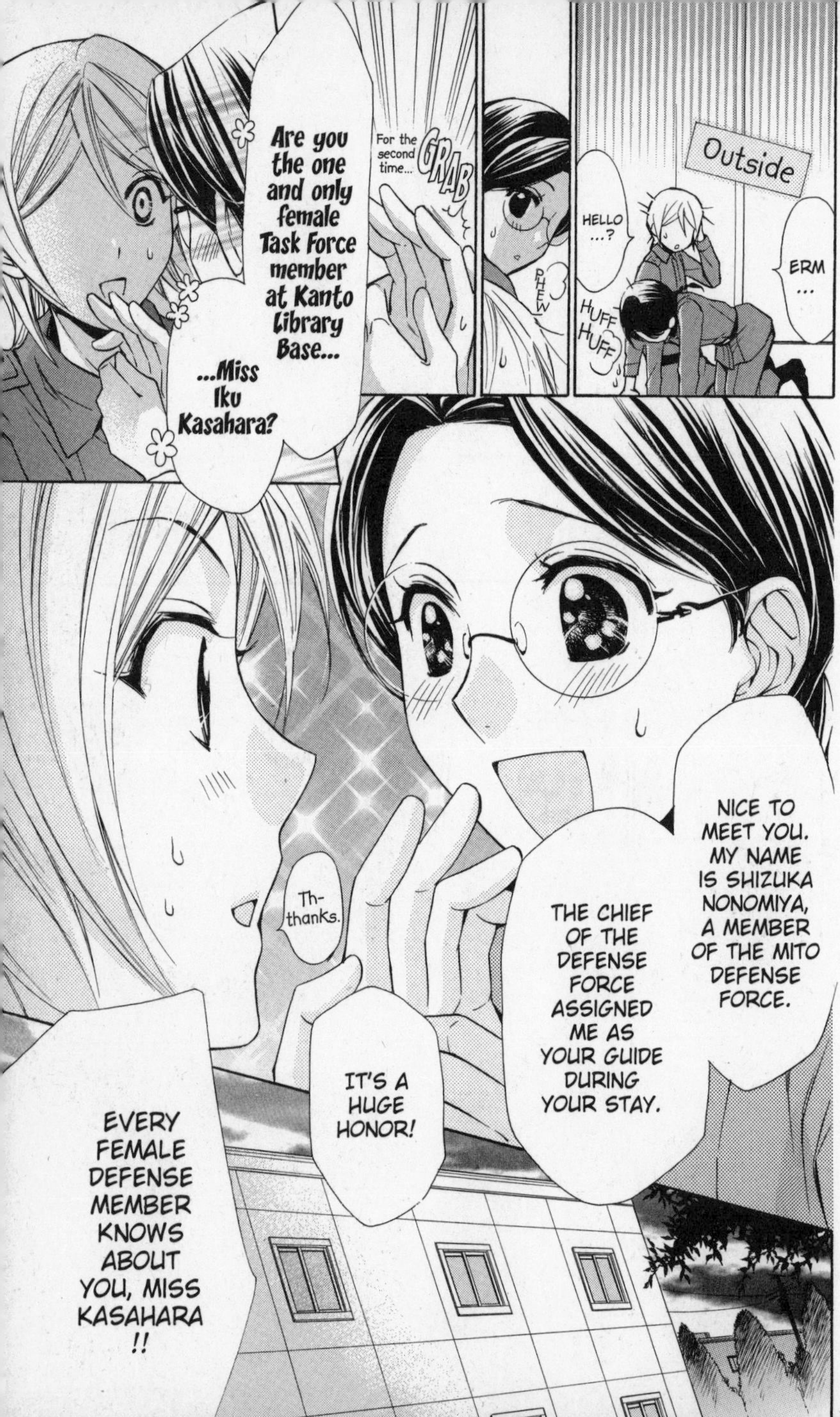
Outside
ERM ...
HELLO ...?
HUFF HUFF
PHEW
For the second time...
GRAB
Are you the one and only female Task Force member at Kanto Library Base...
...Miss Iku Kasahara?
NICE TO MEET YOU. MY NAME IS SHIZUKA NONOMIYA, A MEMBER OF THE MITO DEFENSE FORCE.
THE CHIEF OF THE DEFENSE FORCE ASSIGNED ME AS YOUR GUIDE DURING YOUR STAY.
Th-thanks.
IT'S A HUGE HONOR!
EVERY FEMALE DEFENSE MEMBER KNOWS ABOUT YOU, MISS KASAHARA!!

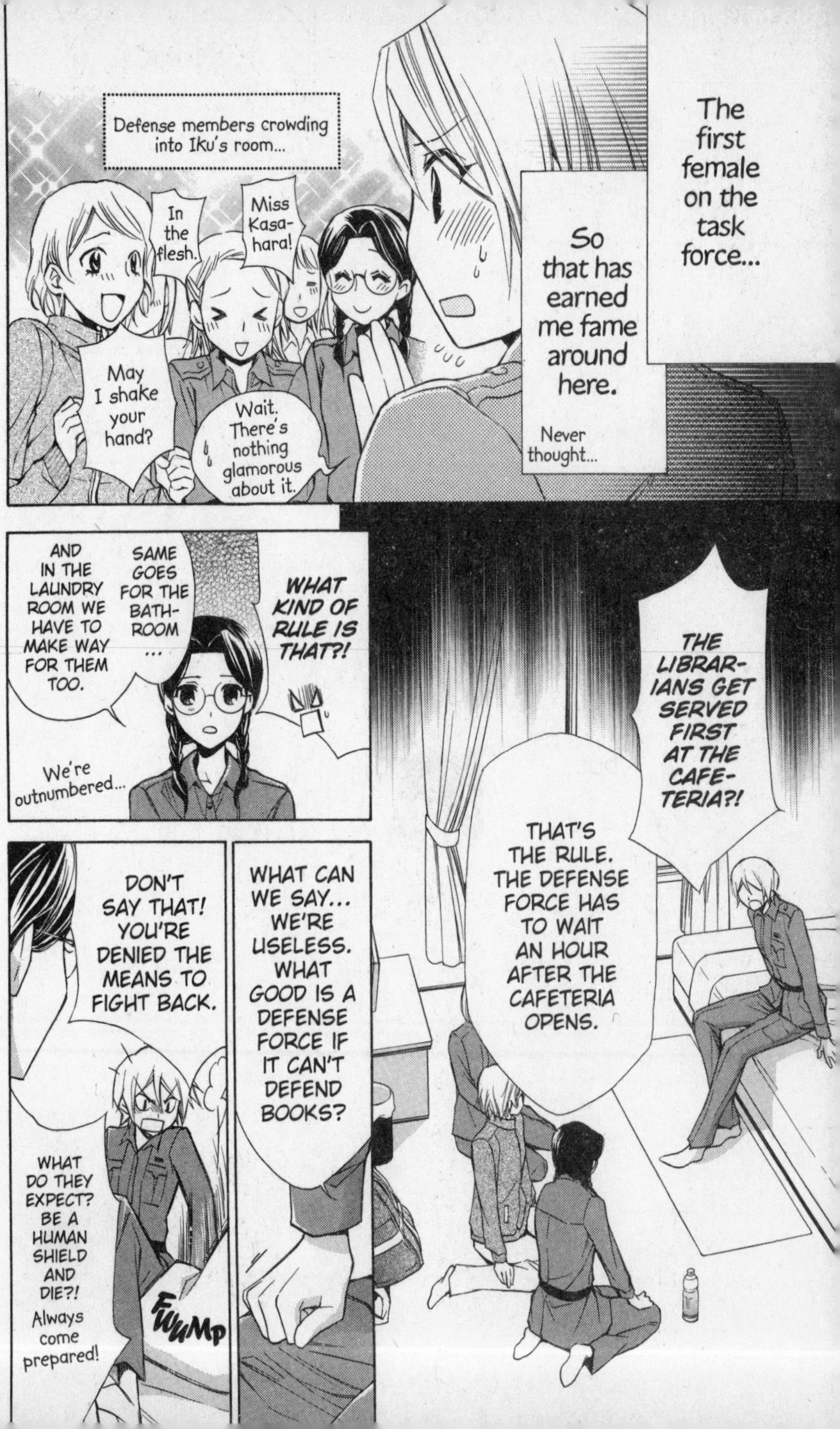
The first female on the task force...
So that has earned me fame around here.
Never thought...
Defense members crowding into Iku's room...
Miss Kasa-hara!
In the flesh.
May I shake your hand?
Wait. There's nothing glamorous about it.
THE LIBRAR-IANS GET SERVED FIRST AT THE CAFE-TERIA?!
THAT'S THE RULE. THE DEFENSE FORCE HAS TO WAIT AN HOUR AFTER THE CAFETERIA OPENS.
WHAT KIND OF RULE IS THAT?!
SAME GOES FOR THE BATH-ROOM...
AND IN THE LAUNDRY ROOM WE HAVE TO MAKE WAY FOR THEM TOO.
We're outnumbered...
WHAT CAN WE SAY... WE'RE USELESS. WHAT GOOD IS A DEFENSE FORCE IF IT CAN'T DEFEND BOOKS?
DON'T SAY THAT! YOU'RE DENIED THE MEANS TO FIGHT BACK.
WHAT DO THEY EXPECT? BE A HUMAN SHIELD AND DIE?!
FWUMP
Always come prepared!

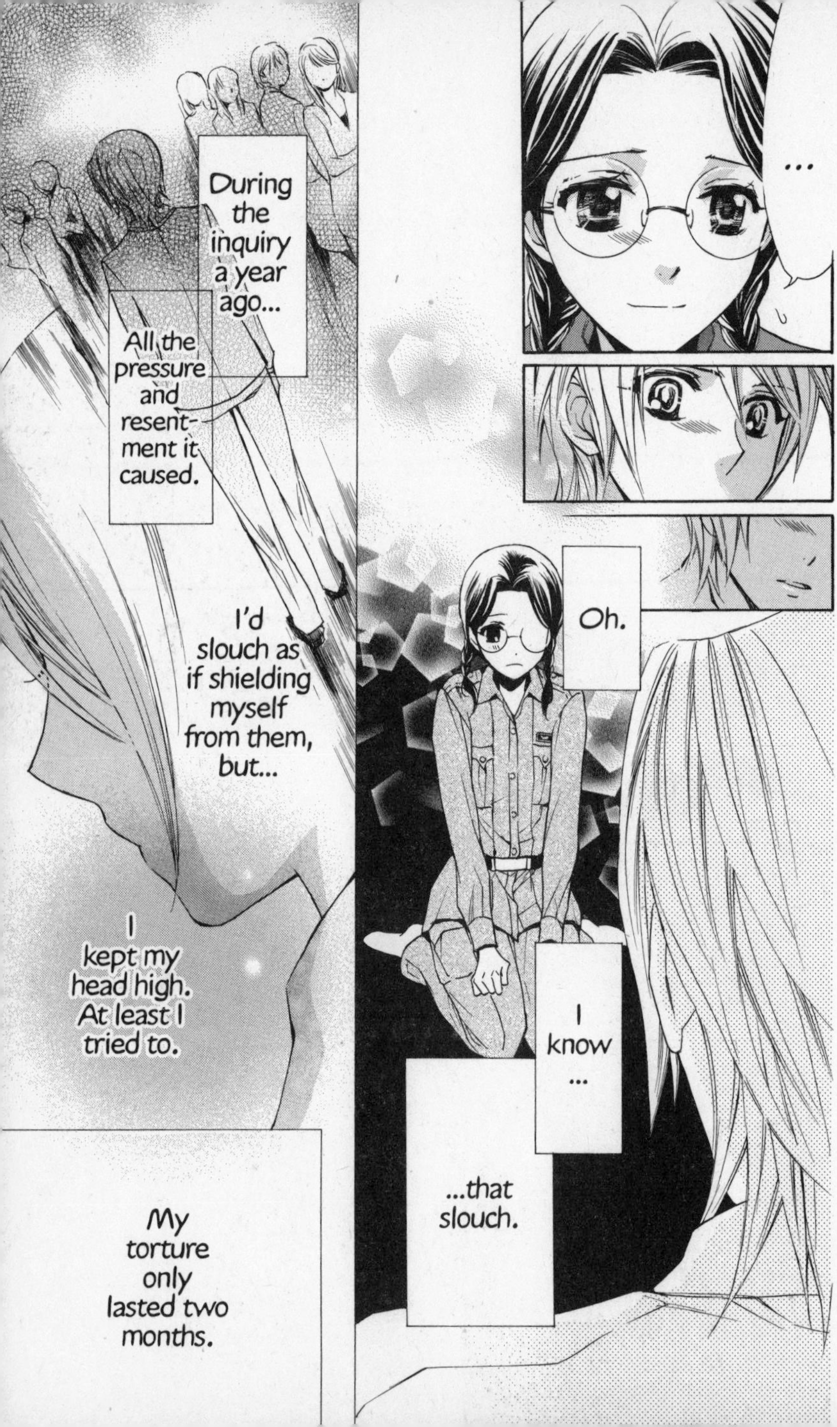
...
Oh.
I know ...
...that slouch.
During the inquiry a year ago...
All the pressure and resentment it caused.
I'd slouch as if shielding myself from them, but...
I kept my head high. At least I tried to.
My torture only lasted two months.

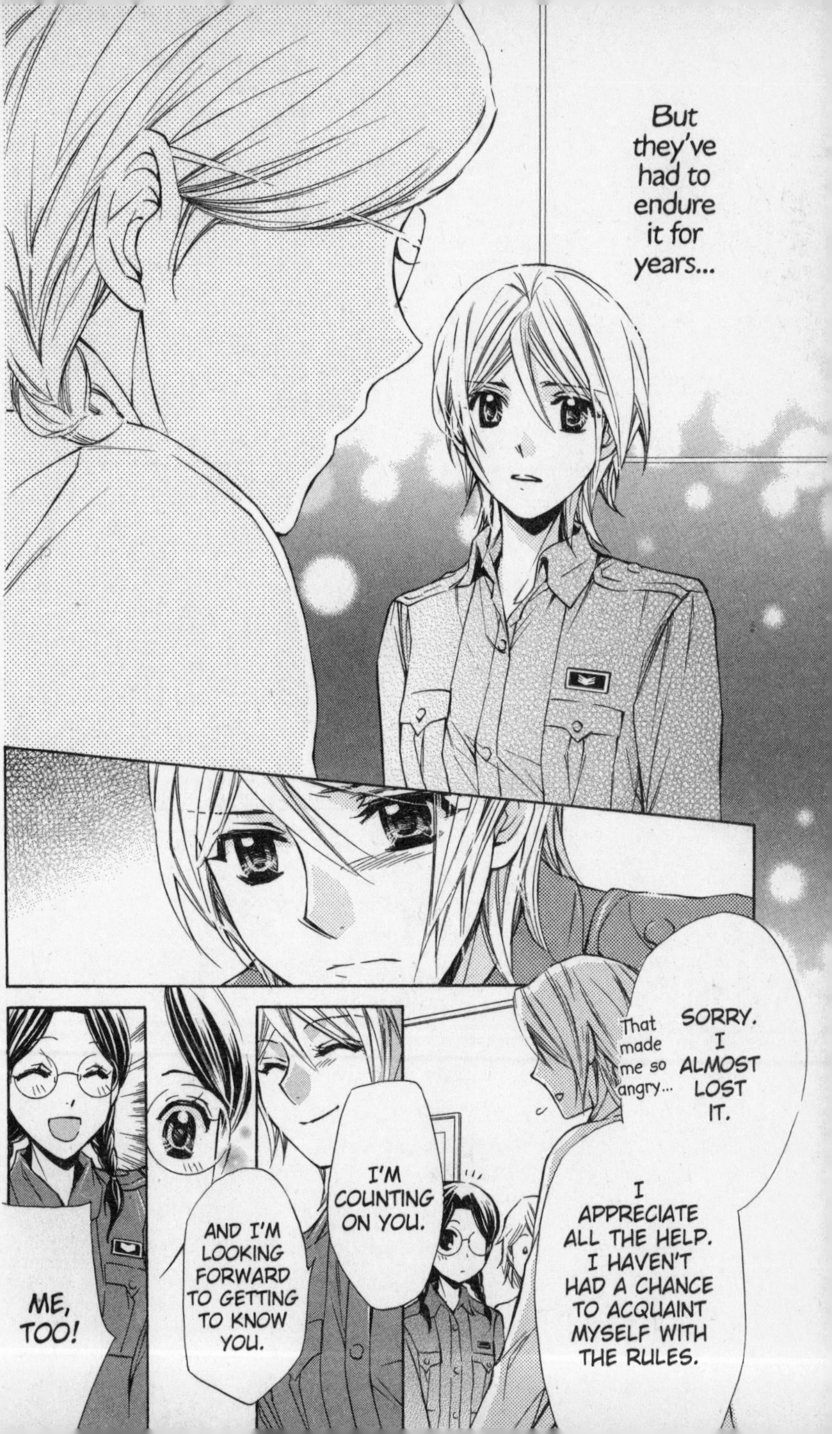
But they've had to endure it for years...
SORRY. I ALMOST LOST IT.
That made me so angry...
I APPRECIATE ALL THE HELP. I HAVEN'T HAD A CHANCE TO ACQUAINT MYSELF WITH THE RULES.
I'M COUNTING ON YOU.
AND I'M LOOKING FORWARD TO GETTING TO KNOW YOU.
ME, TOO!

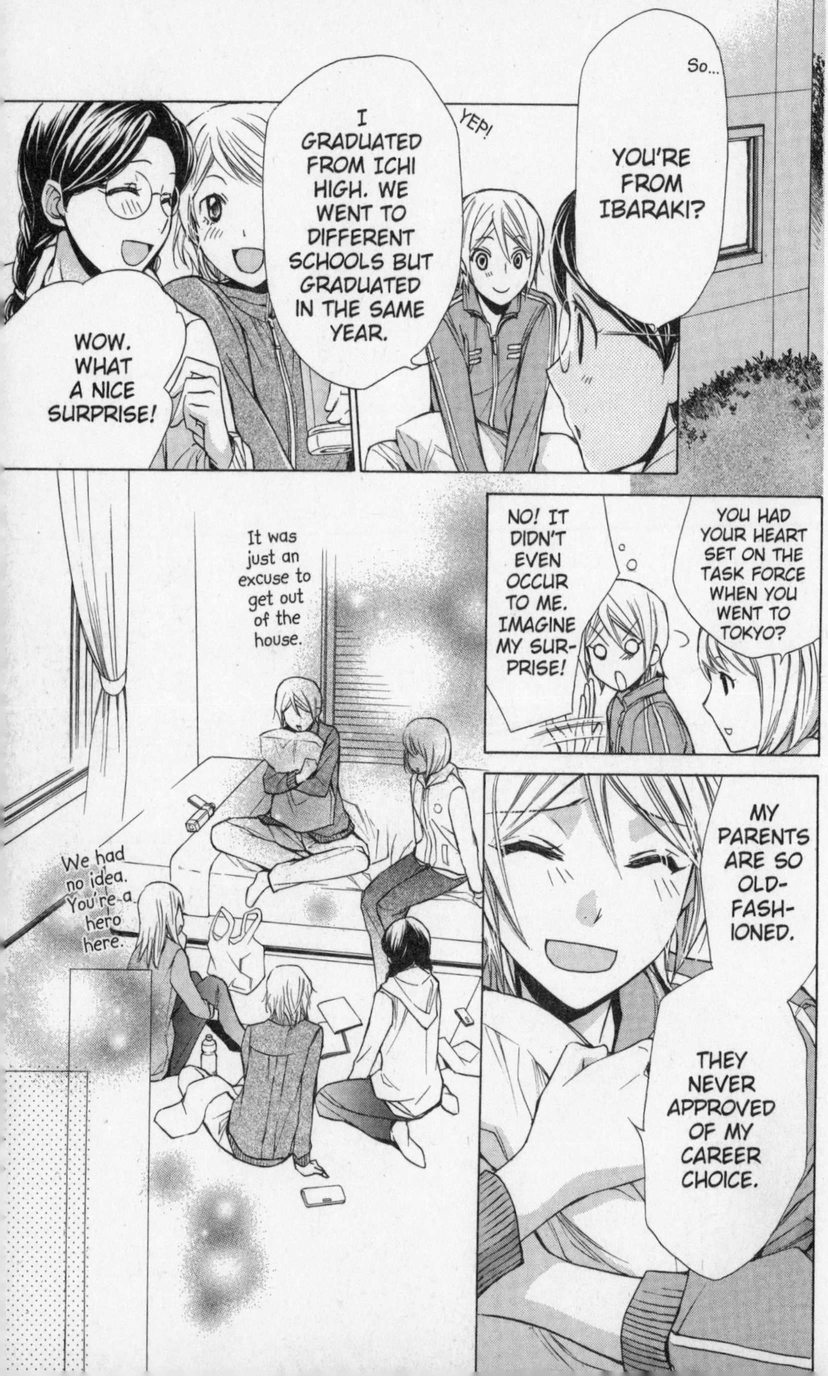
So...
YOU'RE FROM IBARAKI?
YEP!
I GRADUATED FROM ICHI HIGH. WE WENT TO DIFFERENT SCHOOLS BUT GRADUATED IN THE SAME YEAR.
WOW. WHAT A NICE SURPRISE!
YOU HAD YOUR HEART SET ON THE TASK FORCE WHEN YOU WENT TO TOKYO?
NO! IT DIDN'T EVEN OCCUR TO ME. IMAGINE MY SUR-PRISE!
MY PARENTS ARE SO OLD-FASH-IONED.
THEY NEVER APPROVED OF MY CAREER CHOICE.
It was just an excuse to get out of the house.
We had no idea. You're a hero here.

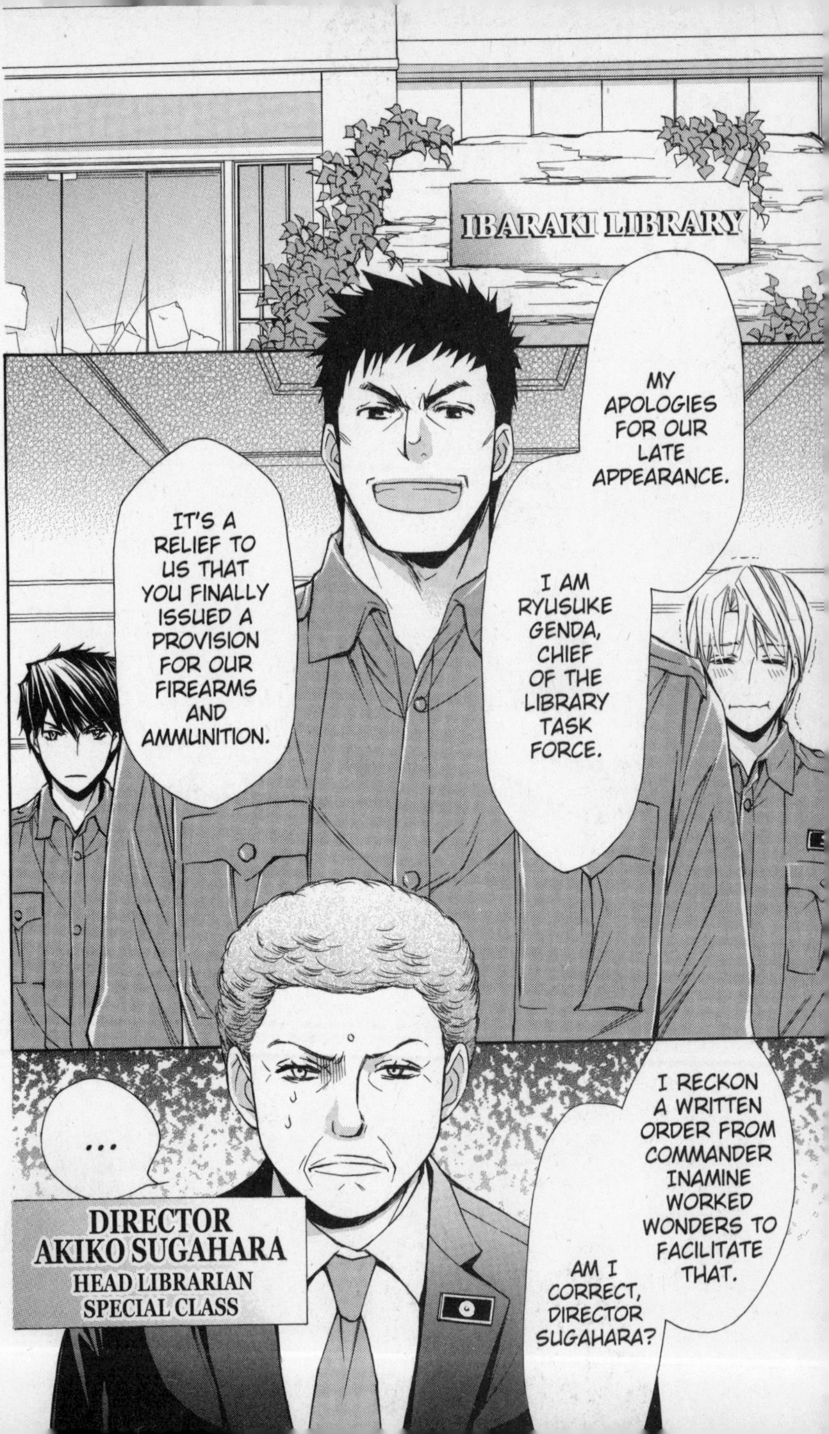
IBARAKI LIBRARY
MY APOLOGIES FOR OUR LATE APPEARANCE.
I AM RYUSUKE GENDA, CHIEF OF THE LIBRARY TASK FORCE.
IT'S A RELIEF TO US THAT YOU FINALLY ISSUED A PROVISION FOR OUR FIREARMS AND AMMUNITION.
I RECKON A WRITTEN ORDER FROM COMMANDER INAMINE WORKED WONDERS TO FACILITATE THAT.
AM I CORRECT, DIRECTOR SUGAHARA?
...
DIRECTOR AKIKO SUGAHARA
HEAD LIBRARIAN SPECIAL CLASS

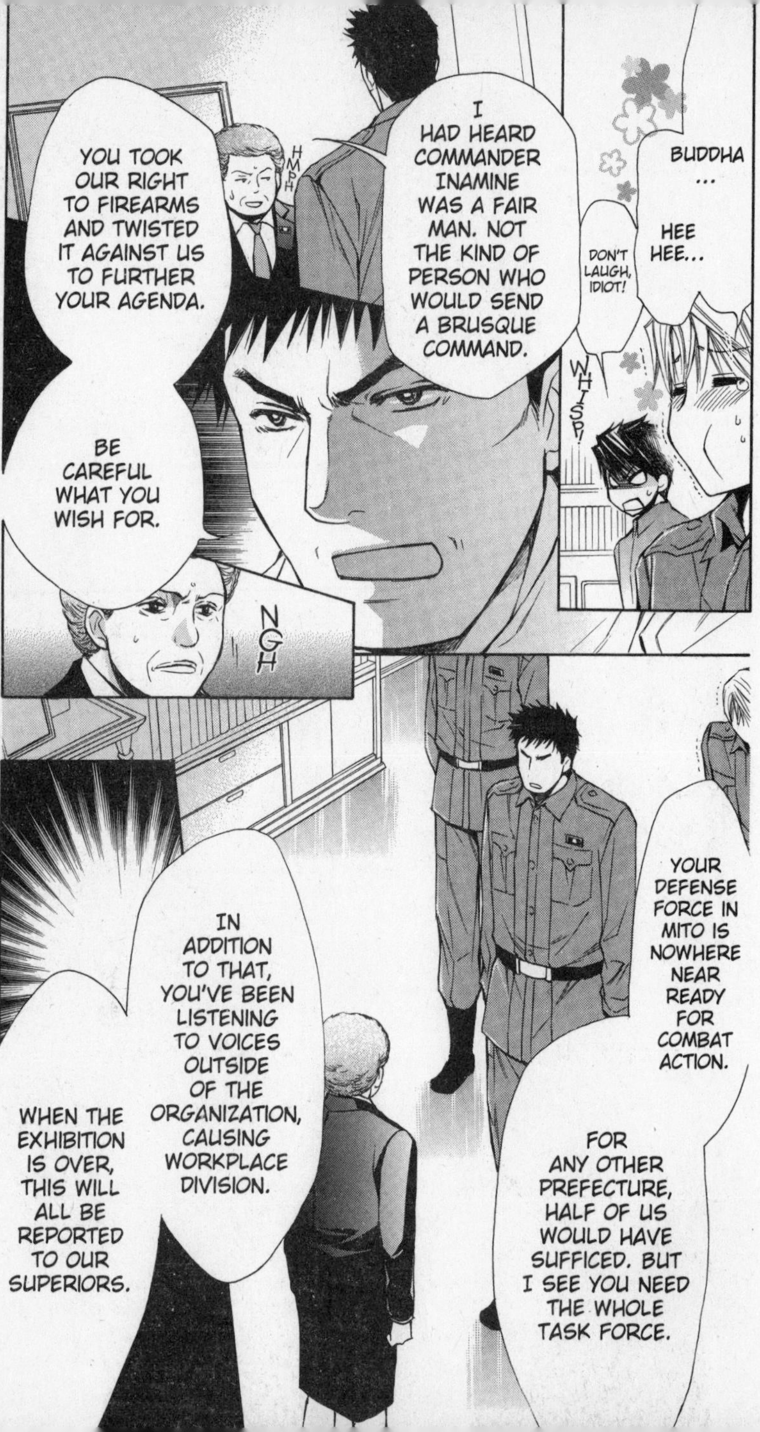
BUDDHA ...
HEE HEE...
DON'T LAUGH, IDIOT!
WHISP!
I HAD HEARD COMMANDER INAMINE WAS A FAIR MAN. NOT THE KIND OF PERSON WHO WOULD SEND A BRUSQUE COMMAND.
HMPH
YOU TOOK OUR RIGHT TO FIREARMS AND TWISTED IT AGAINST US TO FURTHER YOUR AGENDA.
BE CAREFUL WHAT YOU WISH FOR.
NGH
YOUR DEFENSE FORCE IN MITO IS NOWHERE NEAR READY FOR COMBAT ACTION.
FOR ANY OTHER PREFECTURE, HALF OF US WOULD HAVE SUFFICED. BUT I SEE YOU NEED THE WHOLE TASK FORCE.
IN ADDITION TO THAT, YOU'VE BEEN LISTENING TO VOICES OUTSIDE OF THE ORGANIZATION, CAUSING WORKPLACE DIVISION.
WHEN THE EXHIBITION IS OVER, THIS WILL ALL BE REPORTED TO OUR SUPERIORS.

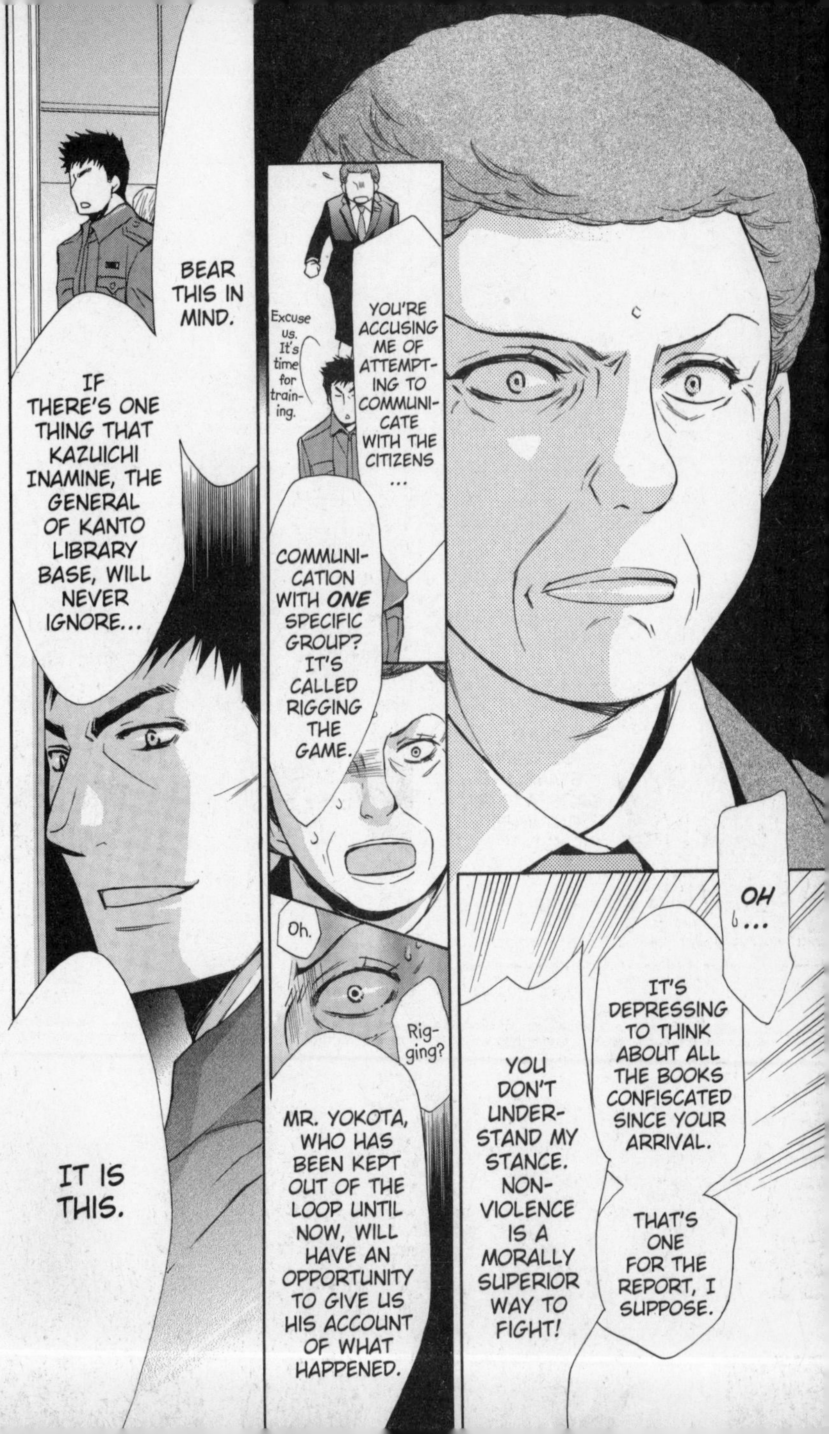
OH...
IT'S DEPRESSING TO THINK ABOUT ALL THE BOOKS CONFISCATED SINCE YOUR ARRIVAL.
THAT'S ONE FOR THE REPORT, I SUPPOSE.
YOU DON'T UNDERSTAND MY STANCE. NON-VIOLENCE IS A MORALLY SUPERIOR WAY TO FIGHT!
YOU'RE ACCUSING ME OF ATTEMPTING TO COMMUNICATE WITH THE CITIZENS...
Excuse us. It's time for training.
COMMUNICATION WITH ***ONE*** SPECIFIC GROUP? IT'S CALLED RIGGING THE GAME.
Oh.
Rigging?
MR. YOKOTA, WHO HAS BEEN KEPT OUT OF THE LOOP UNTIL NOW, WILL HAVE AN OPPORTUNITY TO GIVE US HIS ACCOUNT OF WHAT HAPPENED.
BEAR THIS IN MIND.
IF THERE'S ONE THING THAT KAZUICHI INAMINE, THE GENERAL OF KANTO LIBRARY BASE, WILL NEVER IGNORE...
IT IS THIS.

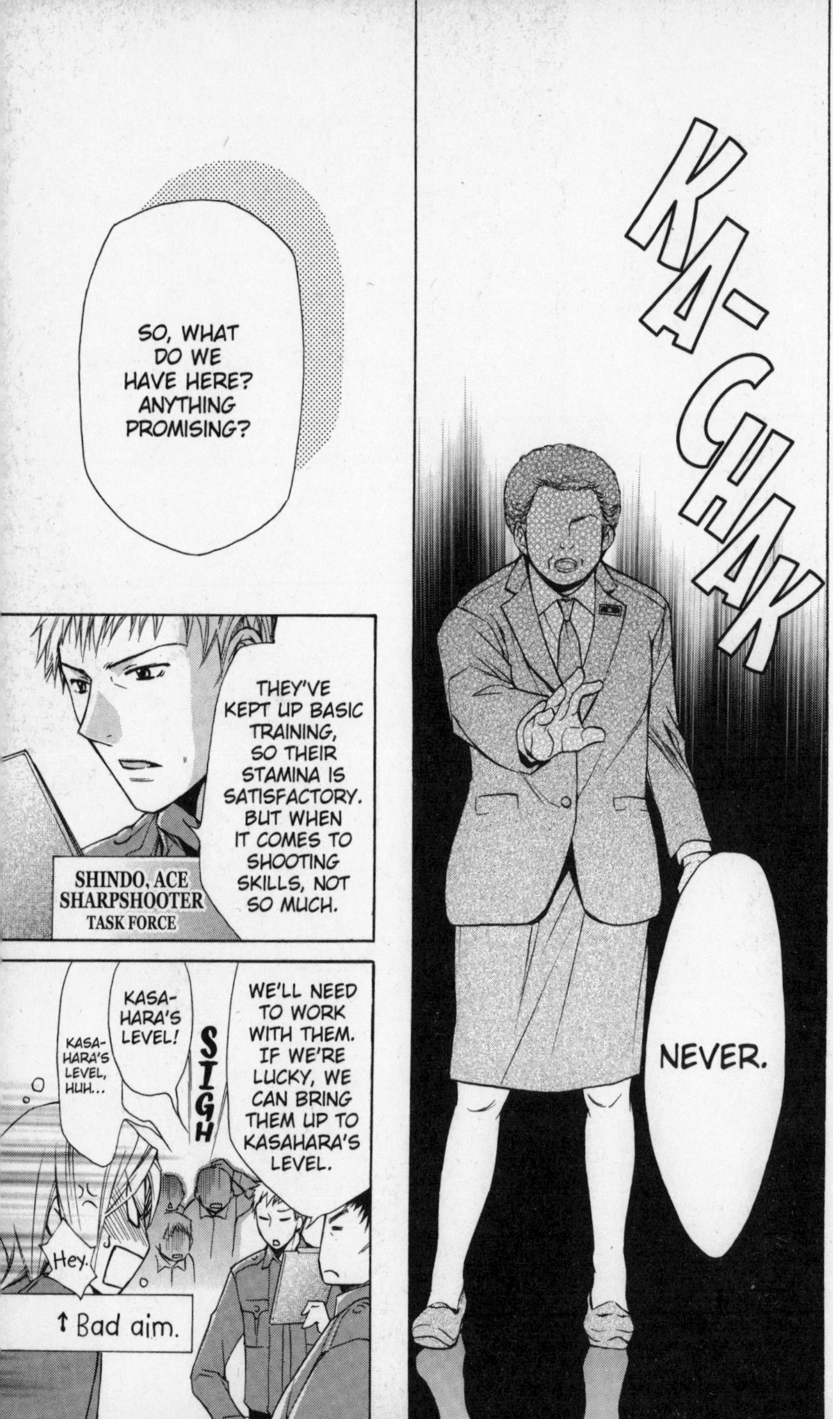
KA-CHAK
NEVER.
SO, WHAT DO WE HAVE HERE? ANYTHING PROMISING?
THEY'VE KEPT UP BASIC TRAINING, SO THEIR STAMINA IS SATISFACTORY. BUT WHEN IT COMES TO SHOOTING SKILLS, NOT SO MUCH.
SHINDO, ACE SHARPSHOOTER TASK FORCE
WE'LL NEED TO WORK WITH THEM. IF WE'RE LUCKY, WE CAN BRING THEM UP TO KASAHARA'S LEVEL.
SIGH
KASA-HARA'S LEVEL!
KASA-HARA'S LEVEL, HUH...
Hey.
↑ Bad aim.

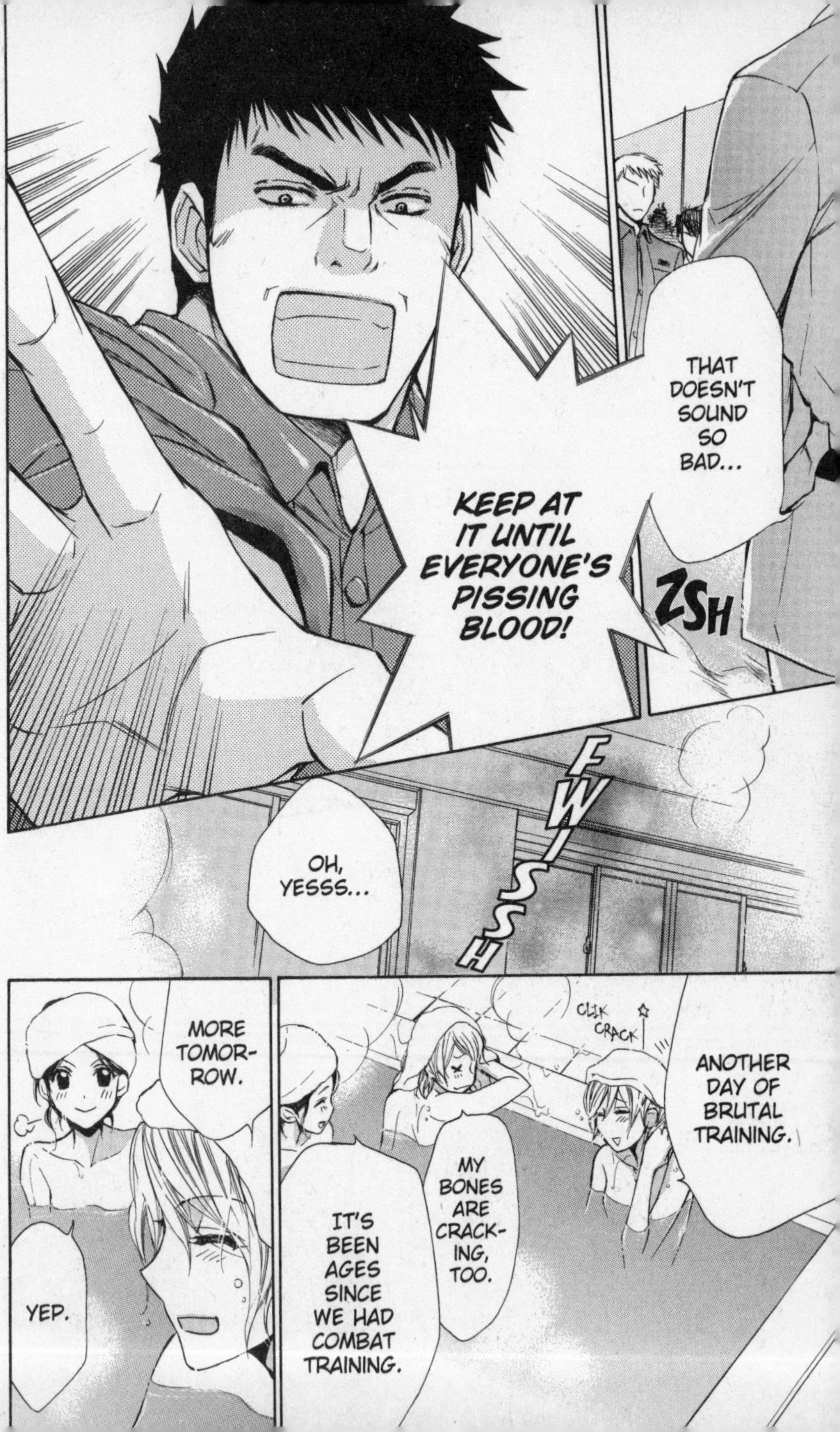
THAT DOESN'T SOUND SO BAD...
KEEP AT IT UNTIL EVERYONE'S PISSING BLOOD!
ZSH
FWISSSH
OH, YESSS...
ANOTHER DAY OF BRUTAL TRAINING.
CLIK CRACK
MY BONES ARE CRACKING, TOO.
IT'S BEEN AGES SINCE WE HAD COMBAT TRAINING.
MORE TOMORROW.
YEP.

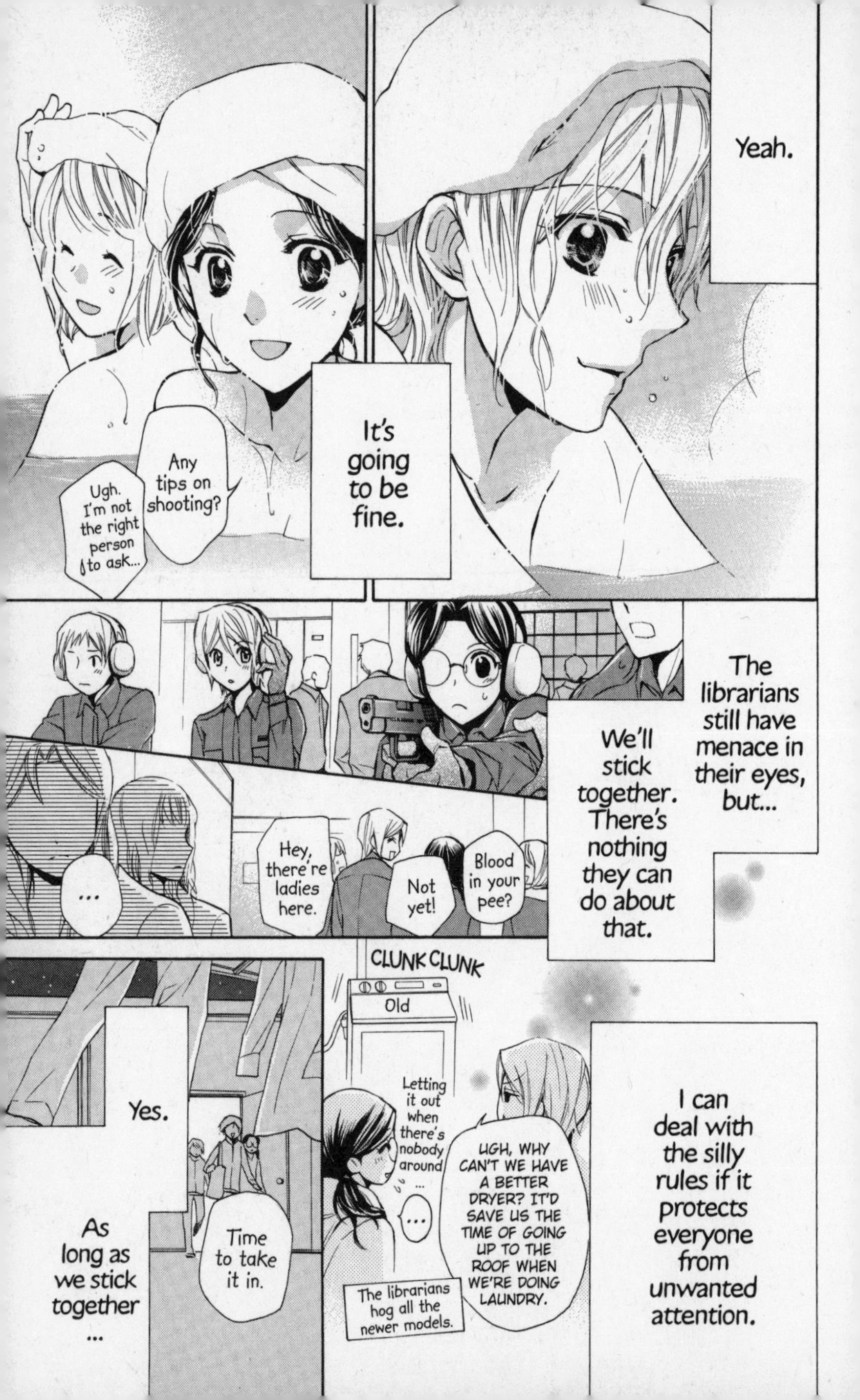
Yeah.
It's going to be fine.
Any tips on shooting?
Ugh. I'm not the right person to ask...
The librarians still have menace in their eyes, but...
We'll stick together. There's nothing they can do about that.
Blood in your pee?
Not yet!
Hey, there're ladies here.
...
CLUNK CLUNK
Old
I can deal with the silly rules if it protects everyone from unwanted attention.
UGH, WHY CAN'T WE HAVE A BETTER DRYER? IT'D SAVE US THE TIME OF GOING UP TO THE ROOF WHEN WE'RE DOING LAUNDRY.
The librarians hog all the newer models.
Letting it out when there's nobody around ...
...
Time to take it in.
Yes.
As long as we stick together ...

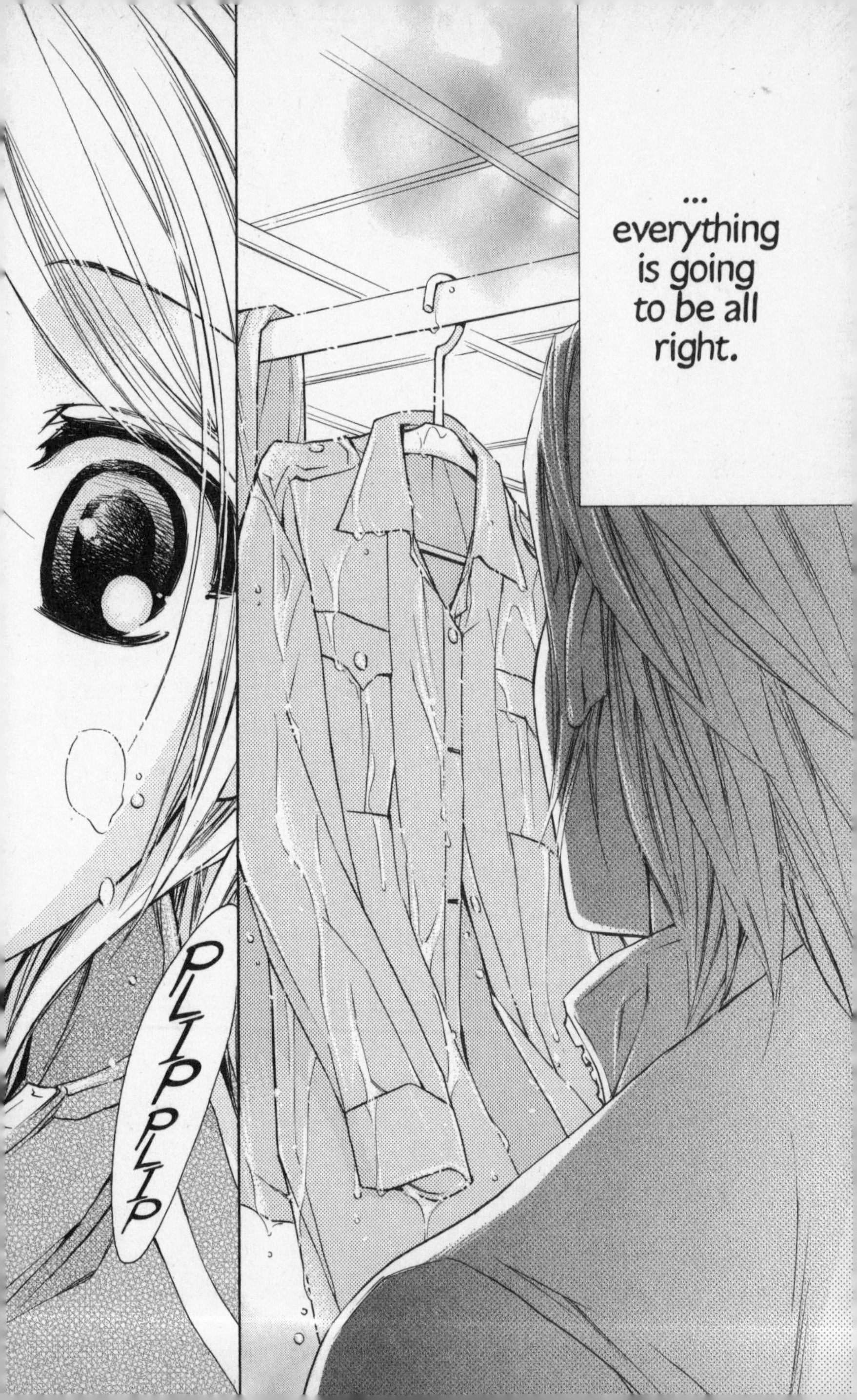
...everything is going to be all right.
PLIP PLIP

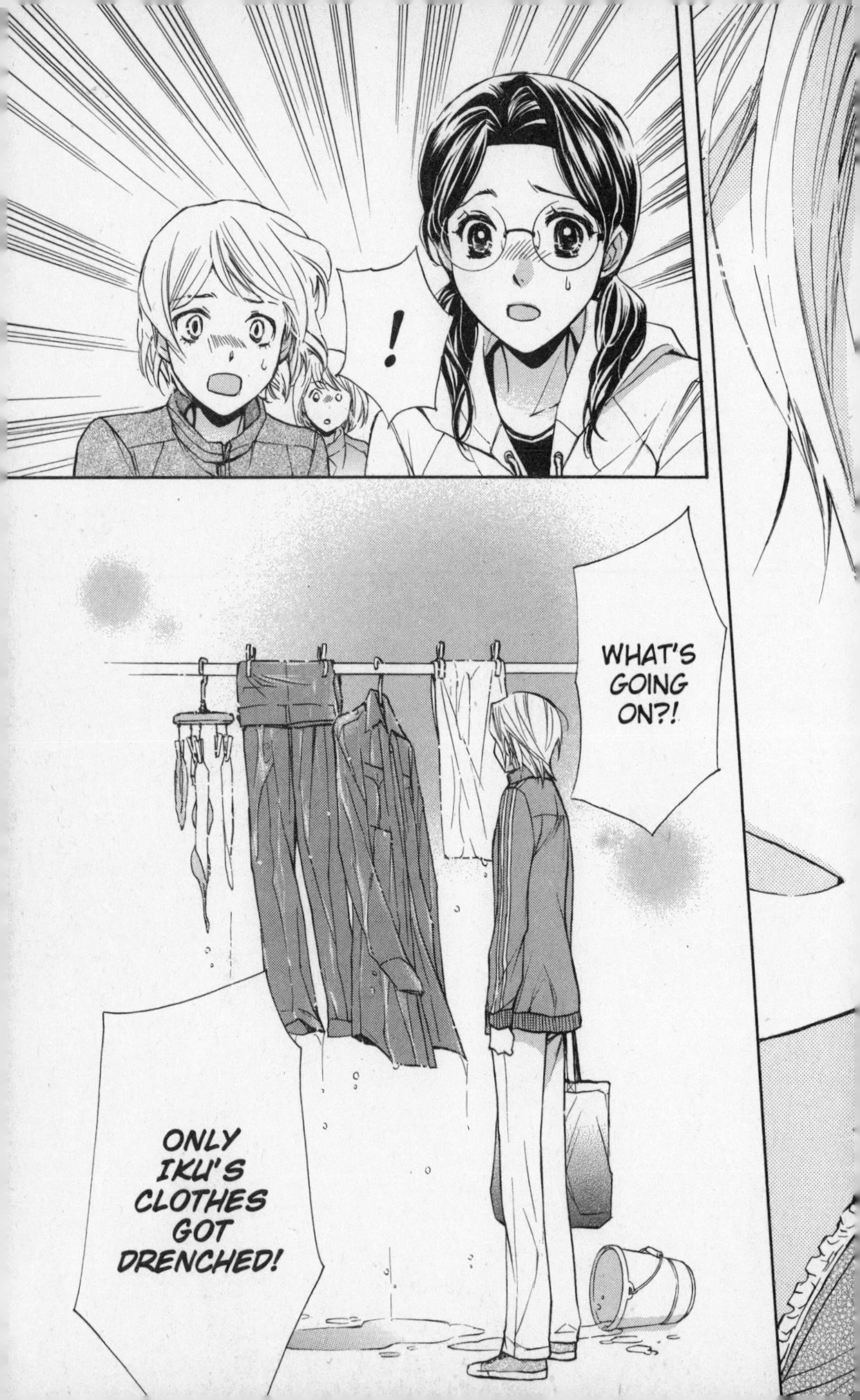
!
WHAT'S GOING ON?!
ONLY IKU'S CLOTHES GOT DRENCHED!

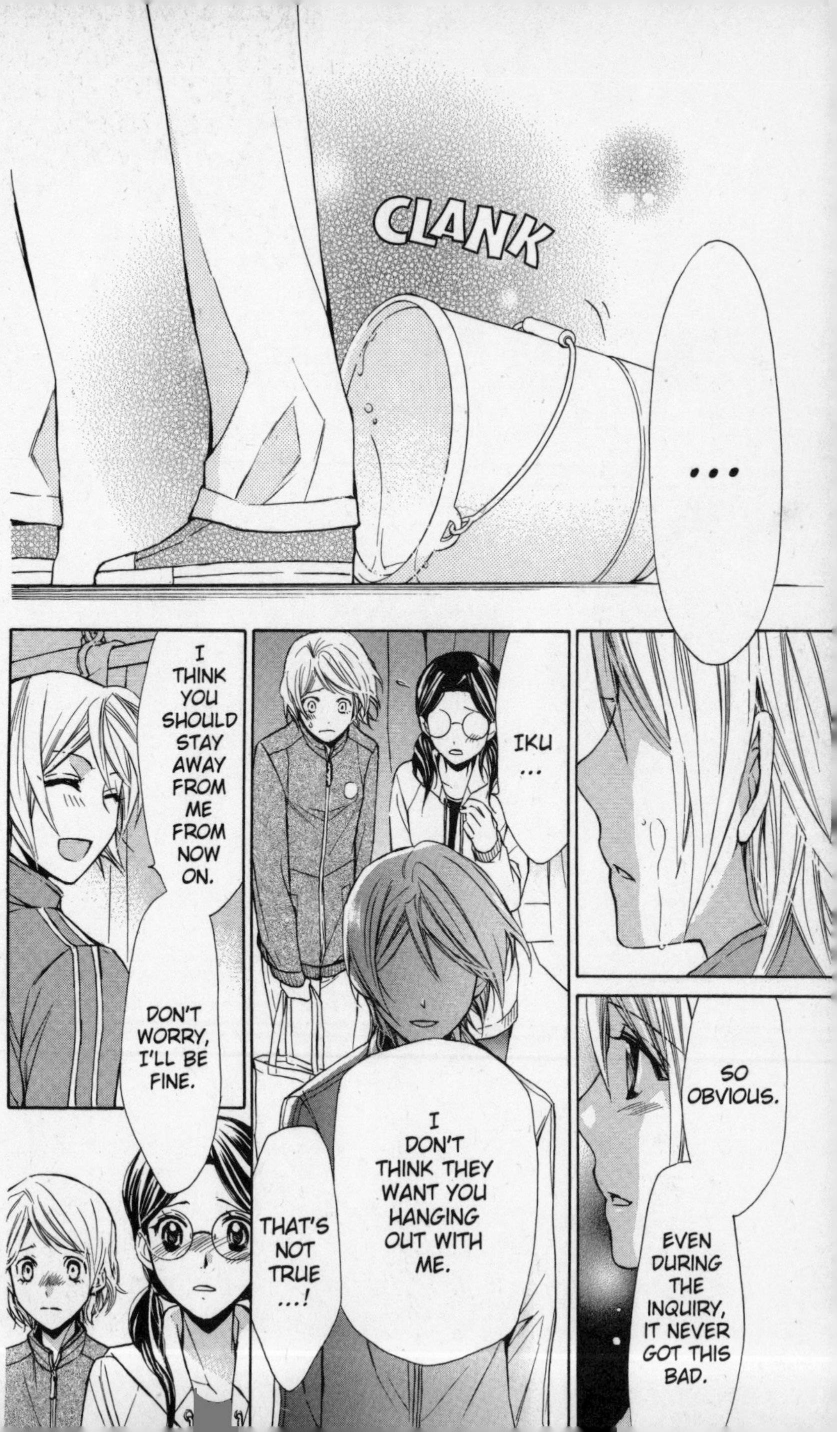
CLANK
...
SO OBVIOUS.
EVEN DURING THE INQUIRY, IT NEVER GOT THIS BAD.
IKU ...
I DON'T THINK THEY WANT YOU HANGING OUT WITH ME.
THAT'S NOT TRUE ...!
I THINK YOU SHOULD STAY AWAY FROM ME FROM NOW ON.
DON'T WORRY, I'LL BE FINE.

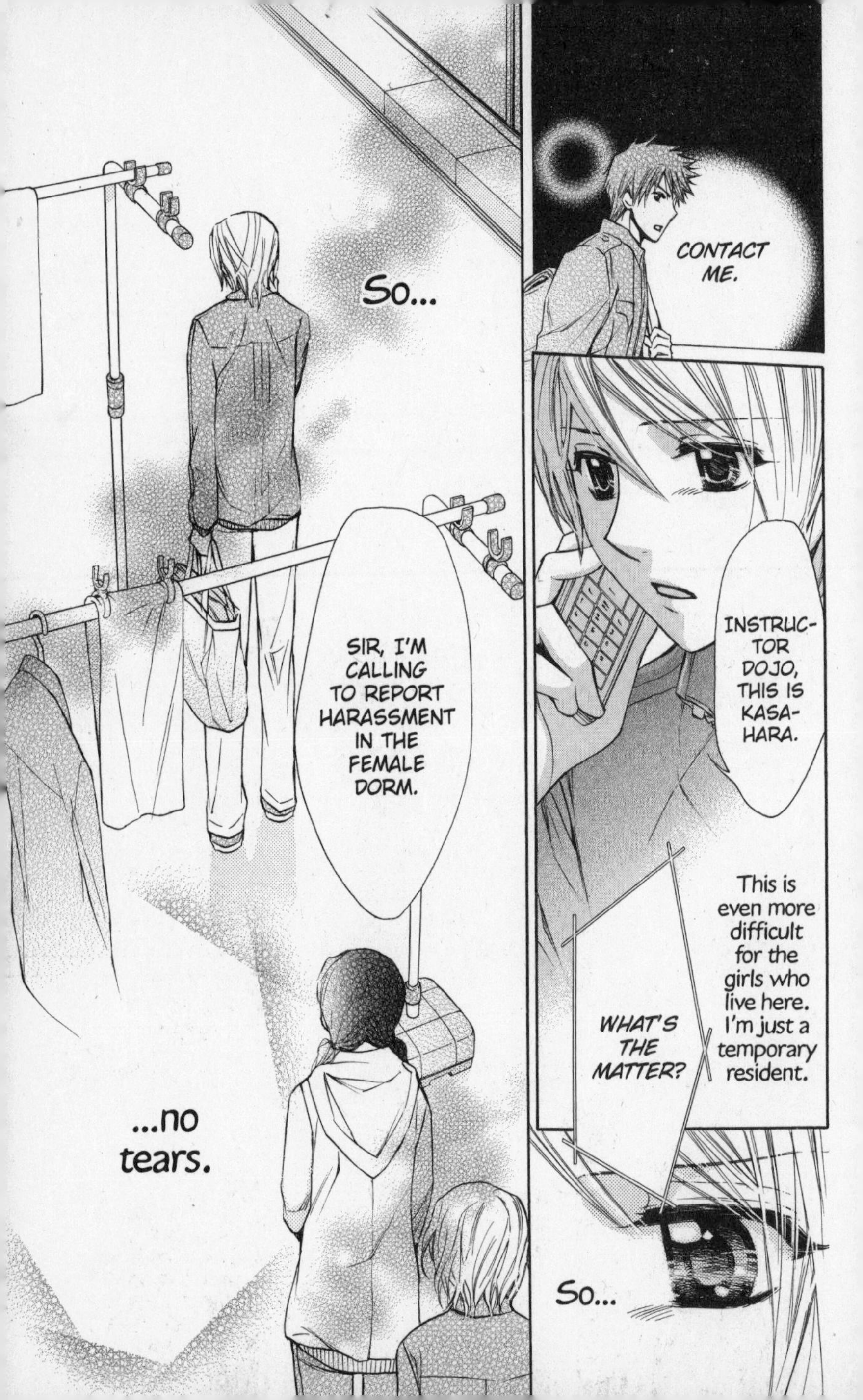
CONTACT ME.
INSTRUCTOR DOJO, THIS IS KASAHARA.
This is even more difficult for the girls who live here. I'm just a temporary resident.
WHAT'S THE MATTER?
So...
So...
SIR, I'M CALLING TO REPORT HARASSMENT IN THE FEMALE DORM.
...no tears.

The King and the princess, on the road.

SNAP
SMIRK
ZZZ
Oh, you're up.
GRIN
SNAP
GRIN
SNAP
SNAPSNAP
SMIRK
SNAPSNAP
SNAP
SMIRKSMIRK
Almost every Task Force member on that bus now has a nice souvenir on their cell phone...
ZZZ
Oh, they'll find out sooner or later.
Maybe I'll take video
Not a Kodak moment for me.
The one exception.

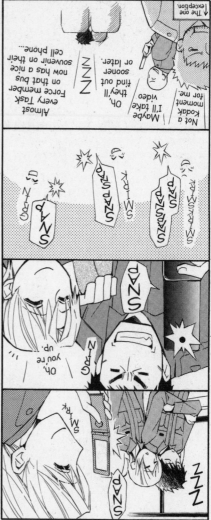

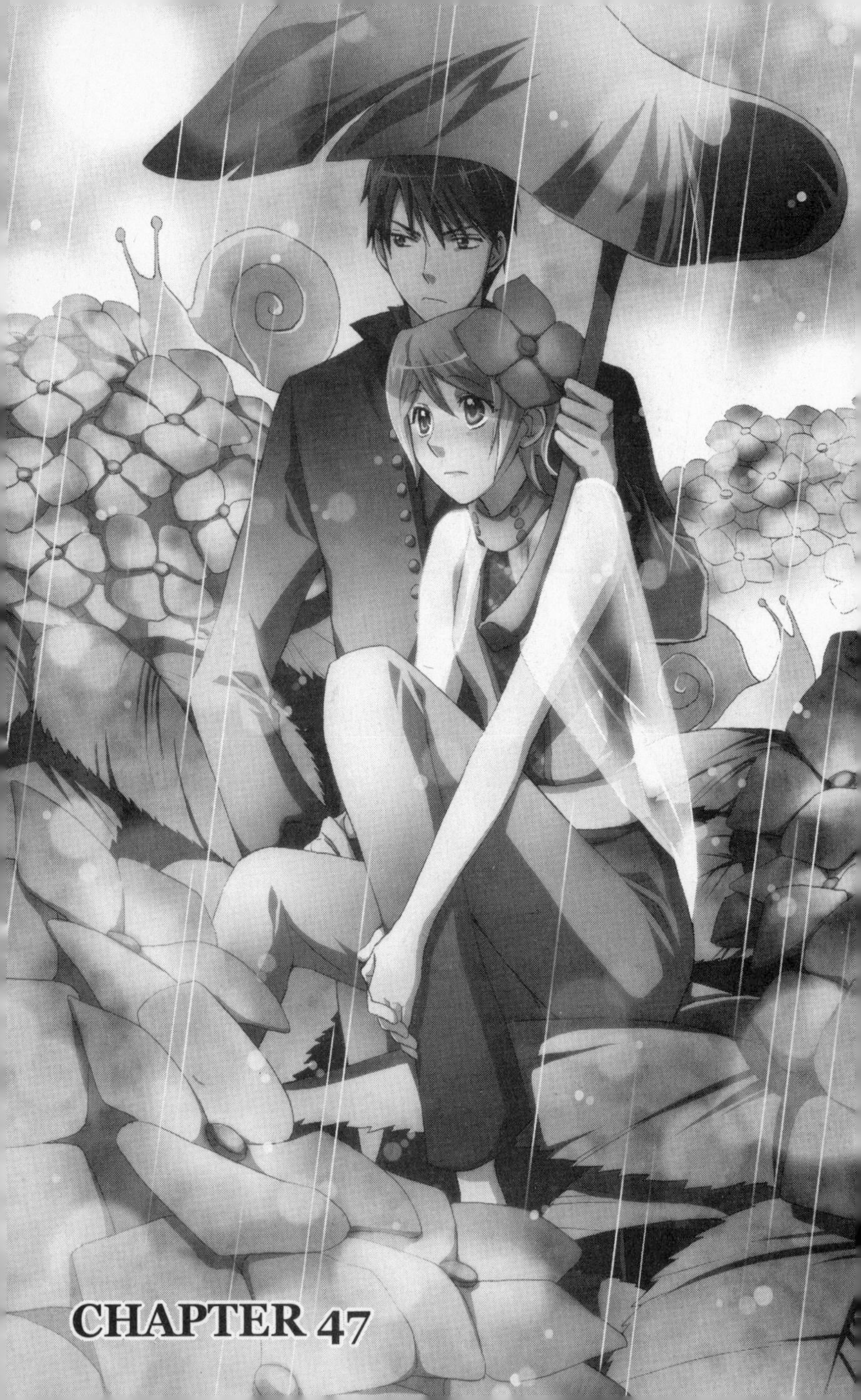
CHAPTER 47

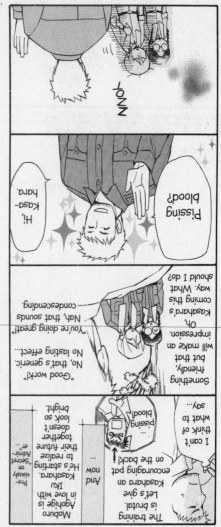

Secret Admirer part 9

Previously on "Secret Admirer"...
Moburo Agohige is in love with Iku Kasahara. He's starting to realize their future together doesn't look so bright.
And now ...
The training is brutal. Let's give Kasahara an encouraging pat on the back!
... pissing blood!
I can't think of what to say...
"Good work!" No, that's generic. No lasting effect...
"You're doing great!" Nah, that sounds condescending.
Something friendly, but that will make an impression. Oh, Kasahara's coming this way. What should I do?
Hi, Kasahara.
Pissing blood?
ZZOT

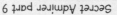

Well, that went well... At least he knows he said the wrong thing!

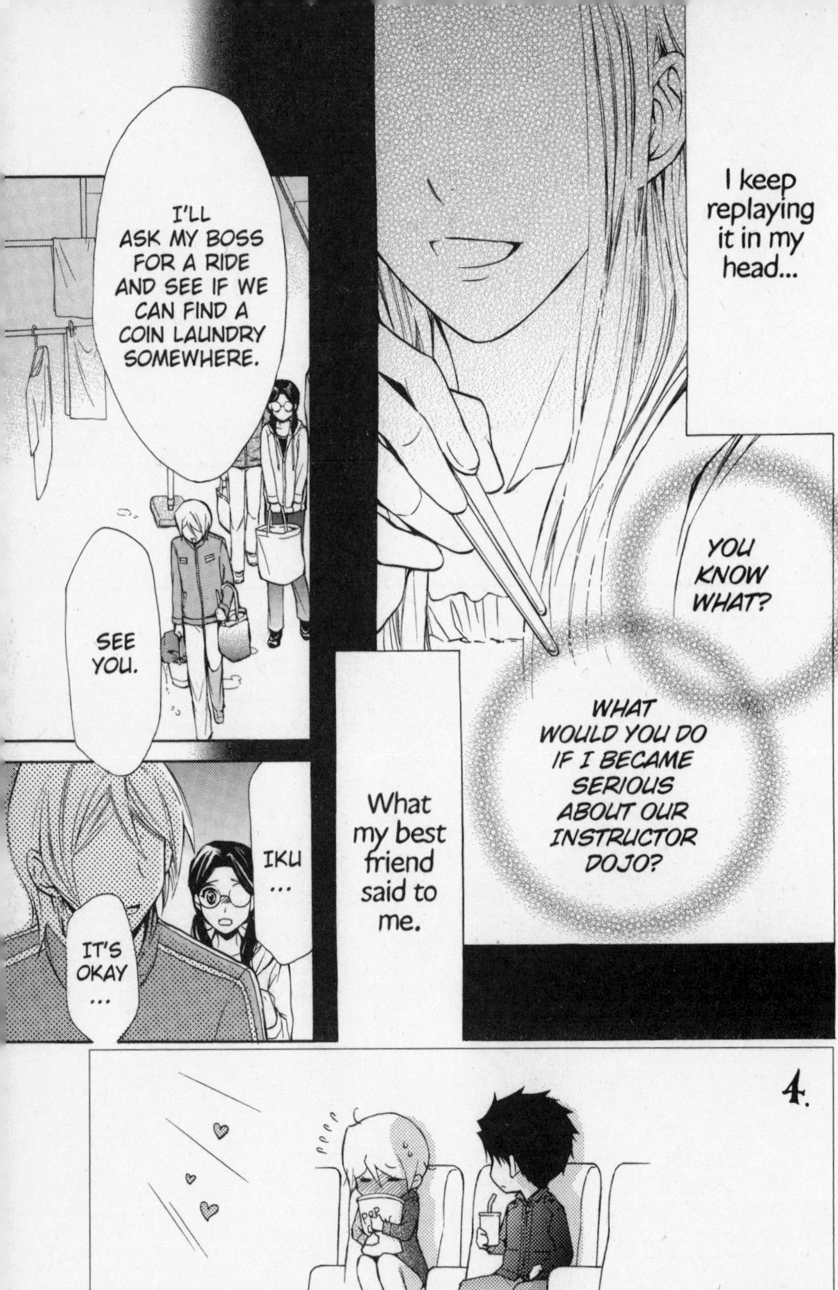
I keep replaying it in my head...
YOU KNOW WHAT?
WHAT WOULD YOU DO IF I BECAME SERIOUS ABOUT OUR INSTRUCTOR DOJO?
What my best friend said to me.
I'LL ASK MY BOSS FOR A RIDE AND SEE IF WE CAN FIND A COIN LAUNDRY SOMEWHERE.
SEE YOU.
IKU ...
IT'S OKAY ...
4.

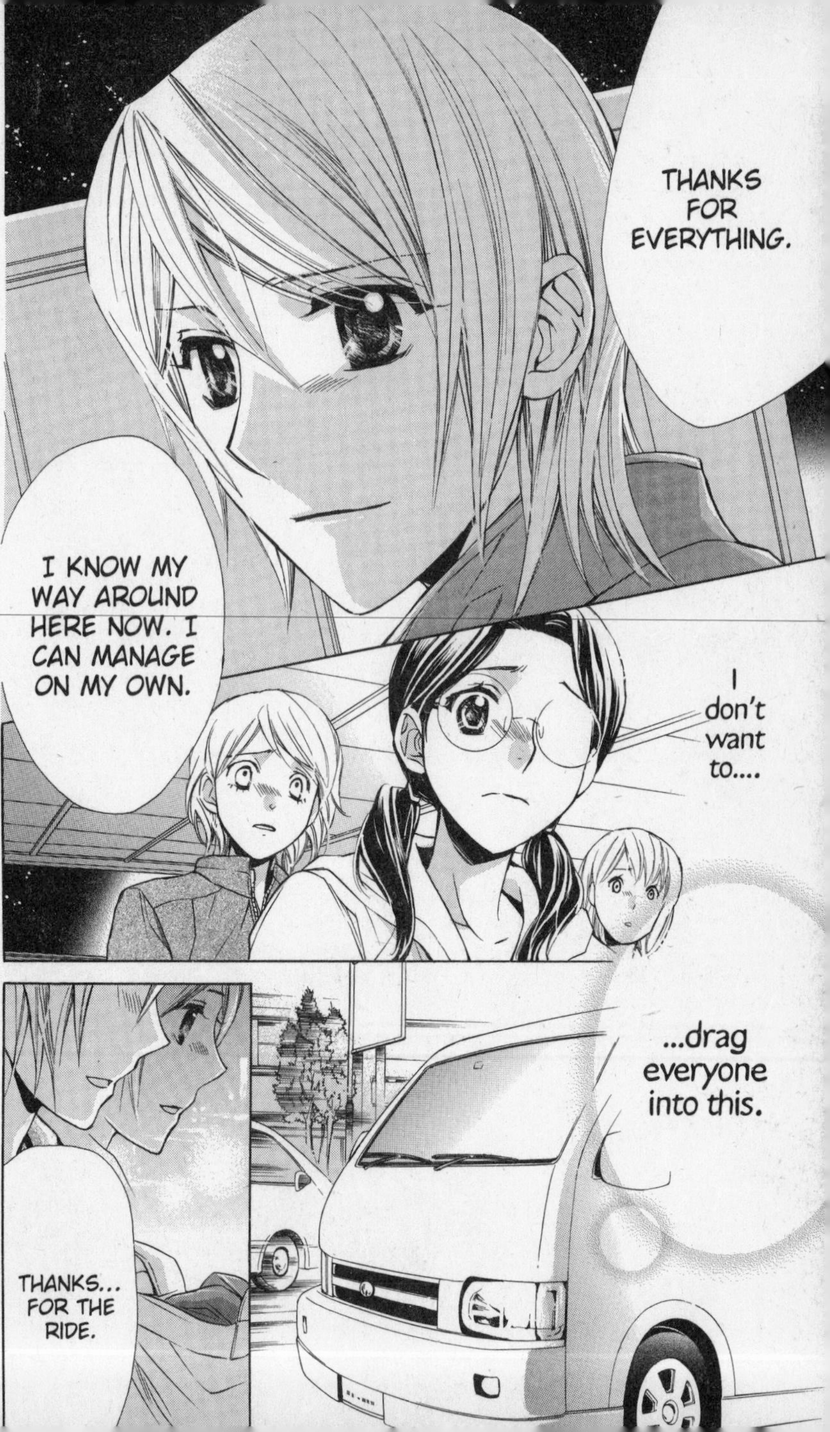
THANKS FOR EVERYTHING.
I KNOW MY WAY AROUND HERE NOW. I CAN MANAGE ON MY OWN.
I don't want to....
...drag everyone into this.
THANKS... FOR THE RIDE.

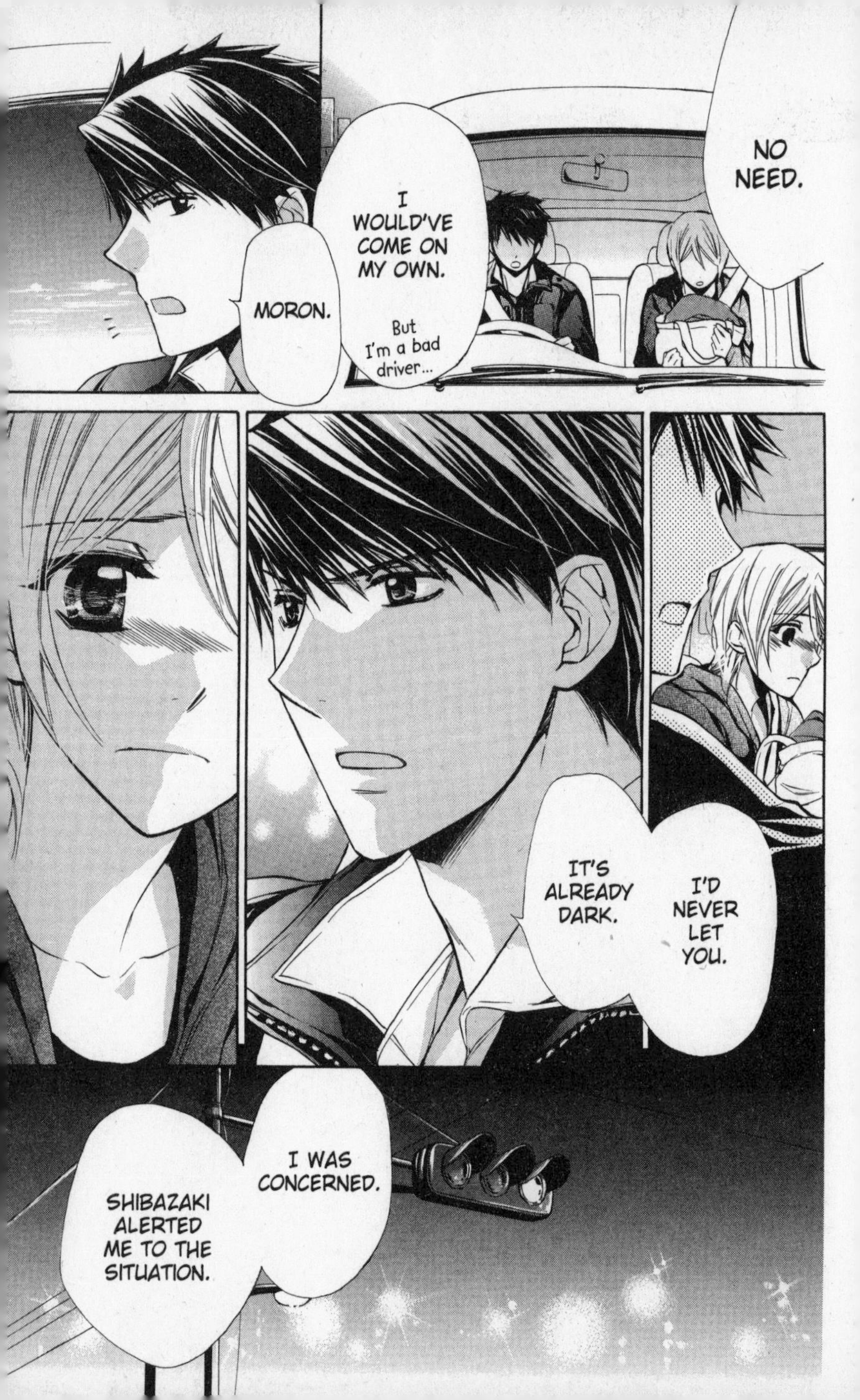
NO NEED.
I WOULD'VE COME ON MY OWN.
But I'm a bad driver...
MORON.
I'D NEVER LET YOU.
IT'S ALREADY DARK.
I WAS CONCERNED.
SHIBAZAKI ALERTED ME TO THE SITUATION.

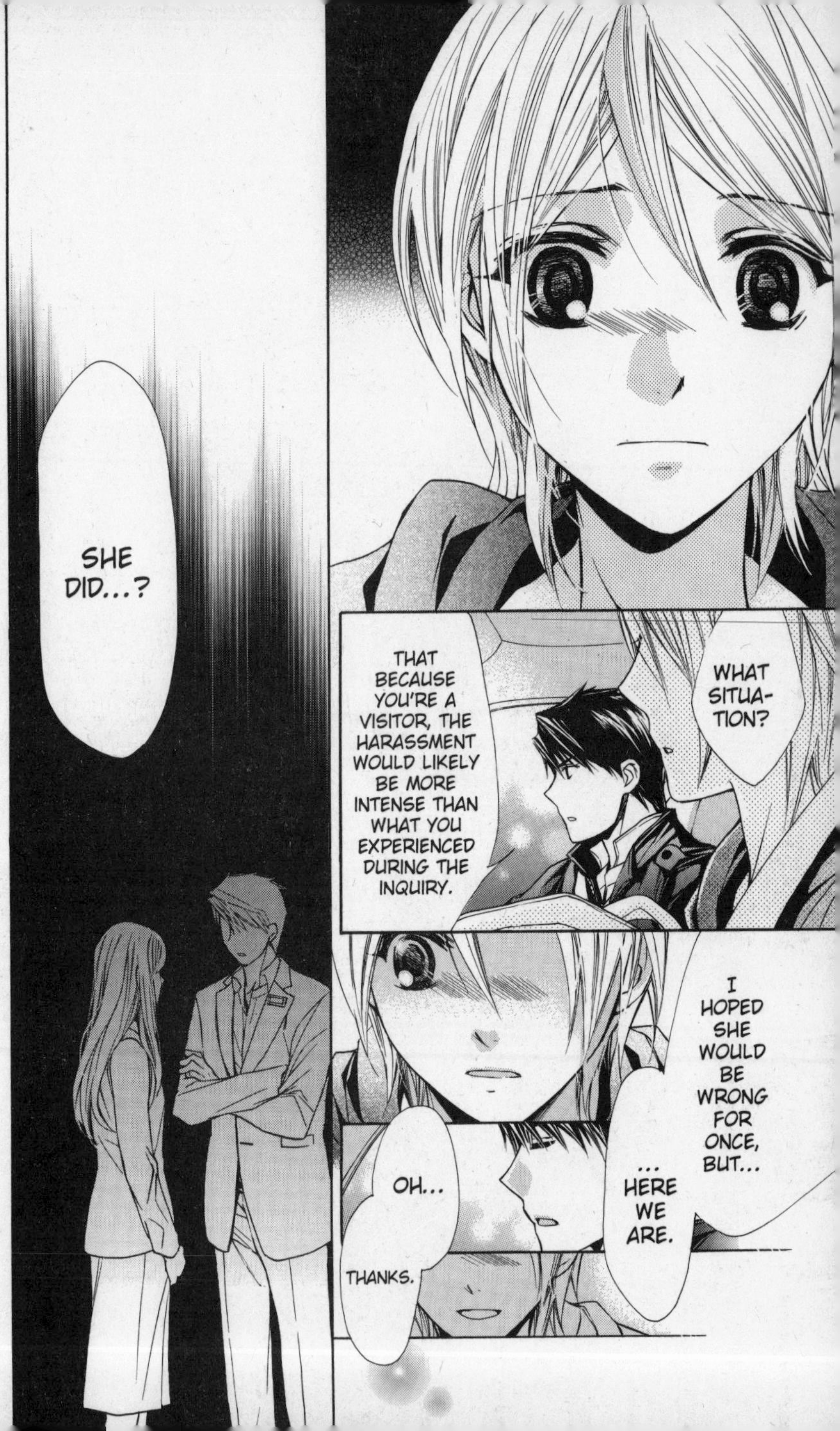
WHAT SITUATION?
THAT BECAUSE YOU'RE A VISITOR, THE HARASSMENT WOULD LIKELY BE MORE INTENSE THAN WHAT YOU EXPERIENCED DURING THE INQUIRY.
I HOPED SHE WOULD BE WRONG FOR ONCE, BUT...
... HERE WE ARE.
OH...
THANKS.
SHE DID...?

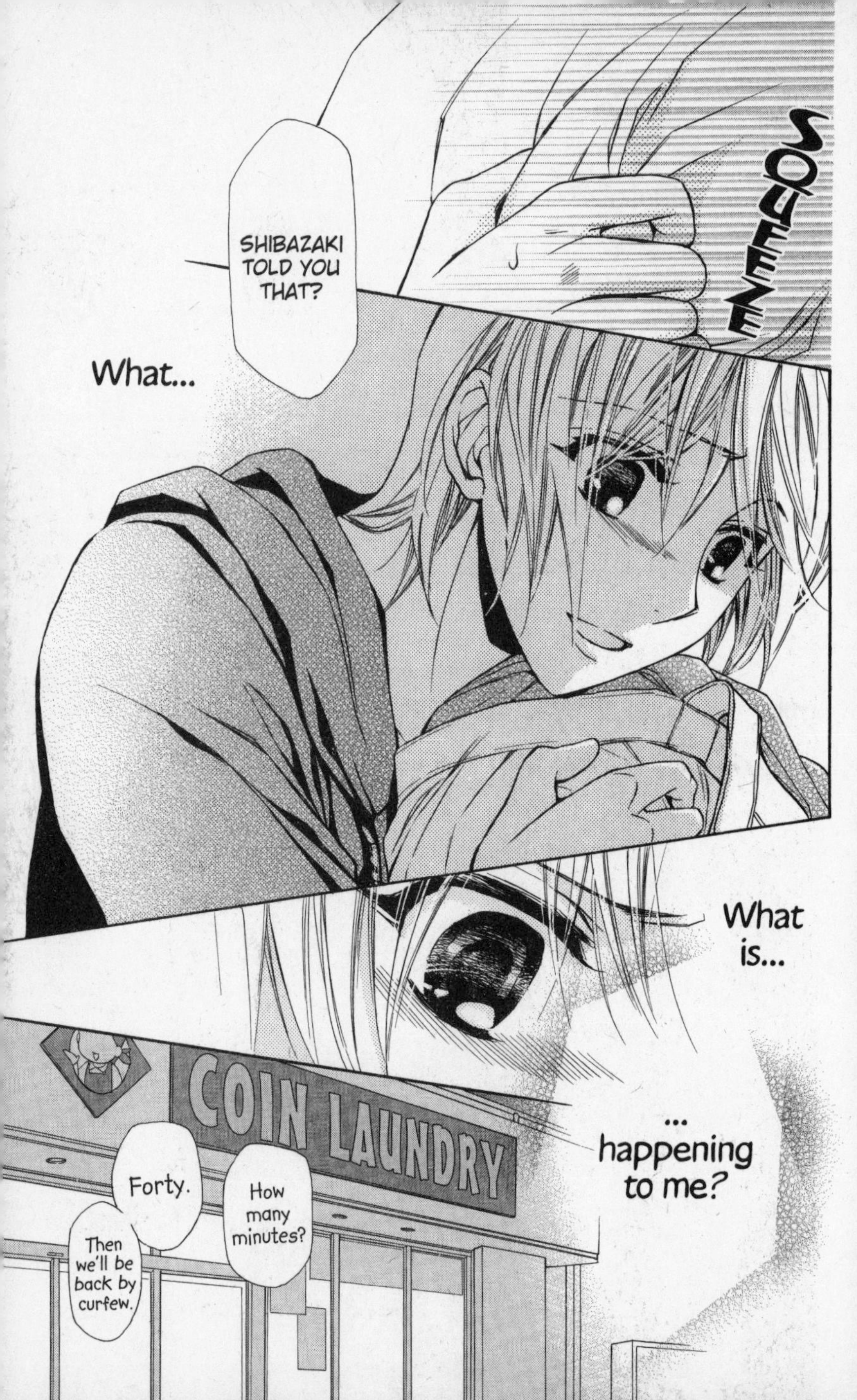
SQUEEZE
SHIBAZAKI TOLD YOU THAT?
What...
What is...
... happening to me?
COIN LAUNDRY
How many minutes?
Forty.
Then we'll be back by curfew.

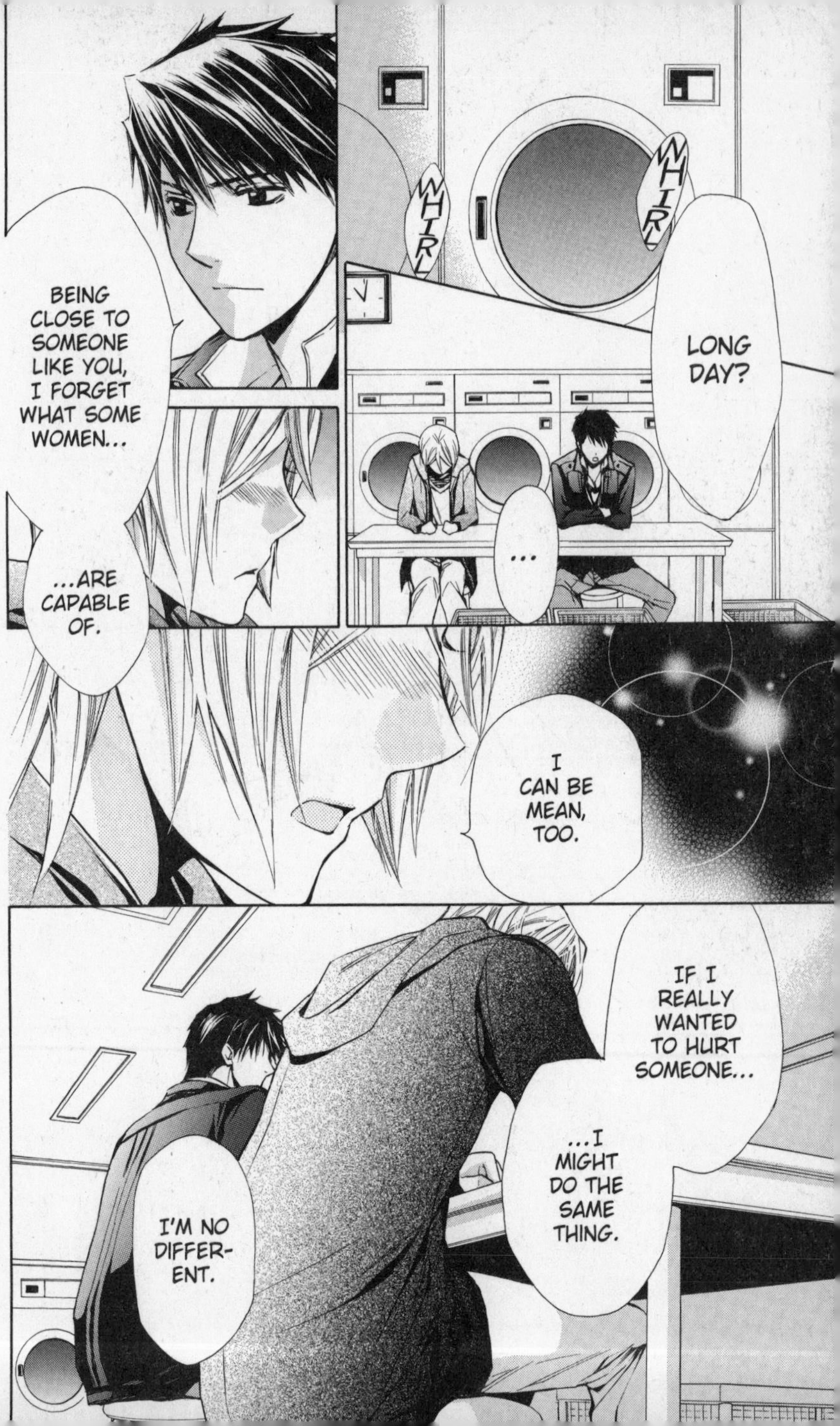
WHIRL
WHIRL
LONG DAY?
...
BEING CLOSE TO SOMEONE LIKE YOU, I FORGET WHAT SOME WOMEN...
...ARE CAPABLE OF.
I CAN BE MEAN, TOO.
IF I REALLY WANTED TO HURT SOMEONE...
...I MIGHT DO THE SAME THING.
I'M NO DIFFER-ENT.

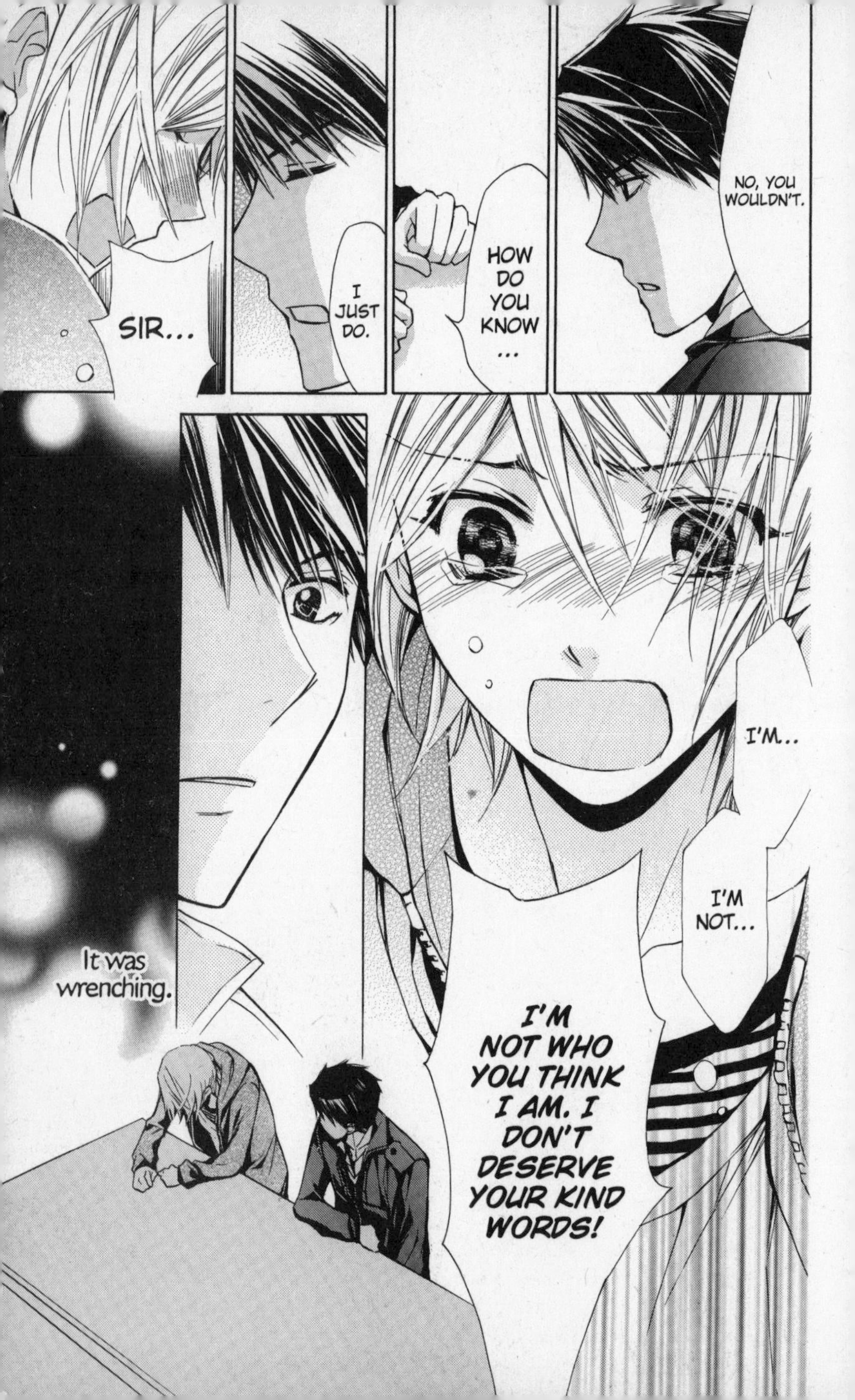
NO, YOU WOULDN'T.
HOW DO YOU KNOW ...
I JUST DO.
SIR...
I'M...
I'M NOT...
I'M NOT WHO YOU THINK I AM. I DON'T DESERVE YOUR KIND WORDS!
It was wrenching.

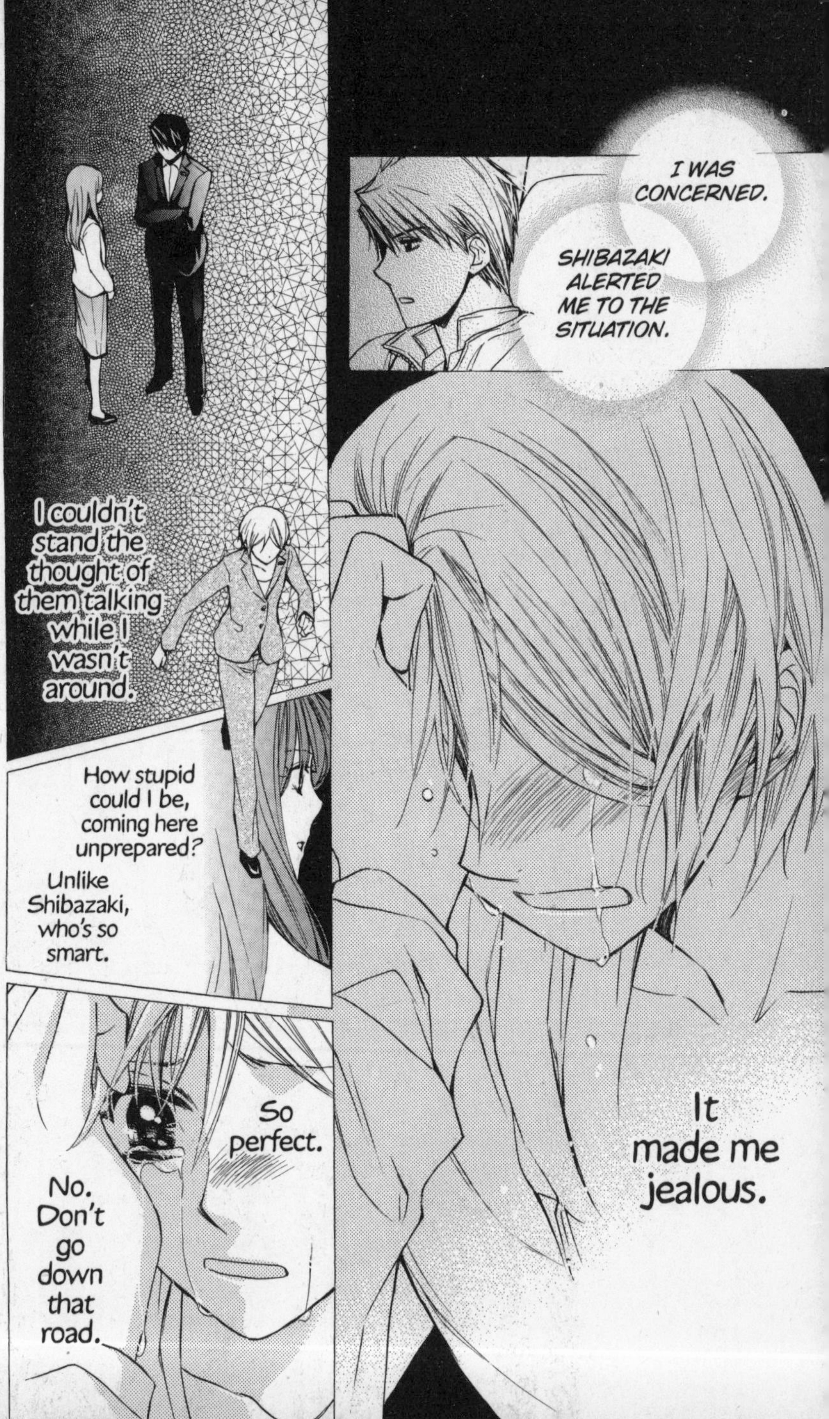
I WAS CONCERNED.
SHIBAZAKI ALERTED ME TO THE SITUATION.
It made me jealous.
I couldn't stand the thought of them talking while I wasn't around.
How stupid could I be, coming here unprepared?
Unlike Shibazaki, who's so smart.
So perfect.
No. Don't go down that road.

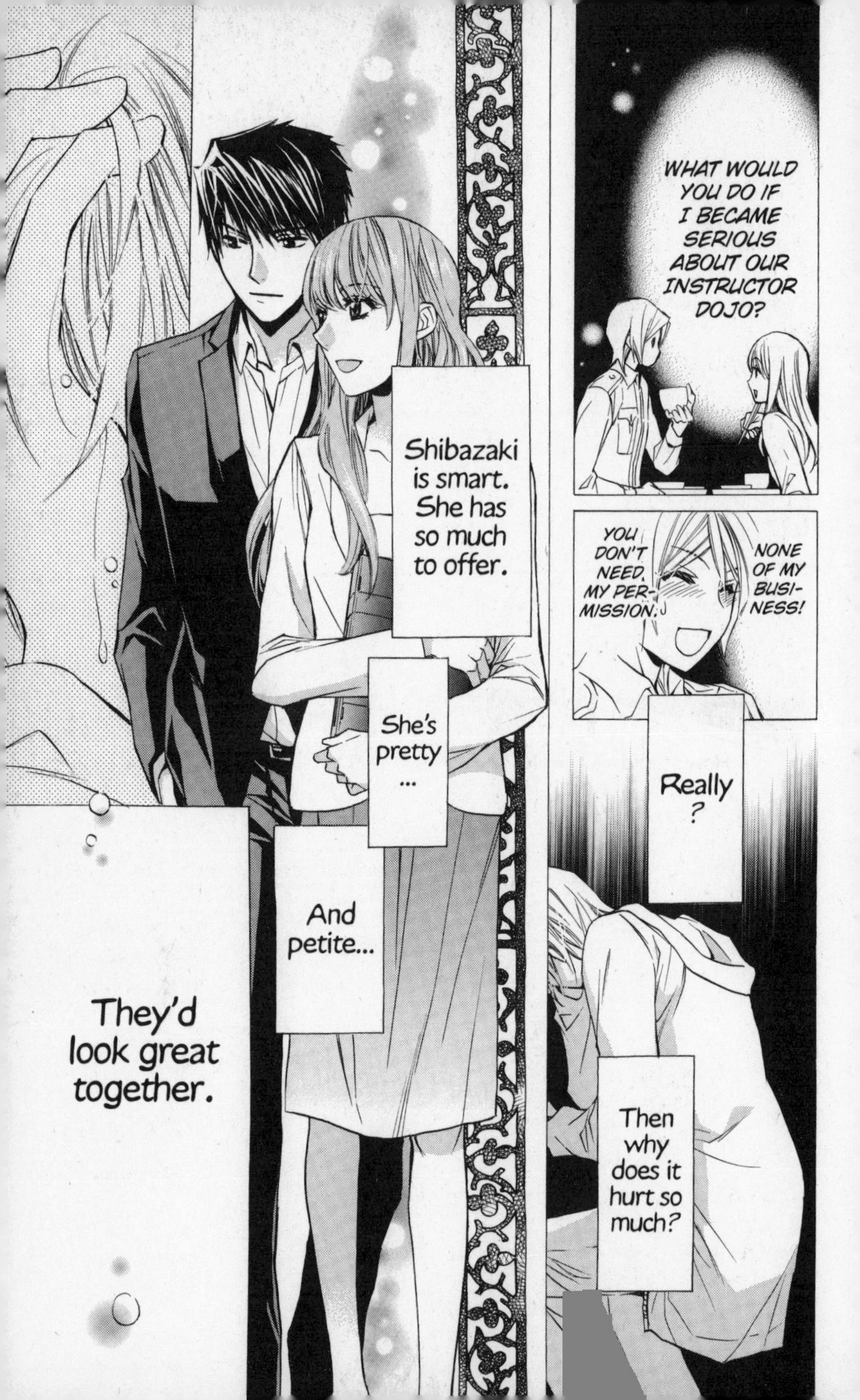
WHAT WOULD YOU DO IF I BECAME SERIOUS ABOUT OUR INSTRUCTOR DOJO?
NONE OF MY BUSINESS!
YOU DON'T NEED MY PERMISSION.
Really?
Then why does it hurt so much?
Shibazaki is smart. She has so much to offer.
She's pretty...
And petite...
They'd look great together.

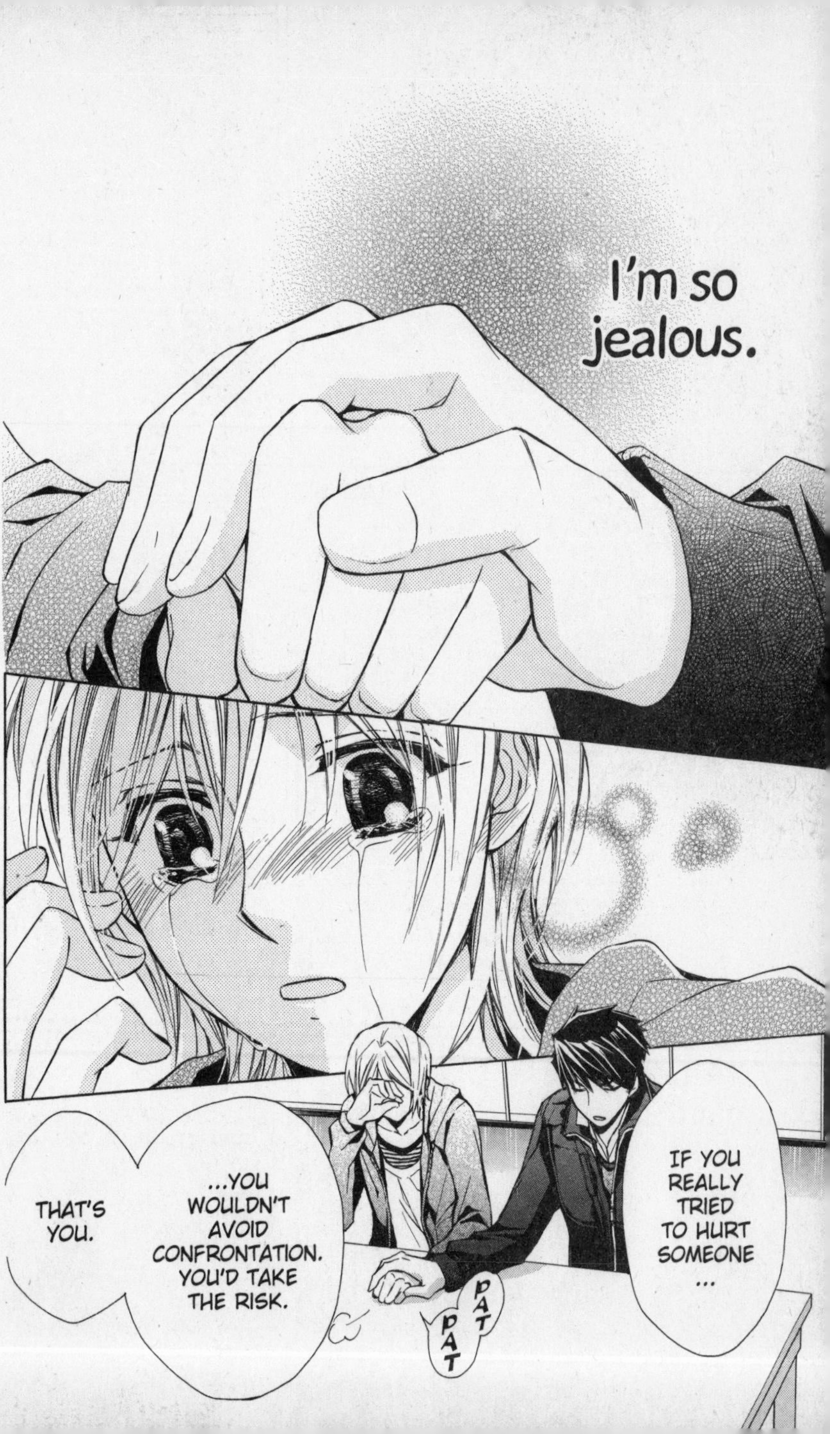
I'm so jealous.
IF YOU REALLY TRIED TO HURT SOMEONE ...
PAT PAT
...YOU WOULDN'T AVOID CONFRONTATION. YOU'D TAKE THE RISK.
THAT'S YOU.

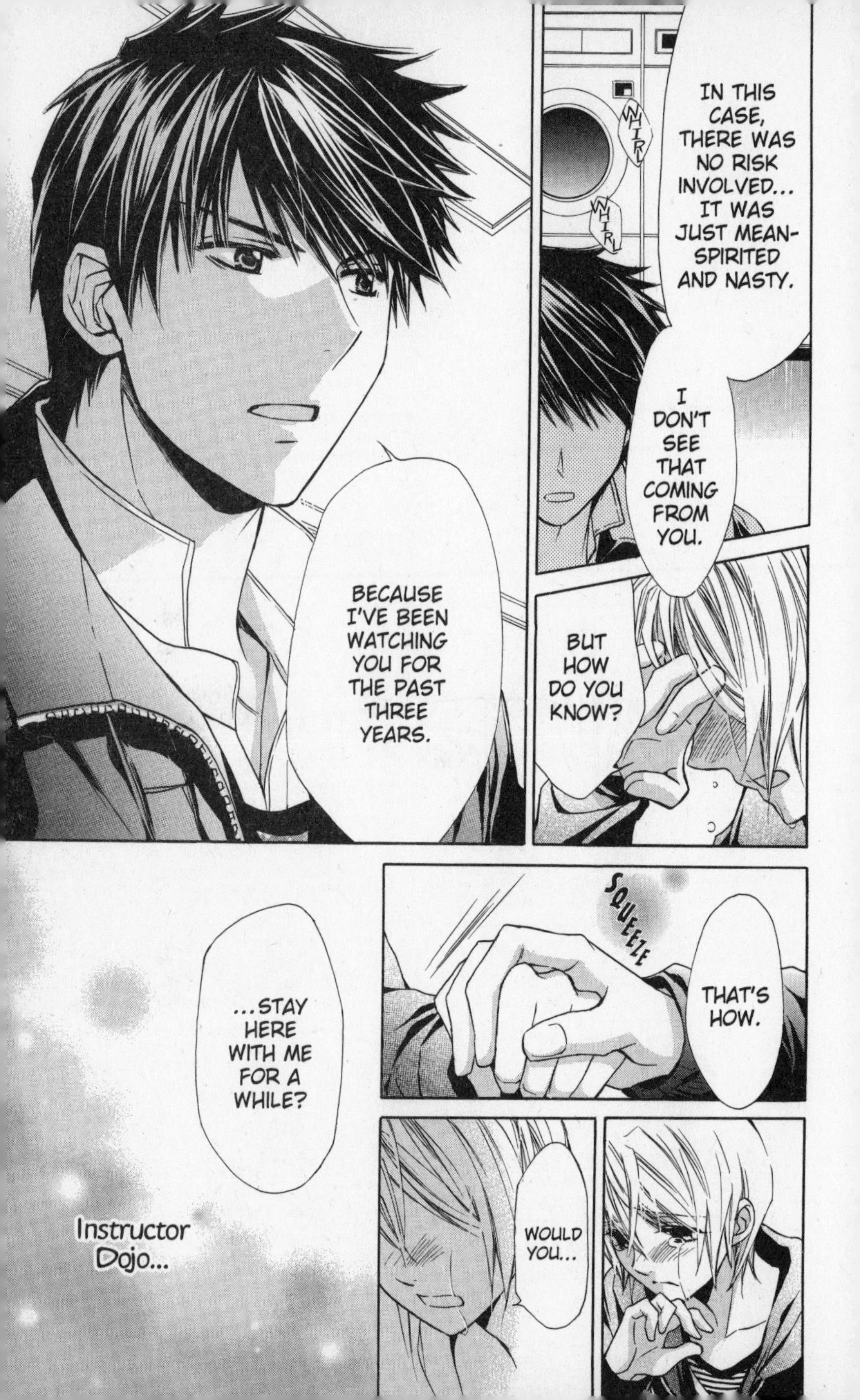
IN THIS CASE, THERE WAS NO RISK INVOLVED... IT WAS JUST MEAN-SPIRITED AND NASTY.
WHIRL
WHIRL
I DON'T SEE THAT COMING FROM YOU.
BUT HOW DO YOU KNOW?
BECAUSE I'VE BEEN WATCHING YOU FOR THE PAST THREE YEARS.
SQUEEZE
THAT'S HOW.
WOULD YOU...
...STAY HERE WITH ME FOR A WHILE?
Instructor Dojo...

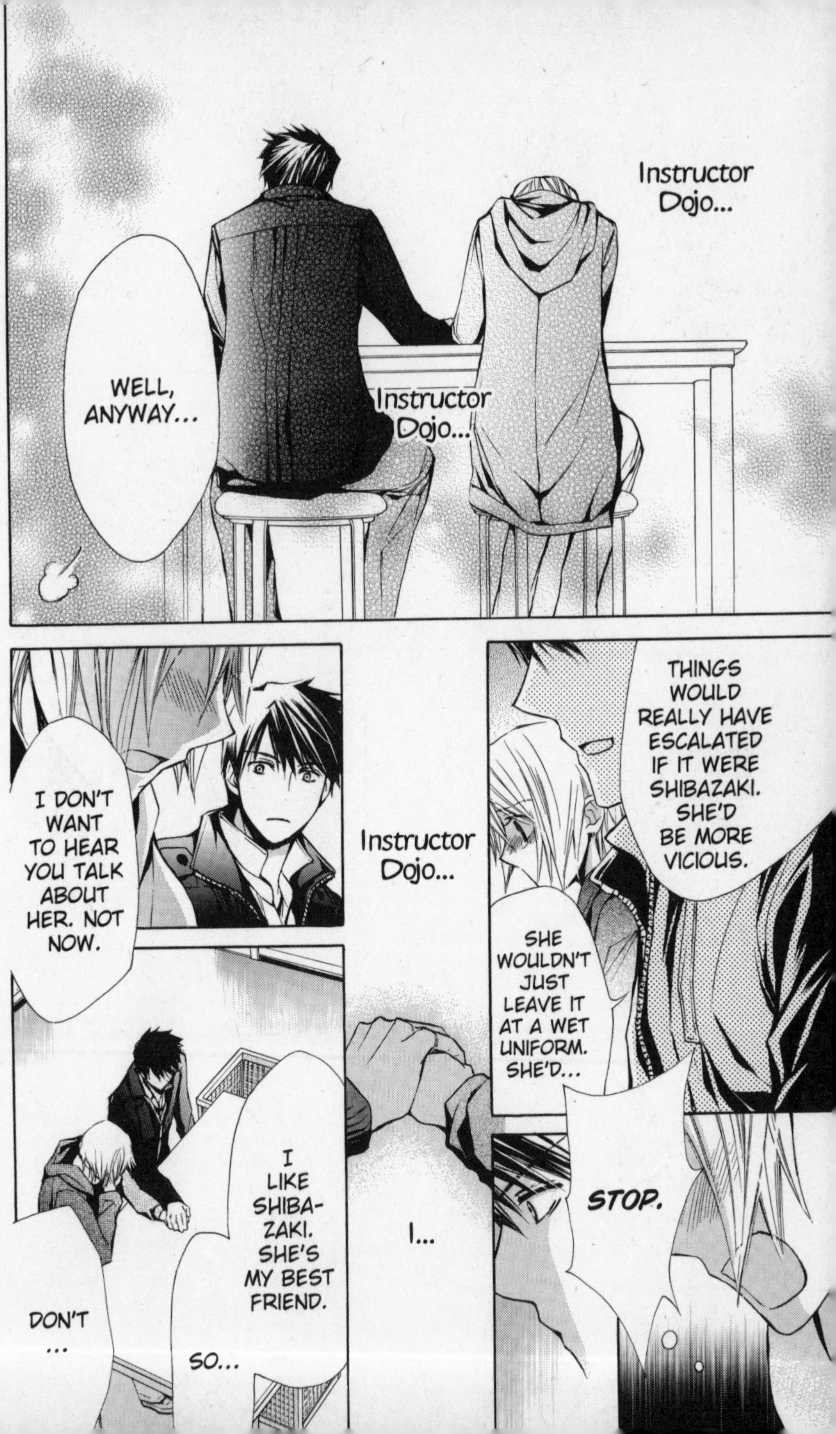
Instructor Dojo...
Instructor Dojo...
WELL, ANYWAY...
THINGS WOULD REALLY HAVE ESCALATED IF IT WERE SHIBAZAKI. SHE'D BE MORE VICIOUS.
SHE WOULDN'T JUST LEAVE IT AT A WET UNIFORM. SHE'D...
Instructor Dojo...
STOP.
I DON'T WANT TO HEAR YOU TALK ABOUT HER. NOT NOW.
I...
I LIKE SHIBA-ZAKI. SHE'S MY BEST FRIEND.
SO...
DON'T ...

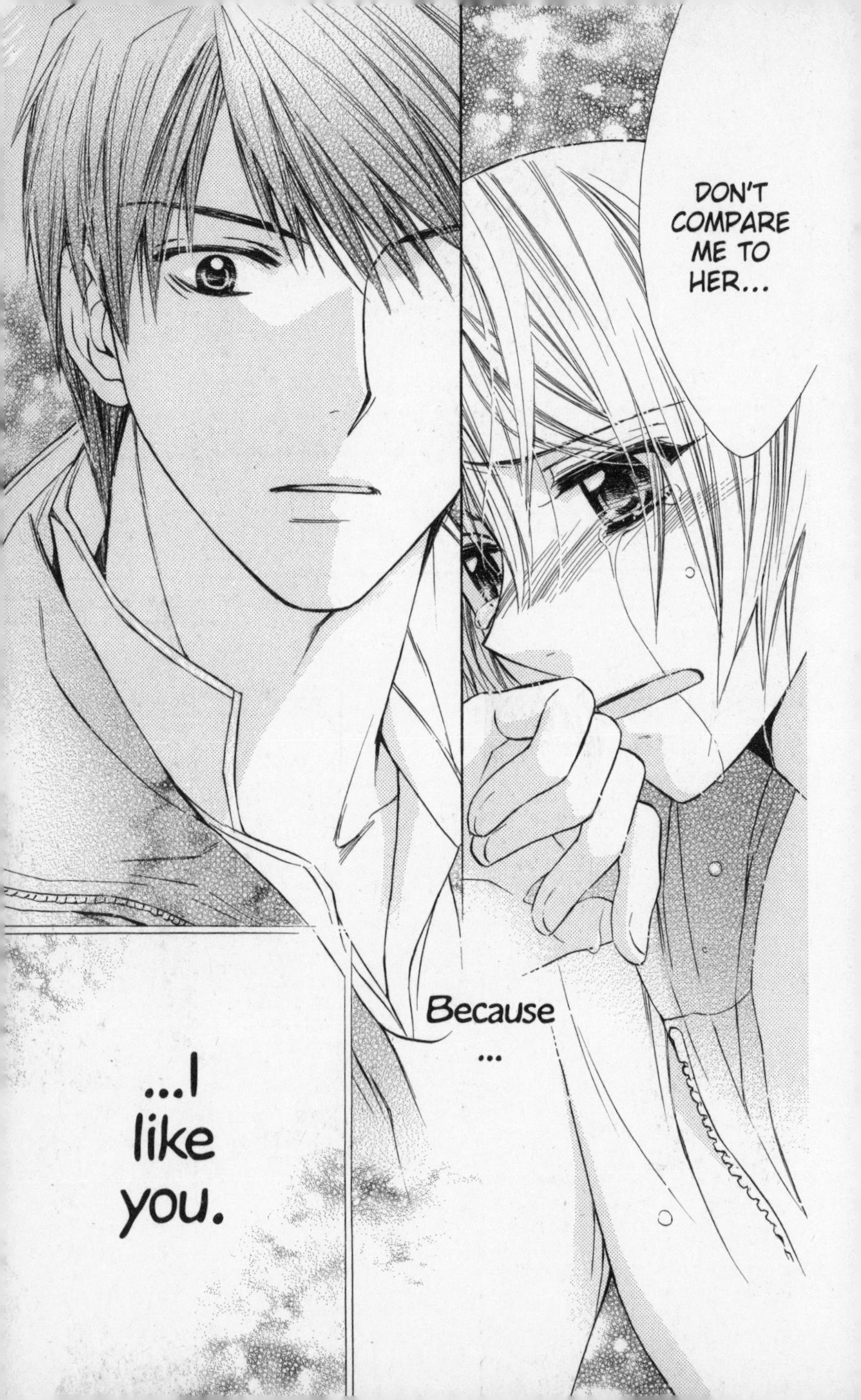
DON'T COMPARE ME TO HER...
Because ...
...I like you.

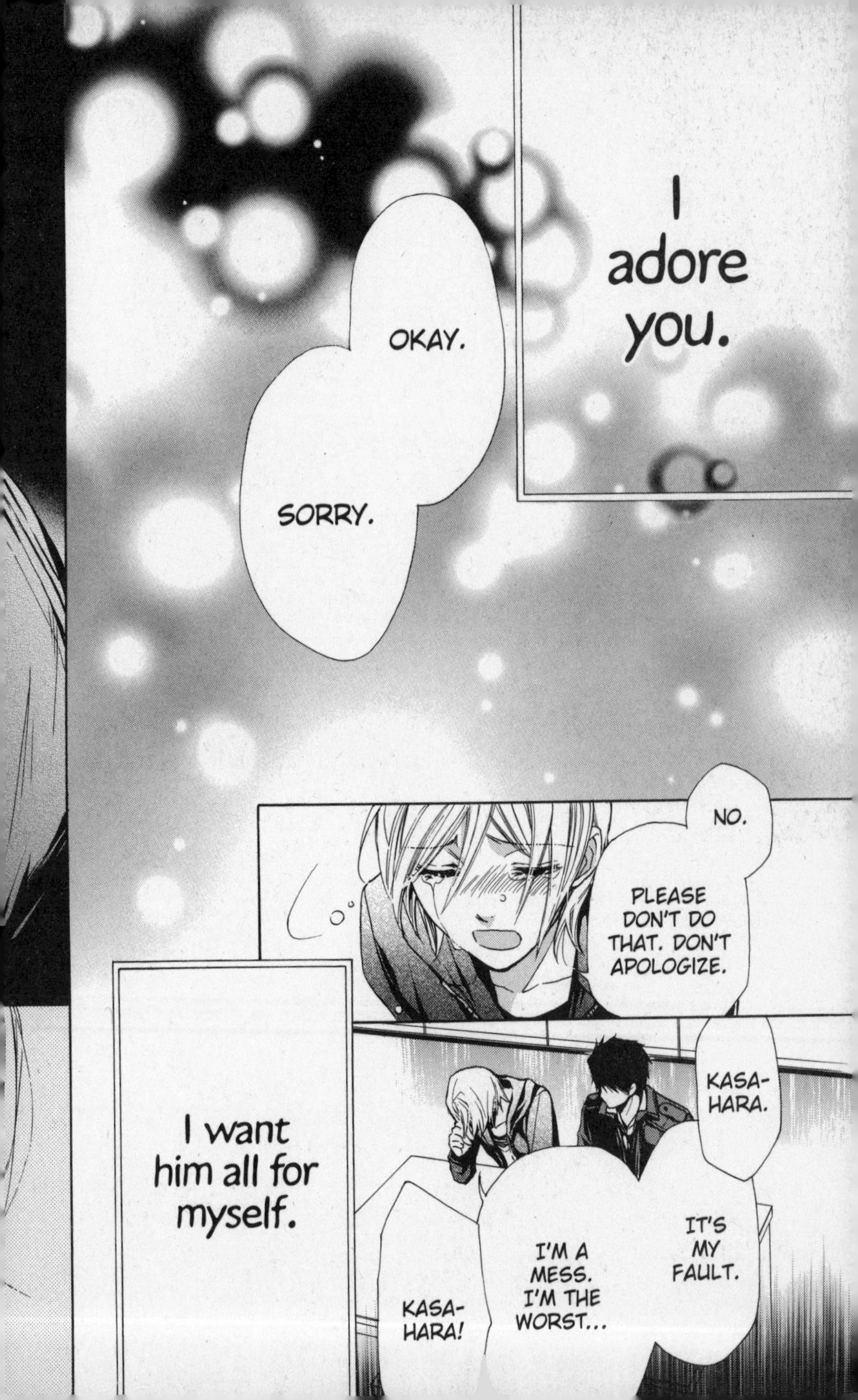

I adore you.
OKAY.
SORRY.
NO.
PLEASE DON'T DO THAT. DON'T APOLOGIZE.
KASA-HARA.
IT'S MY FAULT.
I'M A MESS. I'M THE WORST...
KASA-HARA!
I want him all for myself.

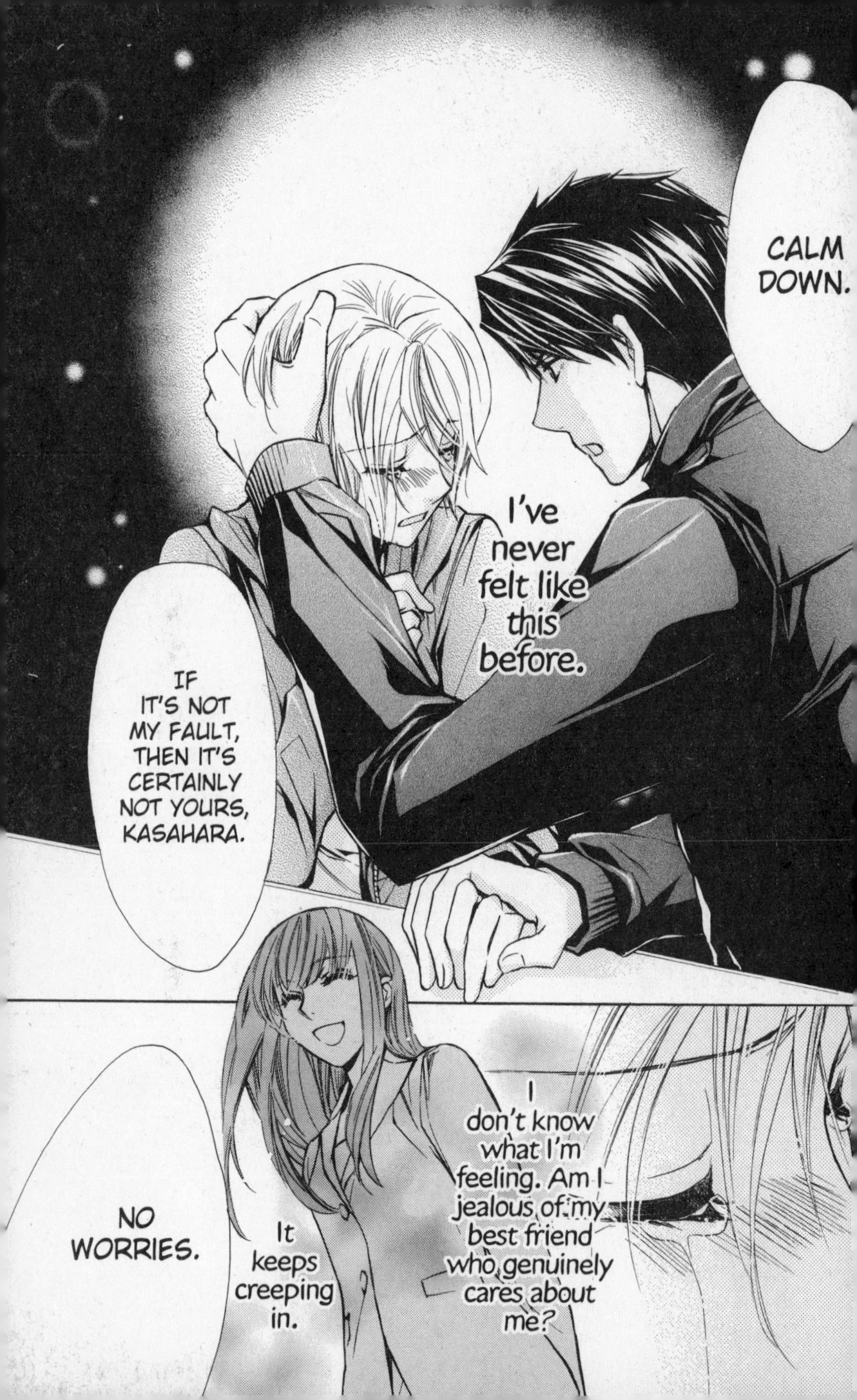
CALM DOWN.
I've never felt like this before.
IF IT'S NOT MY FAULT, THEN IT'S CERTAINLY NOT YOURS, KASAHARA.
I don't know what I'm feeling. Am I jealous of my best friend who genuinely cares about me?
It keeps creeping in.
NO WORRIES.

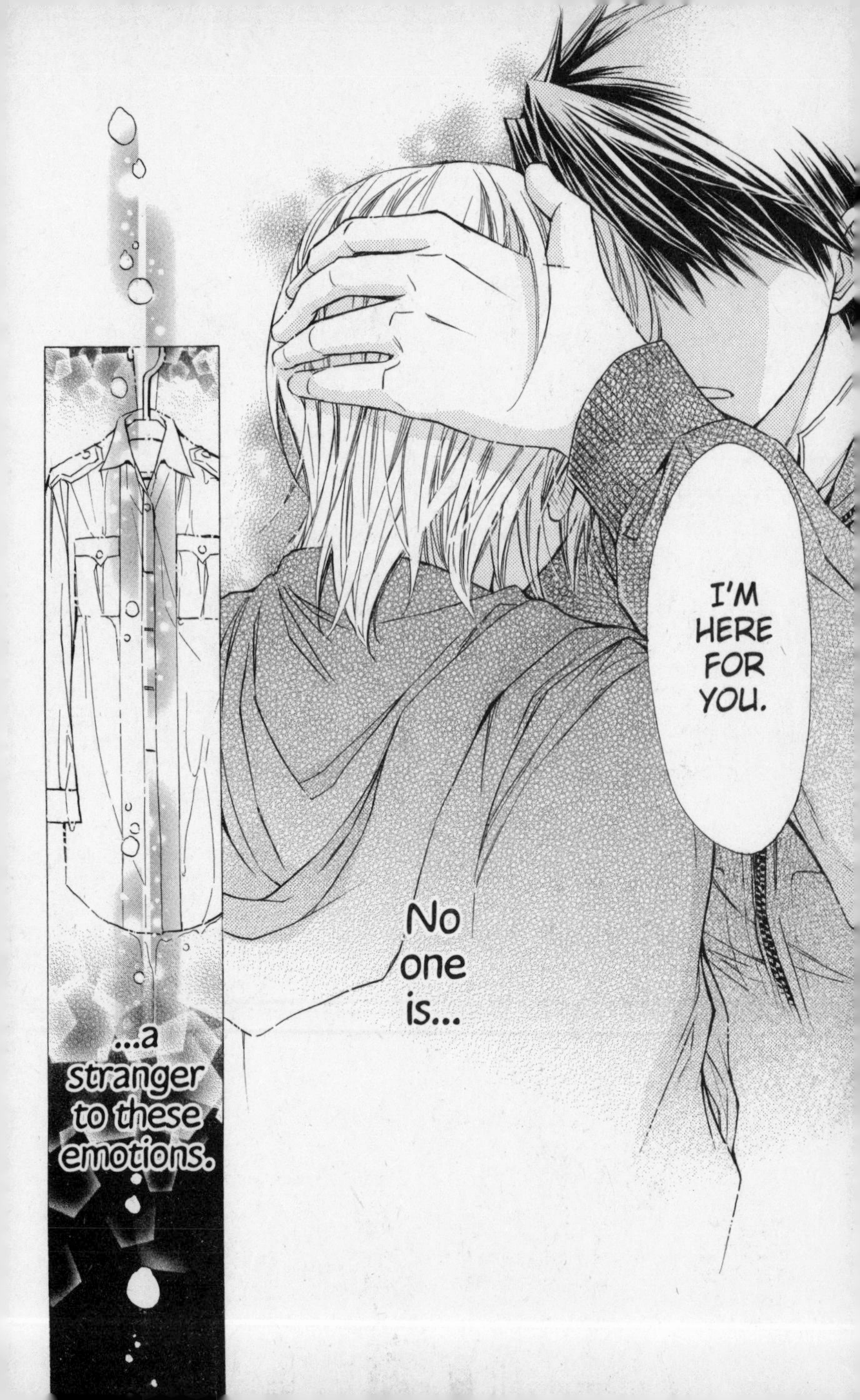
I'M HERE FOR YOU.
No one is...
...a stranger to these emotions.

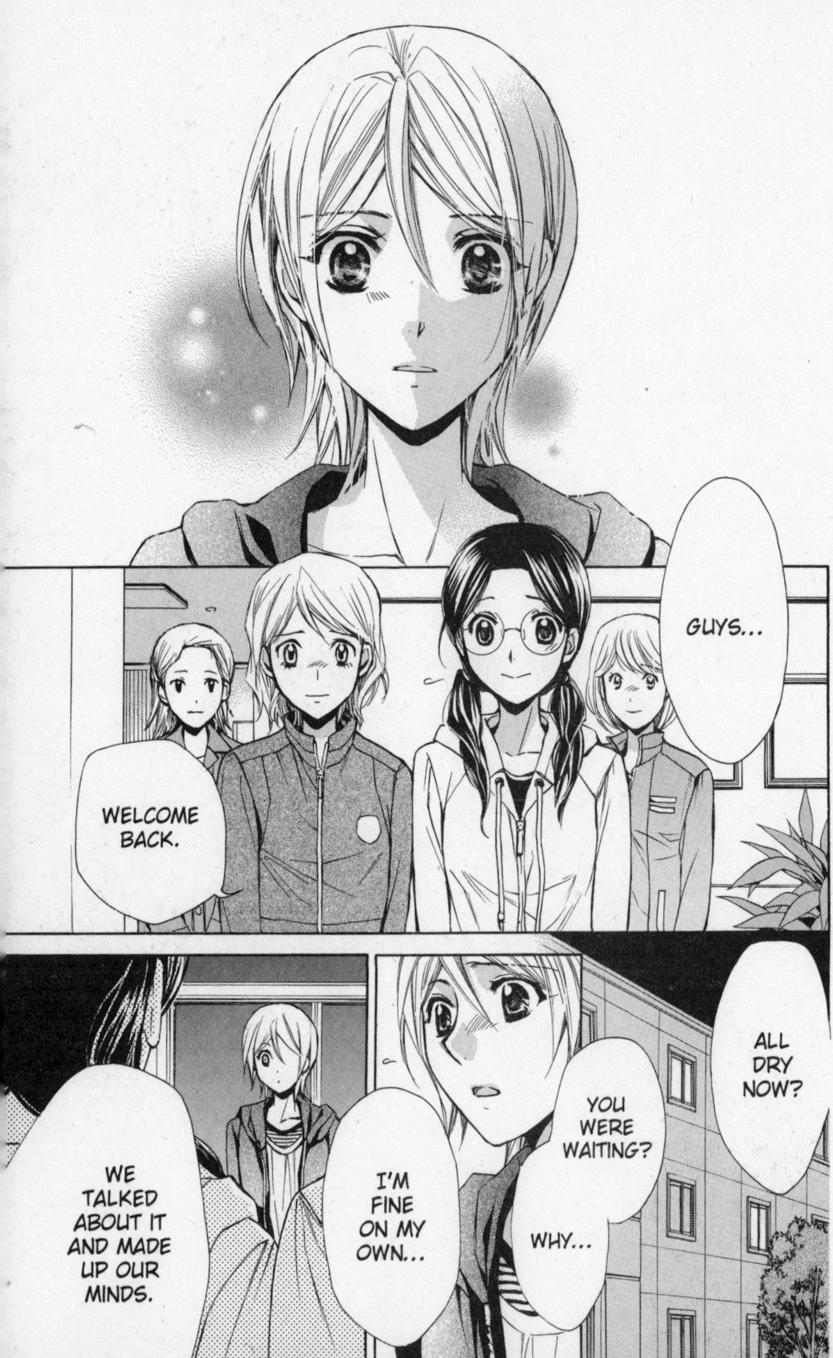
GUYS...
WELCOME BACK.
ALL DRY NOW?
YOU WERE WAITING?
WHY...
I'M FINE ON MY OWN...
WE TALKED ABOUT IT AND MADE UP OUR MINDS.

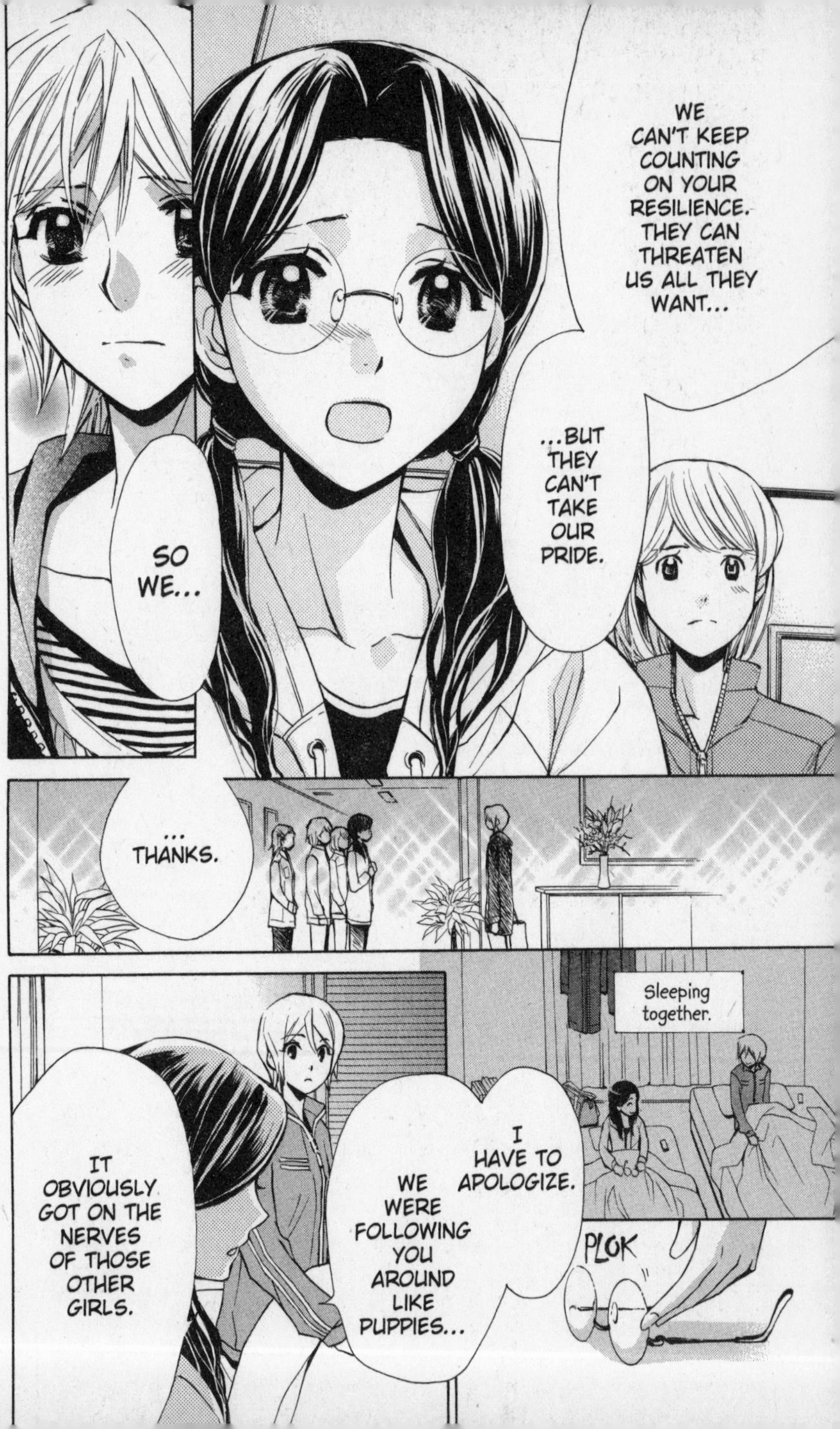
WE CAN'T KEEP COUNTING ON YOUR RESILIENCE. THEY CAN THREATEN US ALL THEY WANT...
...BUT THEY CAN'T TAKE OUR PRIDE.
SO WE...
... THANKS.
Sleeping together.
PLOK
I HAVE TO APOLOGIZE.
WE WERE FOLLOWING YOU AROUND LIKE PUPPIES...
IT OBVIOUSLY GOT ON THE NERVES OF THOSE OTHER GIRLS.

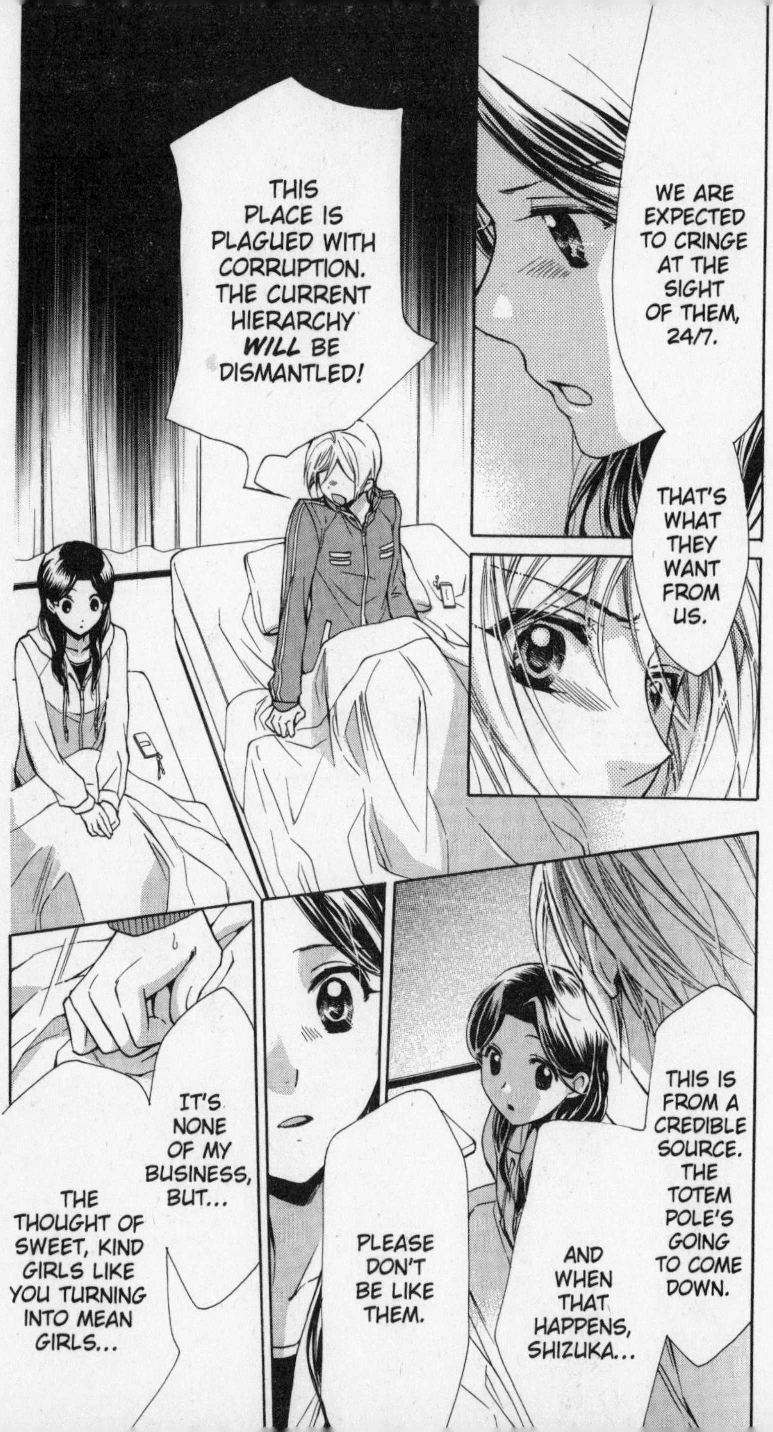
WE ARE EXPECTED TO CRINGE AT THE SIGHT OF THEM, 24/7.
THAT'S WHAT THEY WANT FROM US.
THIS PLACE IS PLAGUED WITH CORRUPTION. THE CURRENT HIERARCHY *WILL* BE DISMANTLED!
THIS IS FROM A CREDIBLE SOURCE. THE TOTEM POLE'S GOING TO COME DOWN.
AND WHEN THAT HAPPENS, SHIZUKA...
PLEASE DON'T BE LIKE THEM.
IT'S NONE OF MY BUSINESS, BUT...
THE THOUGHT OF SWEET, KIND GIRLS LIKE YOU TURNING INTO MEAN GIRLS...

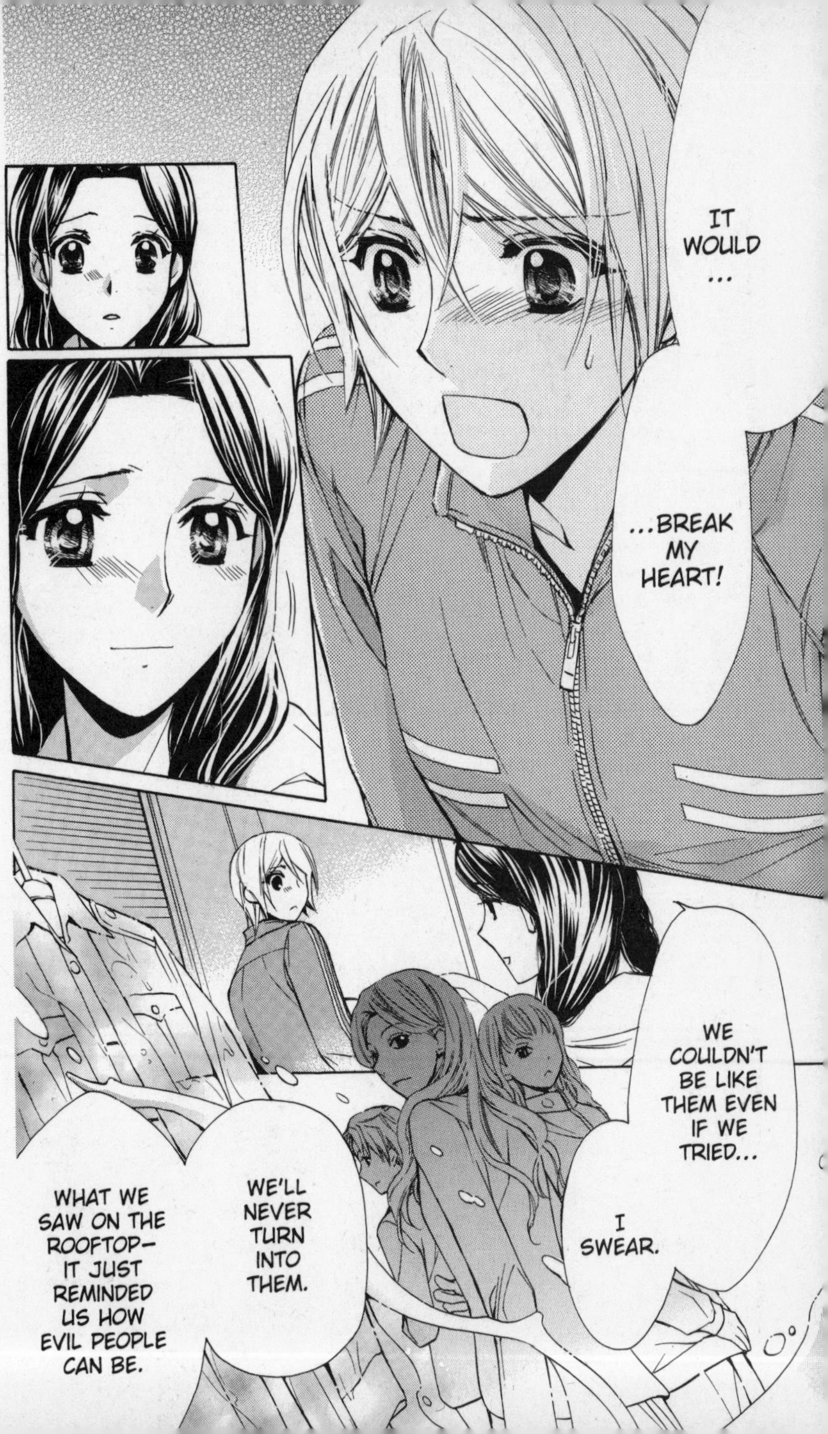
IT WOULD ...
...BREAK MY HEART!
WE COULDN'T BE LIKE THEM EVEN IF WE TRIED...
I SWEAR.
WE'LL NEVER TURN INTO THEM.
WHAT WE SAW ON THE ROOFTOP— IT JUST REMINDED US HOW EVIL PEOPLE CAN BE.

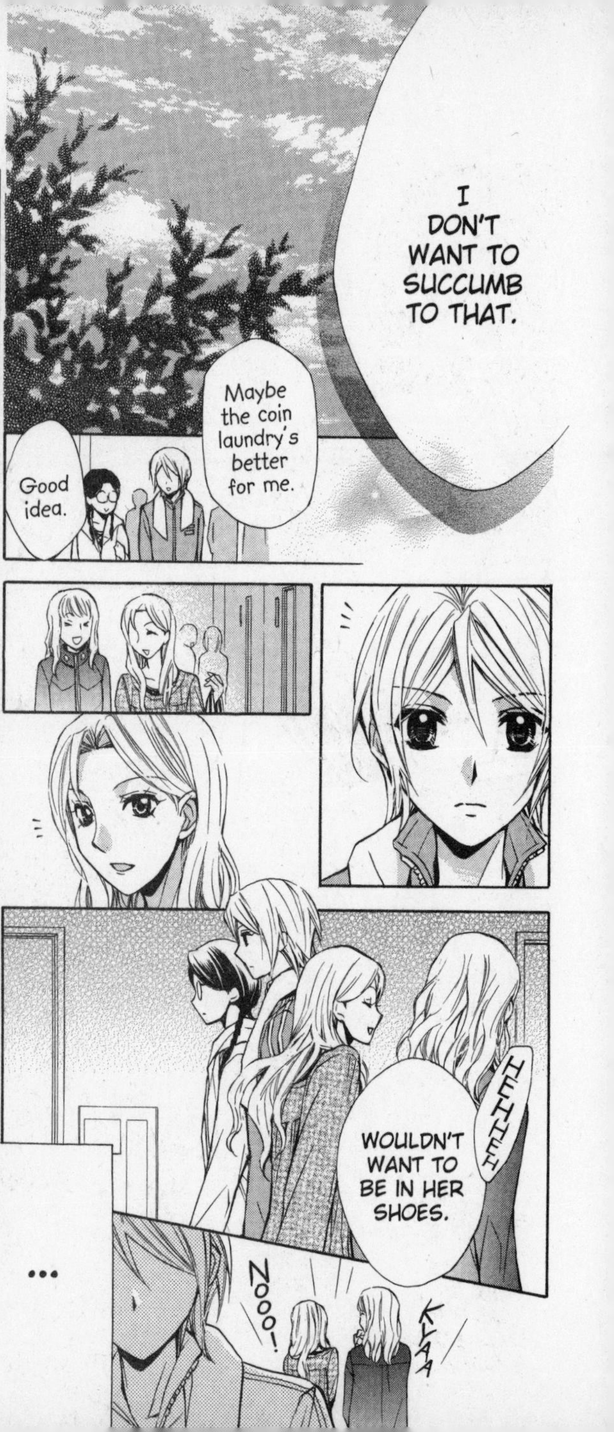
I DON'T WANT TO SUCCUMB TO THAT.
Maybe the coin laundry's better for me.
Good idea.
HEHHEH
WOULDN'T WANT TO BE IN HER SHOES.
...
NOOO!
KLAAA

4

The *Library Wars* movie was released in June, 2012!! It was wonderful, wonderful. The sight of my beloved characters moving about... It made me actually shudder with excitement. It was hard to keep myself in check (*laugh*).
The movie focused on the "Revolution" episode, which is where the original story ends.
It was such a joy to watch. Plenty of action and romance—never a dull moment! My heart was pacing throughout the movie!! I feel so grateful to be part of such a wonderful project. Love for *Library Wars*...!

*

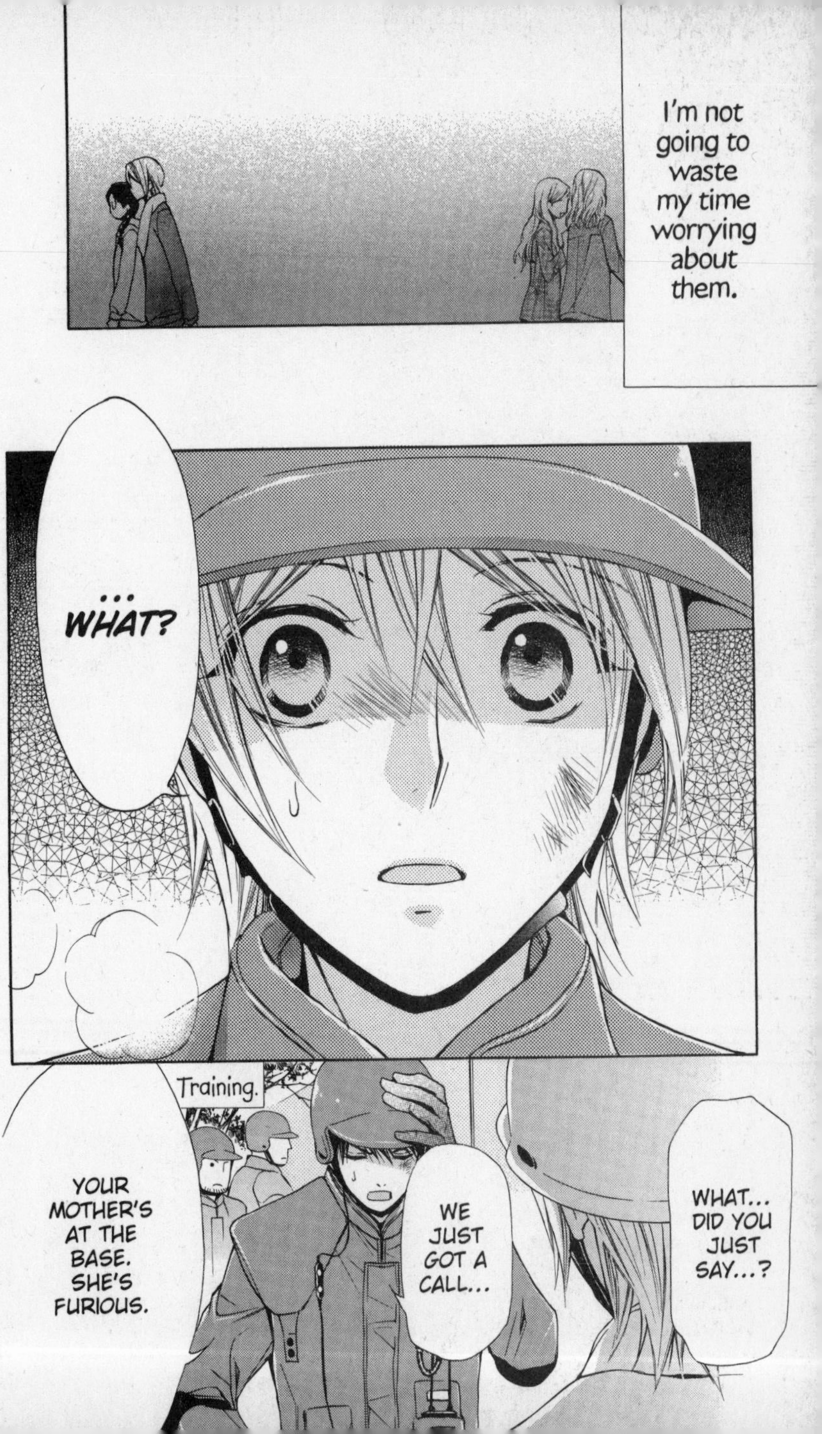
I'm not going to waste my time worrying about them.
...WHAT?
WHAT... DID YOU JUST SAY...?
WE JUST GOT A CALL...
Training.
YOUR MOTHER'S AT THE BASE. SHE'S FURIOUS.

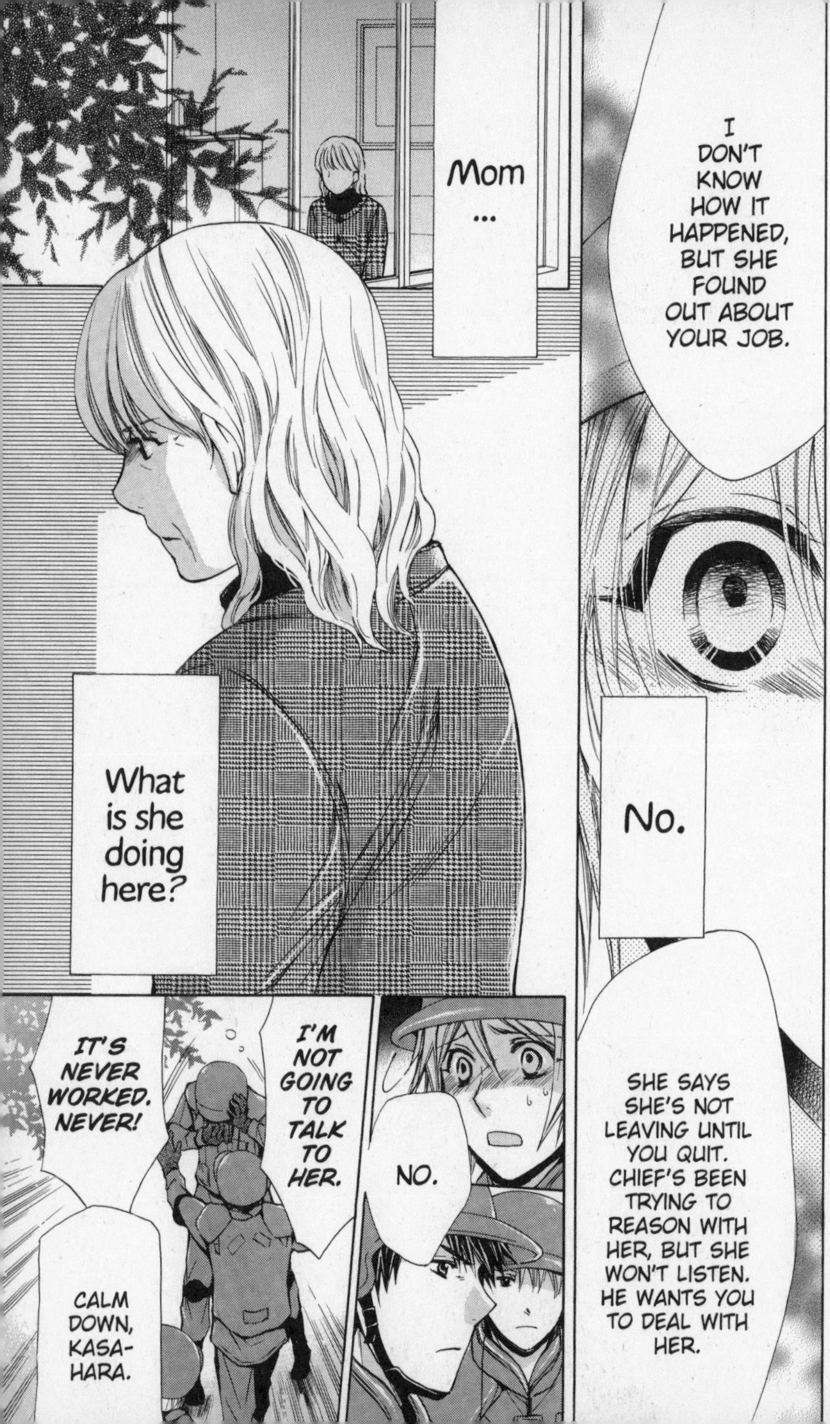
I DON'T KNOW HOW IT HAPPENED, BUT SHE FOUND OUT ABOUT YOUR JOB.
No.
SHE SAYS SHE'S NOT LEAVING UNTIL YOU QUIT. CHIEF'S BEEN TRYING TO REASON WITH HER, BUT SHE WON'T LISTEN. HE WANTS YOU TO DEAL WITH HER.
Mom ...
What is she doing here?
NO.
I'M NOT GOING TO TALK TO HER.
IT'S NEVER WORKED. NEVER!
CALM DOWN, KASA-HARA.

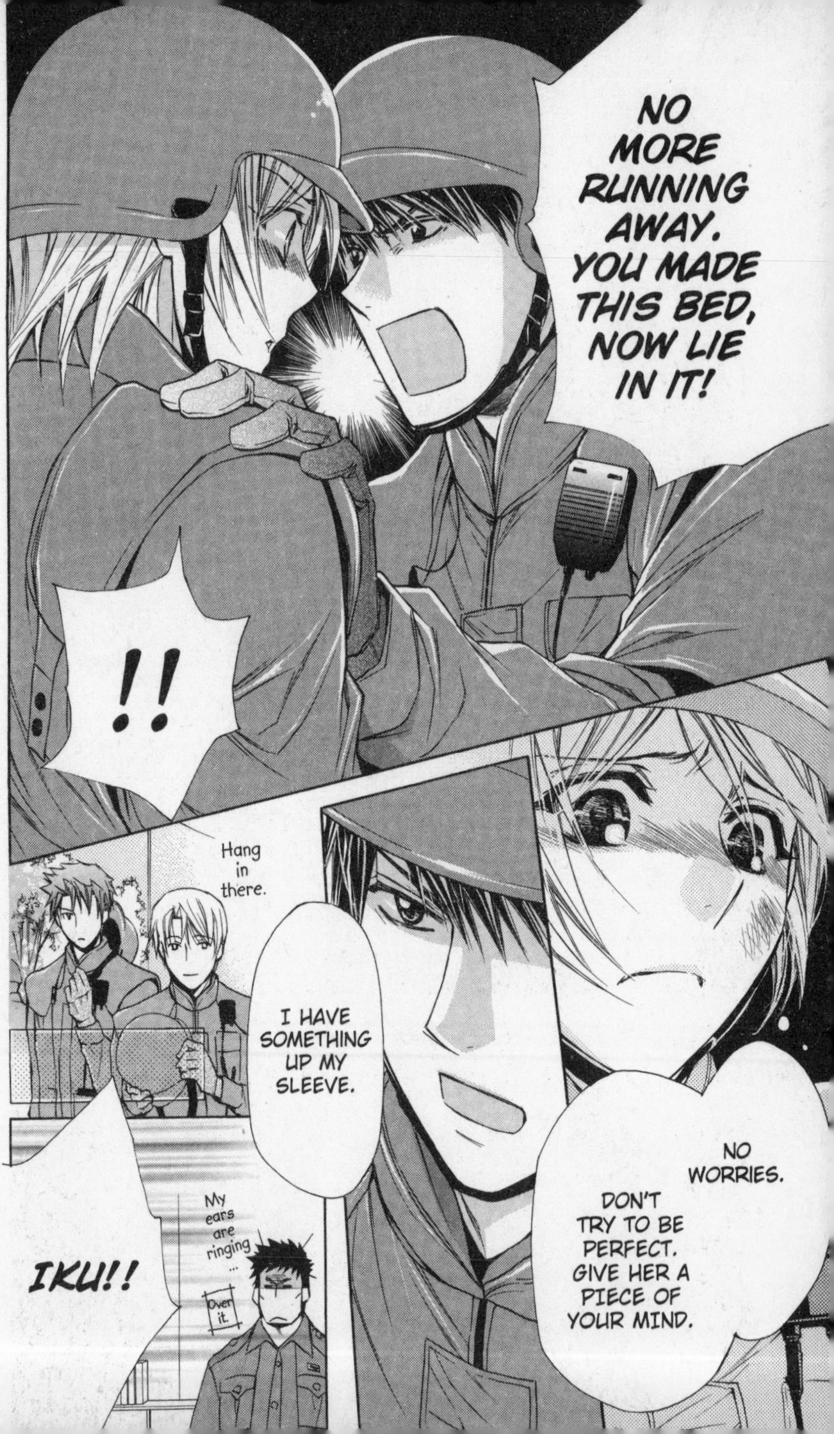
NO MORE RUNNING AWAY. YOU MADE THIS BED, NOW LIE IN IT!
!!
NO WORRIES.
DON'T TRY TO BE PERFECT. GIVE HER A PIECE OF YOUR MIND.
I HAVE SOMETHING UP MY SLEEVE.
Hang in there.
My ears are ringing...
Over it.
IKU!!

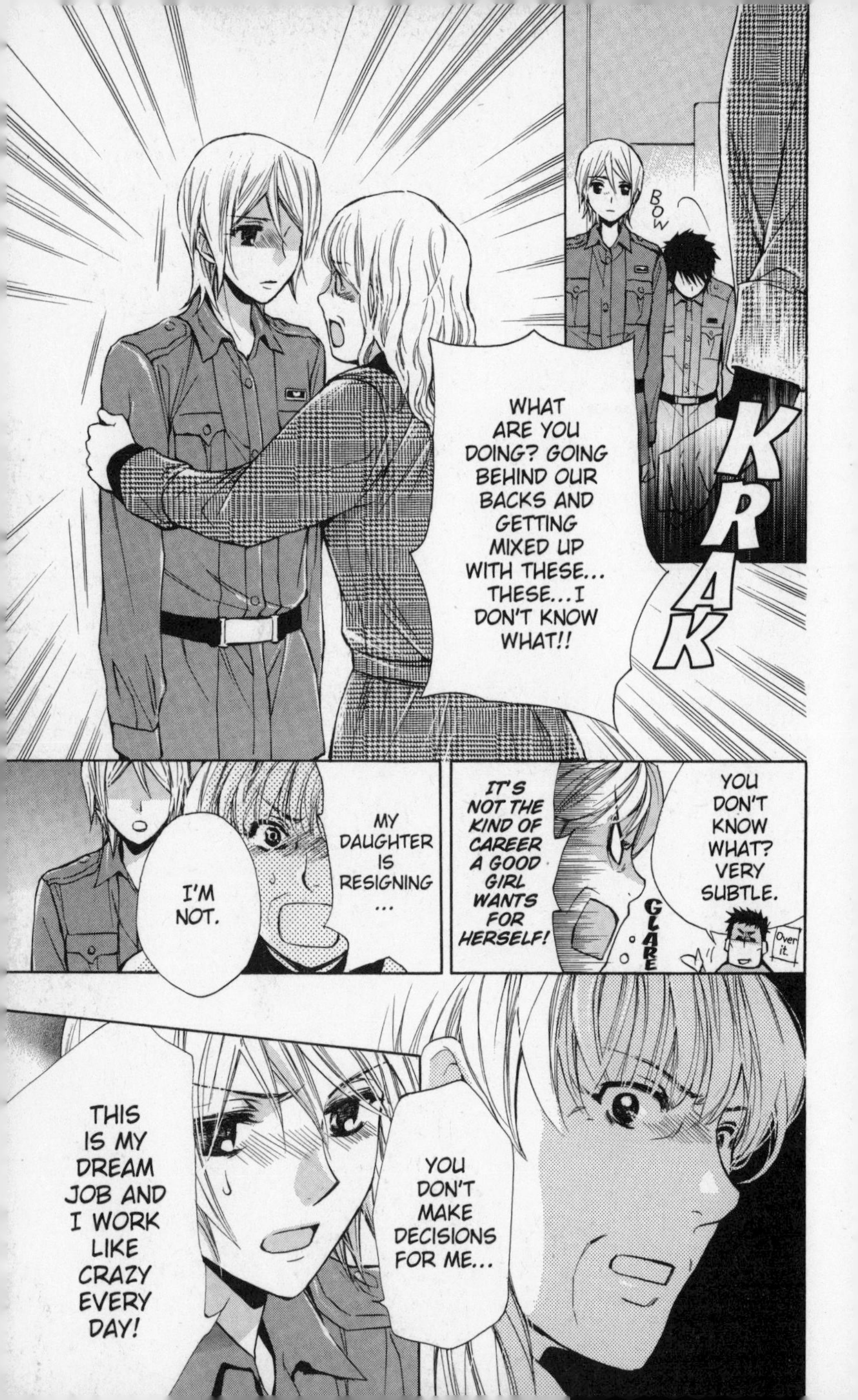
BOW
KRAK
WHAT ARE YOU DOING? GOING BEHIND OUR BACKS AND GETTING MIXED UP WITH THESE... THESE...I DON'T KNOW WHAT!!
YOU DON'T KNOW WHAT? VERY SUBTLE.
Over it.
GLARE
IT'S NOT THE KIND OF CAREER A GOOD GIRL WANTS FOR HERSELF!
MY DAUGHTER IS RESIGNING...
I'M NOT.
YOU DON'T MAKE DECISIONS FOR ME...
THIS IS MY DREAM JOB AND I WORK LIKE CRAZY EVERY DAY!

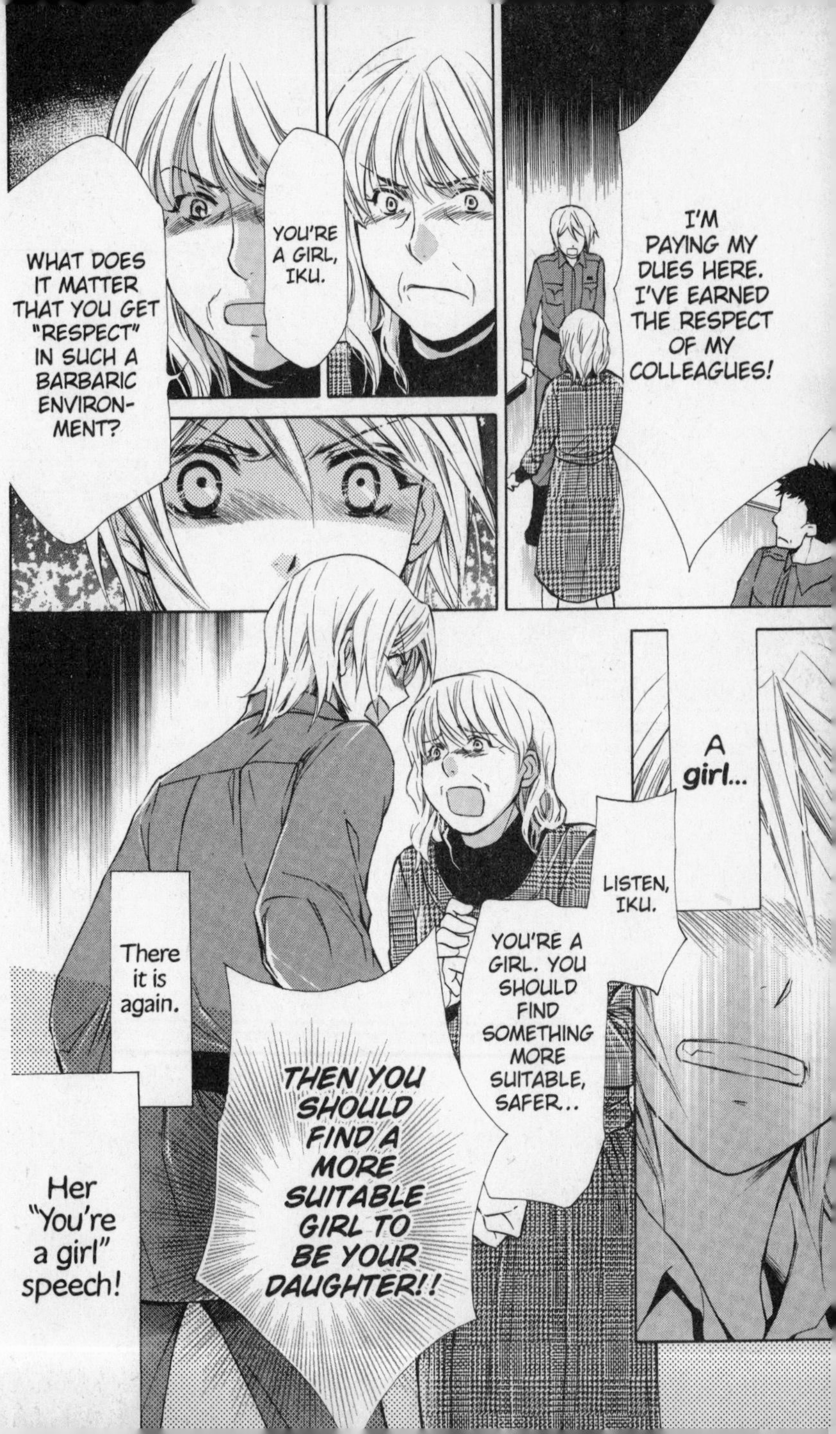
I'M PAYING MY DUES HERE. I'VE EARNED THE RESPECT OF MY COLLEAGUES!
YOU'RE A GIRL, IKU.
WHAT DOES IT MATTER THAT YOU GET "RESPECT" IN SUCH A BARBARIC ENVIRON-MENT?
A girl...
LISTEN, IKU.
YOU'RE A GIRL. YOU SHOULD FIND SOMETHING MORE SUITABLE, SAFER...
THEN YOU SHOULD FIND A MORE SUITABLE GIRL TO BE YOUR DAUGHTER!!
There it is again.
Her "You're a girl" speech!

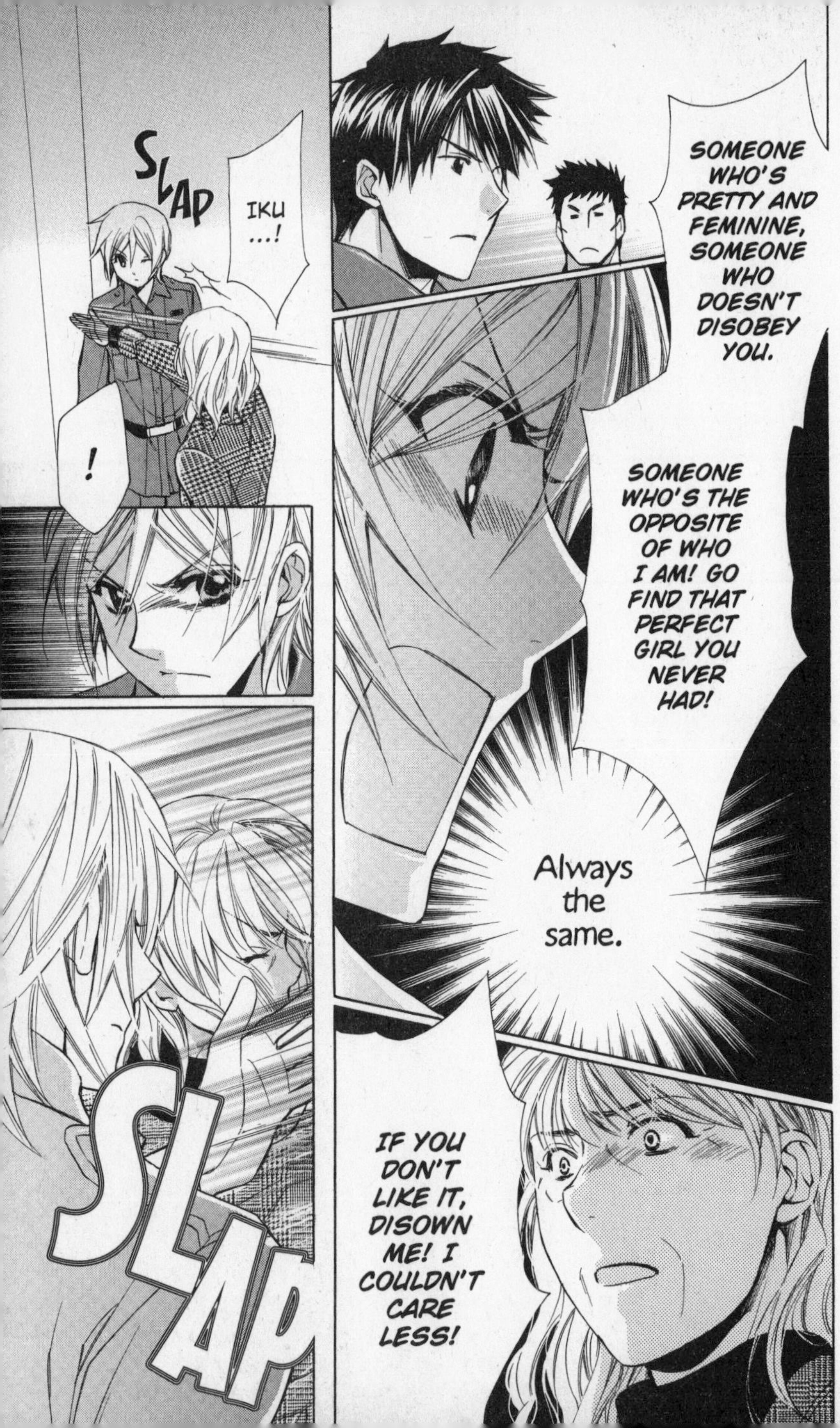
SOMEONE WHO'S PRETTY AND FEMININE, SOMEONE WHO DOESN'T DISOBEY YOU.
SOMEONE WHO'S THE OPPOSITE OF WHO I AM! GO FIND THAT PERFECT GIRL YOU NEVER HAD!
Always the same.
IF YOU DON'T LIKE IT, DISOWN ME! I COULDN'T CARE LESS!
SLAP
IKU ...!
!
SLAP

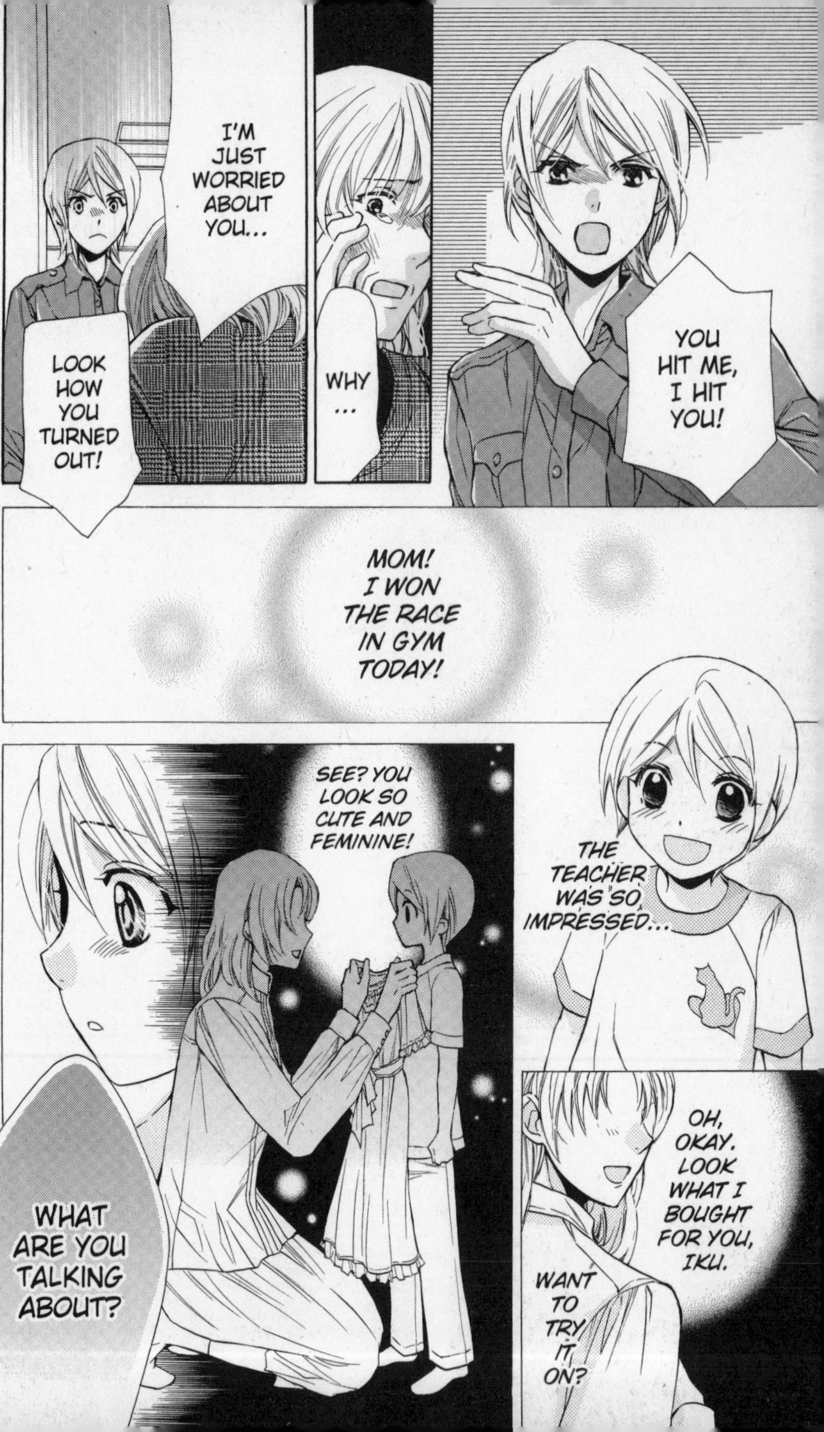
YOU HIT ME, I HIT YOU!
WHY...
I'M JUST WORRIED ABOUT YOU...
LOOK HOW YOU TURNED OUT!
MOM! I WON THE RACE IN GYM TODAY!
THE TEACHER WAS SO IMPRESSED...
OH, OKAY. LOOK WHAT I BOUGHT FOR YOU, IKU.
WANT TO TRY IT ON?
SEE? YOU LOOK SO CUTE AND FEMININE!
WHAT ARE YOU TALKING ABOUT?

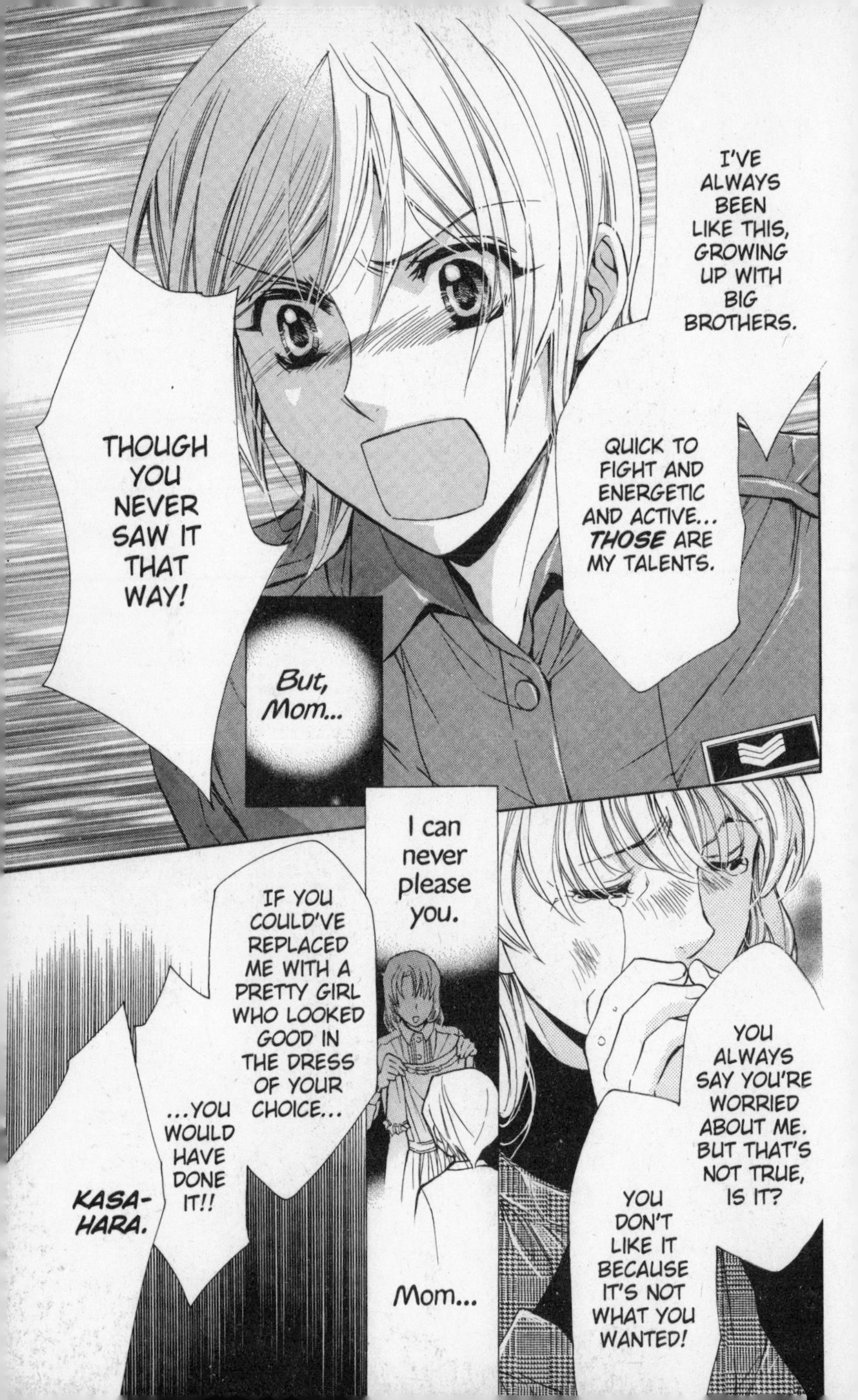
I'VE ALWAYS BEEN LIKE THIS, GROWING UP WITH BIG BROTHERS.
QUICK TO FIGHT AND ENERGETIC AND ACTIVE... *THOSE* ARE MY TALENTS.
THOUGH YOU NEVER SAW IT THAT WAY!
But, Mom...
YOU ALWAYS SAY YOU'RE WORRIED ABOUT ME. BUT THAT'S NOT TRUE, IS IT?
YOU DON'T LIKE IT BECAUSE IT'S NOT WHAT YOU WANTED!
I can never please you.
Mom...
IF YOU COULD'VE REPLACED ME WITH A PRETTY GIRL WHO LOOKED GOOD IN THE DRESS OF YOUR CHOICE...
...YOU WOULD HAVE DONE IT!!
KASA-HARA.

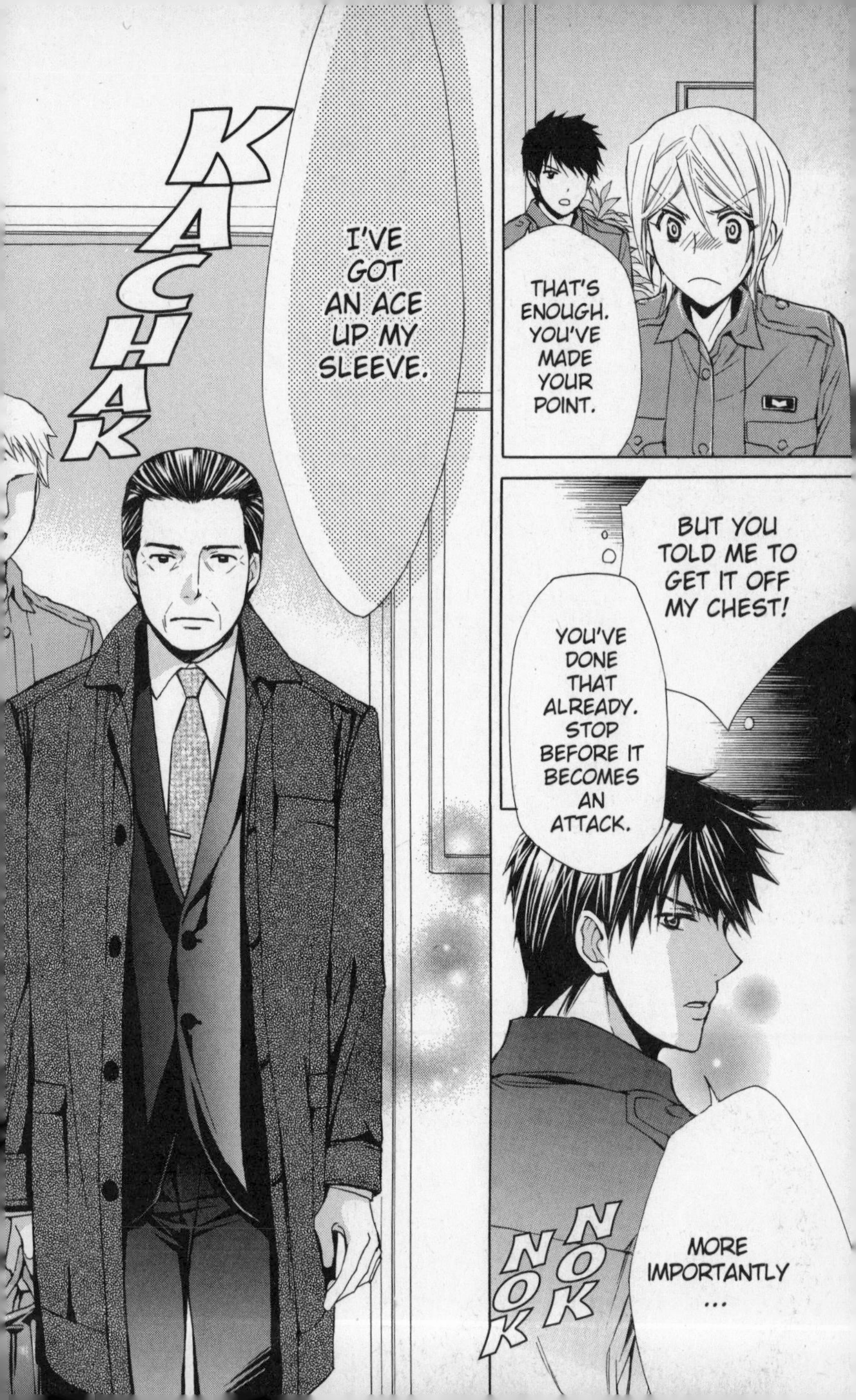
THAT'S ENOUGH. YOU'VE MADE YOUR POINT.
BUT YOU TOLD ME TO GET IT OFF MY CHEST!
YOU'VE DONE THAT ALREADY. STOP BEFORE IT BECOMES AN ATTACK.
MORE IMPORTANTLY ...
NOK NOK
KACHAK
I'VE GOT AN ACE UP MY SLEEVE.

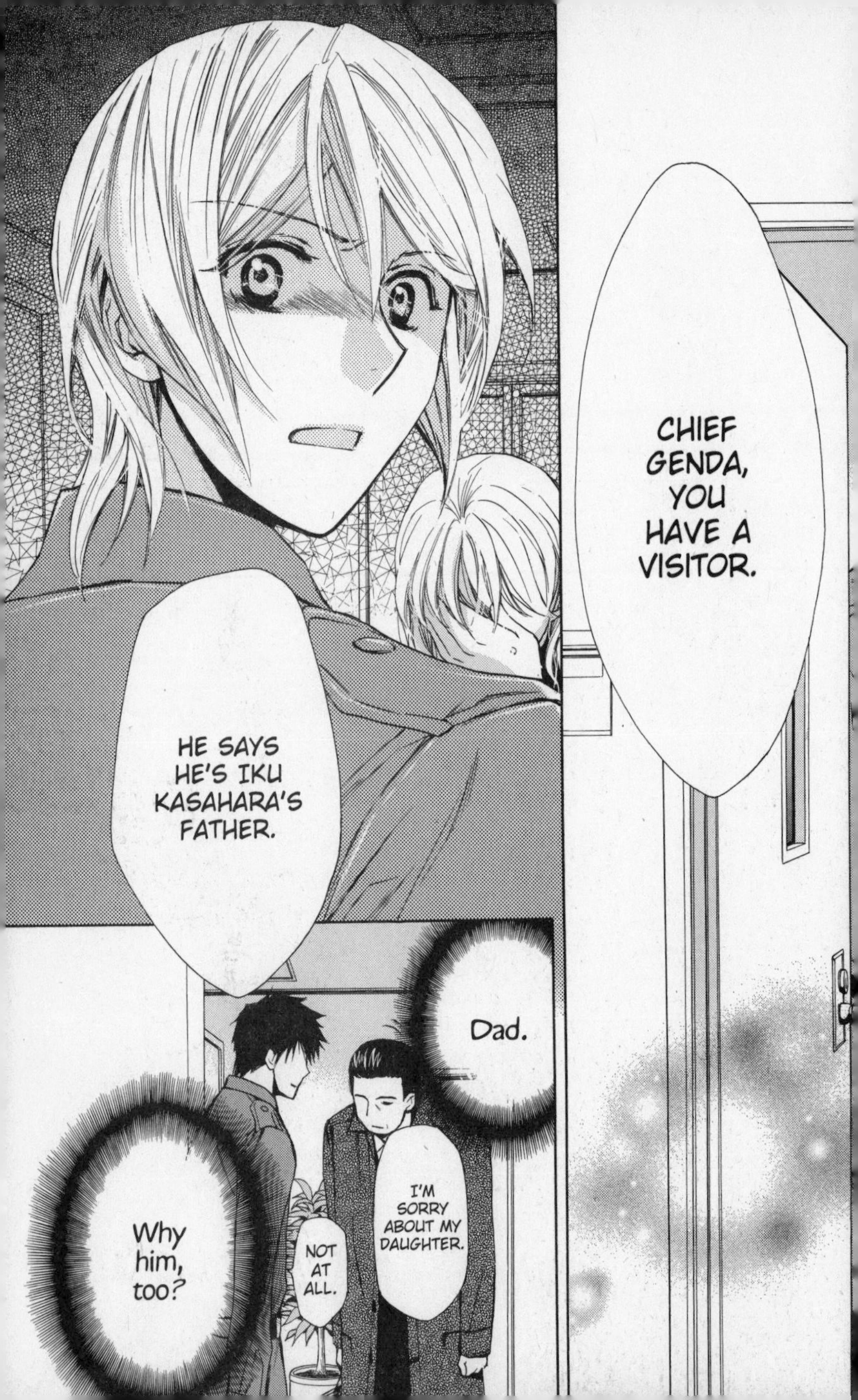
CHIEF GENDA, YOU HAVE A VISITOR.
HE SAYS HE'S IKU KASAHARA'S FATHER.
Dad.
I'M SORRY ABOUT MY DAUGHTER.
NOT AT ALL.
Why him, too?

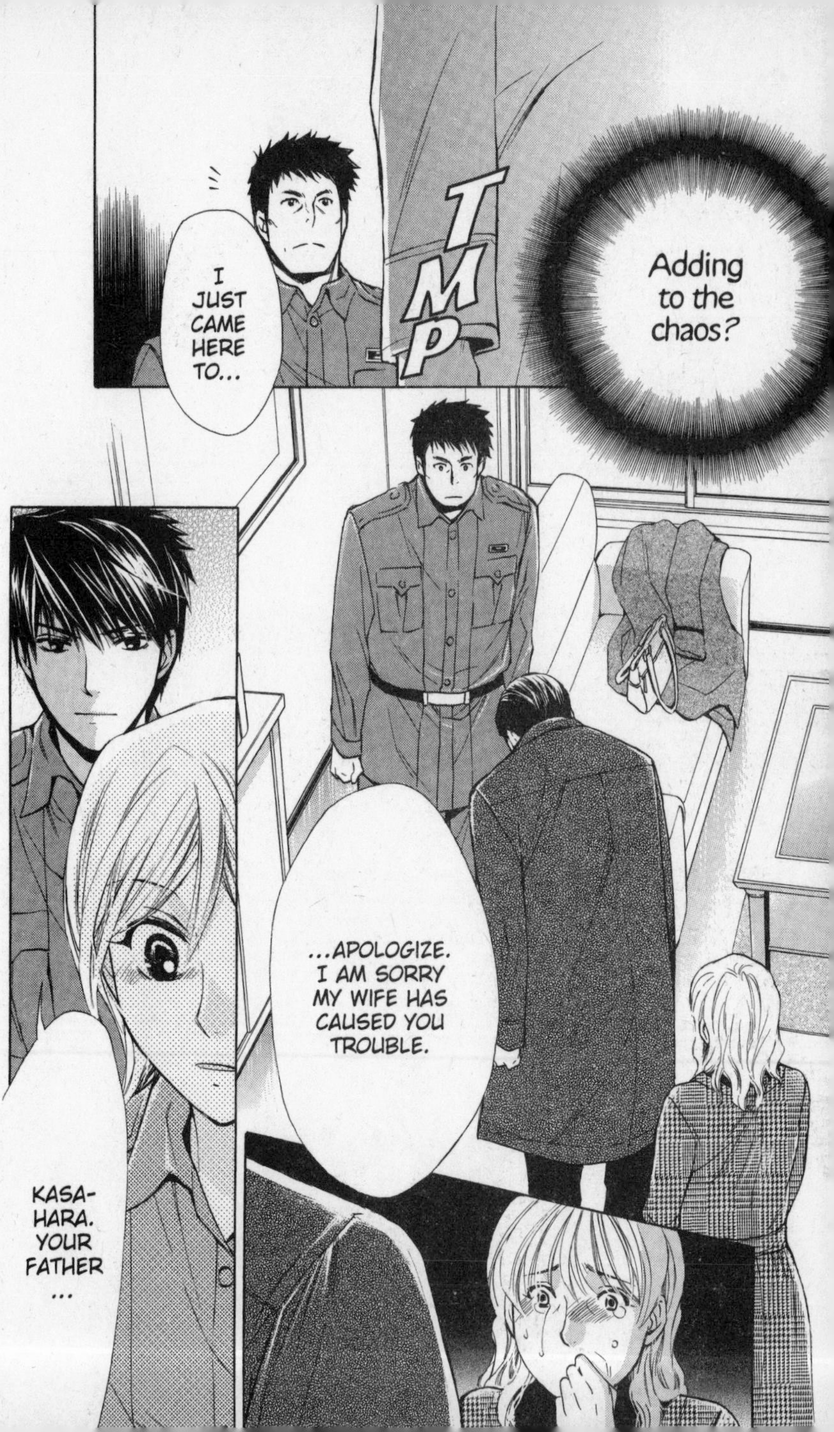
TMP
I JUST CAME HERE TO...
Adding to the chaos?
...APOLOGIZE. I AM SORRY MY WIFE HAS CAUSED YOU TROUBLE.
KASA-HARA. YOUR FATHER ...

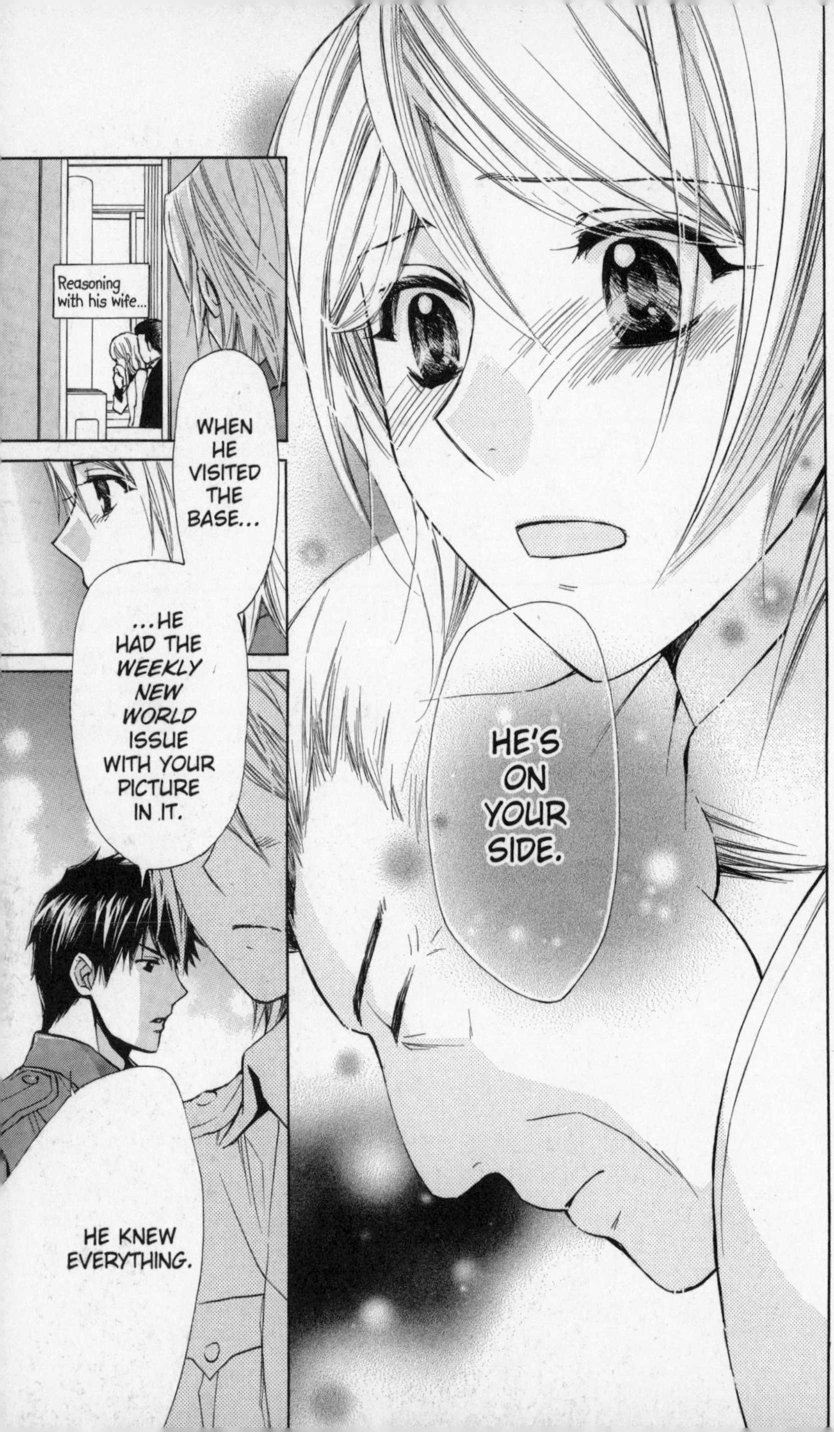
HE'S ON YOUR SIDE.
Reasoning with his wife...
WHEN HE VISITED THE BASE...
...HE HAD THE *WEEKLY NEW WORLD* ISSUE WITH YOUR PICTURE IN IT.
HE KNEW EVERYTHING.

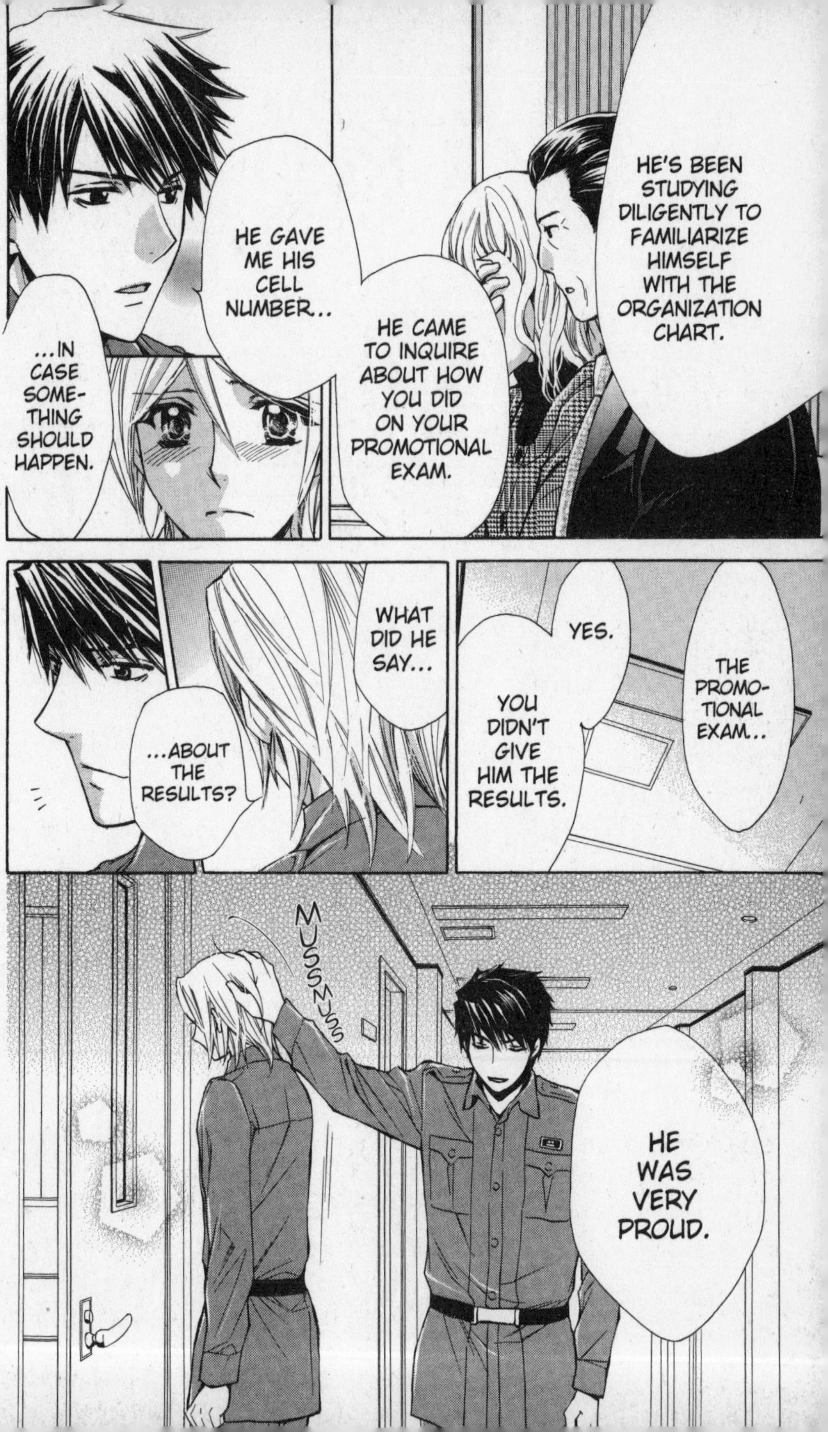
HE'S BEEN STUDYING DILIGENTLY TO FAMILIARIZE HIMSELF WITH THE ORGANIZATION CHART.
HE CAME TO INQUIRE ABOUT HOW YOU DID ON YOUR PROMOTIONAL EXAM.
HE GAVE ME HIS CELL NUMBER...
...IN CASE SOME-THING SHOULD HAPPEN.
THE PROMO-TIONAL EXAM...
YES.
YOU DIDN'T GIVE HIM THE RESULTS.
WHAT DID HE SAY...
...ABOUT THE RESULTS?
MUSSMUSS
HE WAS VERY PROUD.

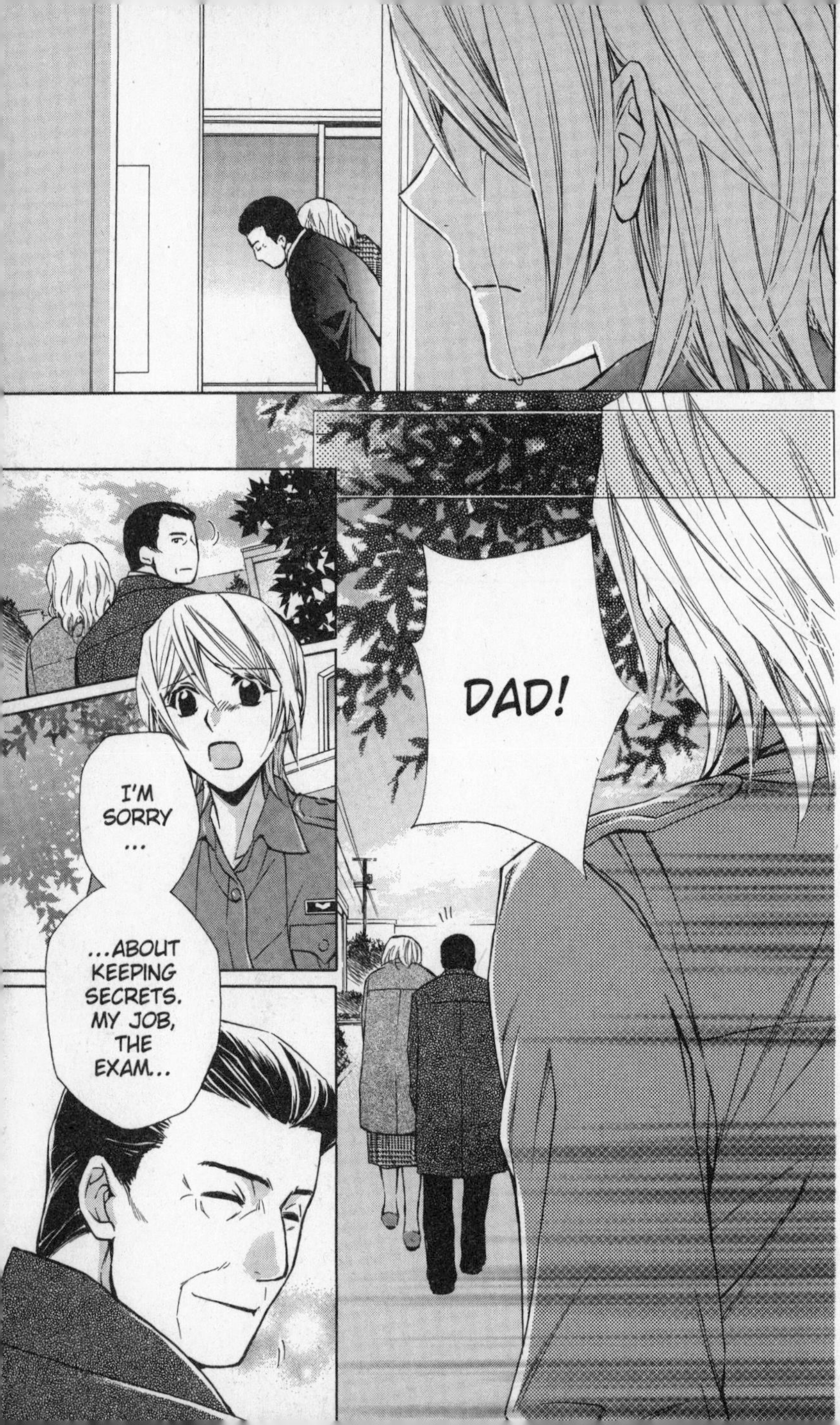
DAD!
I'M SORRY ...
...ABOUT KEEPING SECRETS. MY JOB, THE EXAM...

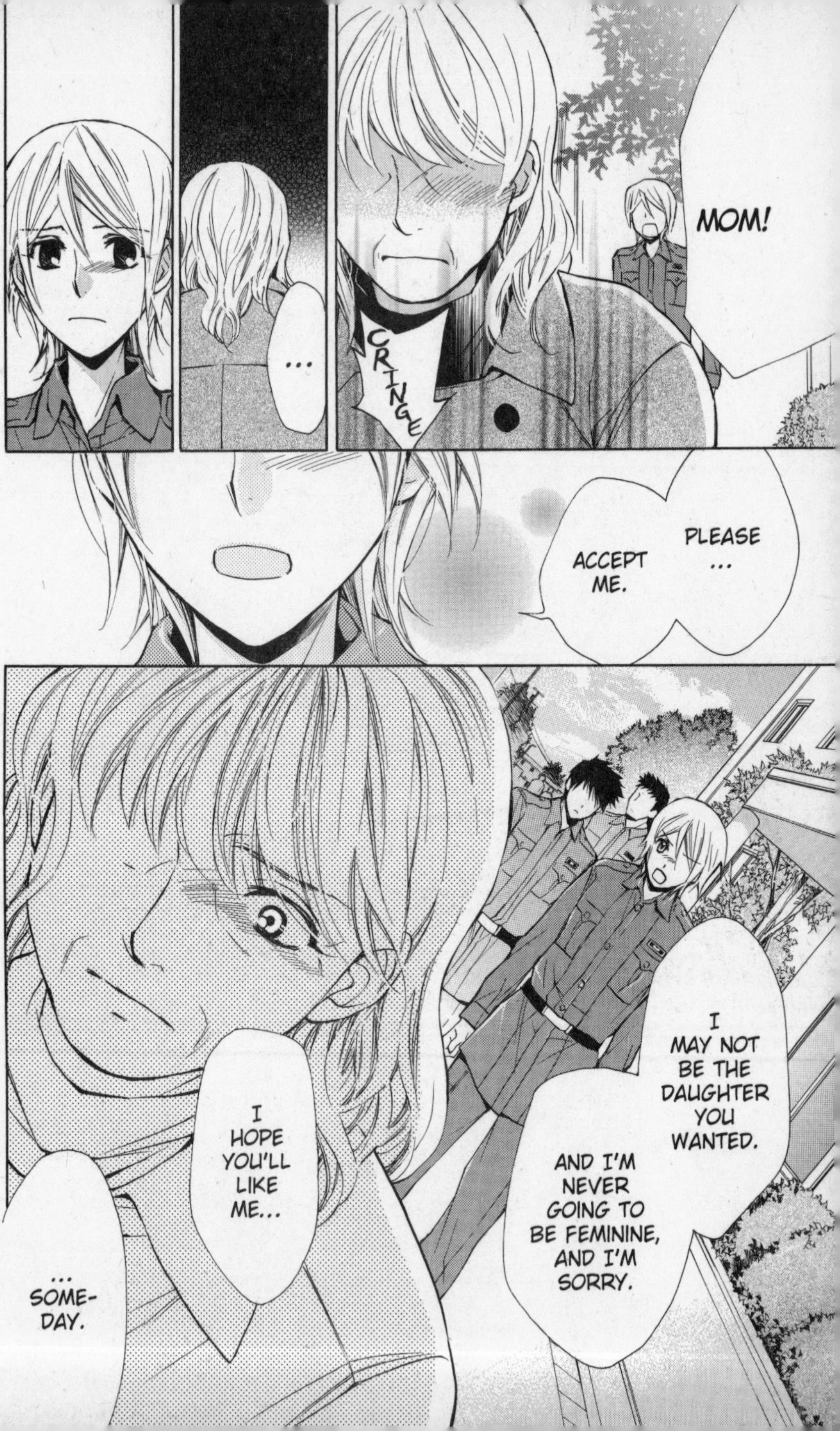
MOM!
CRINGE
...
PLEASE ... ACCEPT ME.
I MAY NOT BE THE DAUGHTER YOU WANTED.
AND I'M NEVER GOING TO BE FEMININE, AND I'M SORRY.
I HOPE YOU'LL LIKE ME...
... SOME-DAY.

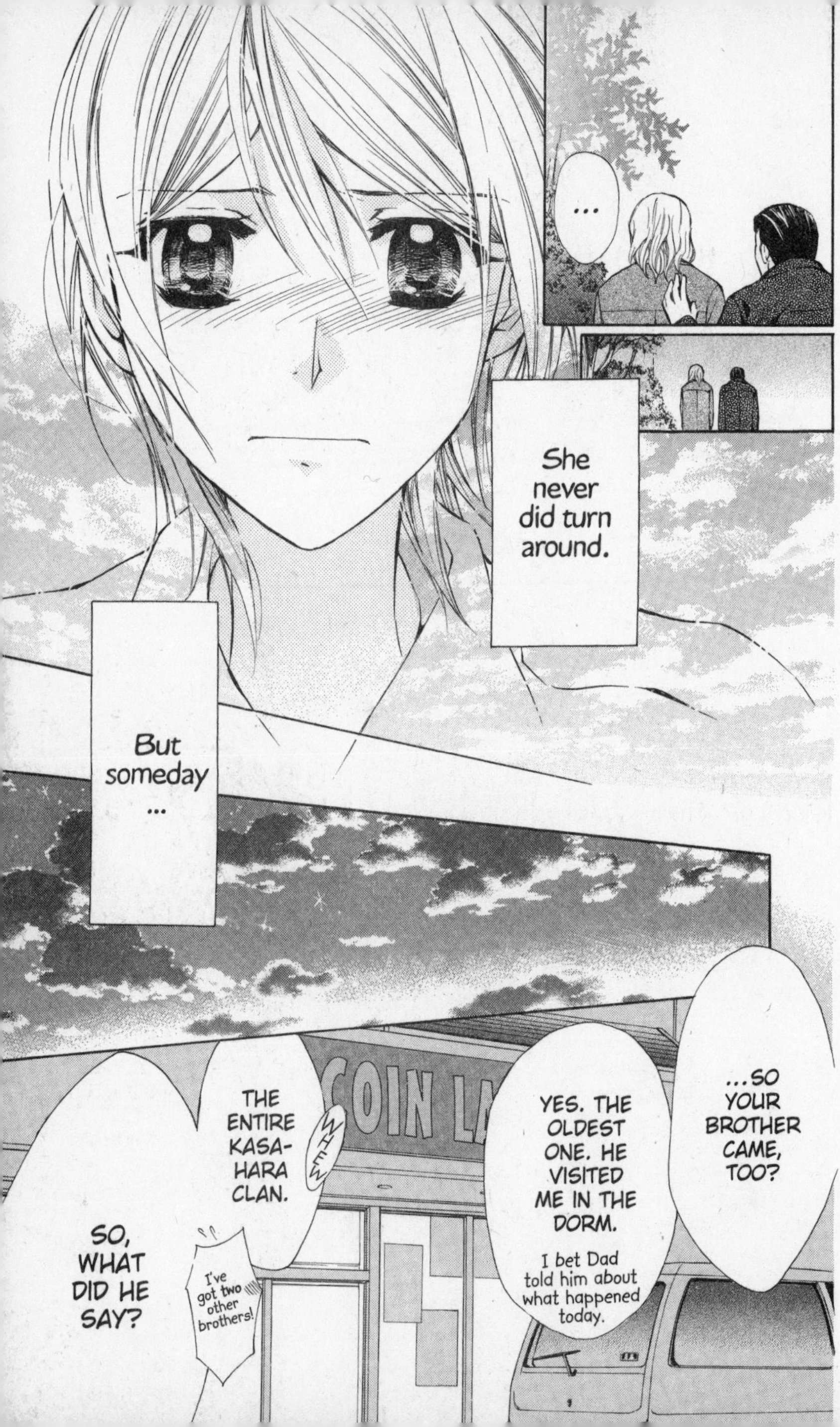
...
She never did turn around.
But someday ...
...SO YOUR BROTHER CAME, TOO?
YES. THE OLDEST ONE. HE VISITED ME IN THE DORM.
I bet Dad told him about what happened today.
THE ENTIRE KASA-HARA CLAN.
WHEW
I've got two other brothers!
SO, WHAT DID HE SAY?
COIN LA

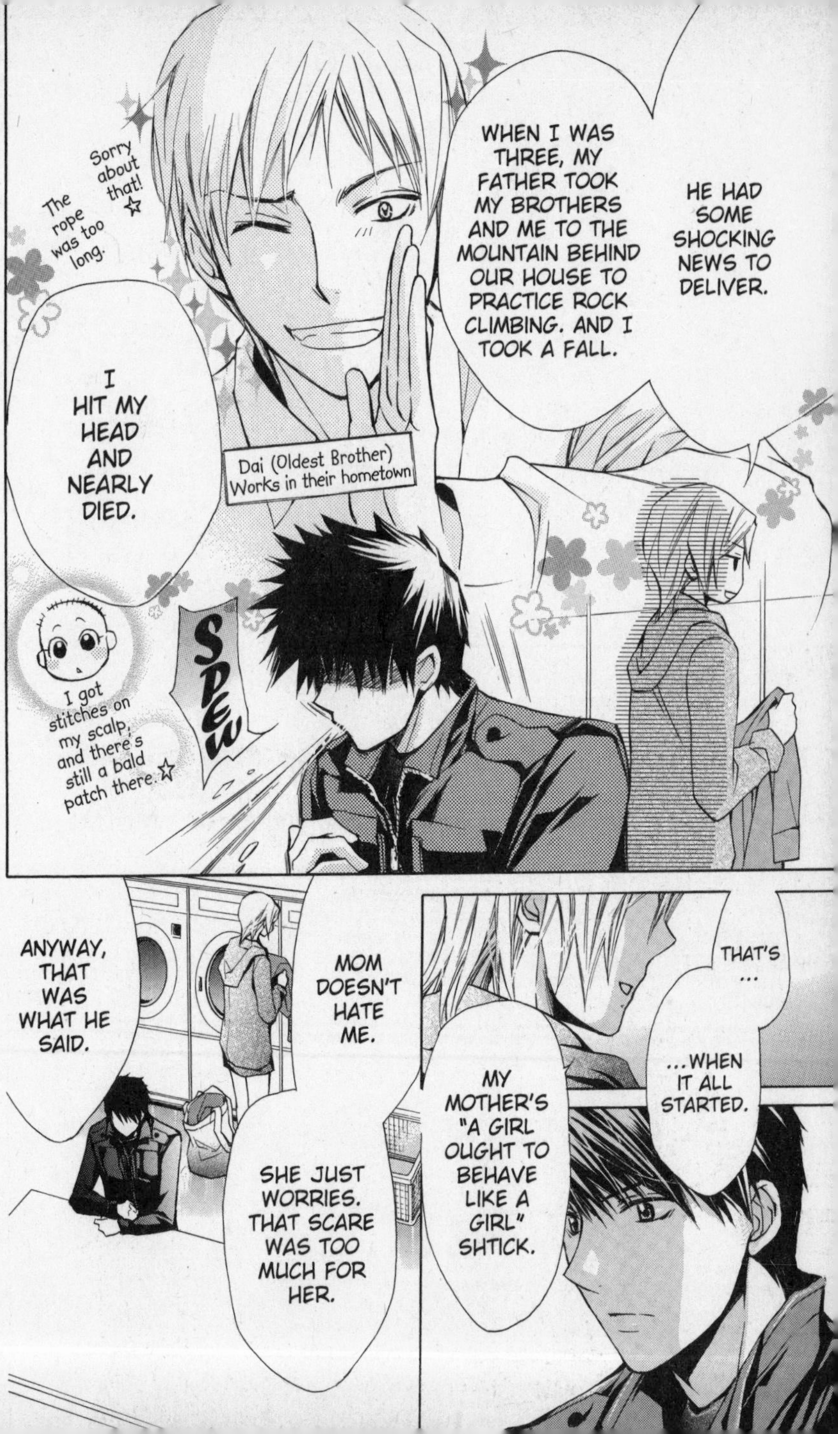
HE HAD SOME SHOCKING NEWS TO DELIVER.
WHEN I WAS THREE, MY FATHER TOOK MY BROTHERS AND ME TO THE MOUNTAIN BEHIND OUR HOUSE TO PRACTICE ROCK CLIMBING. AND I TOOK A FALL.
Sorry about that! ☆
The rope was too long.
I HIT MY HEAD AND NEARLY DIED.
Dai (Oldest Brother) Works in their hometown
SPEW
I got stitches on my scalp, and there's still a bald patch there. ☆
THAT'S ...
...WHEN IT ALL STARTED.
MY MOTHER'S "A GIRL OUGHT TO BEHAVE LIKE A GIRL" SHTICK.
MOM DOESN'T HATE ME.
SHE JUST WORRIES. THAT SCARE WAS TOO MUCH FOR HER.
ANYWAY, THAT WAS WHAT HE SAID.

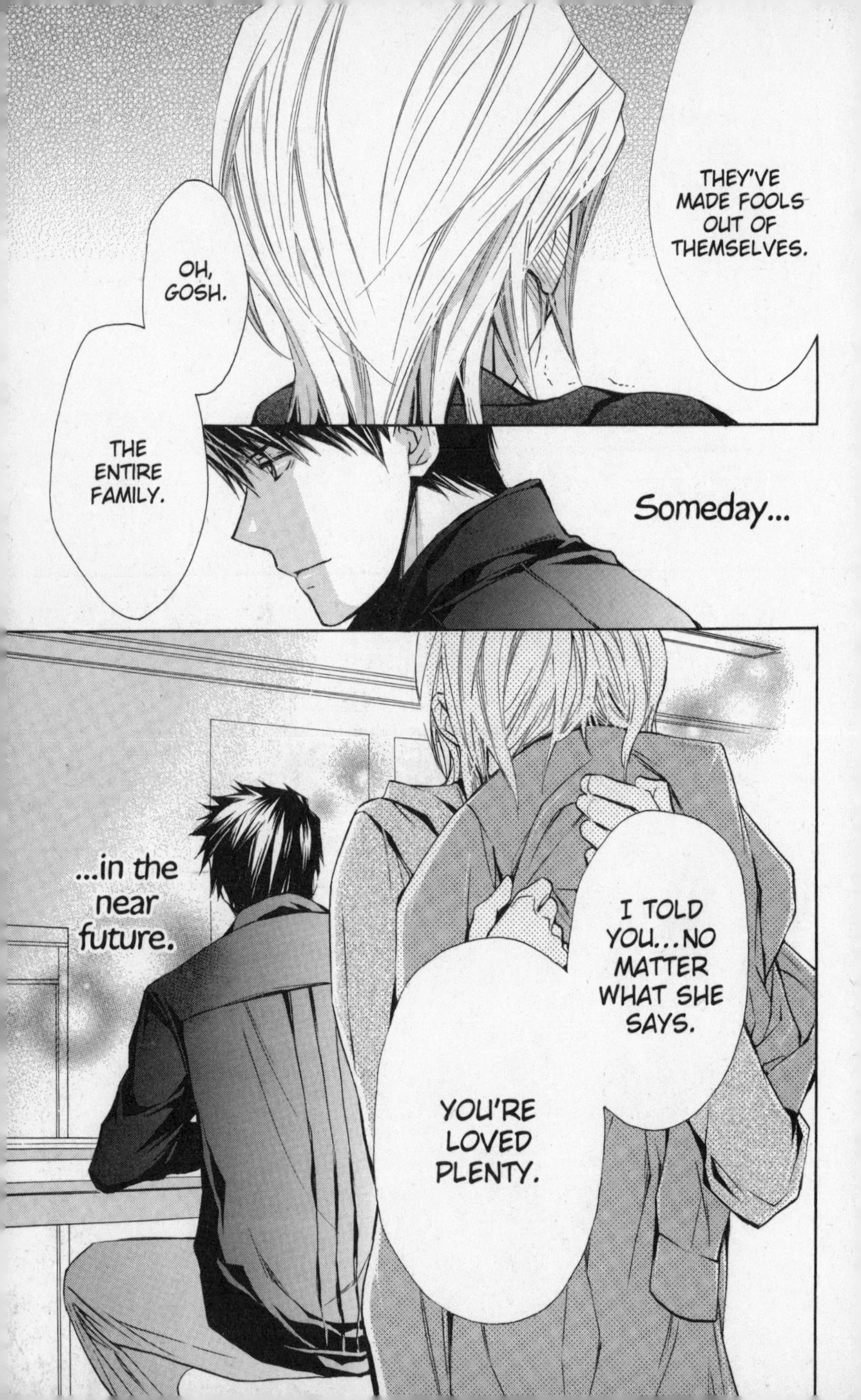
THEY'VE MADE FOOLS OUT OF THEMSELVES.
OH, GOSH.
Someday...
THE ENTIRE FAMILY.
I TOLD YOU...NO MATTER WHAT SHE SAYS.
YOU'RE LOVED PLENTY.
...in the near future.

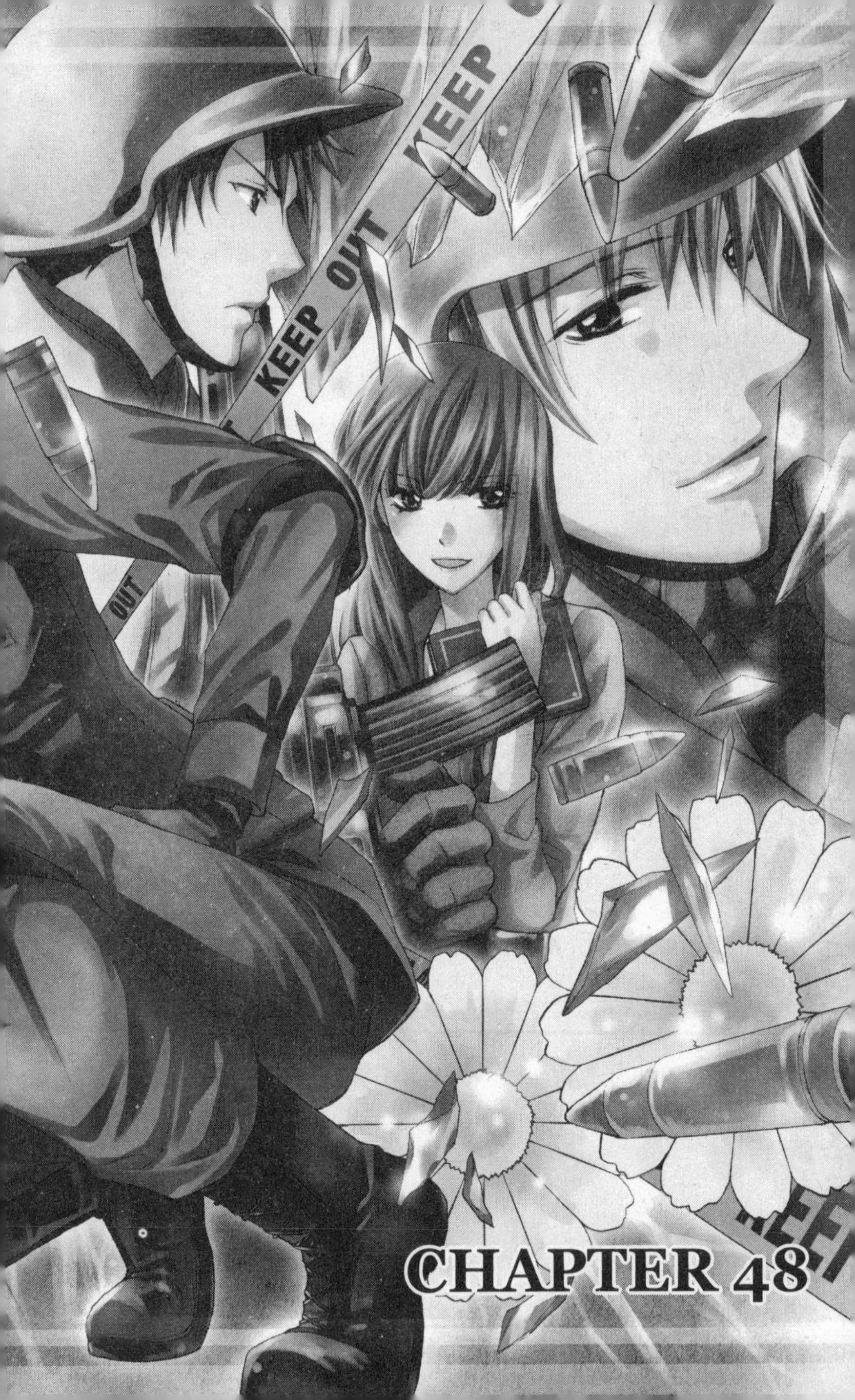
KEEP
KEEP OUT
OUT
CHAPTER 48

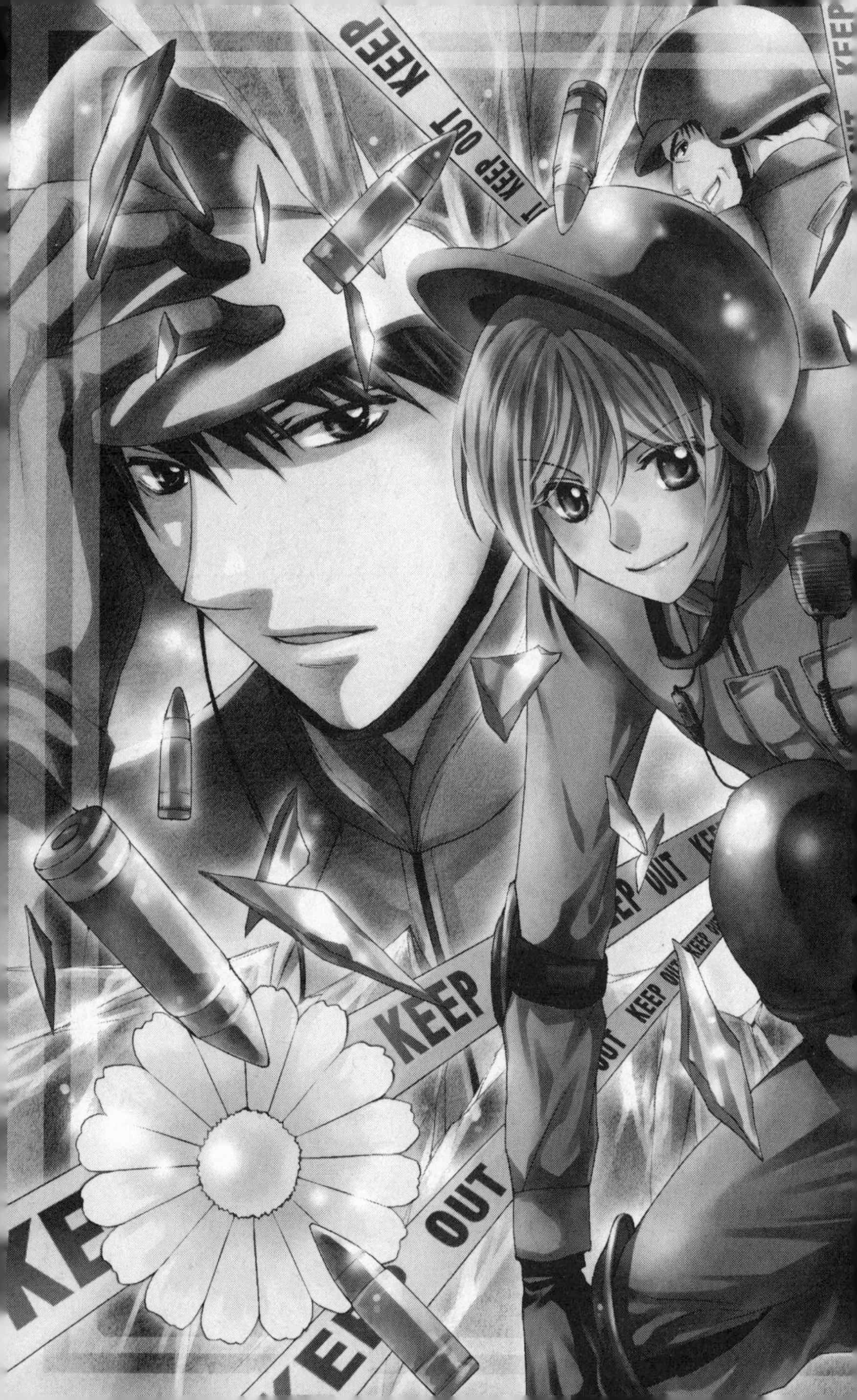
KEEP OUT KEEP
KEEP OUT KEEP
KEEP OUT KEEP OUT KEEP
KEEP
OUT

Mood Swings

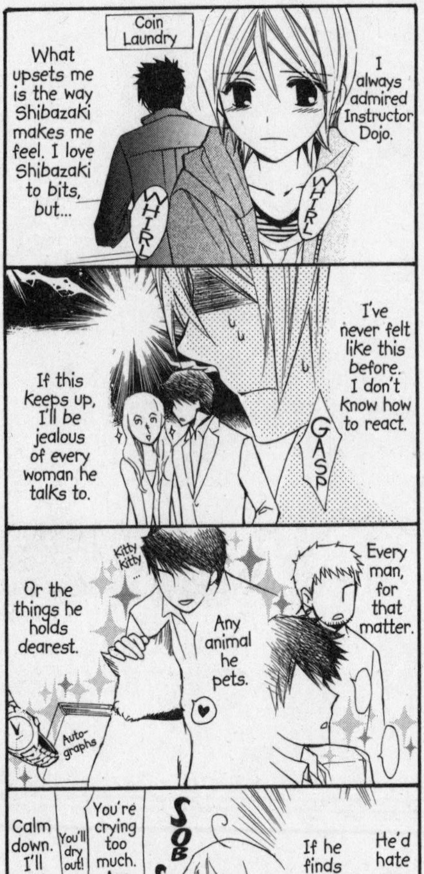
I always admired Instructor Dojo.
Coin Laundry
WHIRL
WHIRL
What upsets me is the way Shibazaki makes me feel. I love Shibazaki to bits, but...
I've never felt like this before. I don't know how to react.
GASP
If this keeps up, I'll be jealous of every woman he talks to.
Every man, for that matter.
Any animal he pets.
Kitty kitty...
Or the things he holds dearest.
Auto-graphs
He'd hate me.
If he finds out what a creep I am, he'll hate me.
SOB SOB SOB SOB
You're crying too much. Are you all right?
You'll dry out!
Calm down. I'll get you a drink.
CRINGE

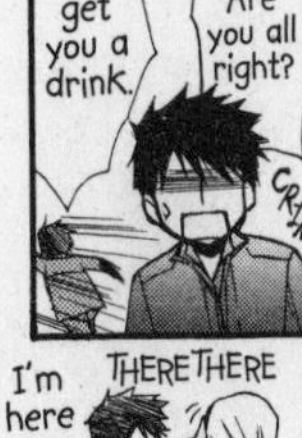
I'm here for you.
THERE THERE
Tea

And he wins her heart all over again. Infinite loop.

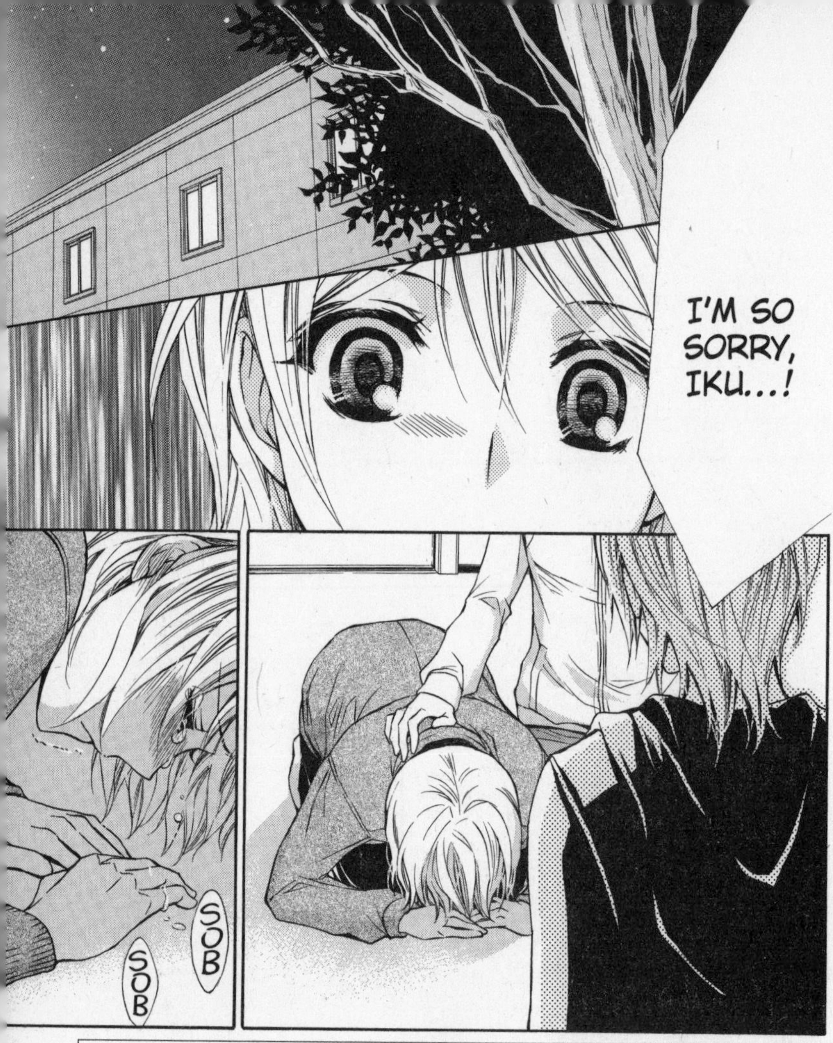
I'M SO SORRY, IKU...!
SOB
SOB

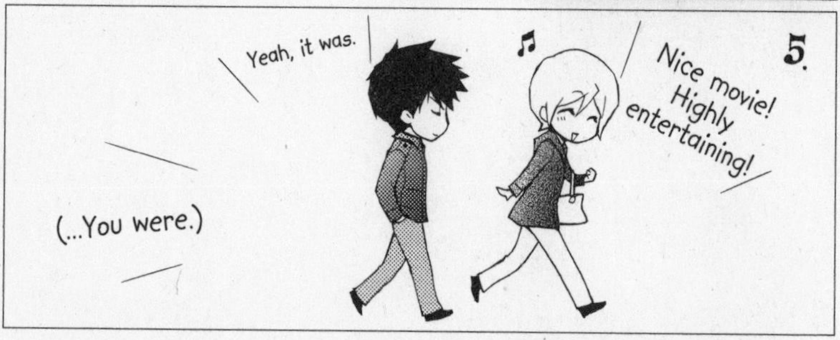
5.
Nice movie! Highly entertaining!
Yeah, it was.
(...You were.)

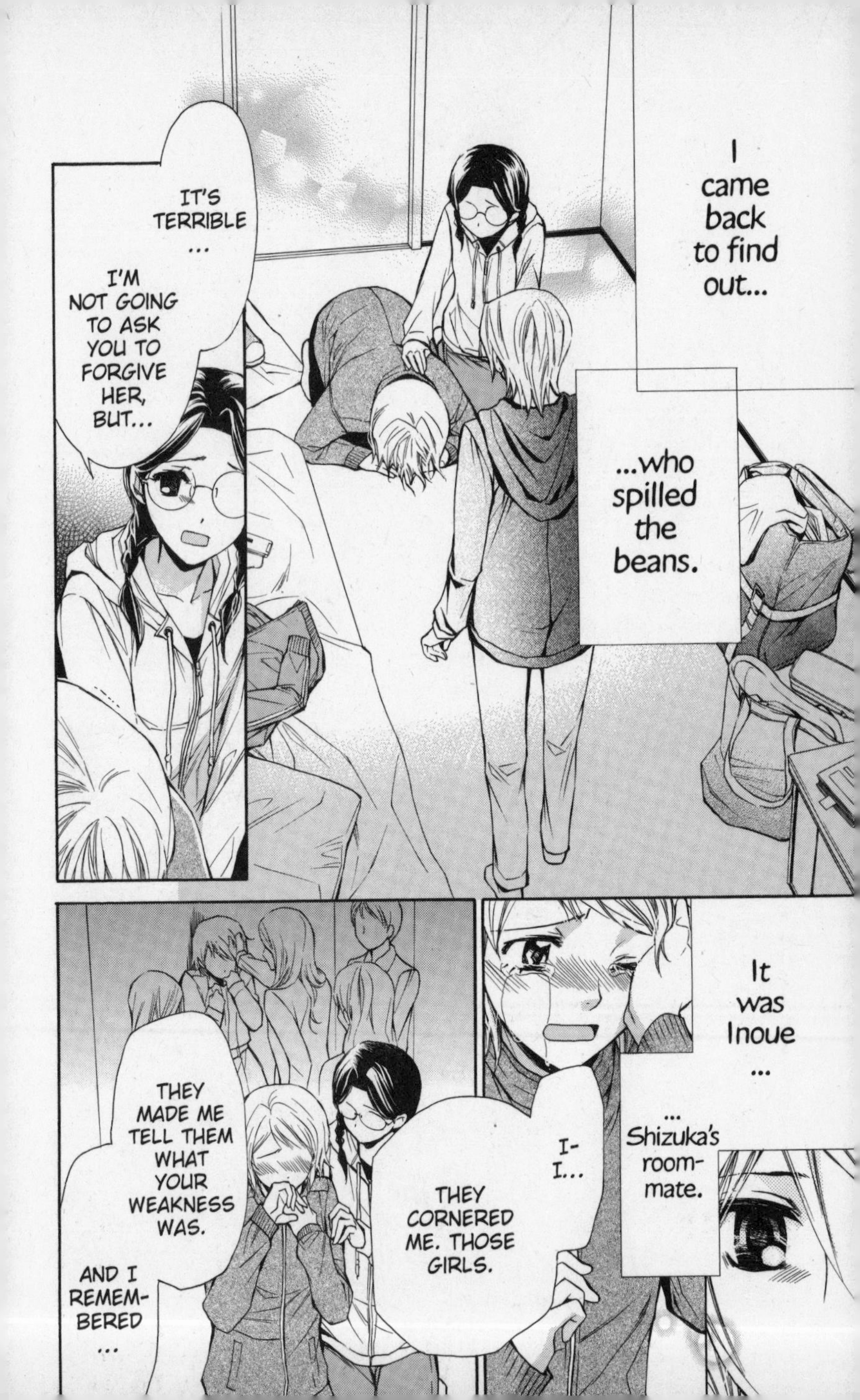
I came back to find out...
...who spilled the beans.
IT'S TERRIBLE ...
I'M NOT GOING TO ASK YOU TO FORGIVE HER, BUT...
It was Inoue ...
... Shizuka's room-mate.
I- I...
THEY CORNERED ME. THOSE GIRLS.
THEY MADE ME TELL THEM WHAT YOUR WEAKNESS WAS.
AND I REMEM-BERED ...

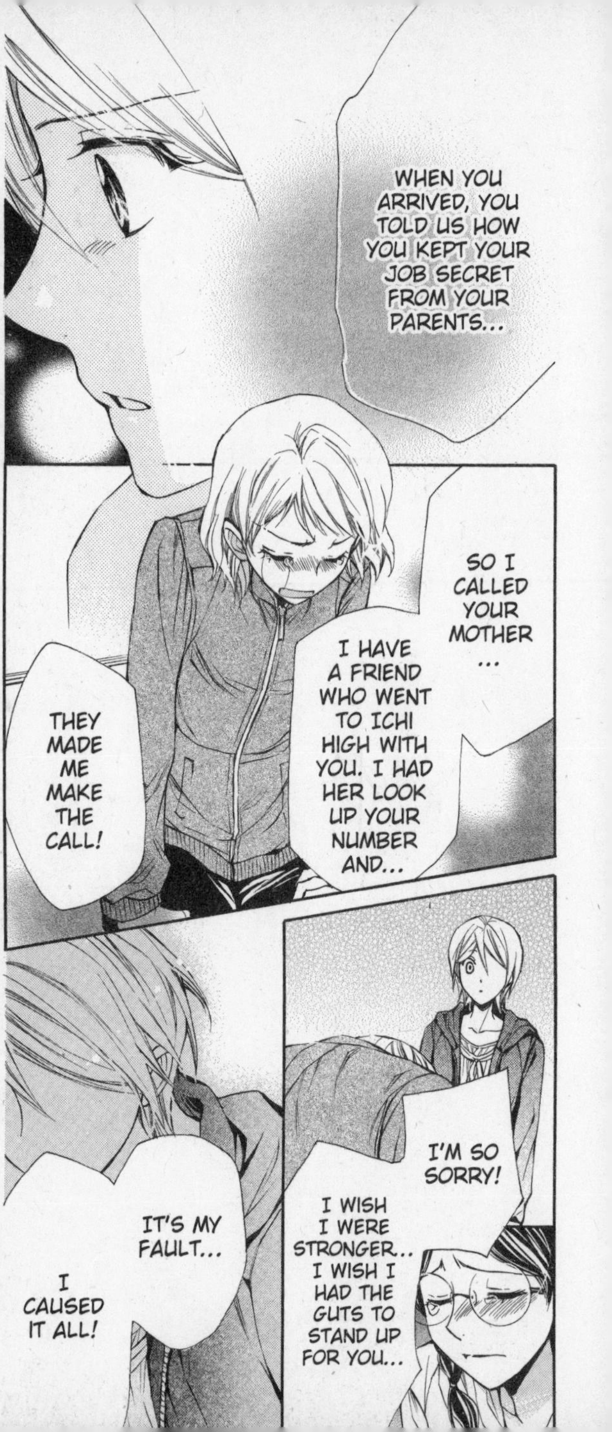
WHEN YOU ARRIVED, YOU TOLD US HOW YOU KEPT YOUR JOB SECRET FROM YOUR PARENTS...
SO I CALLED YOUR MOTHER ...
I HAVE A FRIEND WHO WENT TO ICHI HIGH WITH YOU. I HAD HER LOOK UP YOUR NUMBER AND...
THEY MADE ME MAKE THE CALL!
I'M SO SORRY!
I WISH I WERE STRONGER... I WISH I HAD THE GUTS TO STAND UP FOR YOU...
IT'S MY FAULT...
I CAUSED IT ALL!

5

The coin laundry scene in Chapter 47 is my favorite from the novel's "Crisis" episode. The fact that I've come this far makes me so happy. The drafting process was particularly hard. I can't tell if I did a decent job... But I'm happy I could see it through. Iku's illustrations on the cover and flap are dedicated to the episode... Iku crying in the water... It was fun drawing water, too.

*

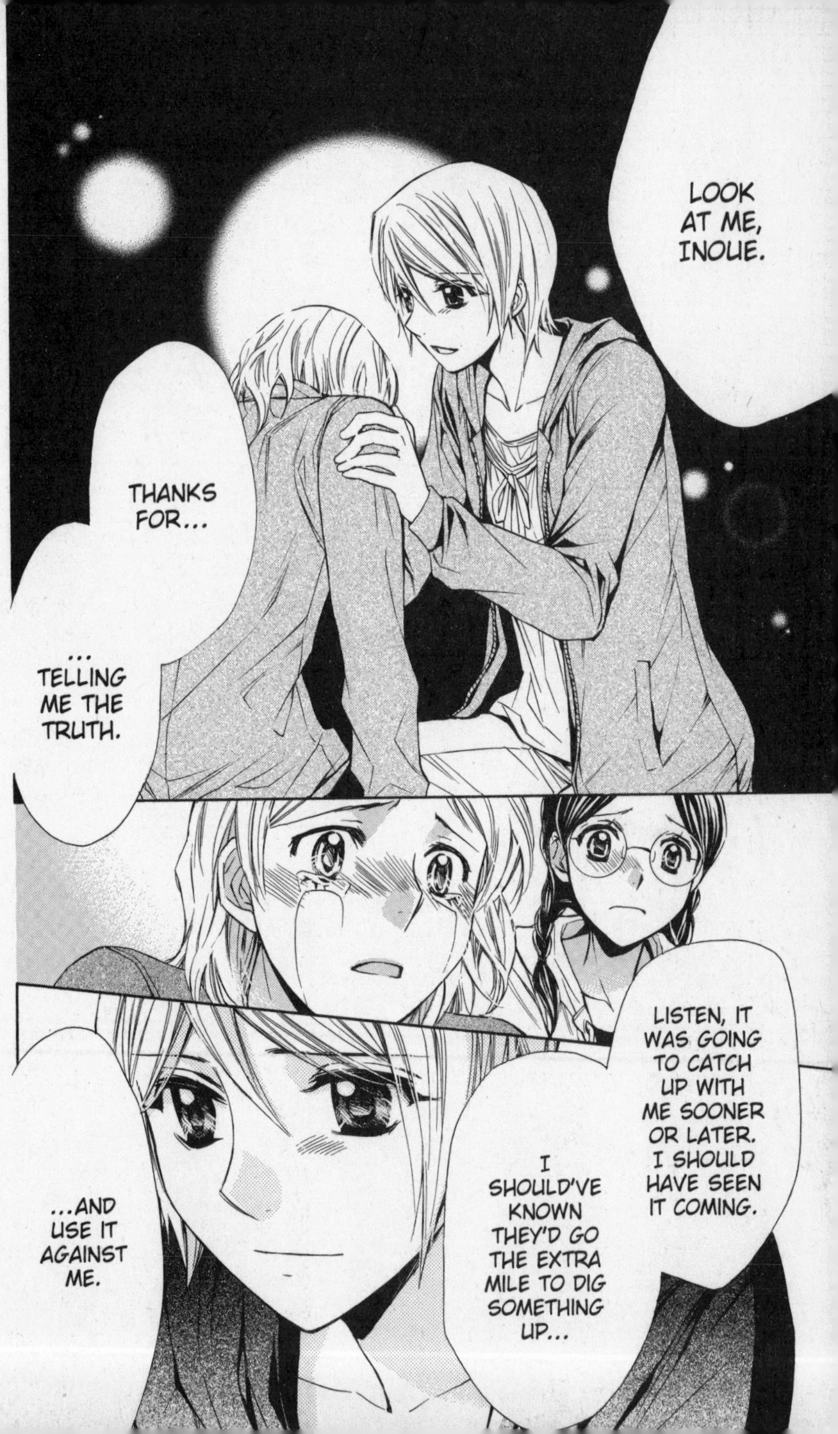
LOOK AT ME, INOUE.
THANKS FOR...
...TELLING ME THE TRUTH.
LISTEN, IT WAS GOING TO CATCH UP WITH ME SOONER OR LATER. I SHOULD HAVE SEEN IT COMING.
I SHOULD'VE KNOWN THEY'D GO THE EXTRA MILE TO DIG SOMETHING UP...
...AND USE IT AGAINST ME.

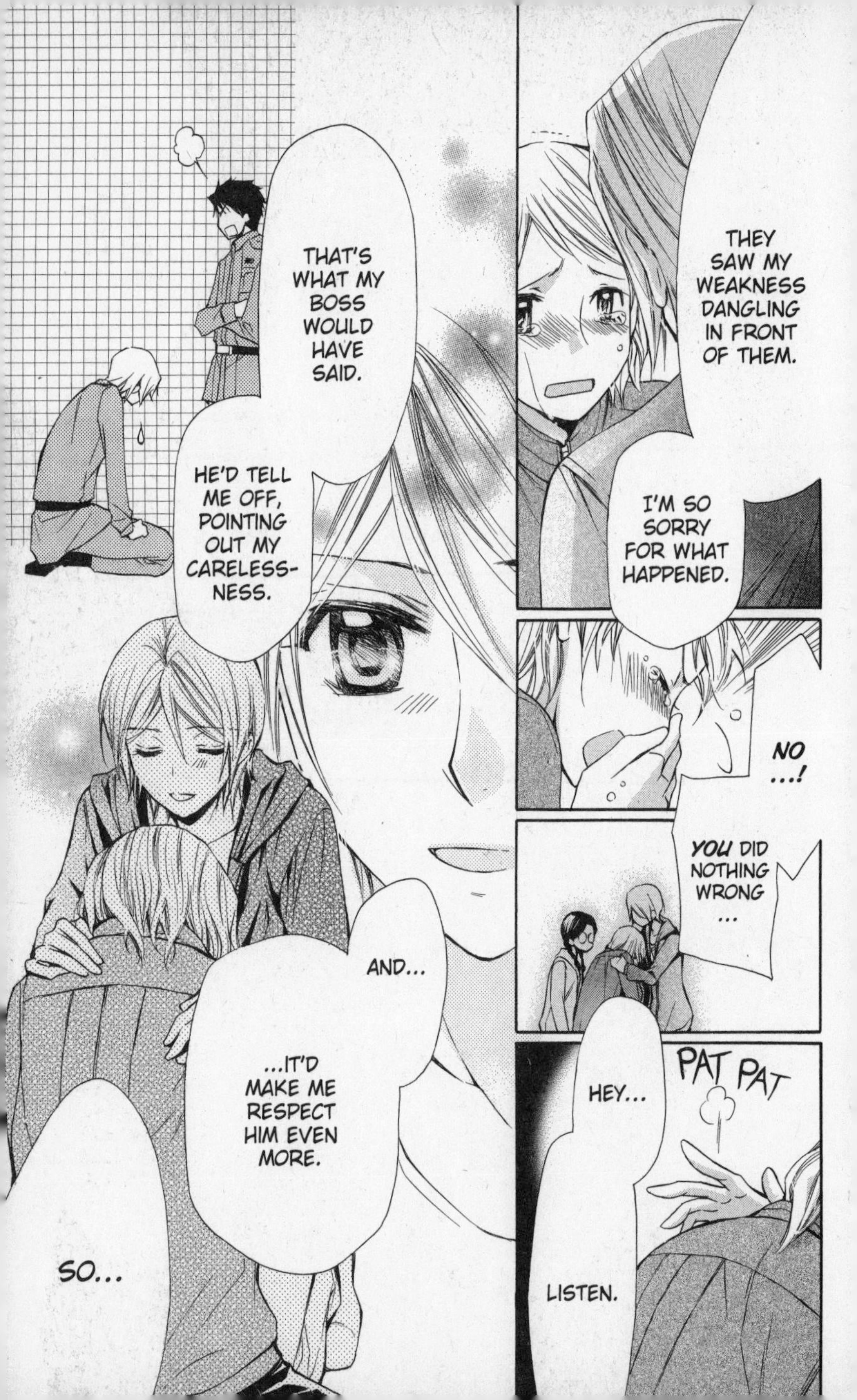
THEY SAW MY WEAKNESS DANGLING IN FRONT OF THEM.
I'M SO SORRY FOR WHAT HAPPENED.
NO ...!
YOU DID NOTHING WRONG ...
PAT PAT
HEY...
LISTEN.
THAT'S WHAT MY BOSS WOULD HAVE SAID.
HE'D TELL ME OFF, POINTING OUT MY CARELESS-NESS.
AND...
...IT'D MAKE ME RESPECT HIM EVEN MORE.
SO...

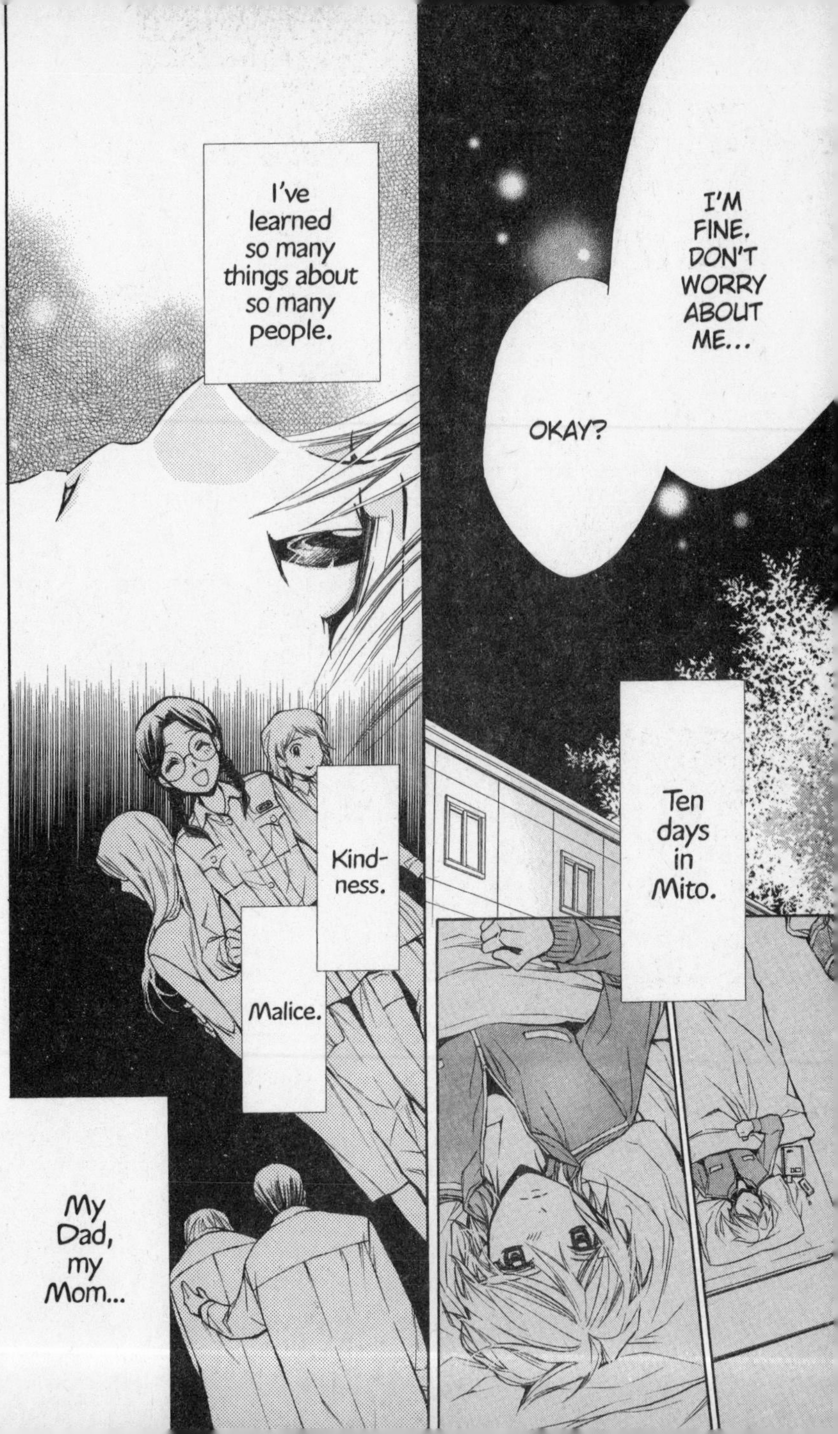
I'M FINE. DON'T WORRY ABOUT ME...
OKAY?
Ten days in Mito.
I've learned so many things about so many people.
Kind-ness.
Malice.
My Dad, my Mom...

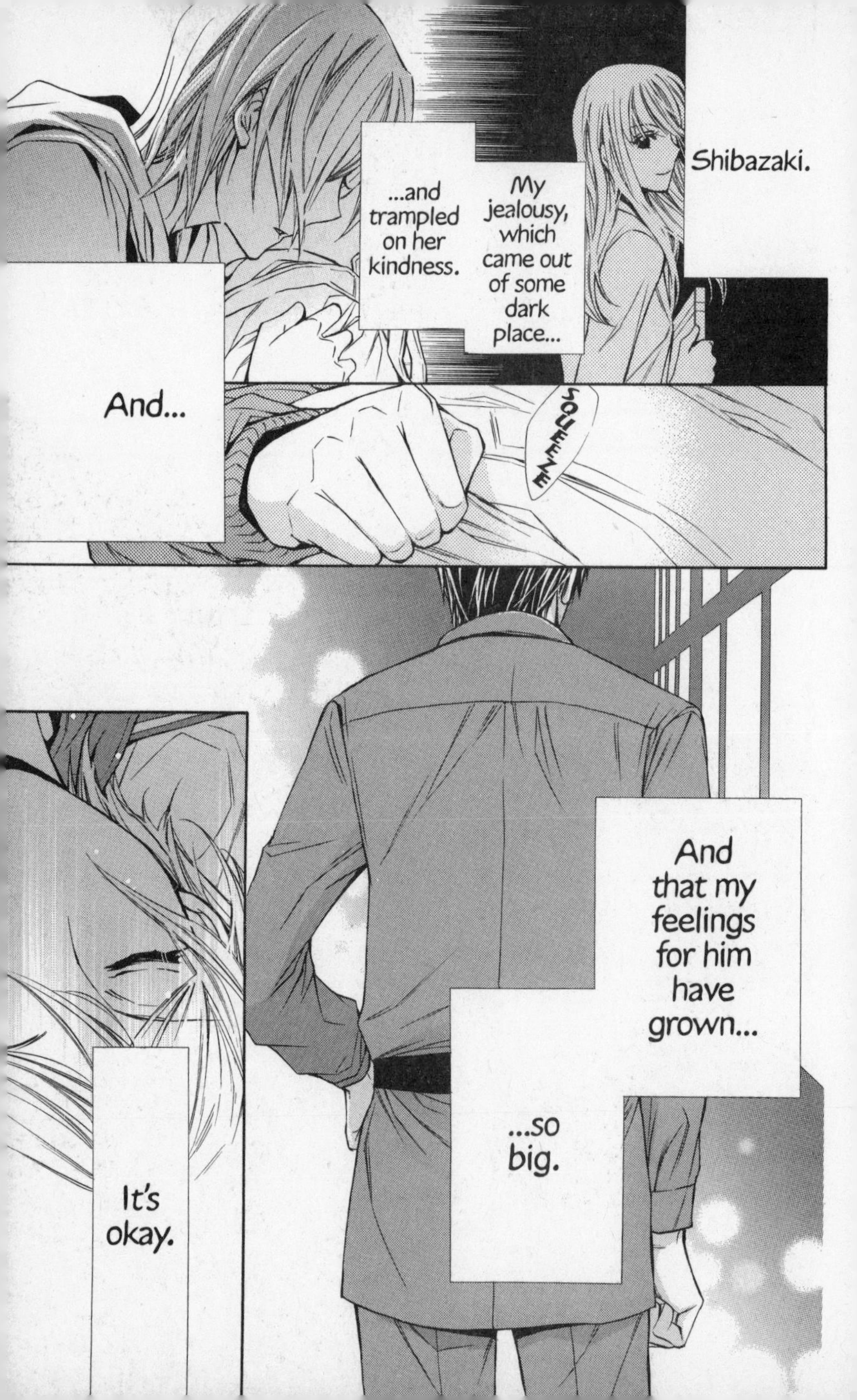
Shibazaki.
My jealousy, which came out of some dark place...
...and trampled on her kindness.
And...
SQUEEZE
And that my feelings for him have grown...
...so big.
It's okay.

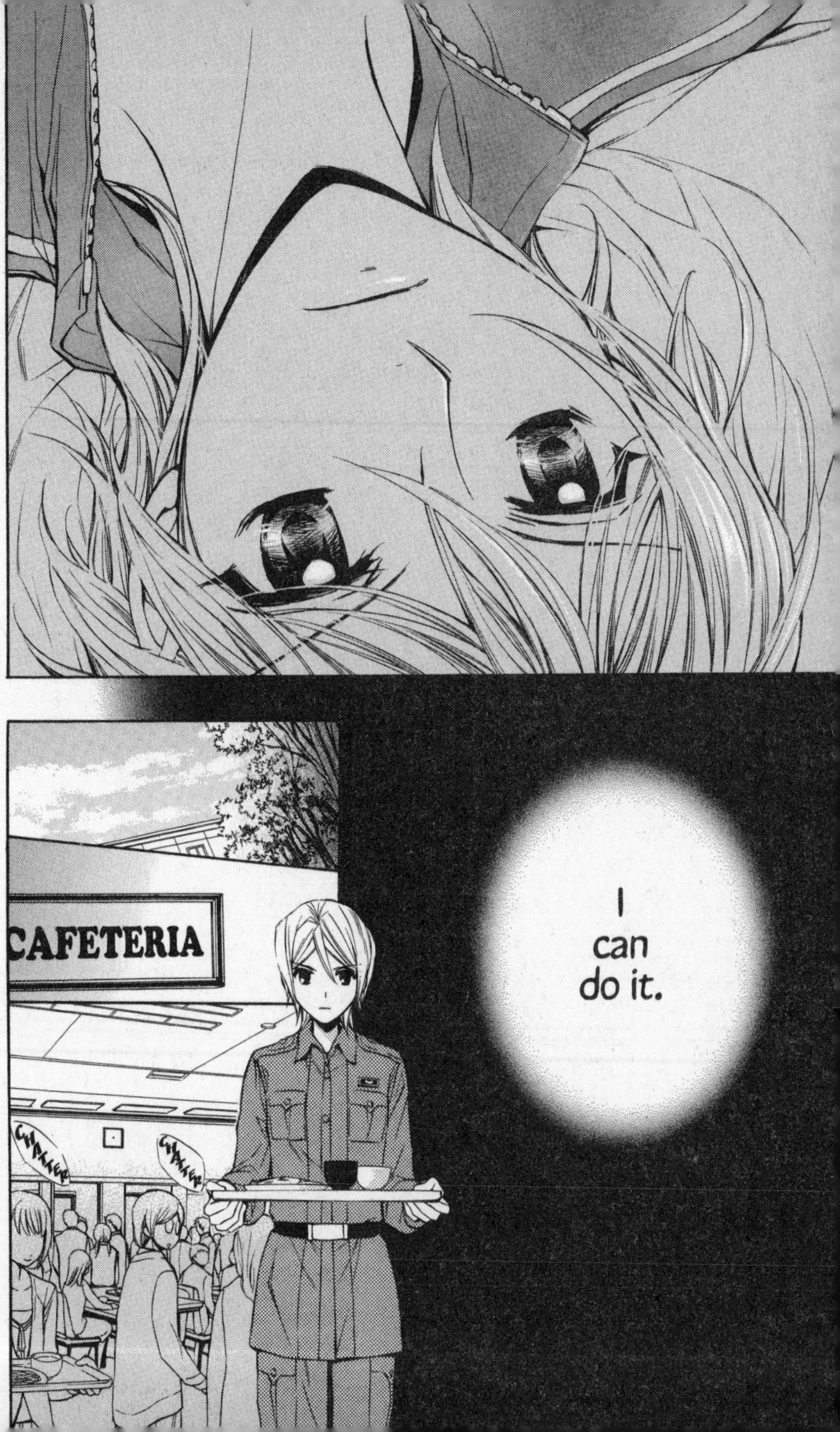
CAFETERIA
I can do it.

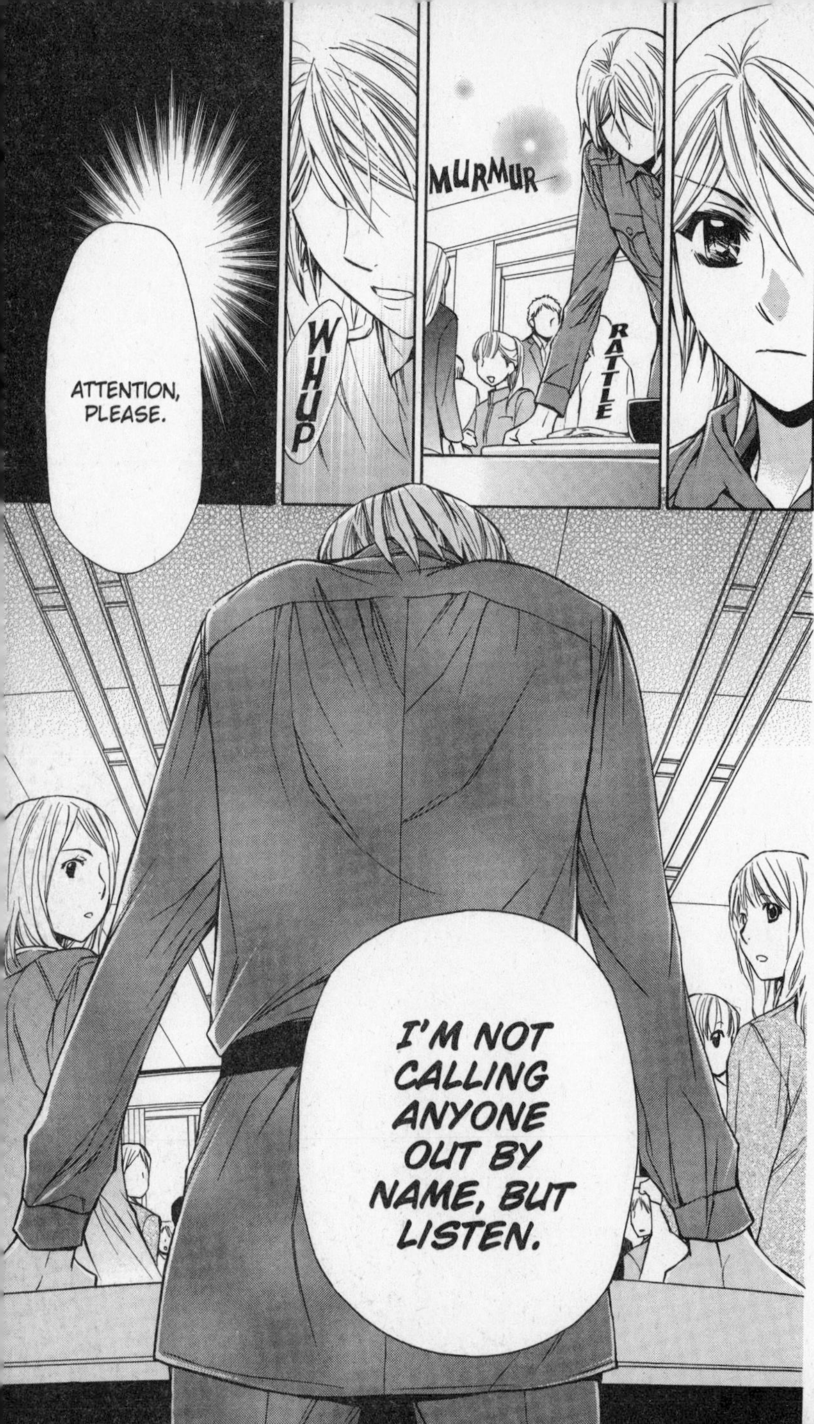
RATTLE
MURMUR
WHUP
ATTENTION, PLEASE.
I'M NOT CALLING ANYONE OUT BY NAME, BUT LISTEN.

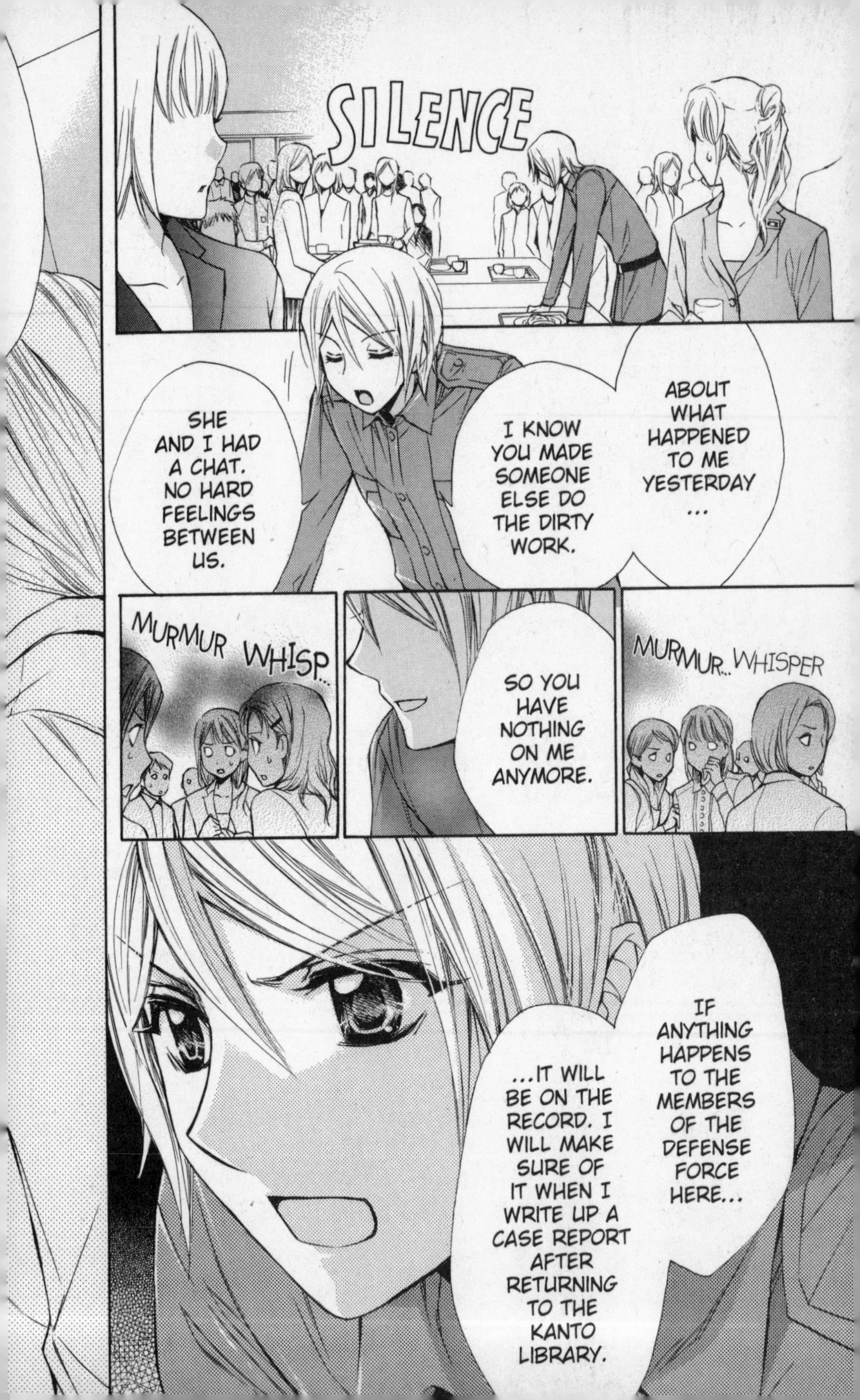
SILENCE
ABOUT WHAT HAPPENED TO ME YESTERDAY...
I KNOW YOU MADE SOMEONE ELSE DO THE DIRTY WORK.
SHE AND I HAD A CHAT. NO HARD FEELINGS BETWEEN US.
MURMUR... WHISPER
SO YOU HAVE NOTHING ON ME ANYMORE.
MURMUR WHISP...
IF ANYTHING HAPPENS TO THE MEMBERS OF THE DEFENSE FORCE HERE...
...IT WILL BE ON THE RECORD. I WILL MAKE SURE OF IT WHEN I WRITE UP A CASE REPORT AFTER RETURNING TO THE KANTO LIBRARY.

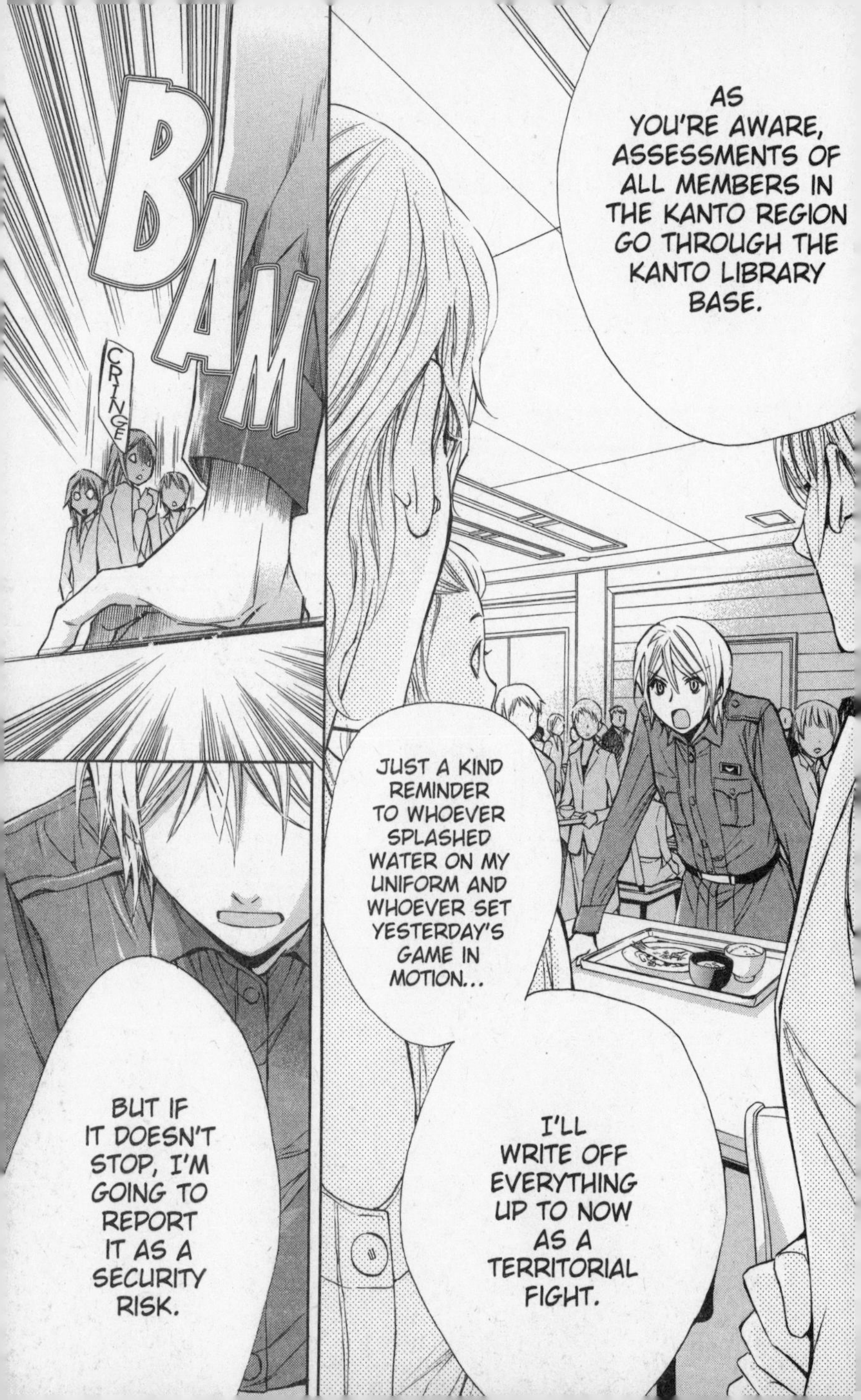
AS YOU'RE AWARE, ASSESSMENTS OF ALL MEMBERS IN THE KANTO REGION GO THROUGH THE KANTO LIBRARY BASE.
JUST A KIND REMINDER TO WHOEVER SPLASHED WATER ON MY UNIFORM AND WHOEVER SET YESTERDAY'S GAME IN MOTION...
I'LL WRITE OFF EVERYTHING UP TO NOW AS A TERRITORIAL FIGHT.
BAM
CRINGE
BUT IF IT DOESN'T STOP, I'M GOING TO REPORT IT AS A SECURITY RISK.

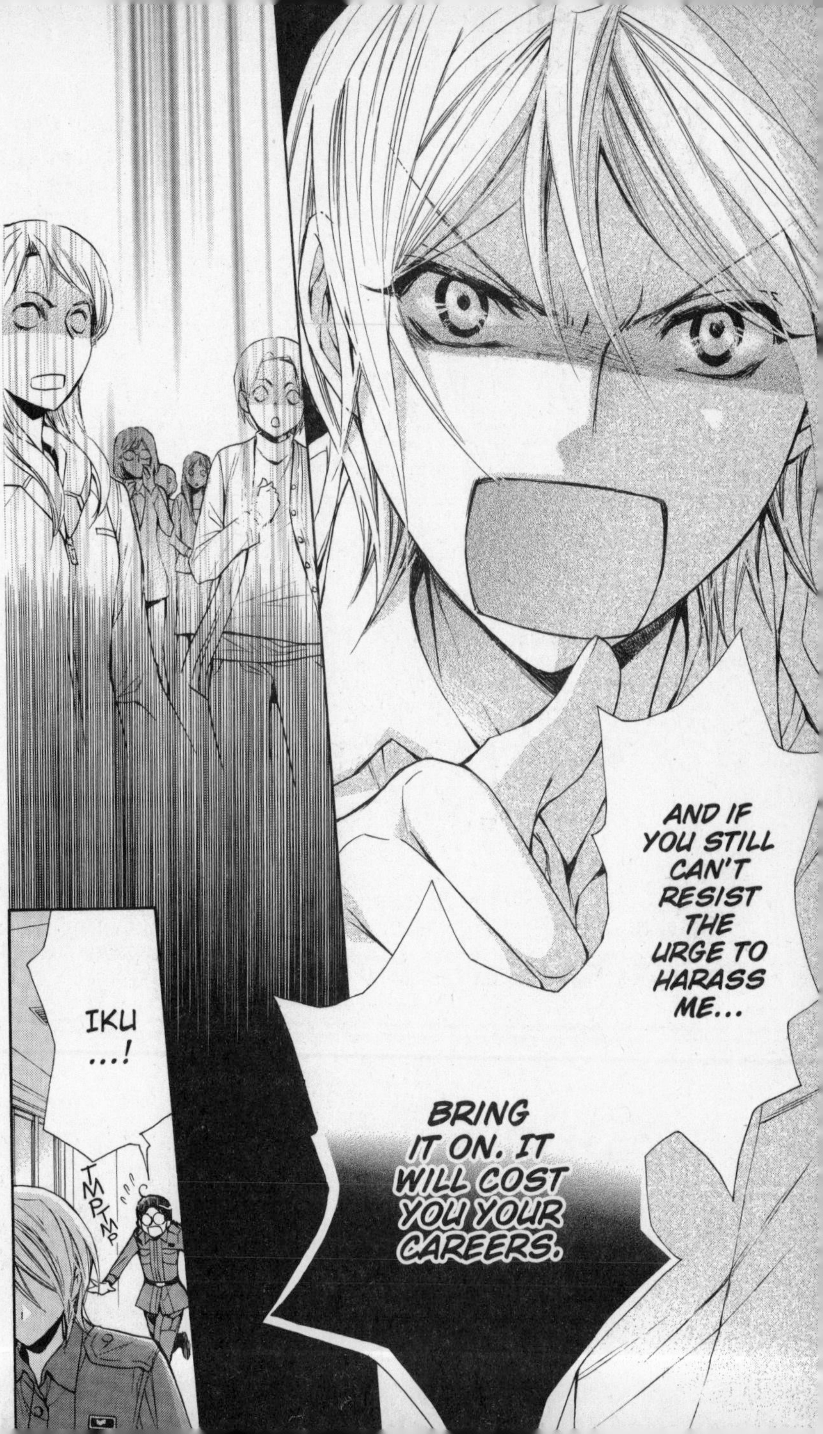
AND IF YOU STILL CAN'T RESIST THE URGE TO HARASS ME...
BRING IT ON. IT WILL COST YOU YOUR CAREERS.
IKU ...!
TMP TMP

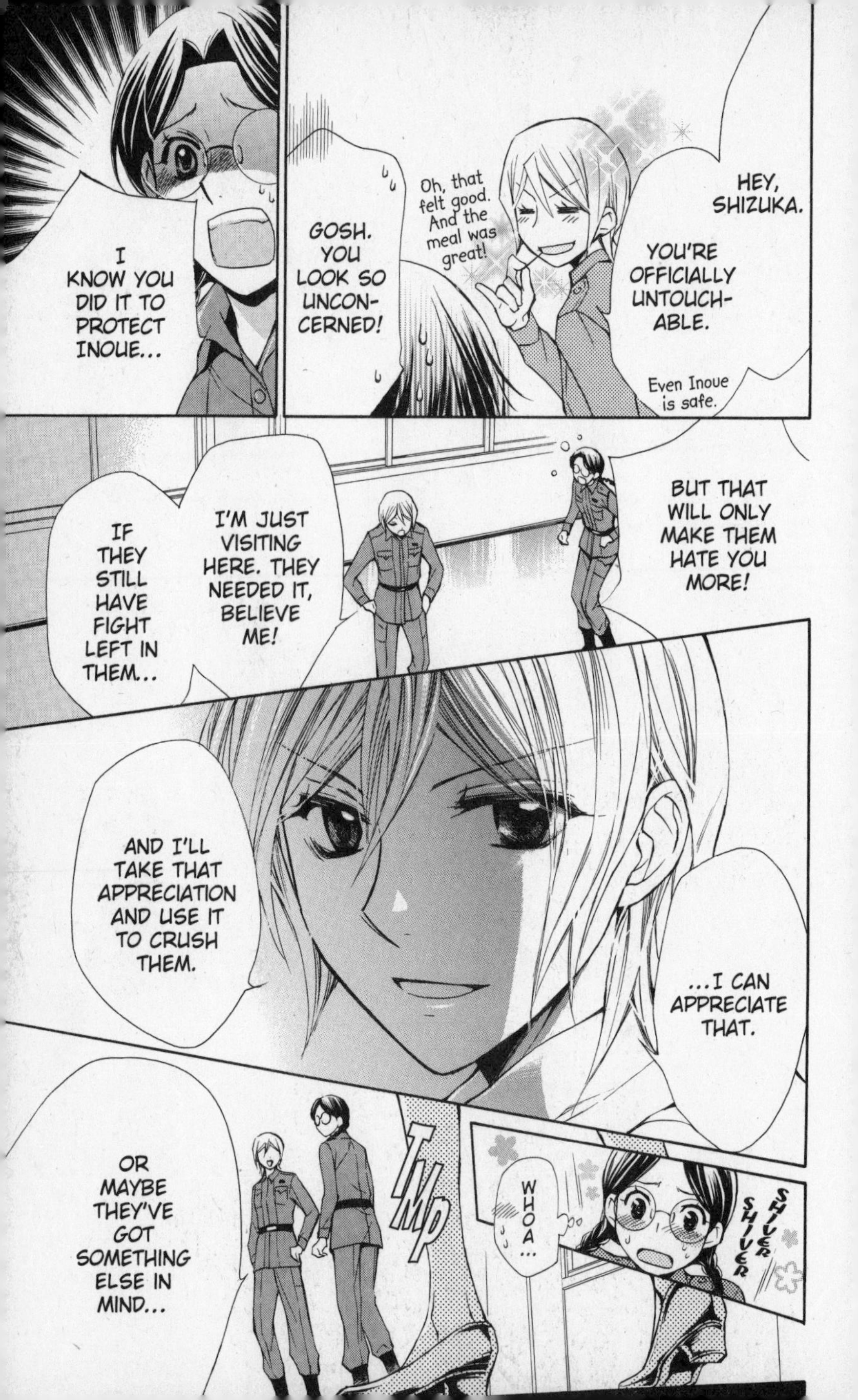
HEY, SHIZUKA.
YOU'RE OFFICIALLY UNTOUCH-ABLE.
Even Inoue is safe.
Oh, that felt good. And the meal was great!
GOSH. YOU LOOK SO UNCON-CERNED!
I KNOW YOU DID IT TO PROTECT INOUE...
BUT THAT WILL ONLY MAKE THEM HATE YOU MORE!
I'M JUST VISITING HERE. THEY NEEDED IT, BELIEVE ME!
IF THEY STILL HAVE FIGHT LEFT IN THEM...
...I CAN APPRECIATE THAT.
AND I'LL TAKE THAT APPRECIATION AND USE IT TO CRUSH THEM.
SHIVER SHIVER
WHOA...
TMP
OR MAYBE THEY'VE GOT SOMETHING ELSE IN MIND...

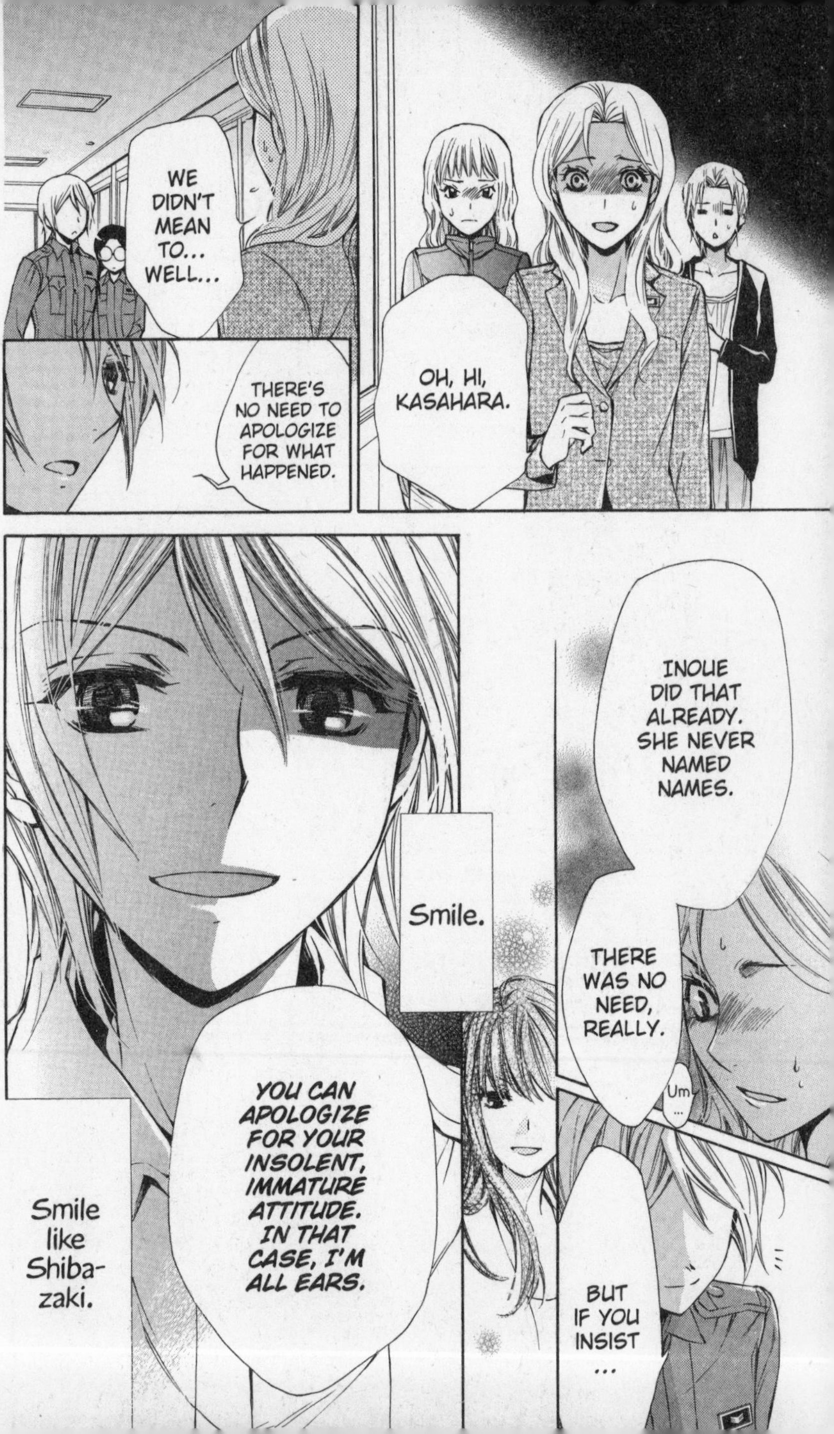
OH, HI, KASAHARA.
WE DIDN'T MEAN TO... WELL...
THERE'S NO NEED TO APOLOGIZE FOR WHAT HAPPENED.
INOUE DID THAT ALREADY. SHE NEVER NAMED NAMES.
THERE WAS NO NEED, REALLY.
Um...
BUT IF YOU INSIST...
Smile.
YOU CAN APOLOGIZE FOR YOUR INSOLENT, IMMATURE ATTITUDE. IN THAT CASE, I'M ALL EARS.
Smile like Shibazaki.

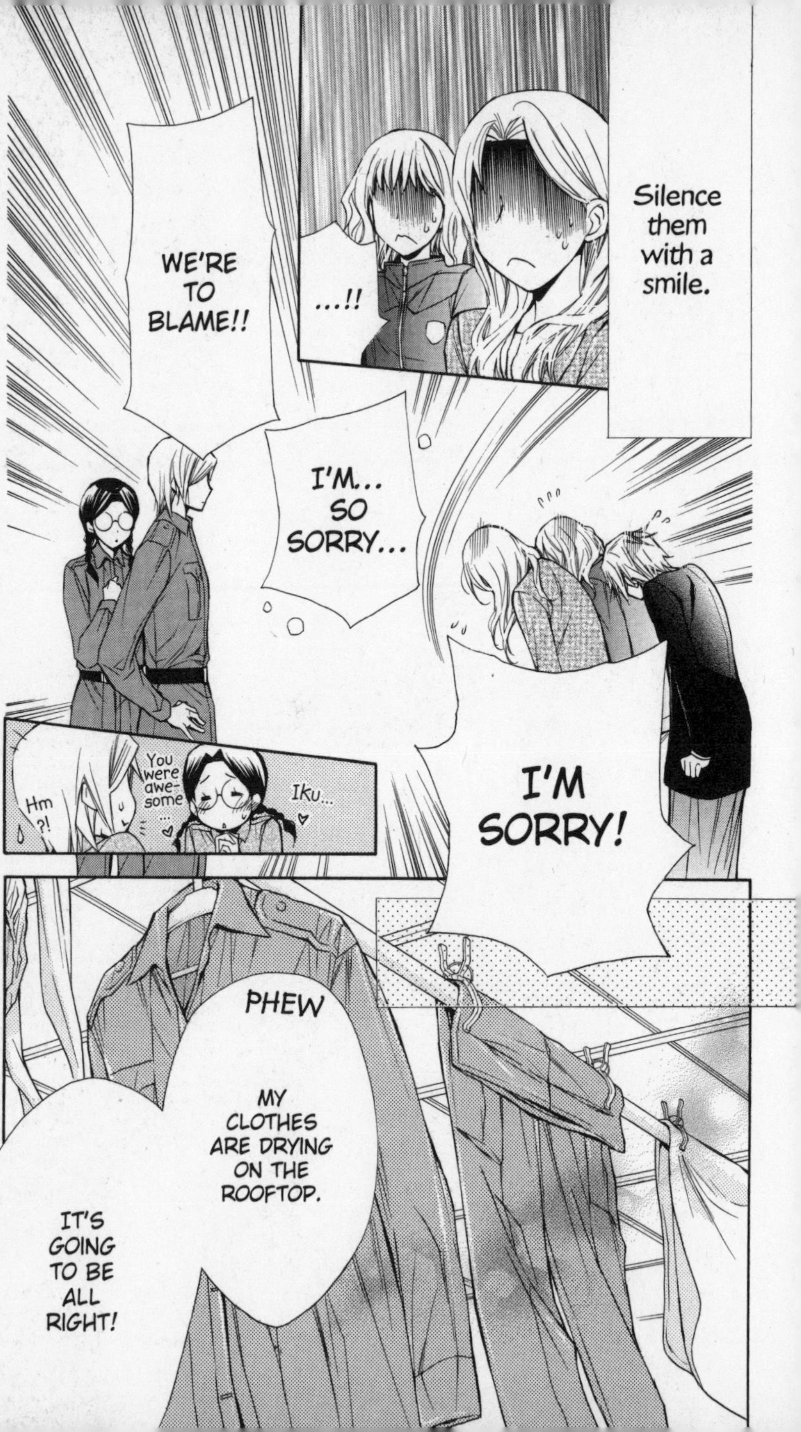
Silence them with a smile.
...!!
WE'RE TO BLAME!!
I'M... SO SORRY...
I'M SORRY!
Iku...
You were awe-some...
Hm ?!
PHEW
MY CLOTHES ARE DRYING ON THE ROOFTOP.
IT'S GOING TO BE ALL RIGHT!

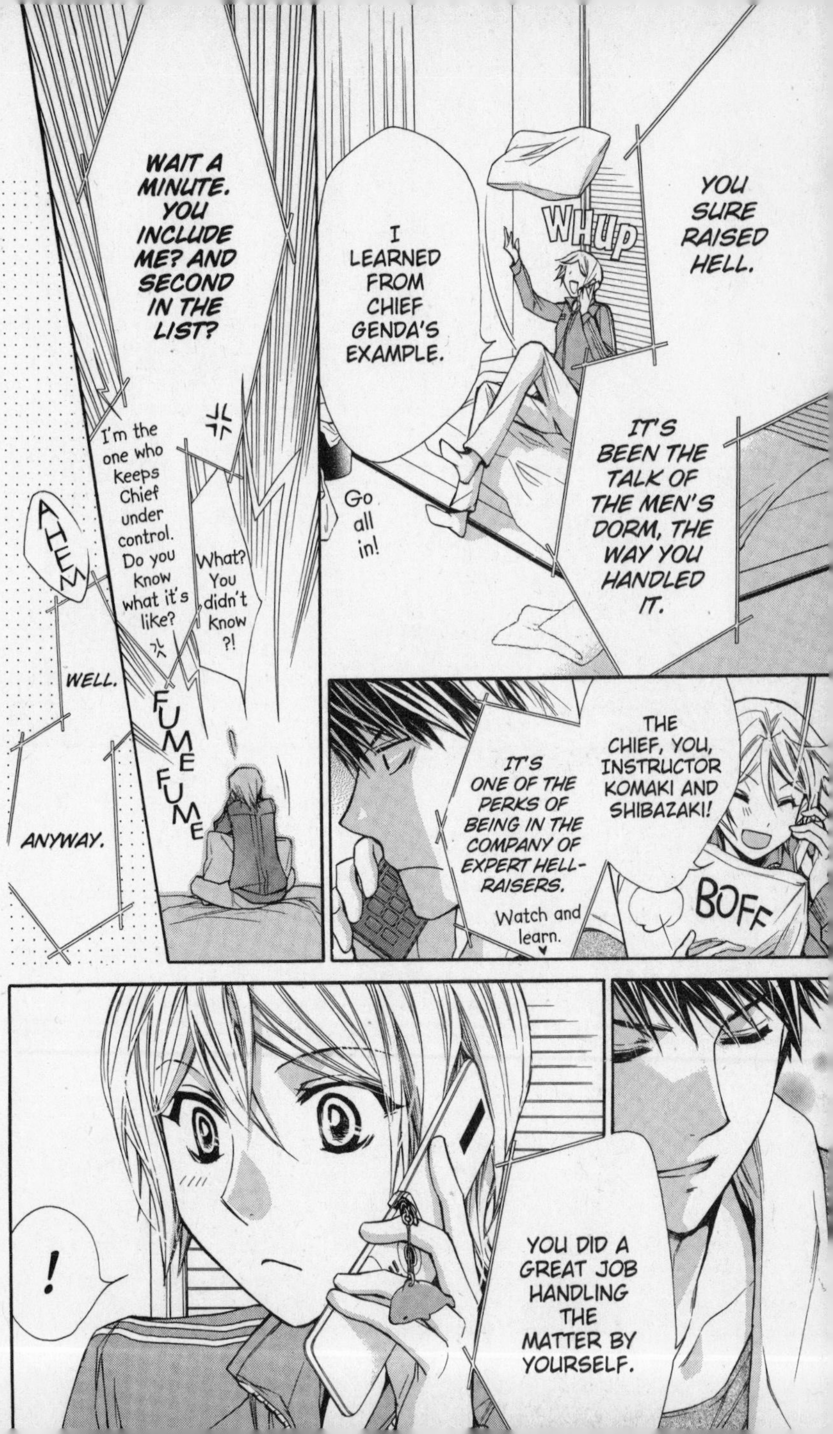
YOU SURE RAISED HELL.
WHUP
I LEARNED FROM CHIEF GENDA'S EXAMPLE.
IT'S BEEN THE TALK OF THE MEN'S DORM, THE WAY YOU HANDLED IT.
Go all in!
WAIT A MINUTE. YOU INCLUDE ME? AND SECOND IN THE LIST?
What? You didn't know?!
I'm the one who keeps Chief under control. Do you know what it's like?
AHEM
WELL.
FUME FUME
ANYWAY.
THE CHIEF, YOU, INSTRUCTOR KOMAKI AND SHIBAZAKI!
BOFF
IT'S ONE OF THE PERKS OF BEING IN THE COMPANY OF EXPERT HELL-RAISERS.
Watch and learn.
YOU DID A GREAT JOB HANDLING THE MATTER BY YOURSELF.
!

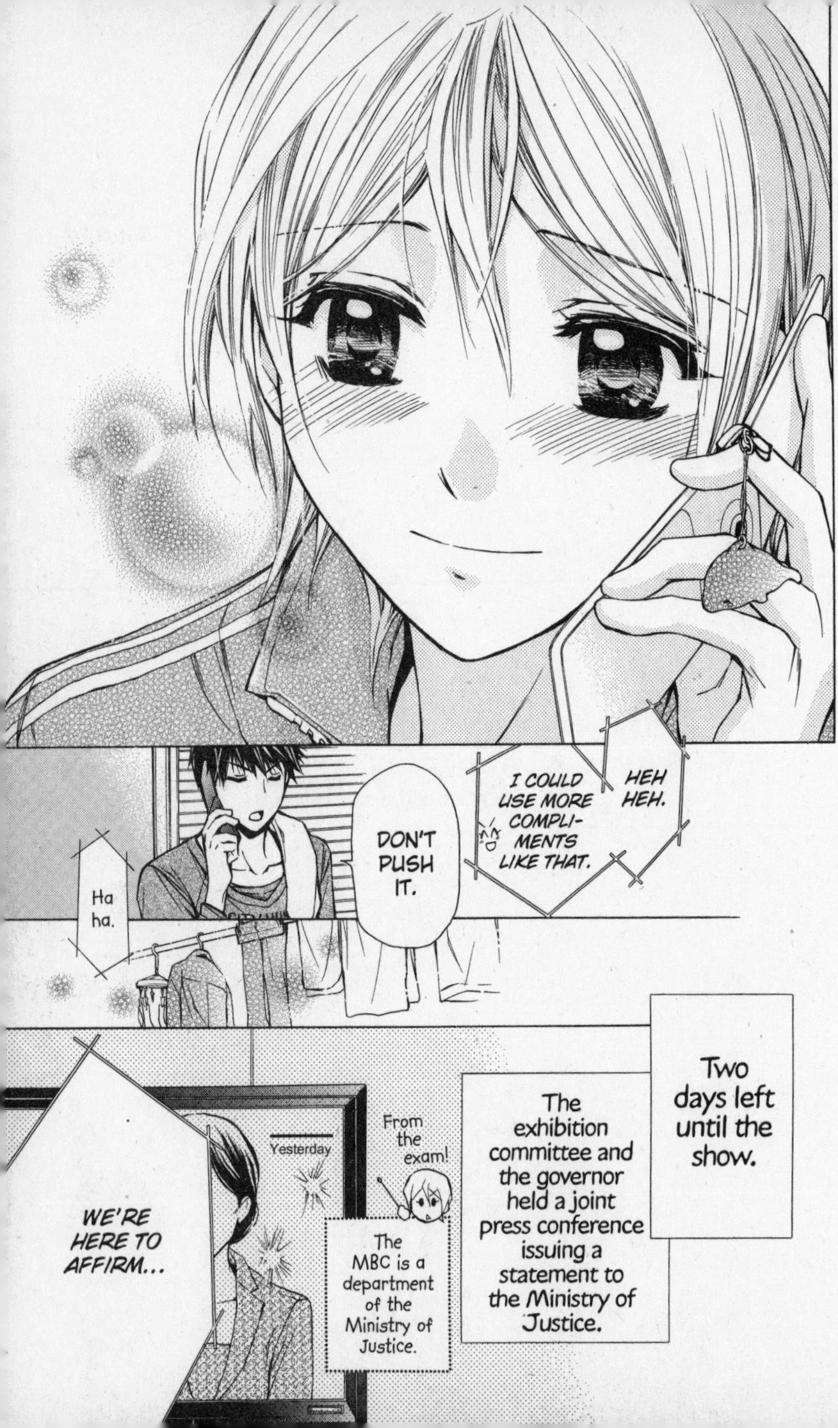
HEH HEH.
I COULD USE MORE COMPLI-MENTS LIKE THAT.
DON'T PUSH IT.
Ha ha.
Two days left until the show.
The exhibition committee and the governor held a joint press conference issuing a statement to the Ministry of Justice.
From the exam!
The MBC is a department of the Ministry of Justice.
Yesterday
WE'RE HERE TO AFFIRM...

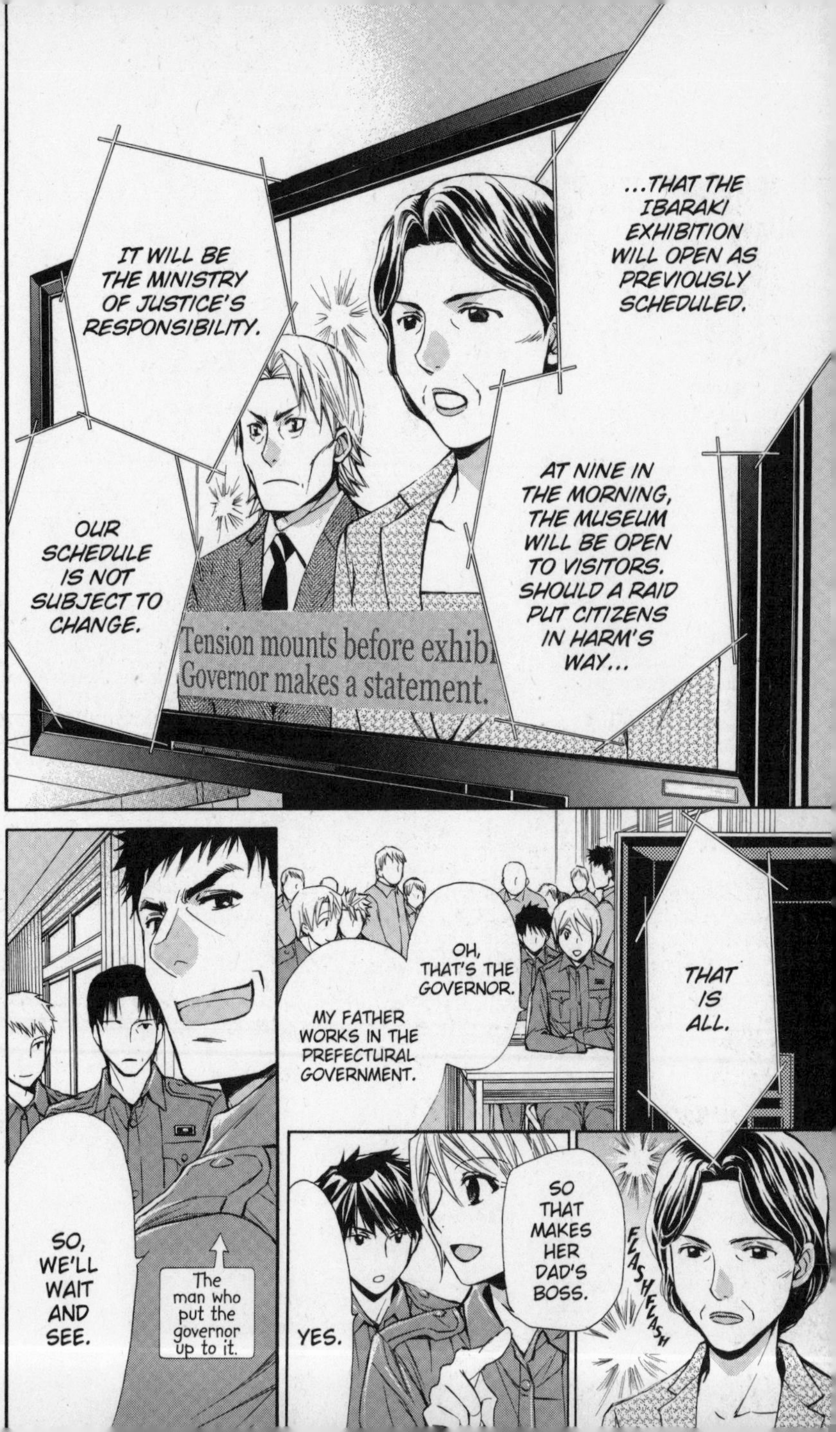
...THAT THE IBARAKI EXHIBITION WILL OPEN AS PREVIOUSLY SCHEDULED.
IT WILL BE THE MINISTRY OF JUSTICE'S RESPONSIBILITY.
AT NINE IN THE MORNING, THE MUSEUM WILL BE OPEN TO VISITORS. SHOULD A RAID PUT CITIZENS IN HARM'S WAY...
OUR SCHEDULE IS NOT SUBJECT TO CHANGE.
Tension mounts before exhibi
Governor makes a statement.
THAT IS ALL.
OH, THAT'S THE GOVERNOR.
MY FATHER WORKS IN THE PREFECTURAL GOVERNMENT.
SO, WE'LL WAIT AND SEE.
The man who put the governor up to it.
FLASH FLASH
SO THAT MAKES HER DAD'S BOSS.
YES.

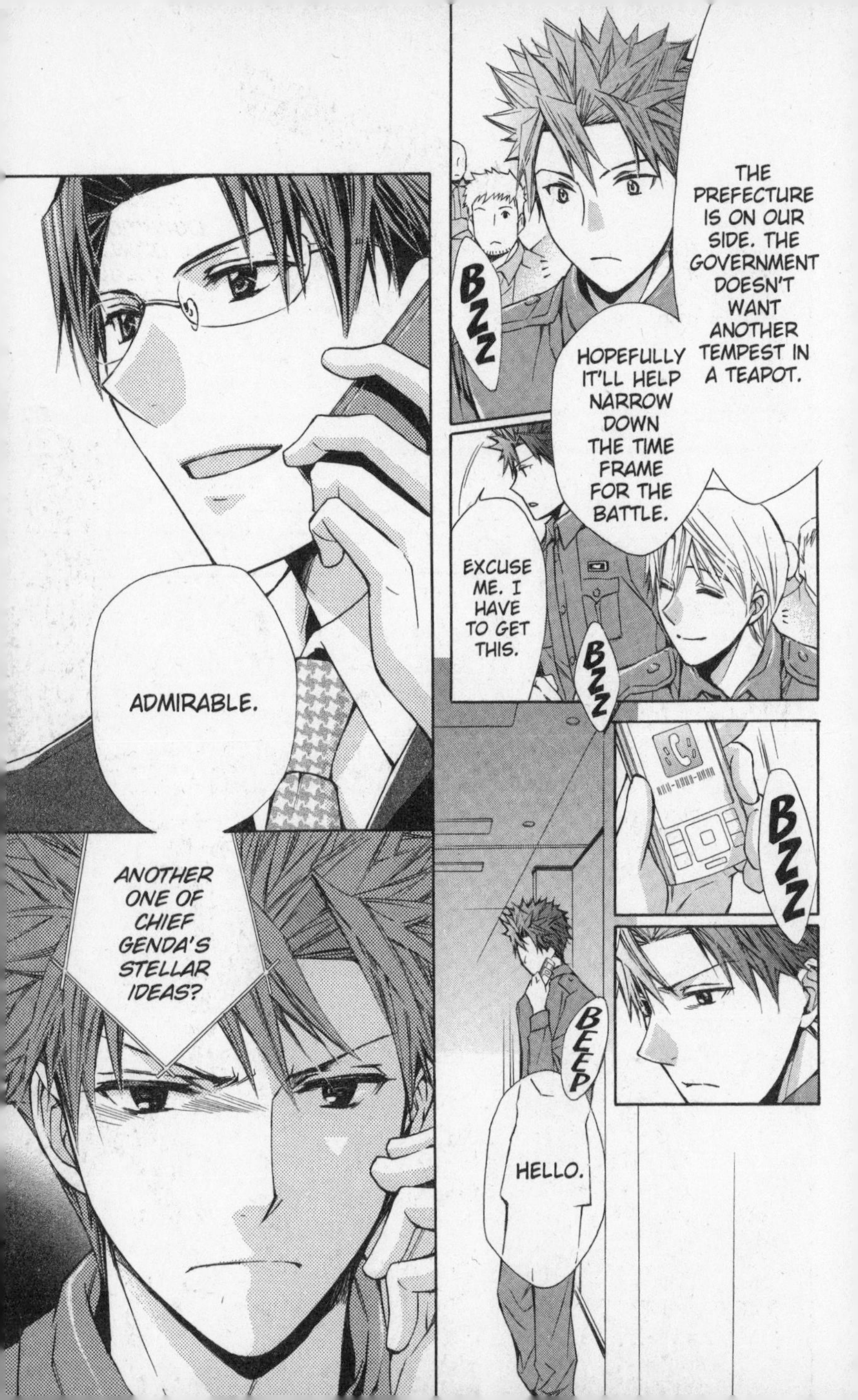
THE PREFECTURE IS ON OUR SIDE. THE GOVERNMENT DOESN'T WANT ANOTHER TEMPEST IN A TEAPOT.
BZZ
HOPEFULLY IT'LL HELP NARROW DOWN THE TIME FRAME FOR THE BATTLE.
EXCUSE ME. I HAVE TO GET THIS.
BZZ
BZZ
BEEP
HELLO.
ADMIRABLE.
ANOTHER ONE OF CHIEF GENDA'S STELLAR IDEAS?

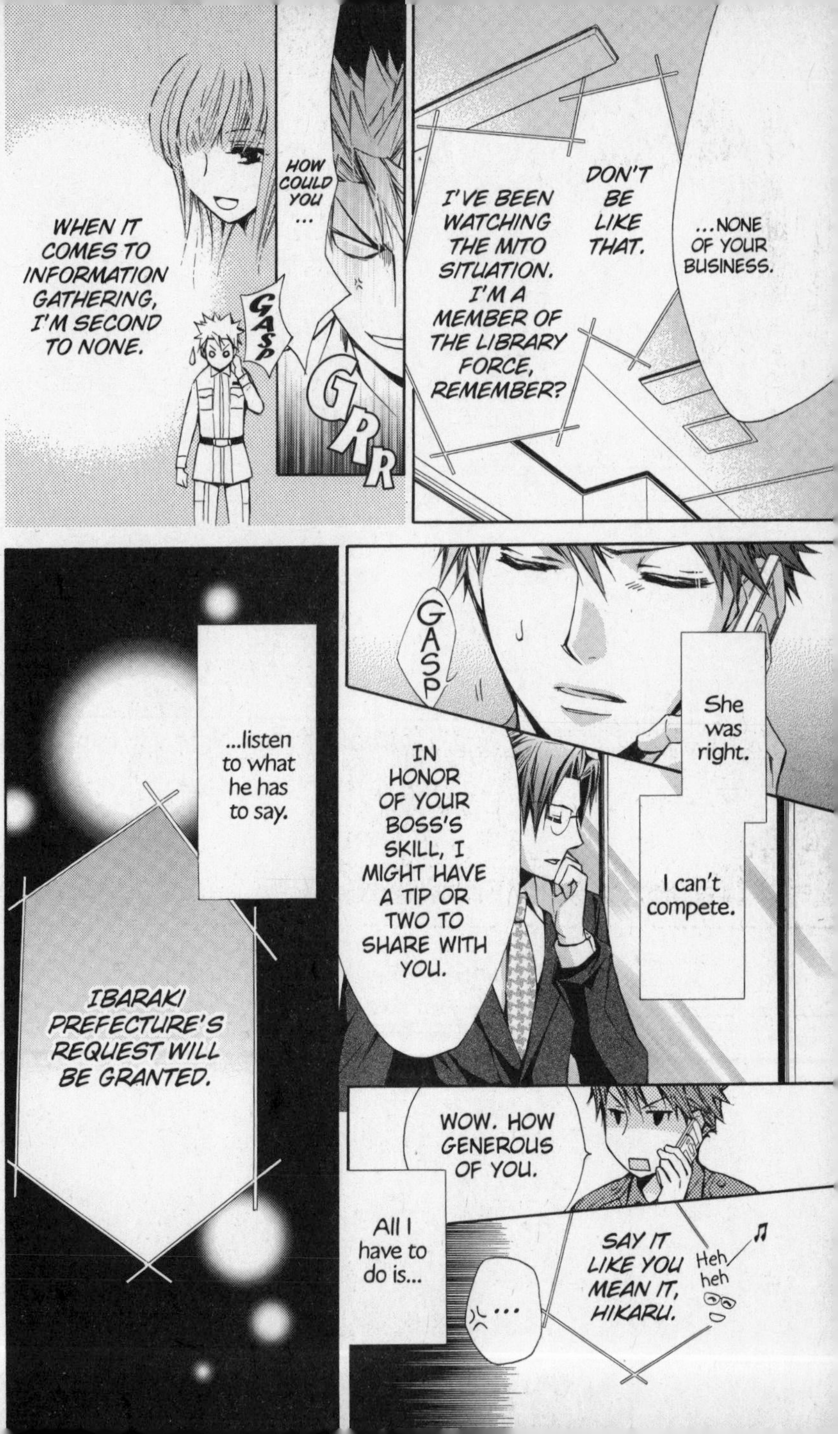
...NONE OF YOUR BUSINESS.
DON'T BE LIKE THAT.
I'VE BEEN WATCHING THE MITO SITUATION. I'M A MEMBER OF THE LIBRARY FORCE, REMEMBER?
HOW COULD YOU ...
GASP
GRR
WHEN IT COMES TO INFORMATION GATHERING, I'M SECOND TO NONE.
She was right.
GASP
I can't compete.
IN HONOR OF YOUR BOSS'S SKILL, I MIGHT HAVE A TIP OR TWO TO SHARE WITH YOU.
WOW. HOW GENEROUS OF YOU.
SAY IT LIKE YOU MEAN IT, HIKARU.
Heh heh
...
All I have to do is...
...listen to what he has to say.
IBARAKI PREFECTURE'S REQUEST WILL BE GRANTED.

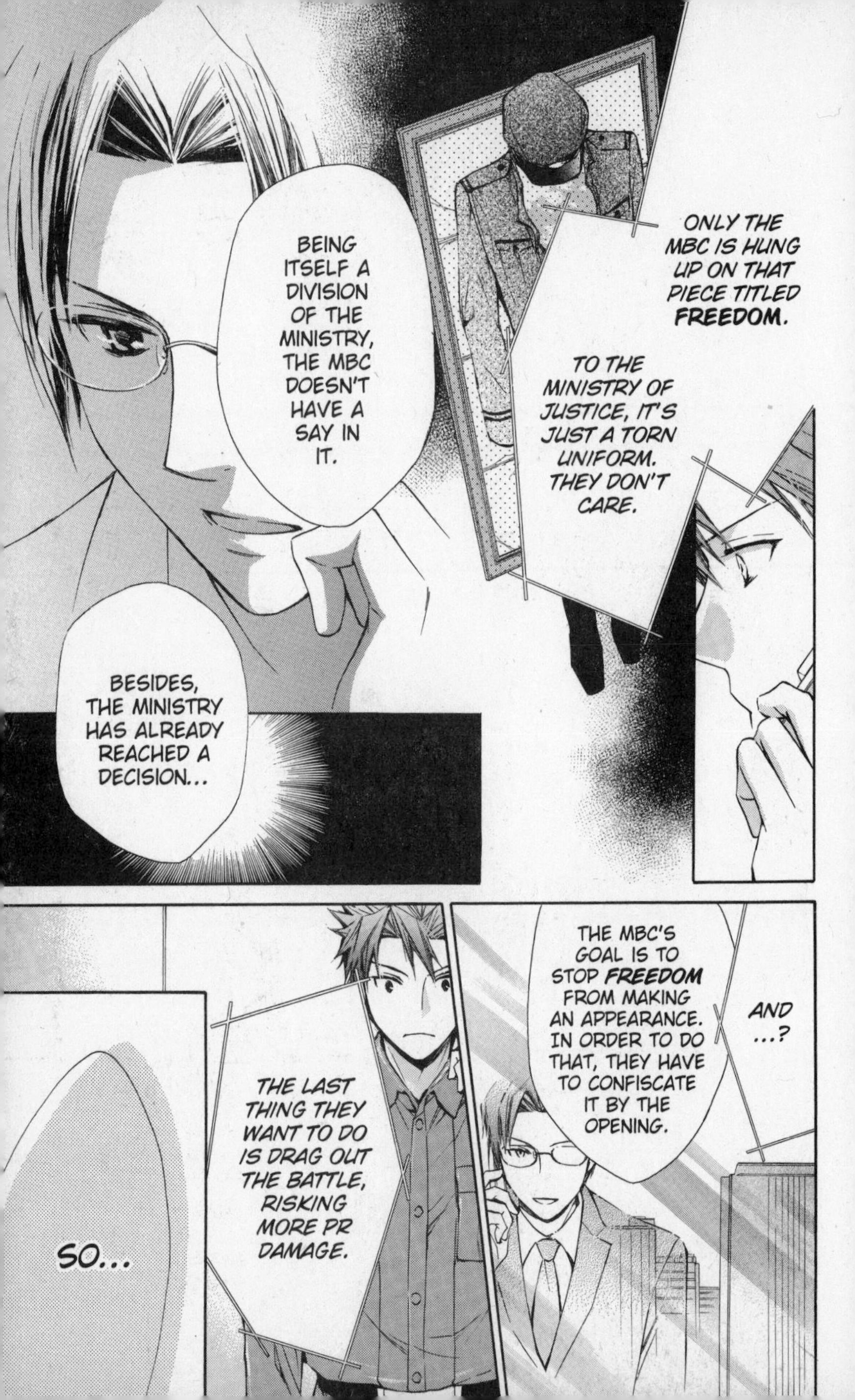
ONLY THE MBC IS HUNG UP ON THAT PIECE TITLED **FREEDOM.**
TO THE MINISTRY OF JUSTICE, IT'S JUST A TORN UNIFORM. THEY DON'T CARE.
BEING ITSELF A DIVISION OF THE MINISTRY, THE MBC DOESN'T HAVE A SAY IN IT.
BESIDES, THE MINISTRY HAS ALREADY REACHED A DECISION...
AND ...?
THE MBC'S GOAL IS TO STOP **FREEDOM** FROM MAKING AN APPEARANCE. IN ORDER TO DO THAT, THEY HAVE TO CONFISCATE IT BY THE OPENING.
THE LAST THING THEY WANT TO DO IS DRAG OUT THE BATTLE, RISKING MORE PR DAMAGE.
SO...

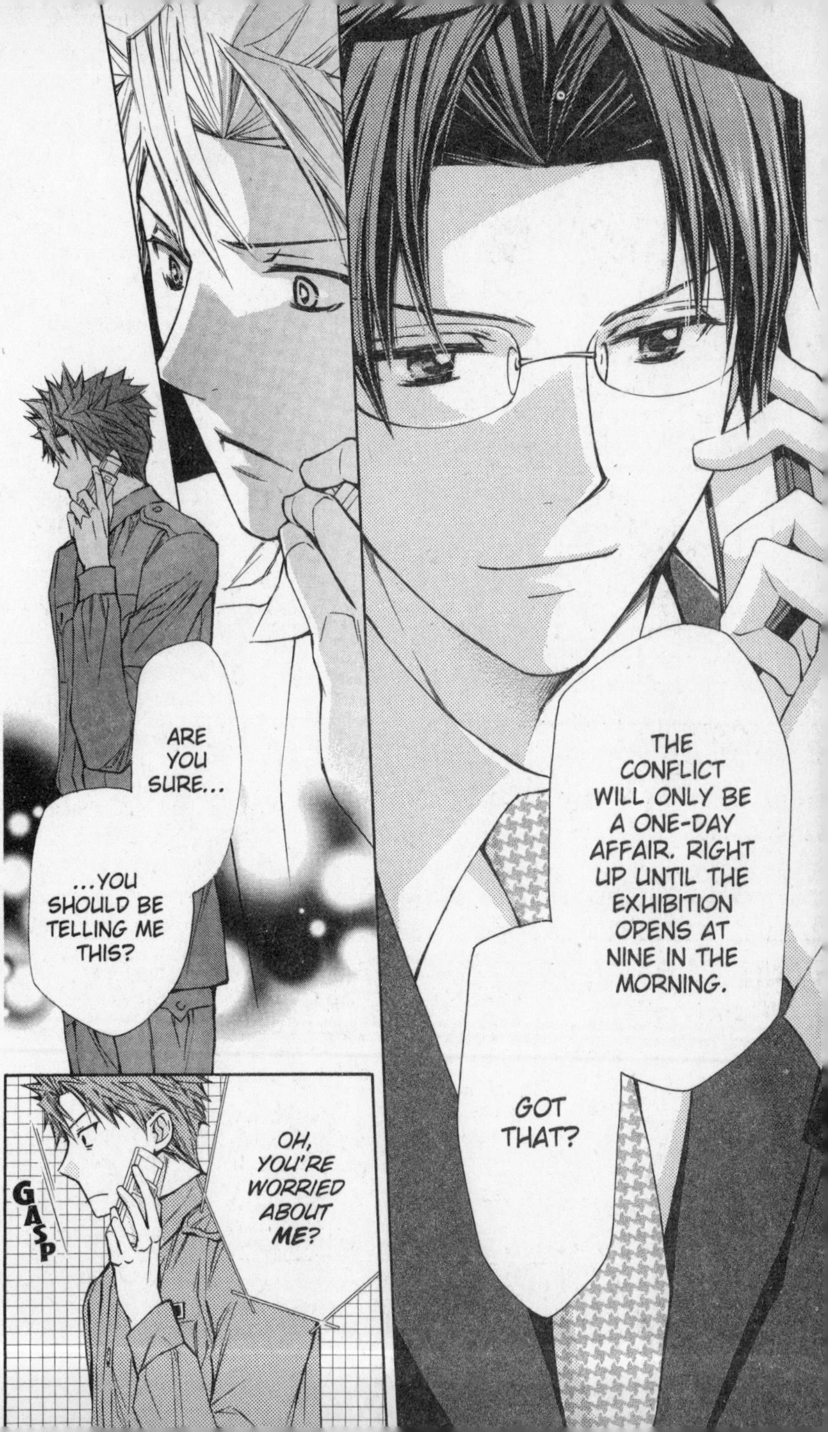
THE CONFLICT WILL ONLY BE A ONE-DAY AFFAIR. RIGHT UP UNTIL THE EXHIBITION OPENS AT NINE IN THE MORNING.
GOT THAT?
ARE YOU SURE...
...YOU SHOULD BE TELLING ME THIS?
GASP
OH, YOU'RE WORRIED ABOUT ME?

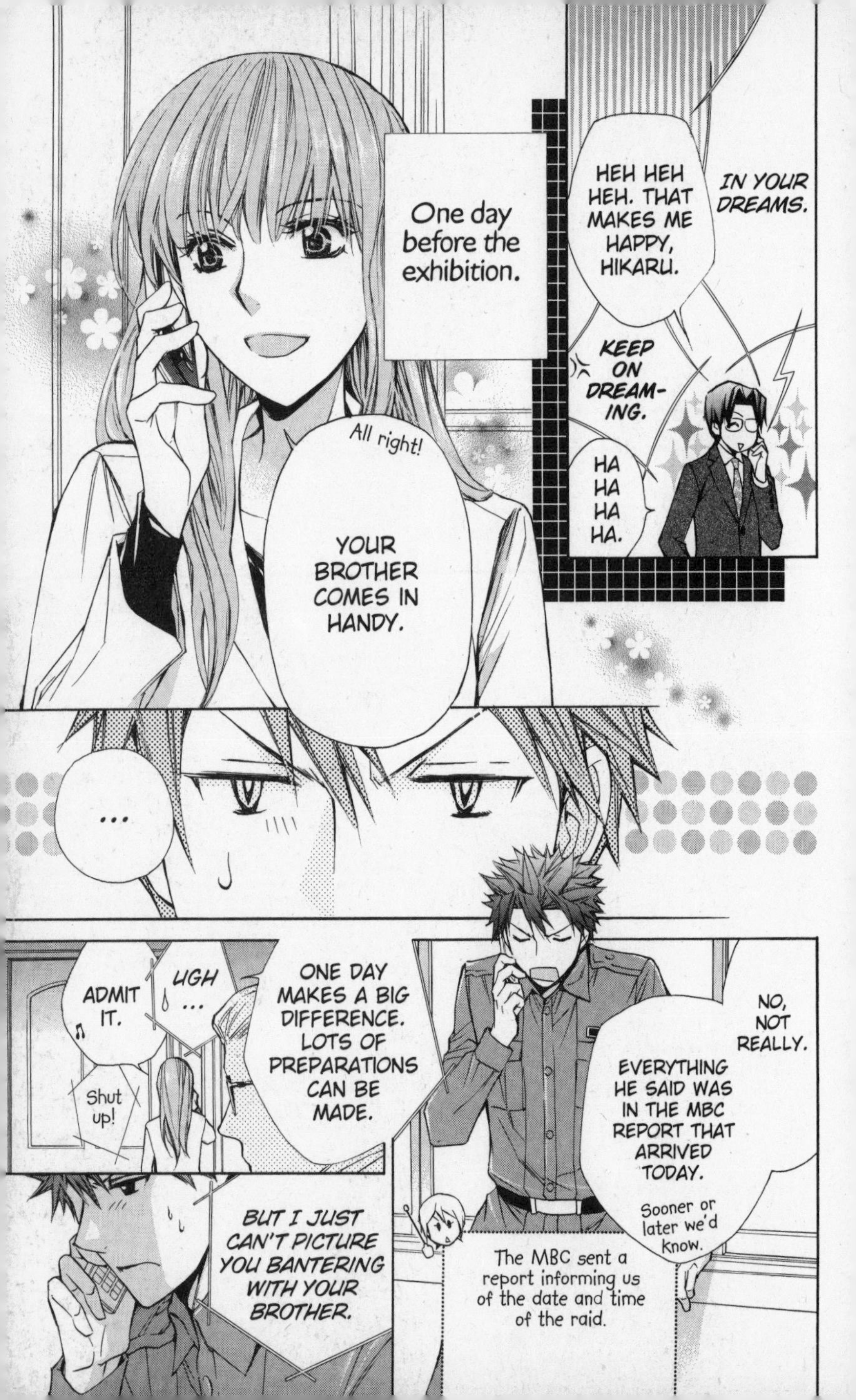
HEH HEH HEH. THAT MAKES ME HAPPY, HIKARU.
IN YOUR DREAMS.
KEEP ON DREAM-ING.
HA HA HA HA.
One day before the exhibition.
All right!
YOUR BROTHER COMES IN HANDY.
...
NO, NOT REALLY.
EVERYTHING HE SAID WAS IN THE MBC REPORT THAT ARRIVED TODAY.
Sooner or later we'd know.
The MBC sent a report informing us of the date and time of the raid.
ONE DAY MAKES A BIG DIFFERENCE. LOTS OF PREPARATIONS CAN BE MADE.
UGH ...
ADMIT IT.
Shut up!
BUT I JUST CAN'T PICTURE YOU BANTERING WITH YOUR BROTHER.

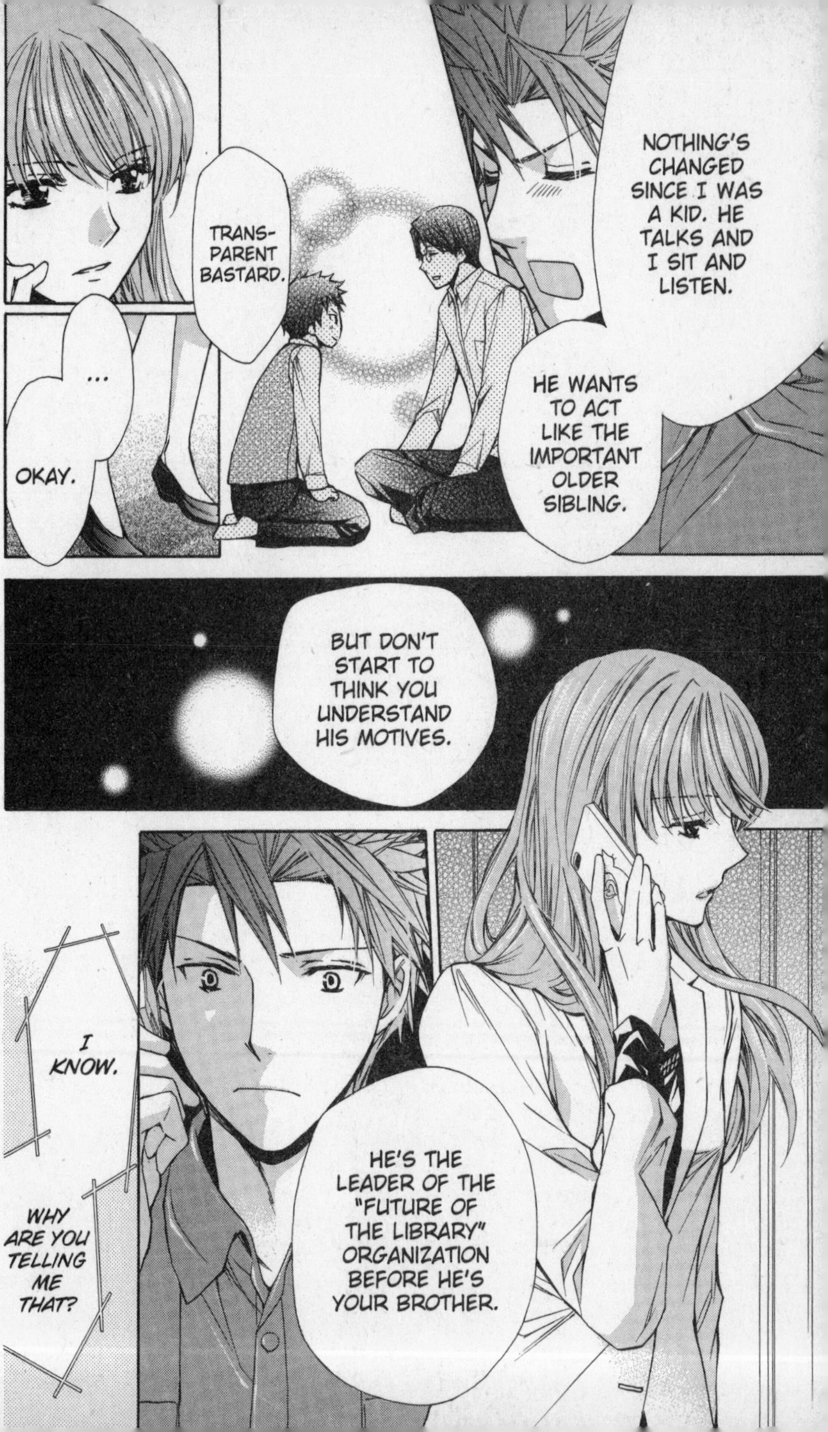
NOTHING'S CHANGED SINCE I WAS A KID. HE TALKS AND I SIT AND LISTEN.
HE WANTS TO ACT LIKE THE IMPORTANT OLDER SIBLING.
TRANS-PARENT BASTARD.
...
OKAY.
BUT DON'T START TO THINK YOU UNDERSTAND HIS MOTIVES.
HE'S THE LEADER OF THE "FUTURE OF THE LIBRARY" ORGANIZATION BEFORE HE'S YOUR BROTHER.
I KNOW.
WHY ARE YOU TELLING ME THAT?

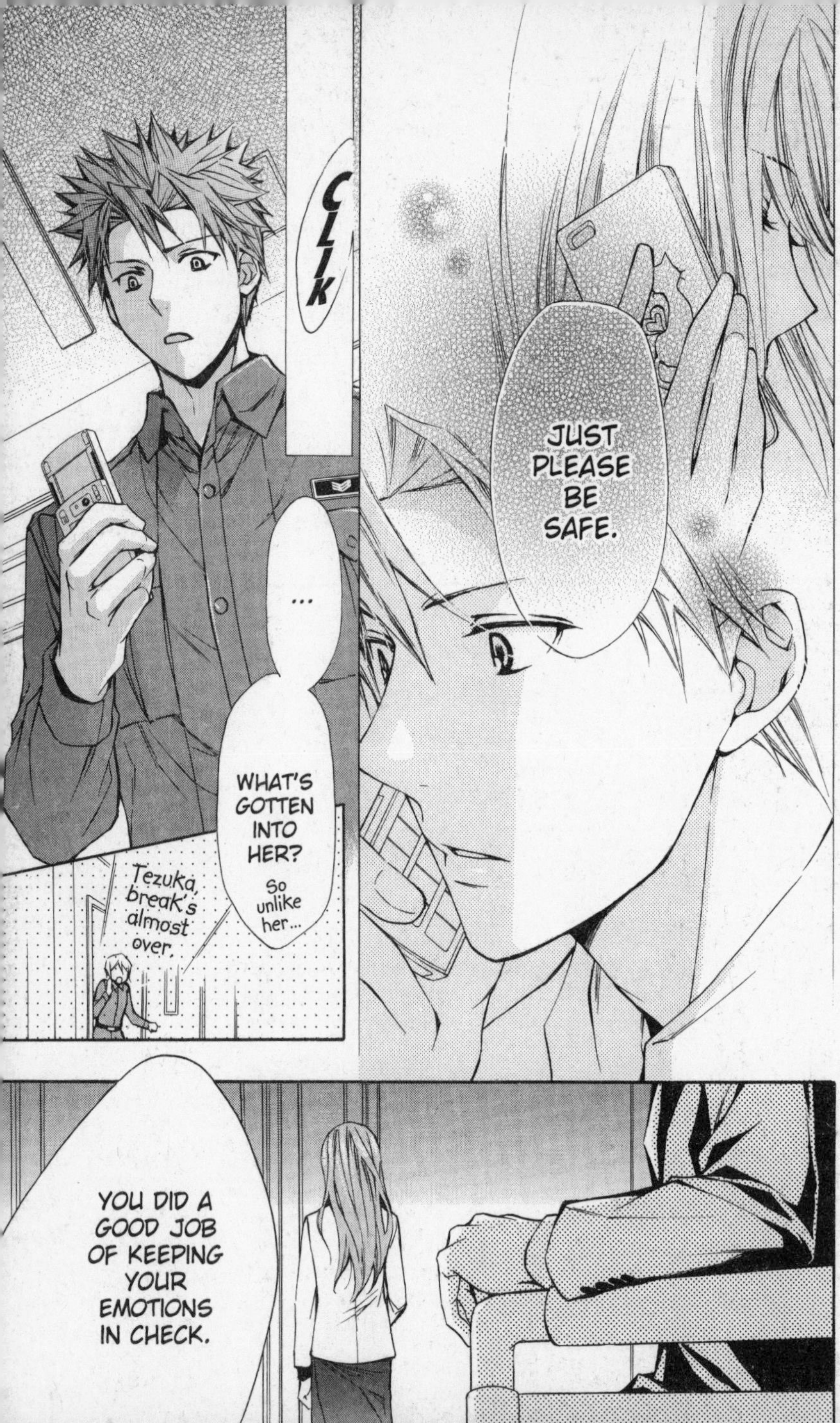
JUST PLEASE BE SAFE.
CLIK
...
WHAT'S GOTTEN INTO HER?
So unlike her...
Tezuka, break's almost over.
YOU DID A GOOD JOB OF KEEPING YOUR EMOTIONS IN CHECK.

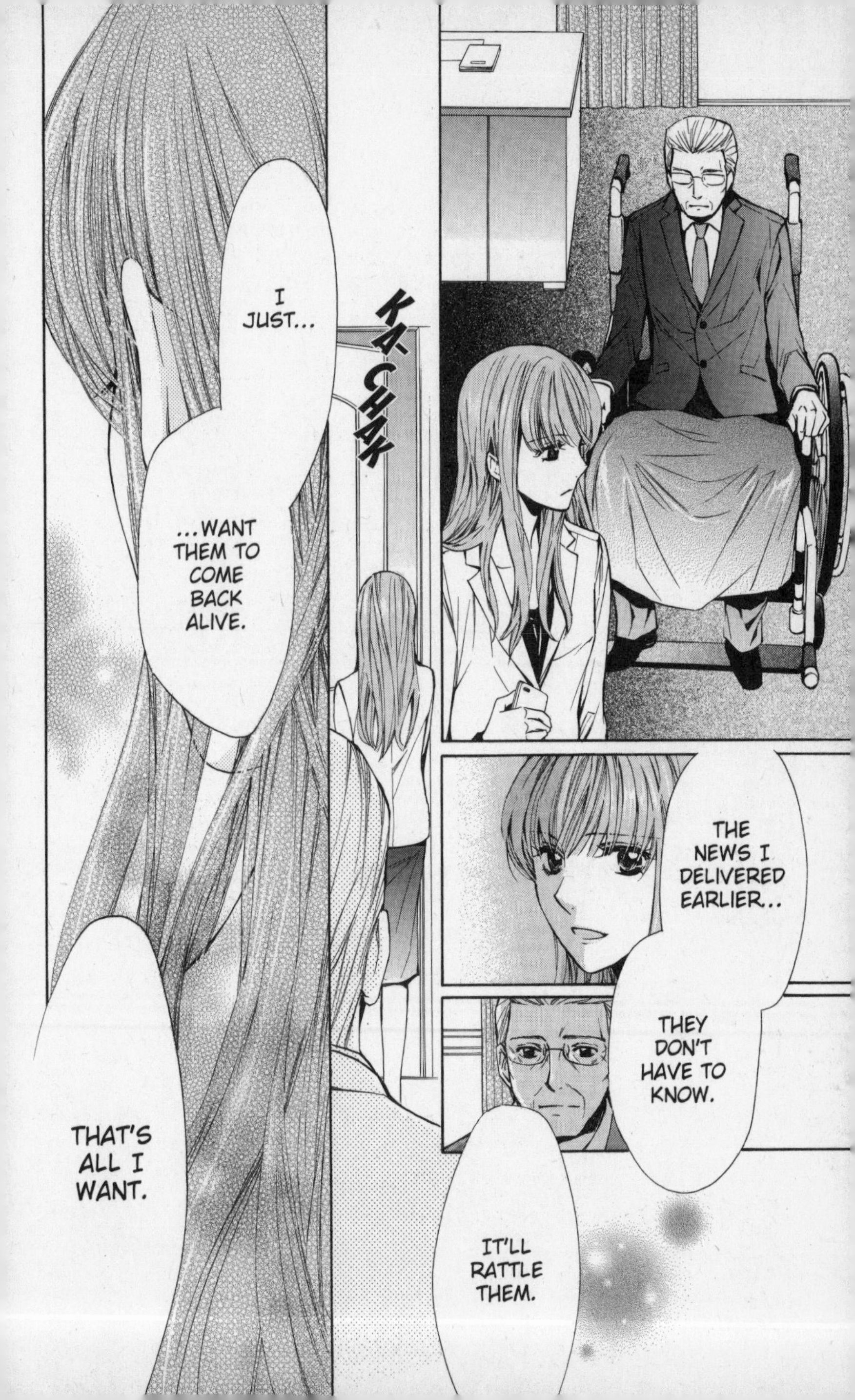
KA-CHAK
THE NEWS I DELIVERED EARLIER...
THEY DON'T HAVE TO KNOW.
IT'LL RATTLE THEM.
I JUST...
...WANT THEM TO COME BACK ALIVE.
THAT'S ALL I WANT.

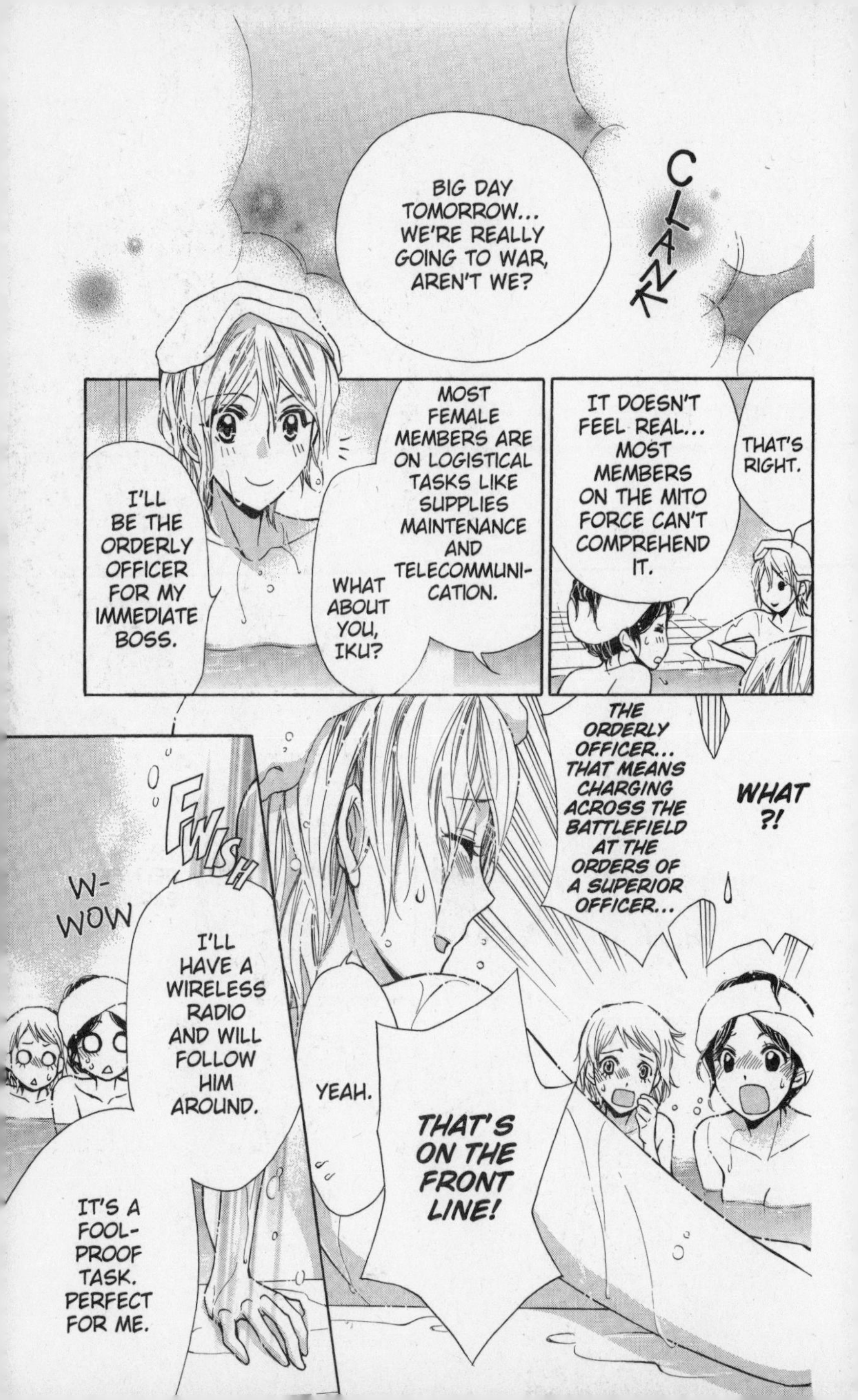
CLANK
BIG DAY TOMORROW... WE'RE REALLY GOING TO WAR, AREN'T WE?
IT DOESN'T FEEL REAL... MOST MEMBERS ON THE MITO FORCE CAN'T COMPREHEND IT.
THAT'S RIGHT.
MOST FEMALE MEMBERS ARE ON LOGISTICAL TASKS LIKE SUPPLIES MAINTENANCE AND TELECOMMUNI-CATION.
WHAT ABOUT YOU, IKU?
I'LL BE THE ORDERLY OFFICER FOR MY IMMEDIATE BOSS.
THE ORDERLY OFFICER... THAT MEANS CHARGING ACROSS THE BATTLEFIELD AT THE ORDERS OF A SUPERIOR OFFICER...
WHAT ?!
YEAH.
THAT'S ON THE FRONT LINE!
FWISH
I'LL HAVE A WIRELESS RADIO AND WILL FOLLOW HIM AROUND.
W-WOW
IT'S A FOOL-PROOF TASK. PERFECT FOR ME.

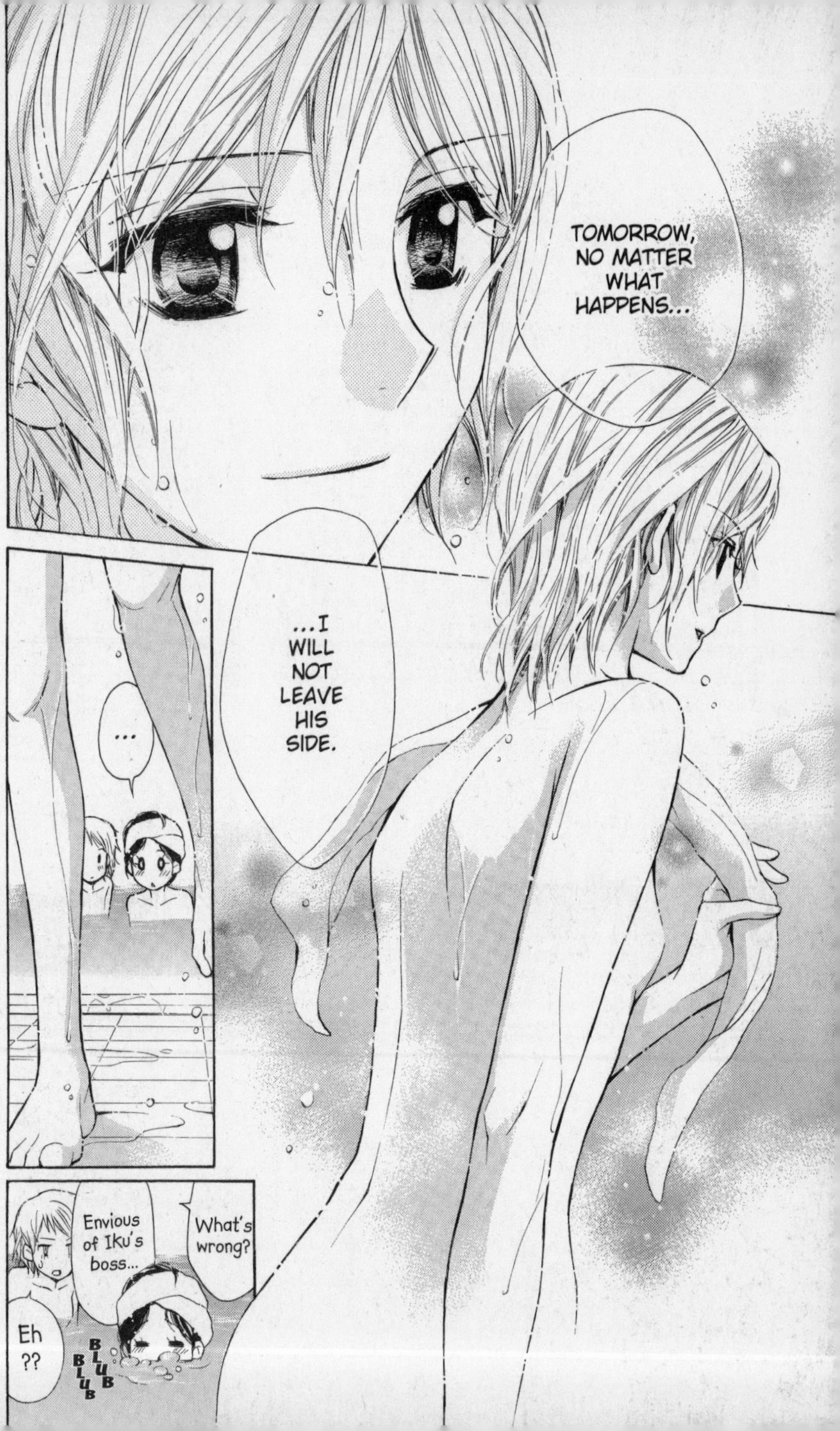
TOMORROW, NO MATTER WHAT HAPPENS...
...I WILL NOT LEAVE HIS SIDE.
...
What's wrong?
Envious of Iku's boss...
Eh ??
BLUB BLUB

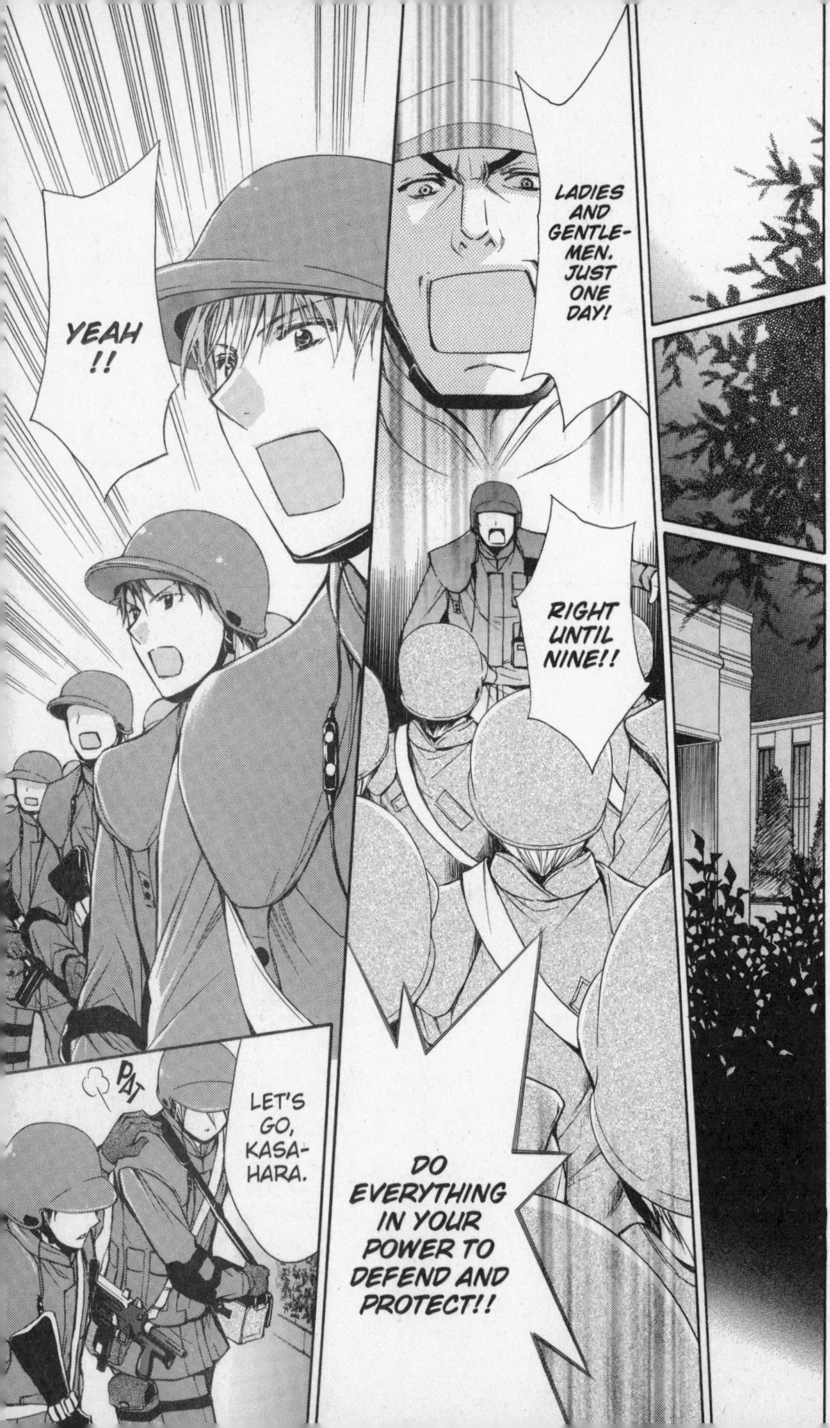
LADIES AND GENTLE-MEN. JUST ONE DAY!
RIGHT UNTIL NINE!!
DO EVERYTHING IN YOUR POWER TO DEFEND AND PROTECT!!
YEAH!!
PAT
LET'S GO, KASA-HARA.

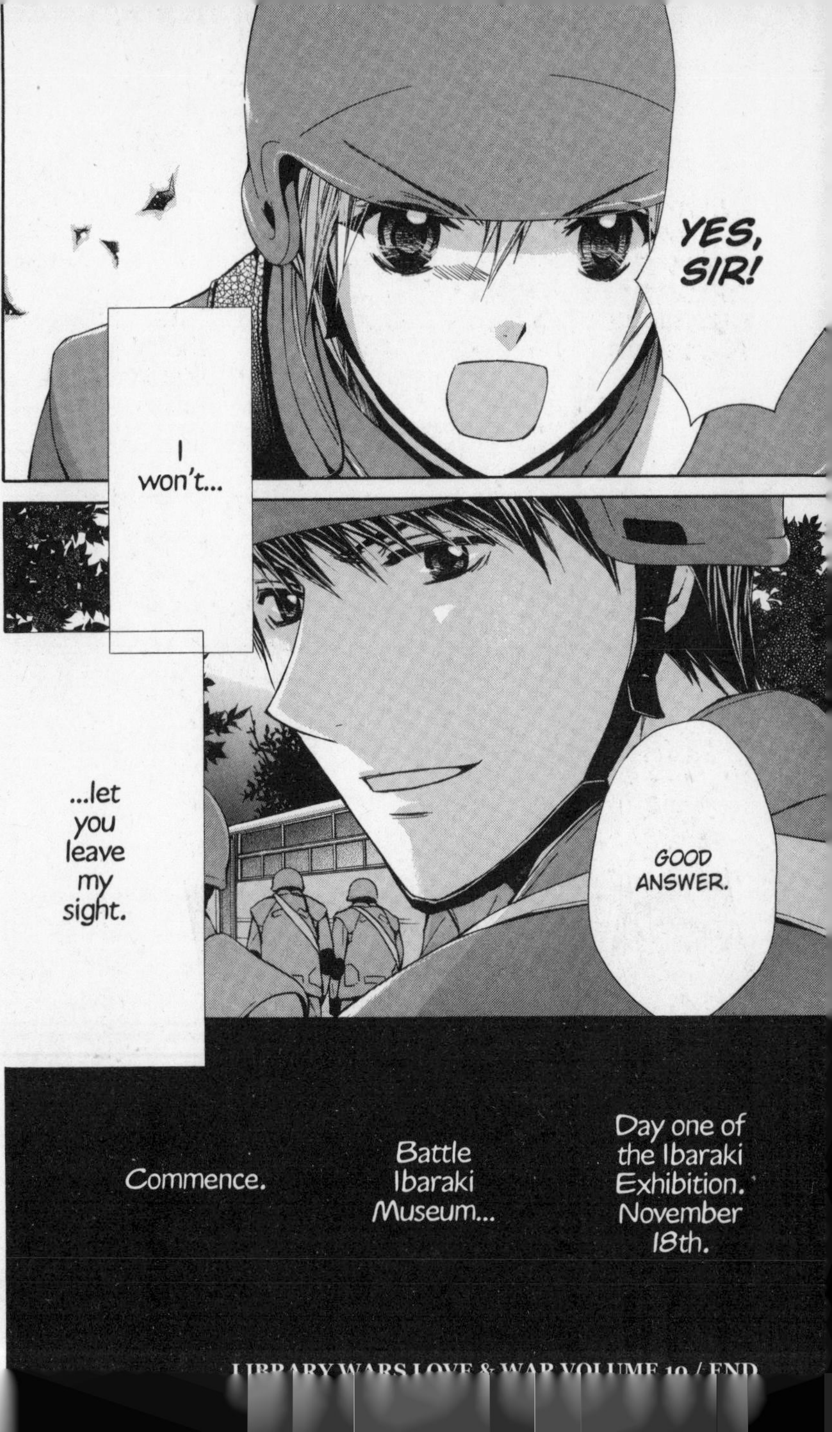
YES, SIR!
I won't...
...let you leave my sight.
GOOD ANSWER.
Day one of the Ibaraki Exhibition. November 18th.
Battle Ibaraki Museum...
Commence.
LIBRARY WARS LOVE & WAR VOLUME 10 / END

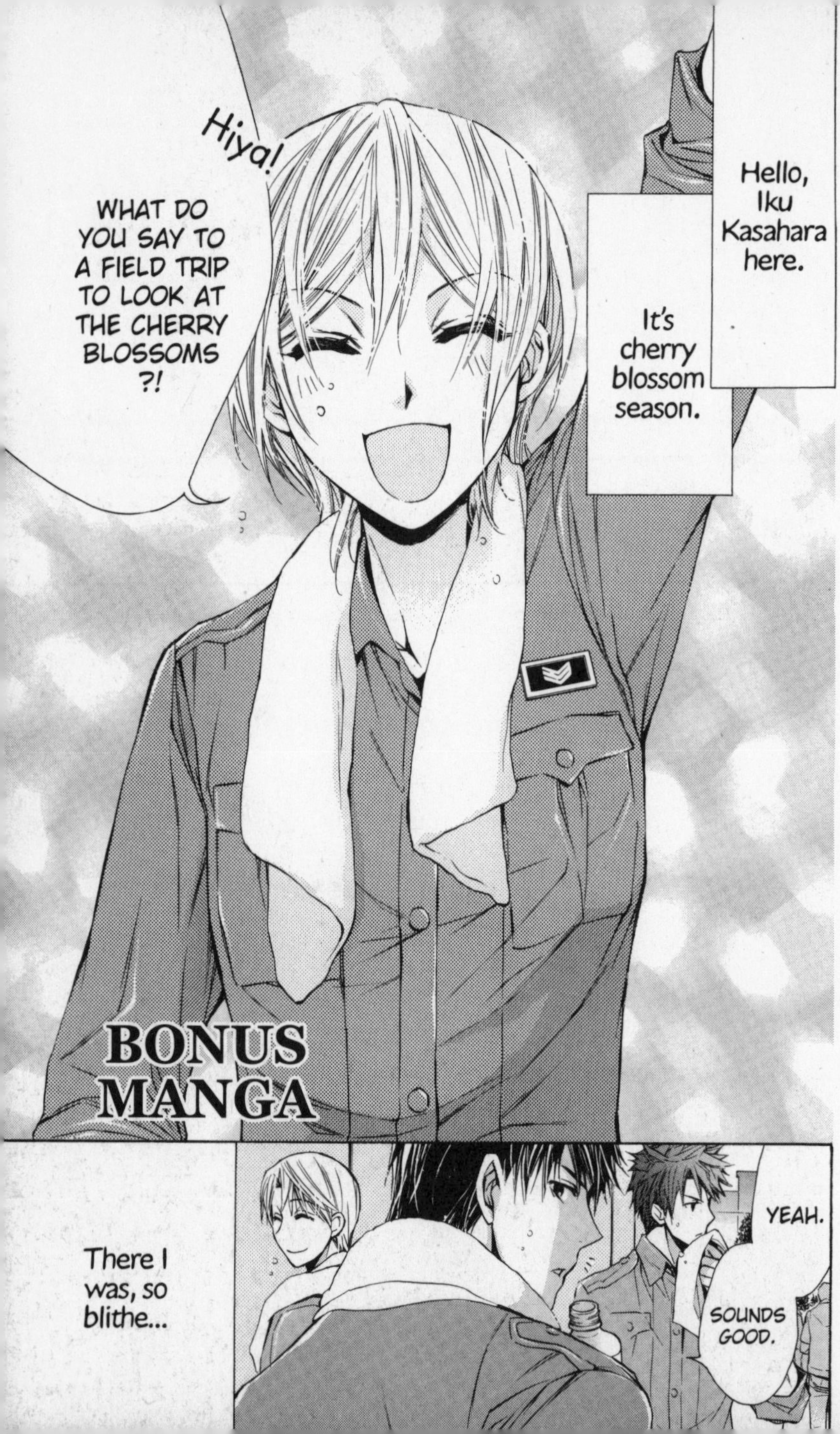
Hello, Iku Kasahara here.
It's cherry blossom season.
Hiya!
WHAT DO YOU SAY TO A FIELD TRIP TO LOOK AT THE CHERRY BLOSSOMS ?!
BONUS MANGA
YEAH.
SOUNDS GOOD.
There I was, so blithe...

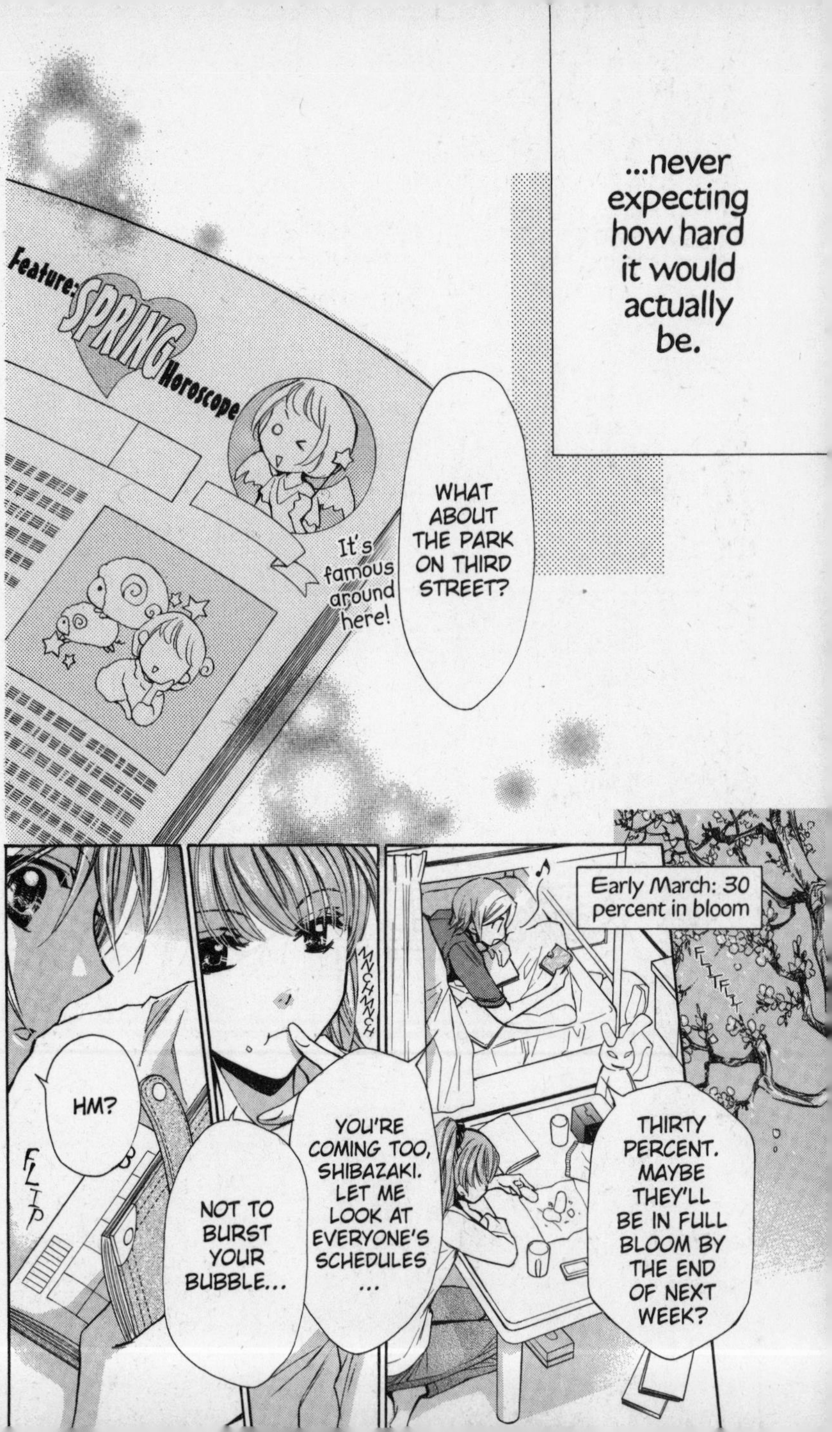
...never expecting how hard it would actually be.
WHAT ABOUT THE PARK ON THIRD STREET?
It's famous around here!
Feature: SPRING Horoscope
Early March: 30 percent in bloom
FLUTTER FLUTTER
THIRTY PERCENT. MAYBE THEY'LL BE IN FULL BLOOM BY THE END OF NEXT WEEK?
MNCHMNCH
YOU'RE COMING TOO, SHIBAZAKI. LET ME LOOK AT EVERYONE'S SCHEDULES...
NOT TO BURST YOUR BUBBLE...
HM?
FLIP

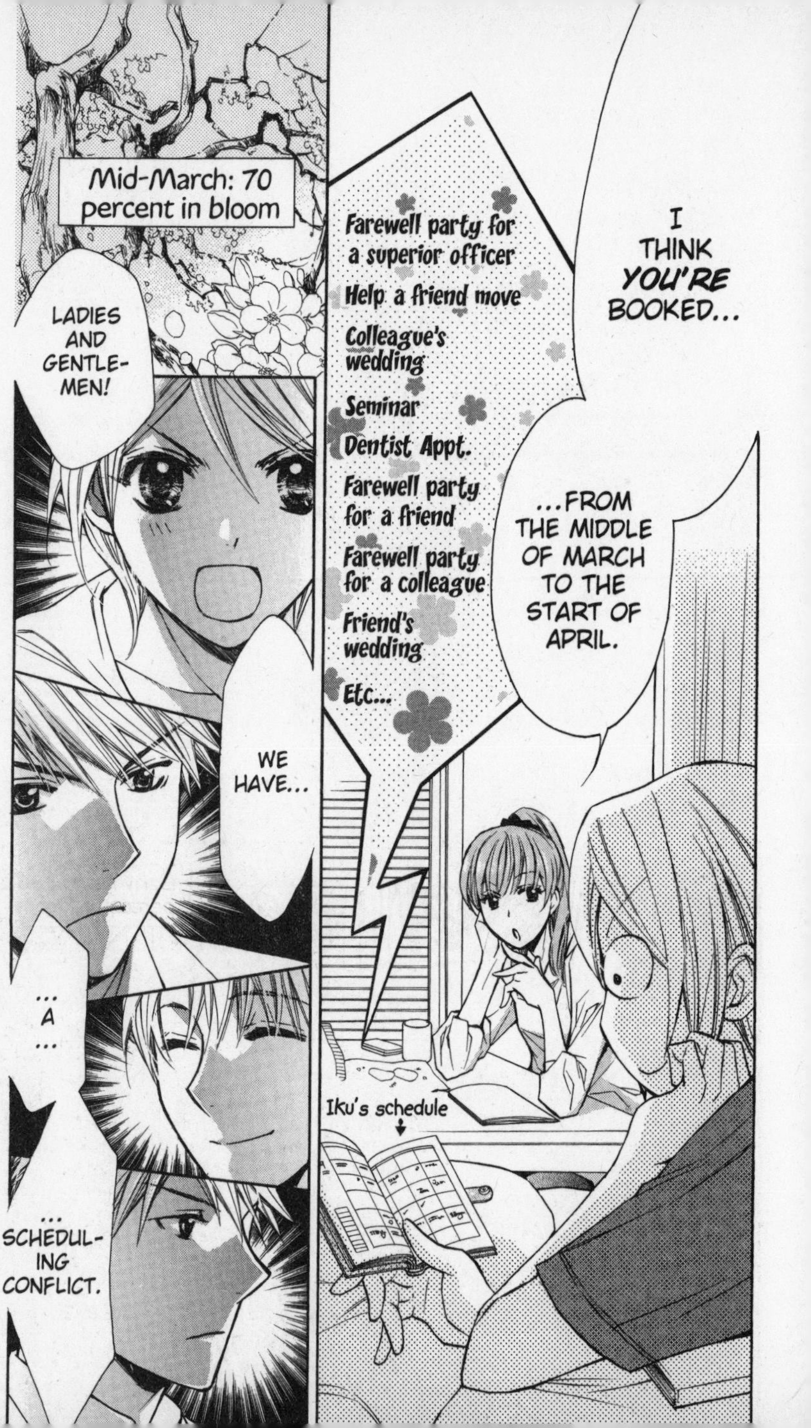
I THINK *YOU'RE* BOOKED...
Farewell party for a superior officer
Help a friend move
Colleague's wedding
Seminar
Dentist Appt.
Farewell party for a friend
Farewell party for a colleague
Friend's wedding
Etc...
...FROM THE MIDDLE OF MARCH TO THE START OF APRIL.
Iku's schedule
Mid-March: 70 percent in bloom
LADIES AND GENTLE-MEN!
WE HAVE...
...A...
...SCHEDUL-ING CONFLICT.

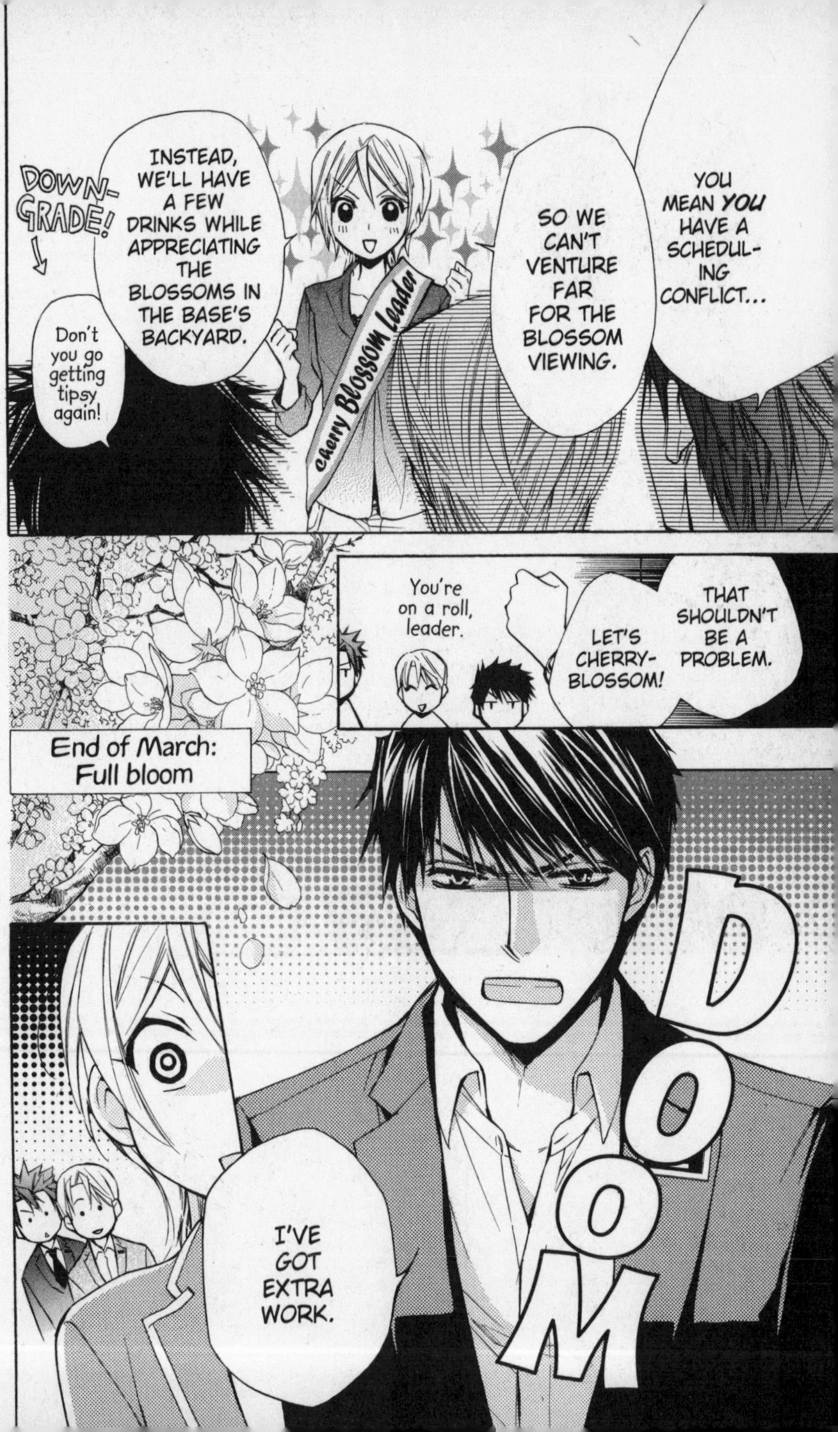
YOU MEAN YOU HAVE A SCHEDUL-ING CONFLICT...
SO WE CAN'T VENTURE FAR FOR THE BLOSSOM VIEWING.
INSTEAD, WE'LL HAVE A FEW DRINKS WHILE APPRECIATING THE BLOSSOMS IN THE BASE'S BACKYARD.
Cherry Blossom Leader
DOWN-GRADE!
Don't you go getting tipsy again!
THAT SHOULDN'T BE A PROBLEM.
LET'S CHERRY-BLOSSOM!
You're on a roll, leader.
End of March: Full bloom
DOOOM
I'VE GOT EXTRA WORK.

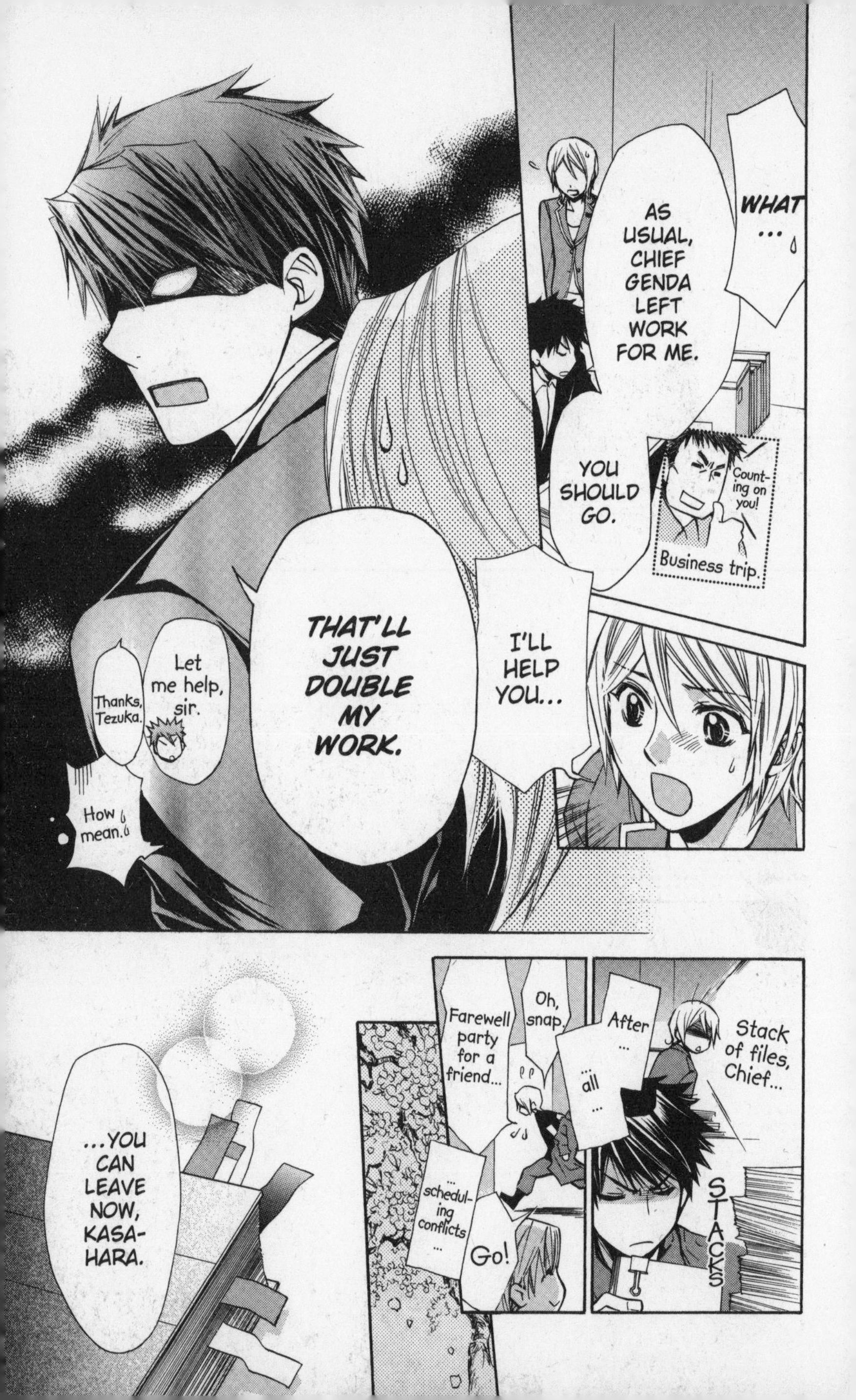
WHAT ...
AS USUAL, CHIEF GENDA LEFT WORK FOR ME.
Counting on you!
Business trip.
YOU SHOULD GO.
I'LL HELP YOU...
THAT'LL JUST DOUBLE MY WORK.
Let me help, sir.
Thanks, Tezuka.
How mean.
Stack of files, Chief...
STACKS
After ...
... all ...
Oh, snap.
Farewell party for a friend...
... scheduling conflicts ...
Go!
...YOU CAN LEAVE NOW, KASAHARA.

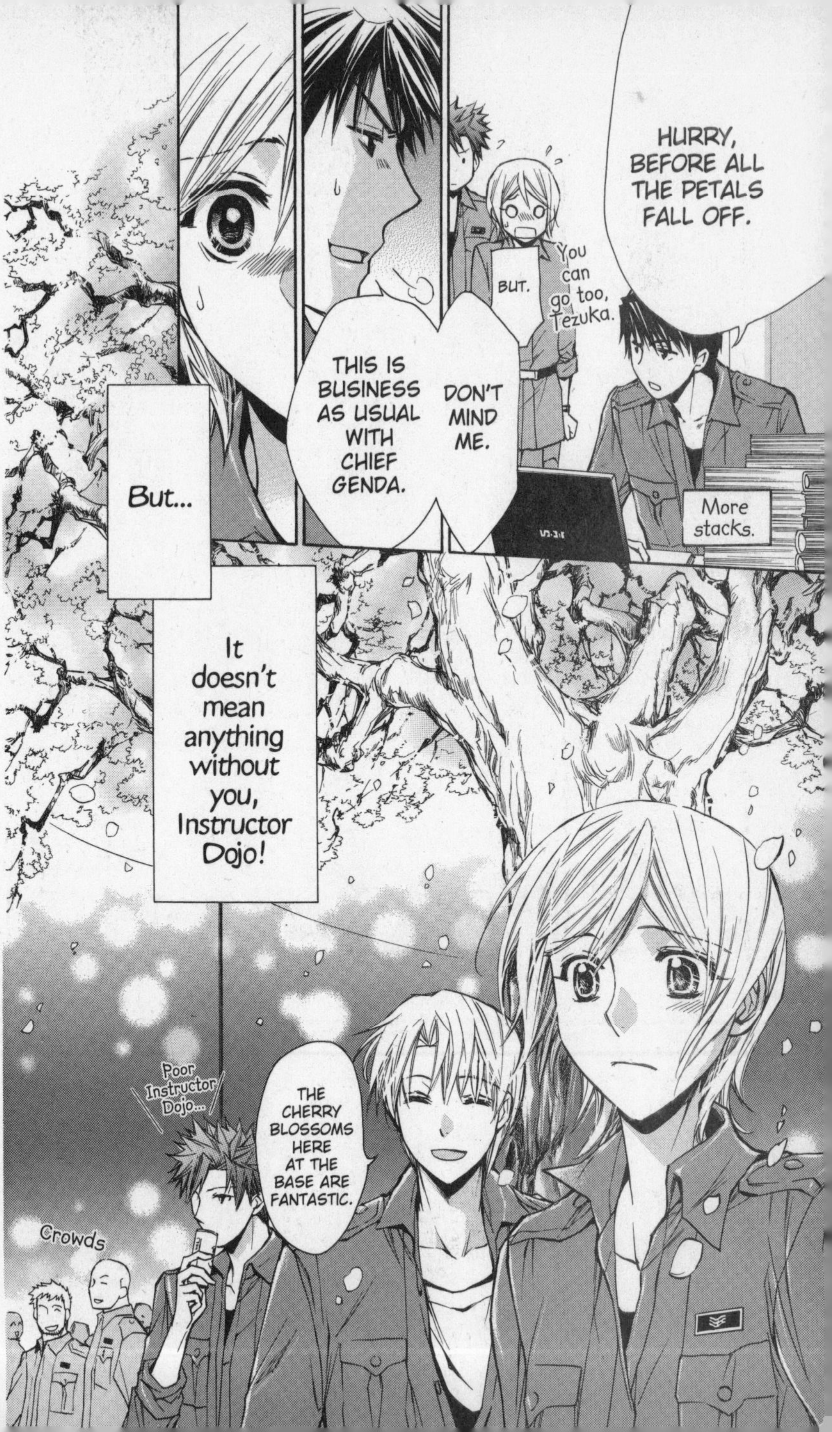
HURRY, BEFORE ALL THE PETALS FALL OFF.
More stacks.
You can go too, Tezuka.
BUT.
DON'T MIND ME.
THIS IS BUSINESS AS USUAL WITH CHIEF GENDA.
But...
It doesn't mean anything without you, Instructor Dojo!
THE CHERRY BLOSSOMS HERE AT THE BASE ARE FANTASTIC.
Poor Instructor Dojo...
Crowds

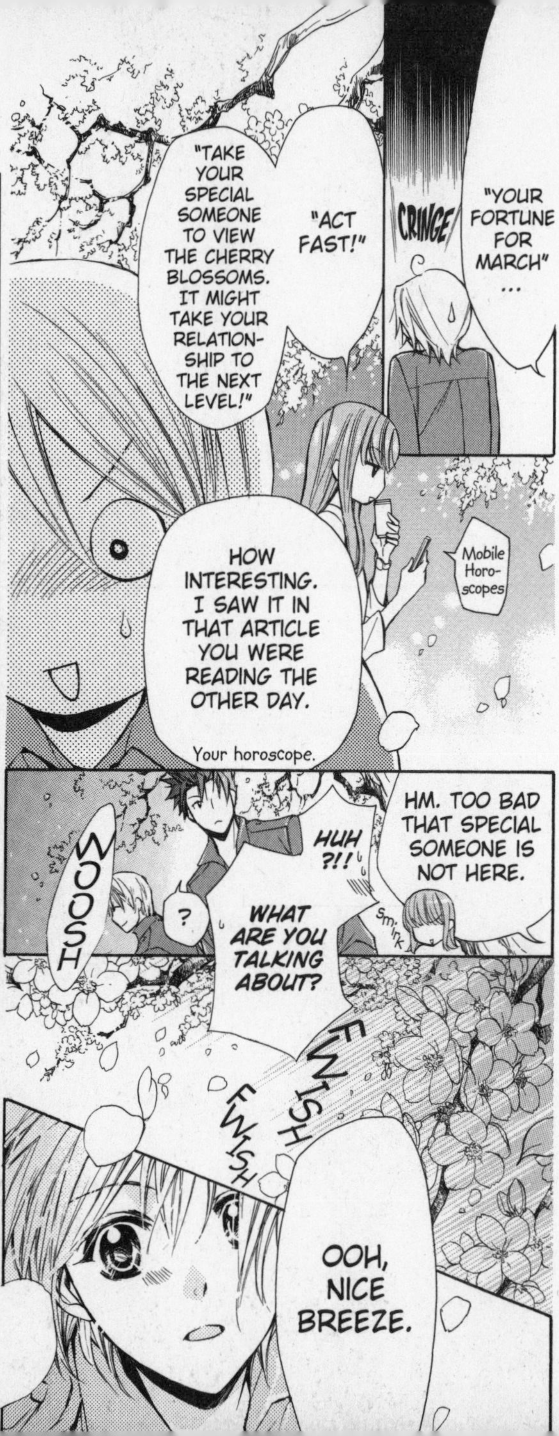
"YOUR FORTUNE FOR MARCH" ...
CRINGE
"TAKE YOUR SPECIAL SOMEONE TO VIEW THE CHERRY BLOSSOMS. IT MIGHT TAKE YOUR RELATIONSHIP TO THE NEXT LEVEL!"
"ACT FAST!"
Mobile Horoscopes
HOW INTERESTING. I SAW IT IN THAT ARTICLE YOU WERE READING THE OTHER DAY.
Your horoscope.
HM. TOO BAD THAT SPECIAL SOMEONE IS NOT HERE.
Smirk
HUH ?!!
WHAT ARE YOU TALKING ABOUT?
?
WOOSH
FWISH
FWISH
OOH, NICE BREEZE.

6

*

This is the final sidebar. Thank you so much for reading this volume! A lot of things happen in this book and it was an exciting experience. I love my work, Sir...!

I still have a lot to learn, but I really appreciate your support. Bye-bye!

Special thanks are at the end of the book.

Kiiro Yumi

*

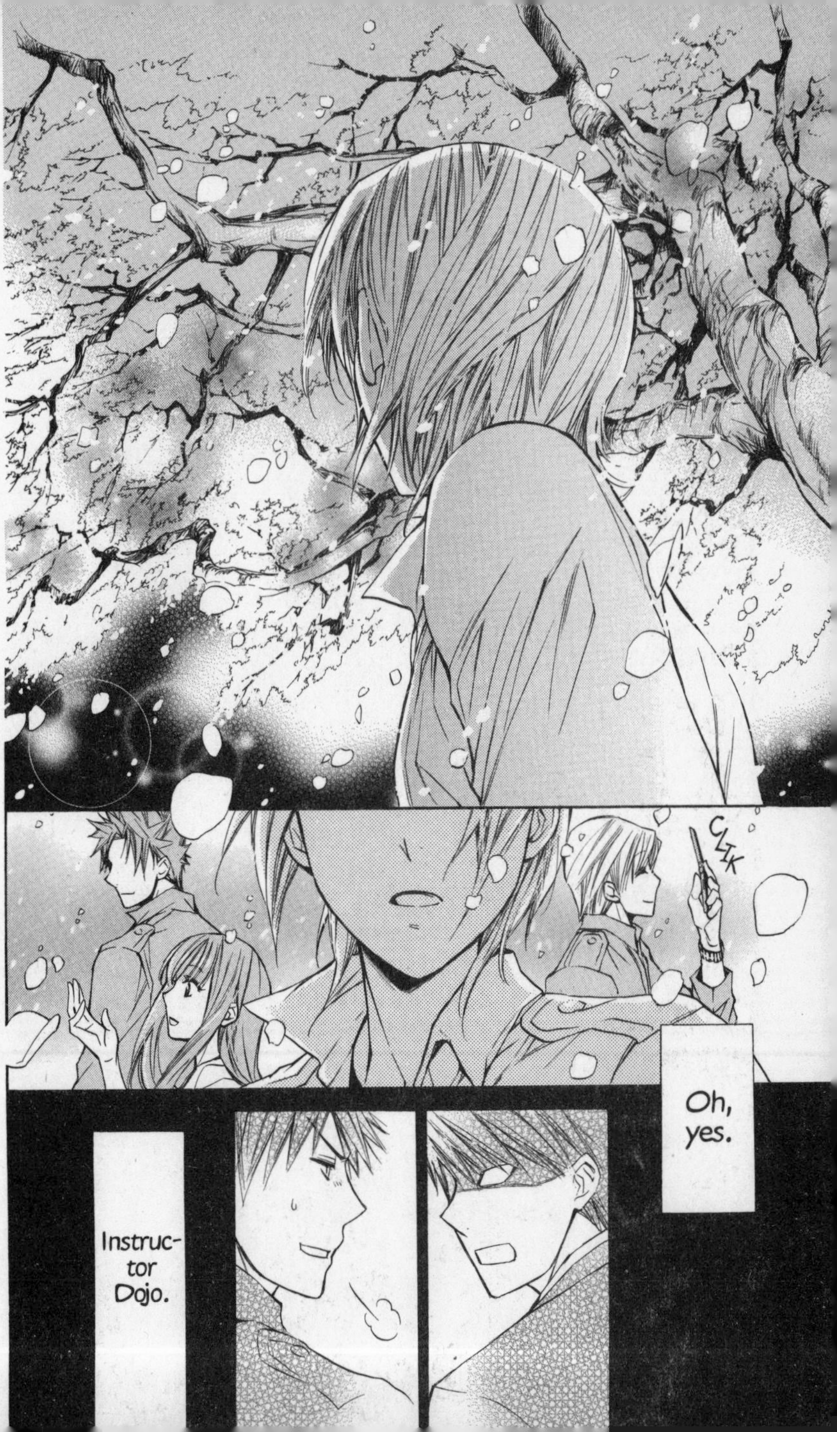
CLIK
Oh, yes.
Instructor Dojo.

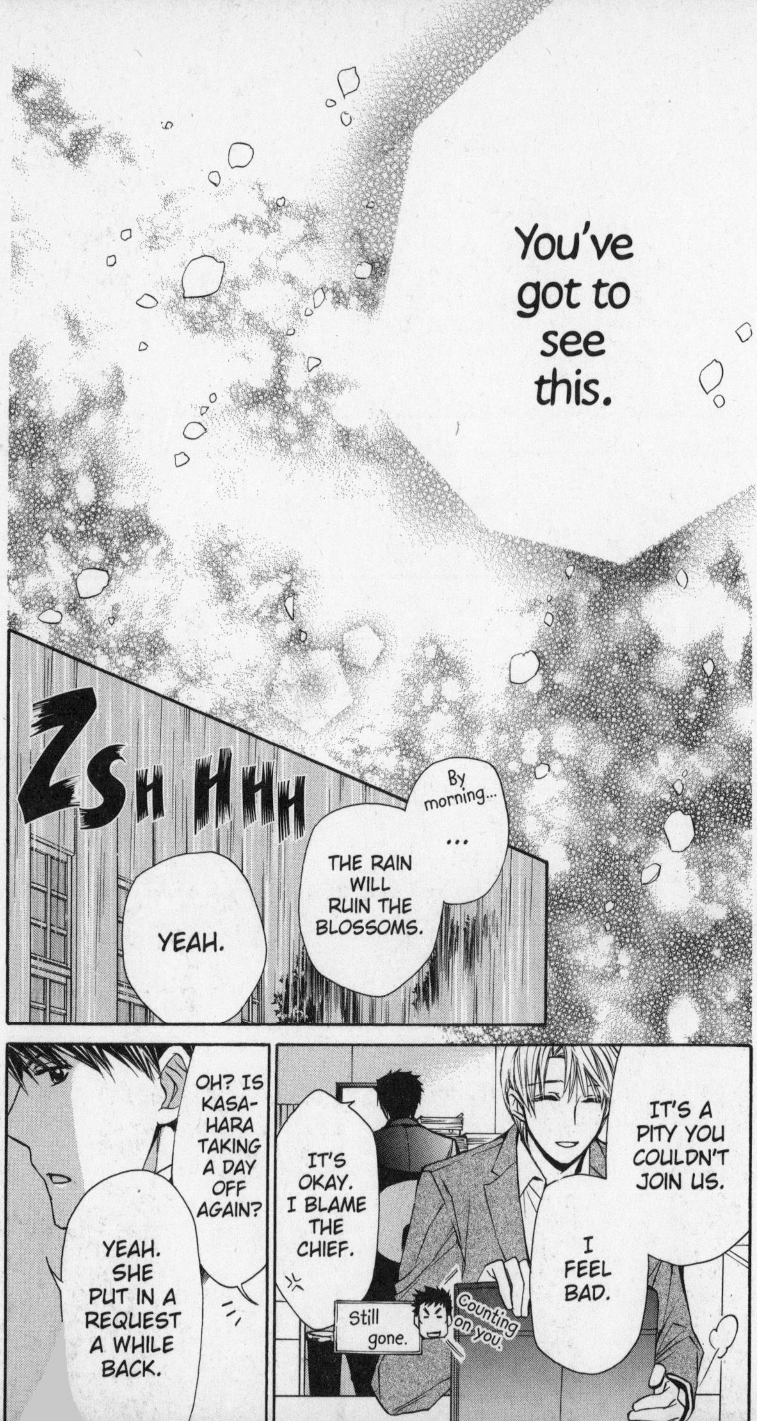
You've got to see this.
By morning...
...
THE RAIN WILL RUIN THE BLOSSOMS.
YEAH.
ZSHHHH
IT'S A PITY YOU COULDN'T JOIN US.
I FEEL BAD.
IT'S OKAY. I BLAME THE CHIEF.
Counting on you.
Still gone.
OH? IS KASA-HARA TAKING A DAY OFF AGAIN?
YEAH. SHE PUT IN A REQUEST A WHILE BACK.

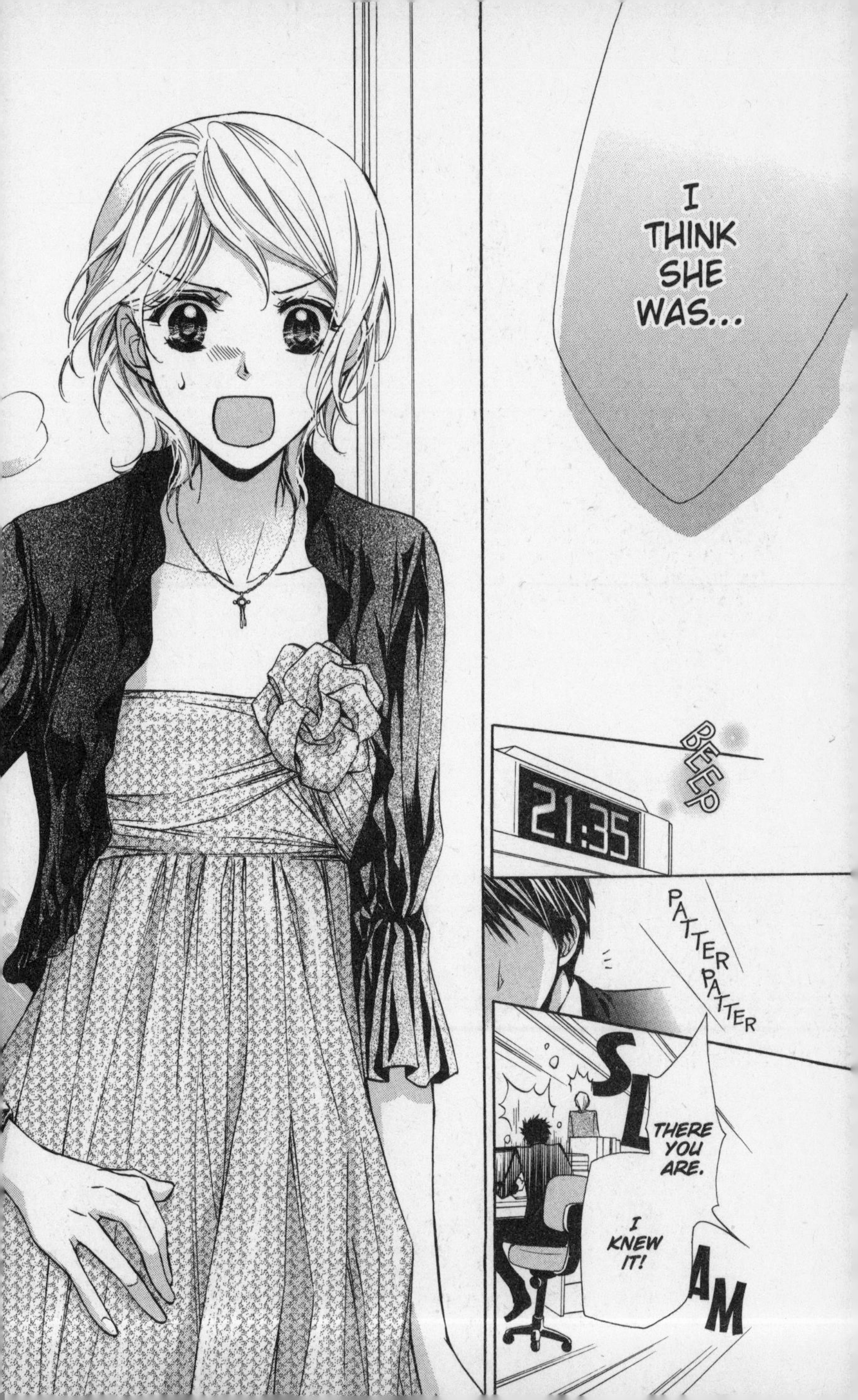
I THINK SHE WAS...
BEEP
21:35
PATTER PATTER
SLAM
THERE YOU ARE.
I KNEW IT!

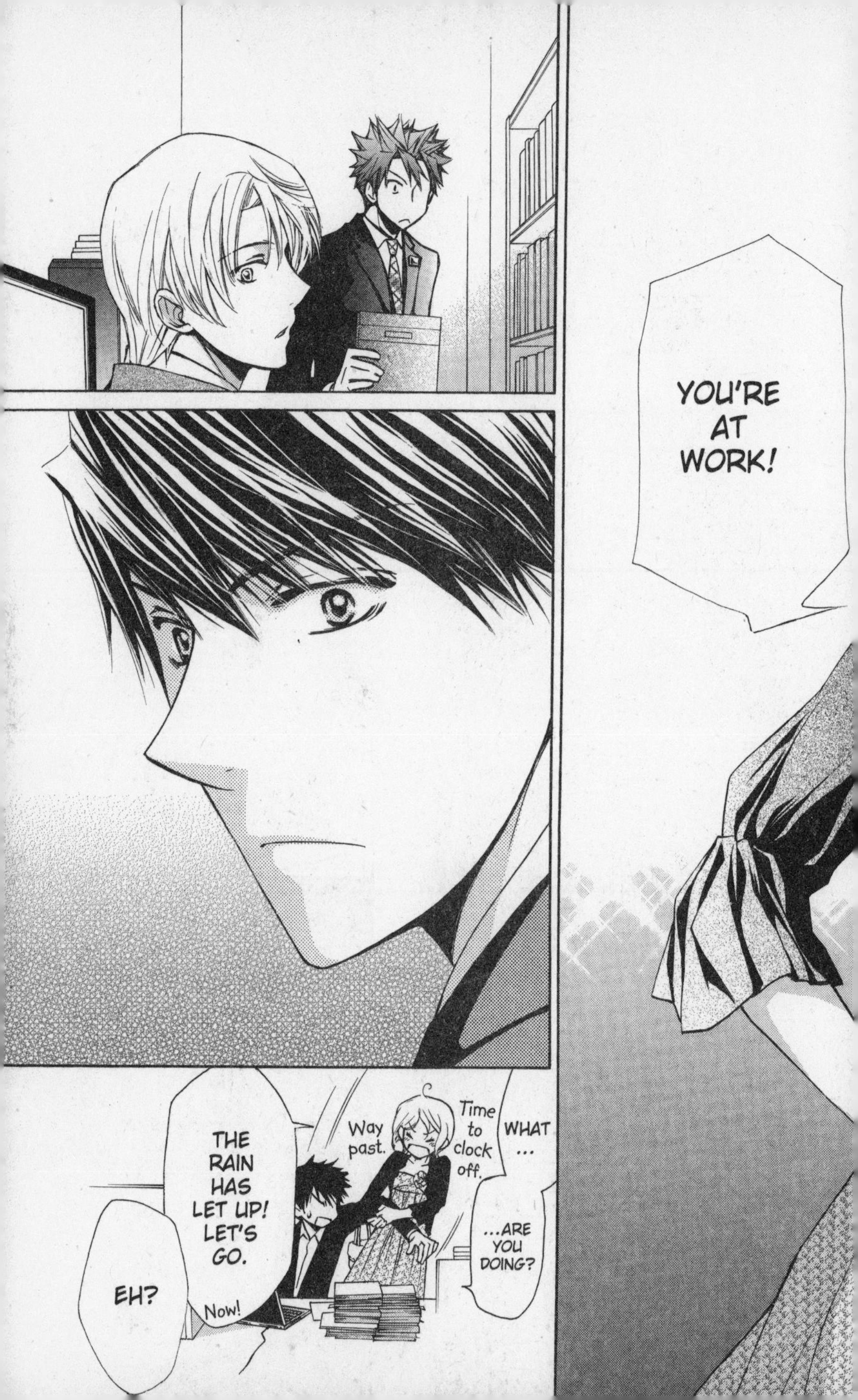
YOU'RE AT WORK!
WHAT ...
...ARE YOU DOING?
Time to clock off.
Way past.
THE RAIN HAS LET UP! LET'S GO.
Now!
EH?

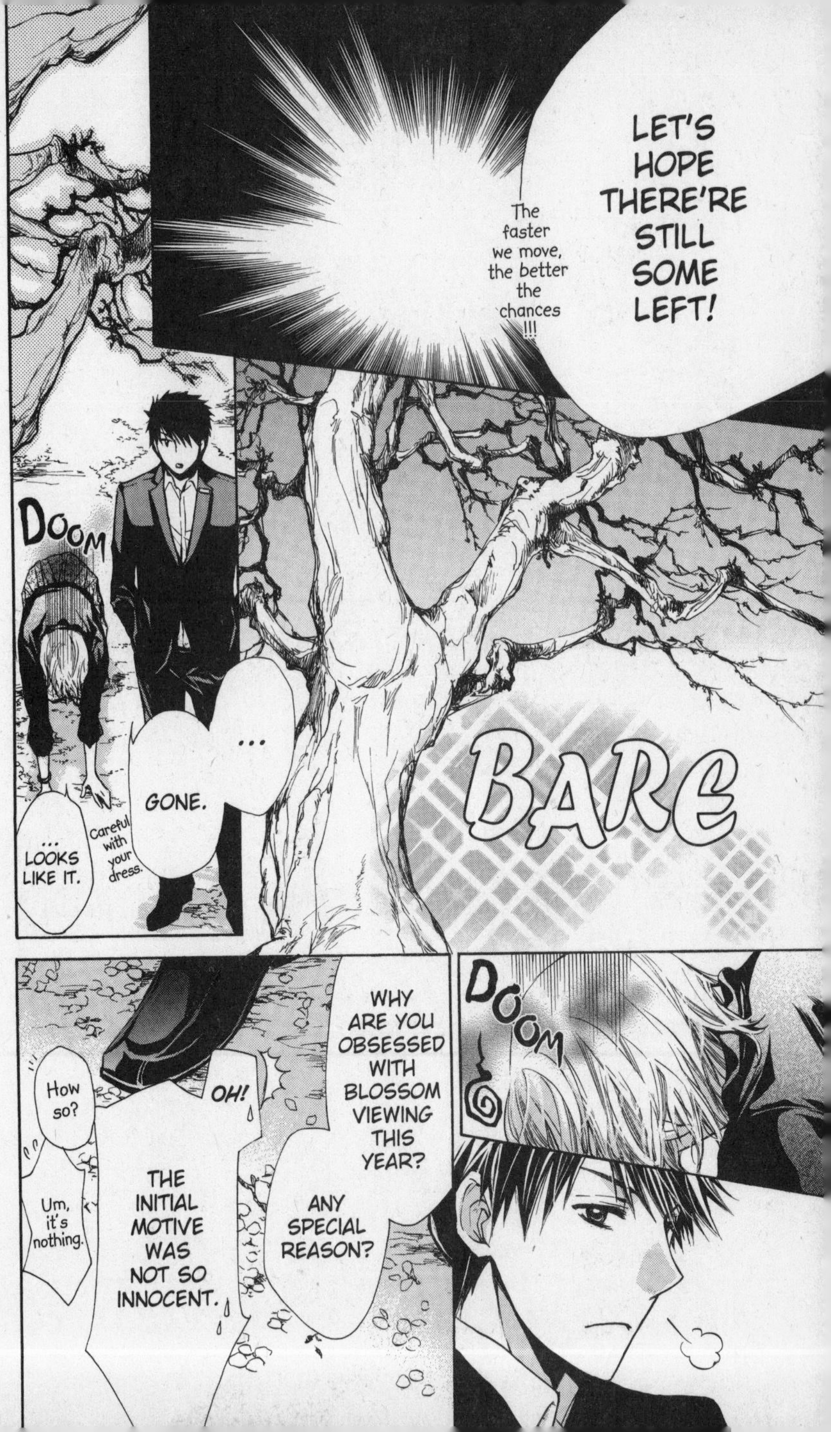
LET'S HOPE THERE'RE STILL SOME LEFT!
The faster we move, the better the chances!!!
BARE
...
GONE.
DOOM
Careful with your dress.
... LOOKS LIKE IT.
DOOM
WHY ARE YOU OBSESSED WITH BLOSSOM VIEWING THIS YEAR?
ANY SPECIAL REASON?
OH!
THE INITIAL MOTIVE WAS NOT SO INNOCENT.
How so?
Um, it's nothing.

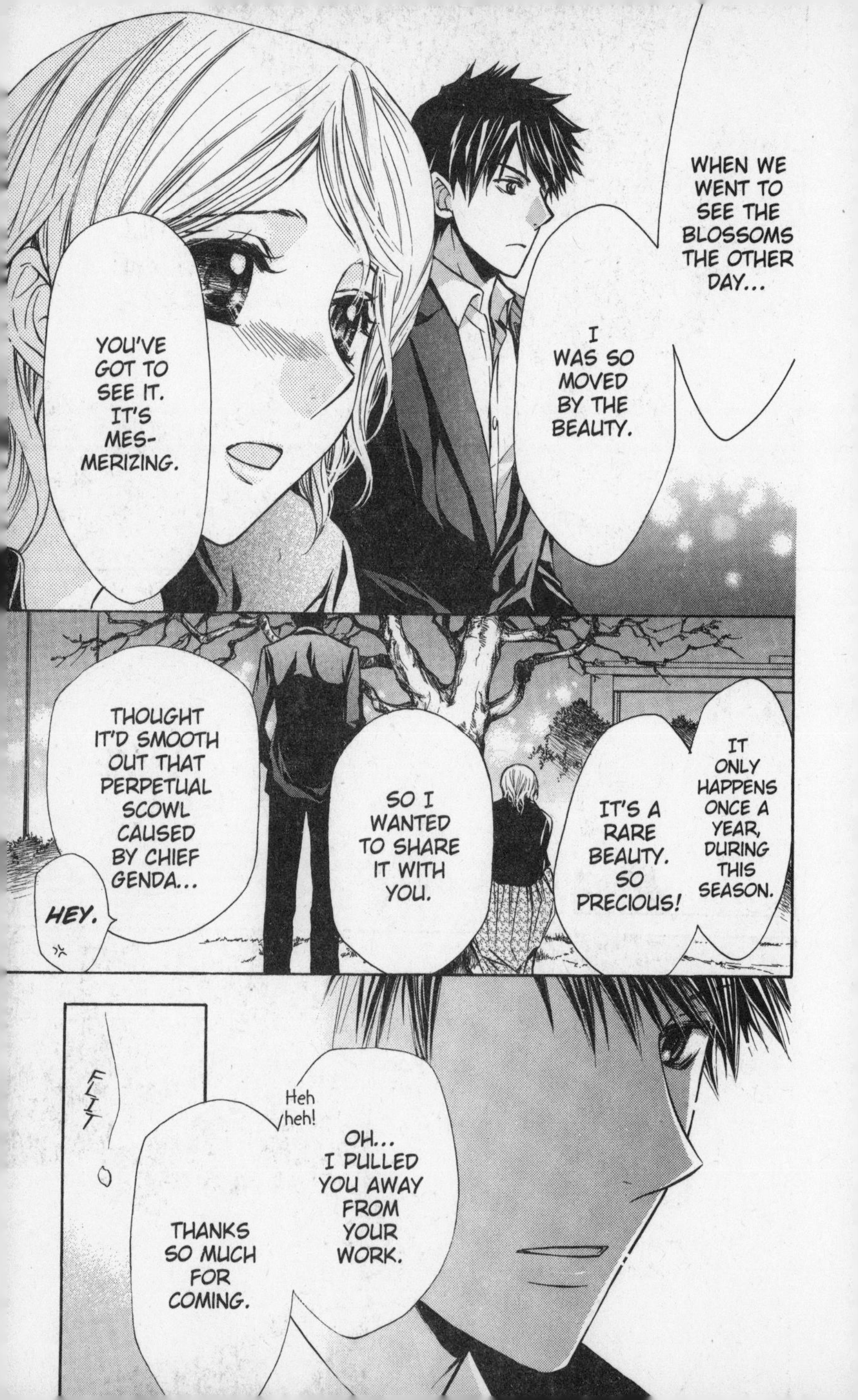
WHEN WE WENT TO SEE THE BLOSSOMS THE OTHER DAY...
I WAS SO MOVED BY THE BEAUTY.
YOU'VE GOT TO SEE IT. IT'S MES-MERIZING.
IT ONLY HAPPENS ONCE A YEAR, DURING THIS SEASON.
IT'S A RARE BEAUTY. SO PRECIOUS!
SO I WANTED TO SHARE IT WITH YOU.
THOUGHT IT'D SMOOTH OUT THAT PERPETUAL SCOWL CAUSED BY CHIEF GENDA...
HEY.
OH... I PULLED YOU AWAY FROM YOUR WORK.
Heh heh!
THANKS SO MUCH FOR COMING.
FLIT

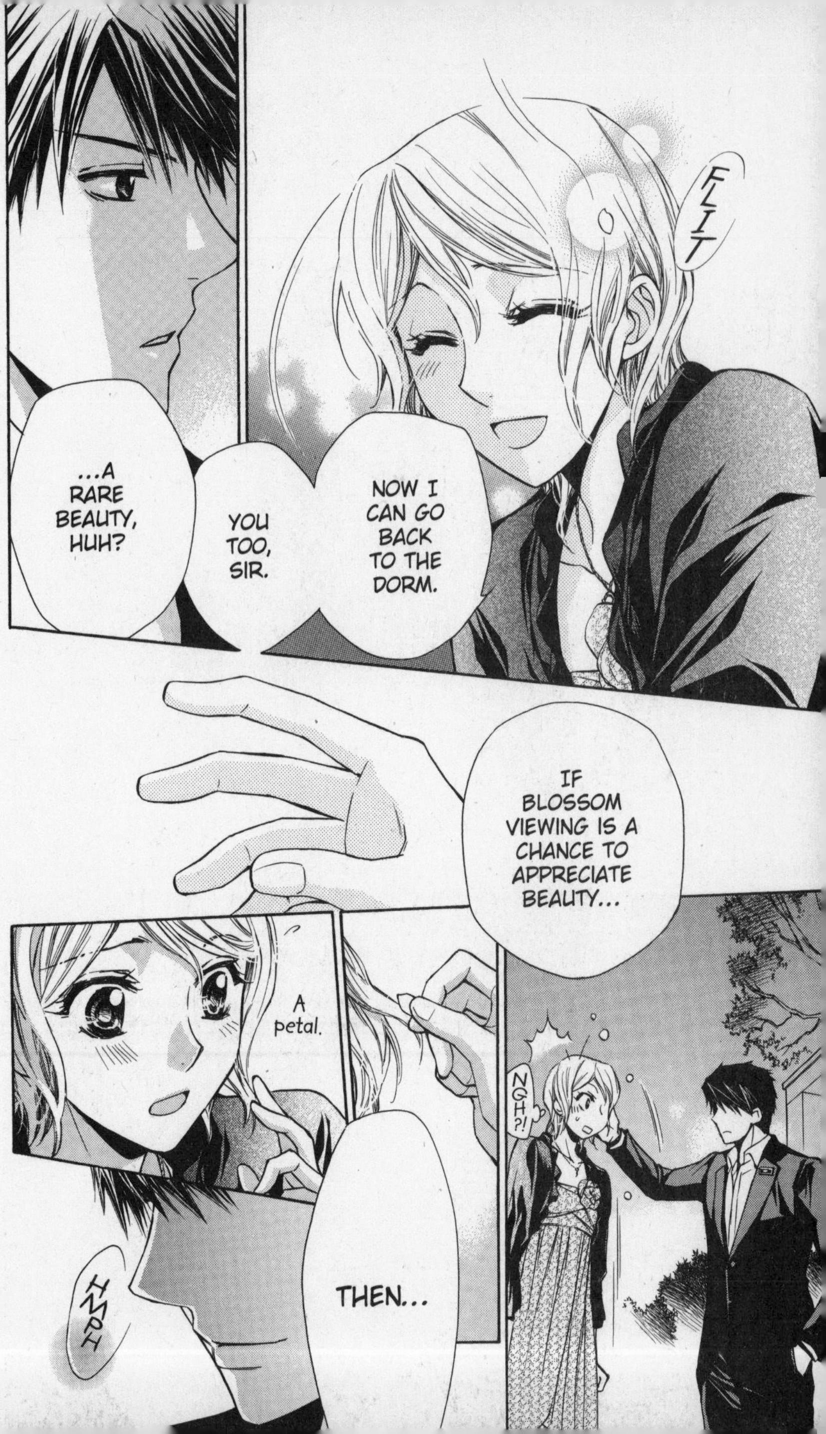
FLIT
NOW I CAN GO BACK TO THE DORM.
YOU TOO, SIR.
...A RARE BEAUTY, HUH?
IF BLOSSOM VIEWING IS A CHANCE TO APPRECIATE BEAUTY...
NGH?!
THEN...
A petal.
HMPH

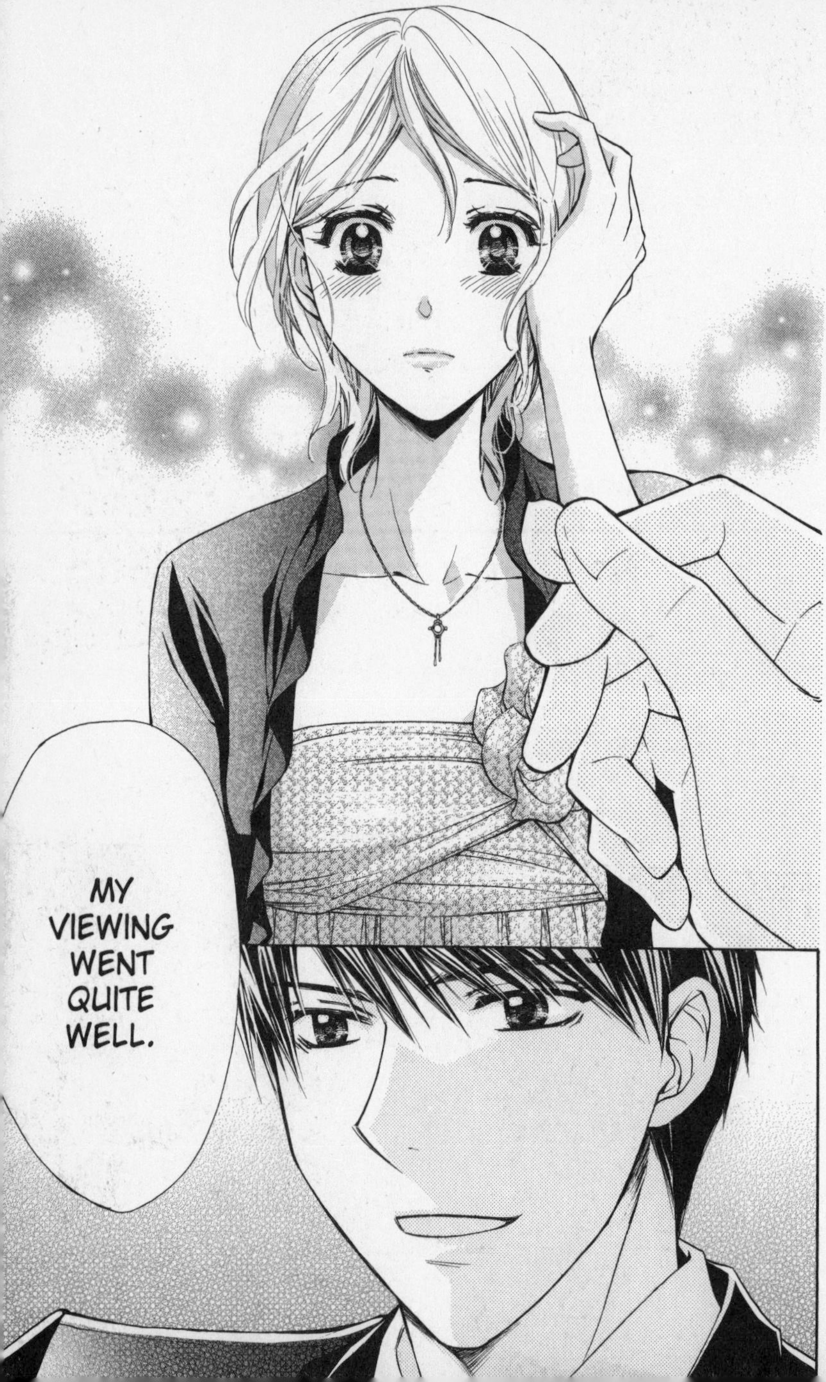
MY VIEWING WENT QUITE WELL.

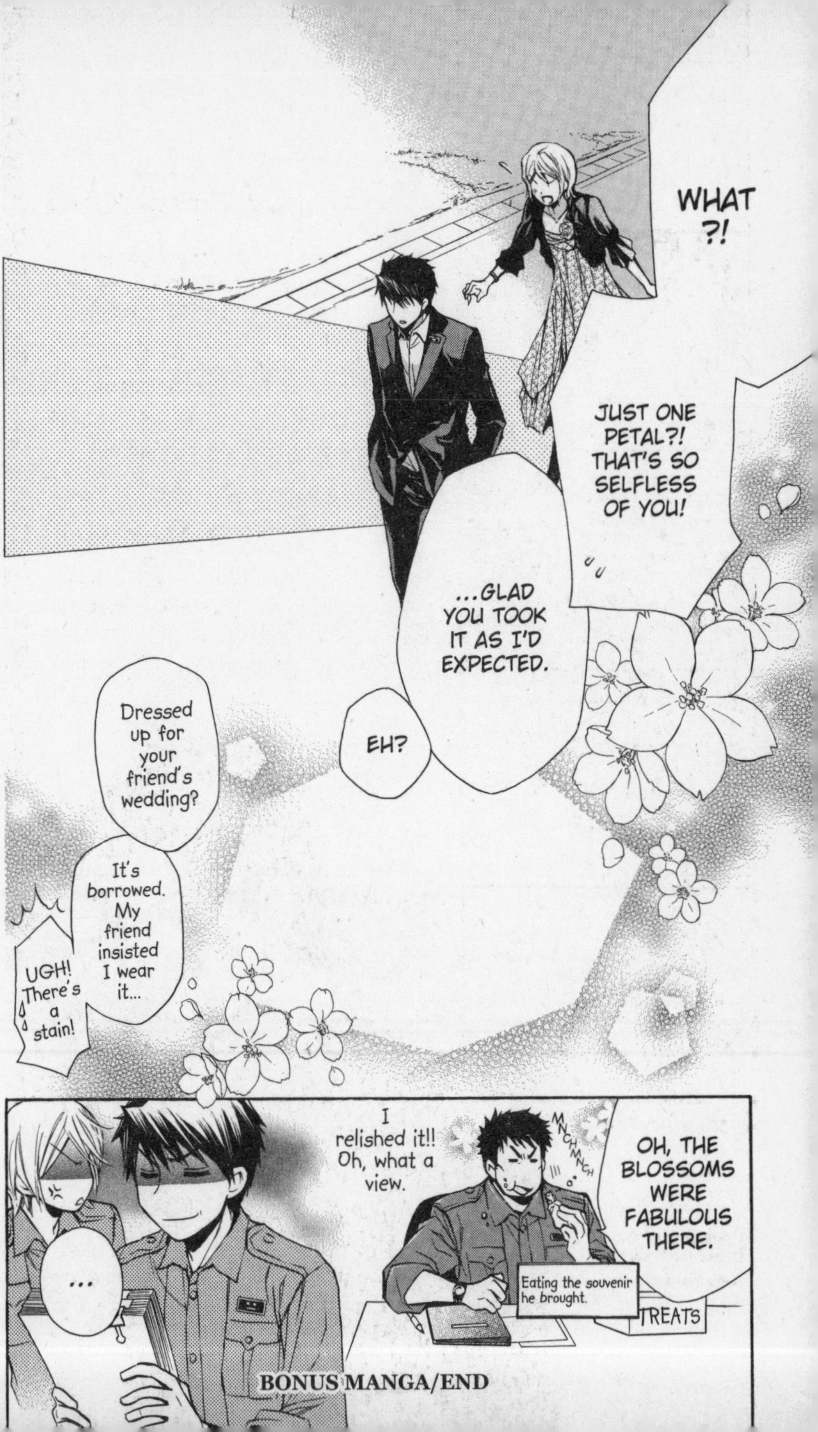
WHAT ?!
JUST ONE PETAL?! THAT'S SO SELFLESS OF YOU!
...GLAD YOU TOOK IT AS I'D EXPECTED.
EH?
Dressed up for your friend's wedding?
It's borrowed. My friend insisted I wear it...
UGH! There's a stain!
OH, THE BLOSSOMS WERE FABULOUS THERE.
MNCH MNCH
Eating the souvenir he brought.
TREATS
I relished it!! Oh, what a view.
...
BONUS MANGA/END

Special Thanks!!

Ms. Arikawa
Ms. Arikawa's editor
(ASCII Media)

★

Mamada, Murakami, Aoki

★

My family

★

My editor, My former editor

★

Everyone who makes
this series possible

★★

Thanks so, so much!

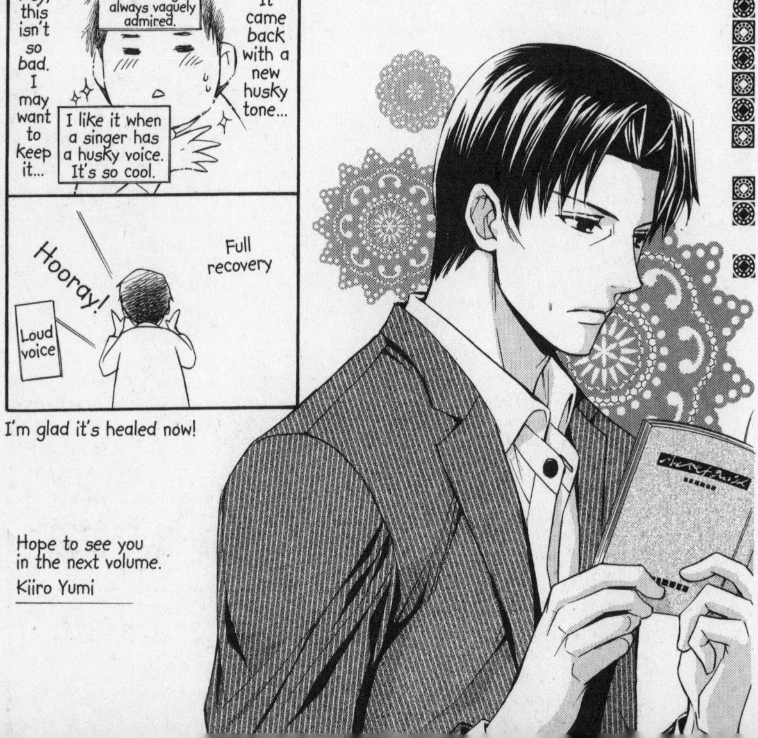

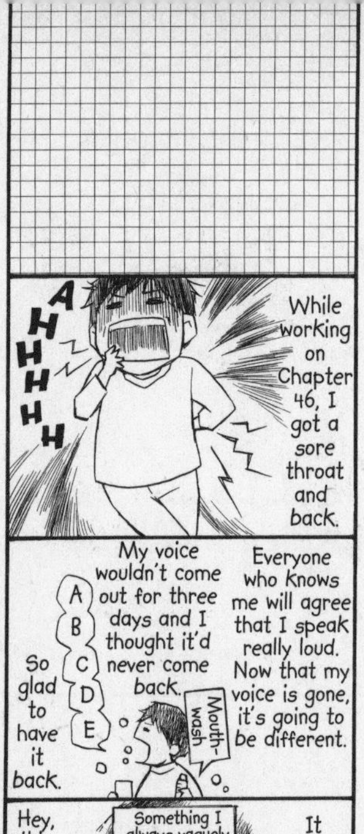
While working on Chapter 46, I got a sore throat and back.
AHHHHHH
Everyone who knows me will agree that I speak really loud. Now that my voice is gone, it's going to be different.
My voice wouldn't come out for three days and I thought it'd never come back.
A B C D E
Mouth-wash
So glad to have it back.
It came back with a new husky tone...
Something I always vaguely admired.
I like it when a singer has a husky voice. It's so cool.
Hey, this isn't so bad. I may want to keep it...
Full recovery
Hooray!
Loud voice

I'm glad it's healed now!

Hope to see you
in the next volume.
Kiiro Yumi

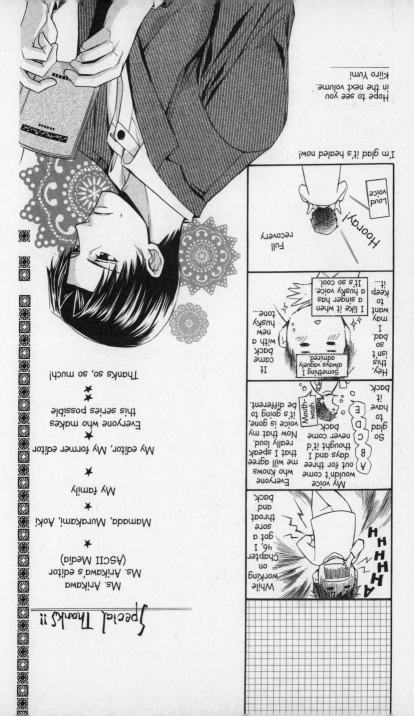

Kiiro Yumi won the 42nd *LaLa* Manga Grand Prix Fresh Debut award for her manga *Billy Bocchan no Yuutsu* (Little Billy's Depression). Her latest series is *Toshokan Senso Love&War* (*Library Wars: Love & War*), which runs in *LaLa* magazine in Japan and is published in English by VIZ Media.

Hiro Arikawa won the 10th Dengeki Novel Prize for her work *Shio no Machi: Wish on My Precious* in 2003 and debuted with the same novel in 2004. Of her many works, Arikawa is best known for the *Library Wars* series and her *Jieitai Sanbusaku* trilogy, which consists of *Sora no Naka* (In the Sky), *Umi no Soko* (The Bottom of the Sea) and *Shio no Machi* (City of Salt).

library wars

Volume 10
Shojo Beat Edition

Story & Art by *Kiiro Yumi*
Original Concept by *Hiro Arikawa*

ENGLISH TRANSLATION Kinami Watabe
LETTERING Annaliese Christman
DESIGN Amy Martin
EDITOR Megan Bates

Toshokan Sensou LOVE&WAR by Kiiro Yumi and Hiro Arikawa
© Kiiro Yumi 2012
© Hiro Arikawa 2012
All rights reserved.
First published in Japan in 2012 by HAKUSENSHA, Inc., Tokyo.
English language translation rights arranged with HAKUSENSHA,
Inc., Tokyo.

Printed in Canada

Published by VIZ Media, LLC
P.O. Box 77010
San Francisco, CA 94107

10 9 8 7 6 5 4 3 2 1
First printing, August 2013

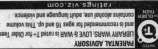

www.shojobeat.com
www.viz.com

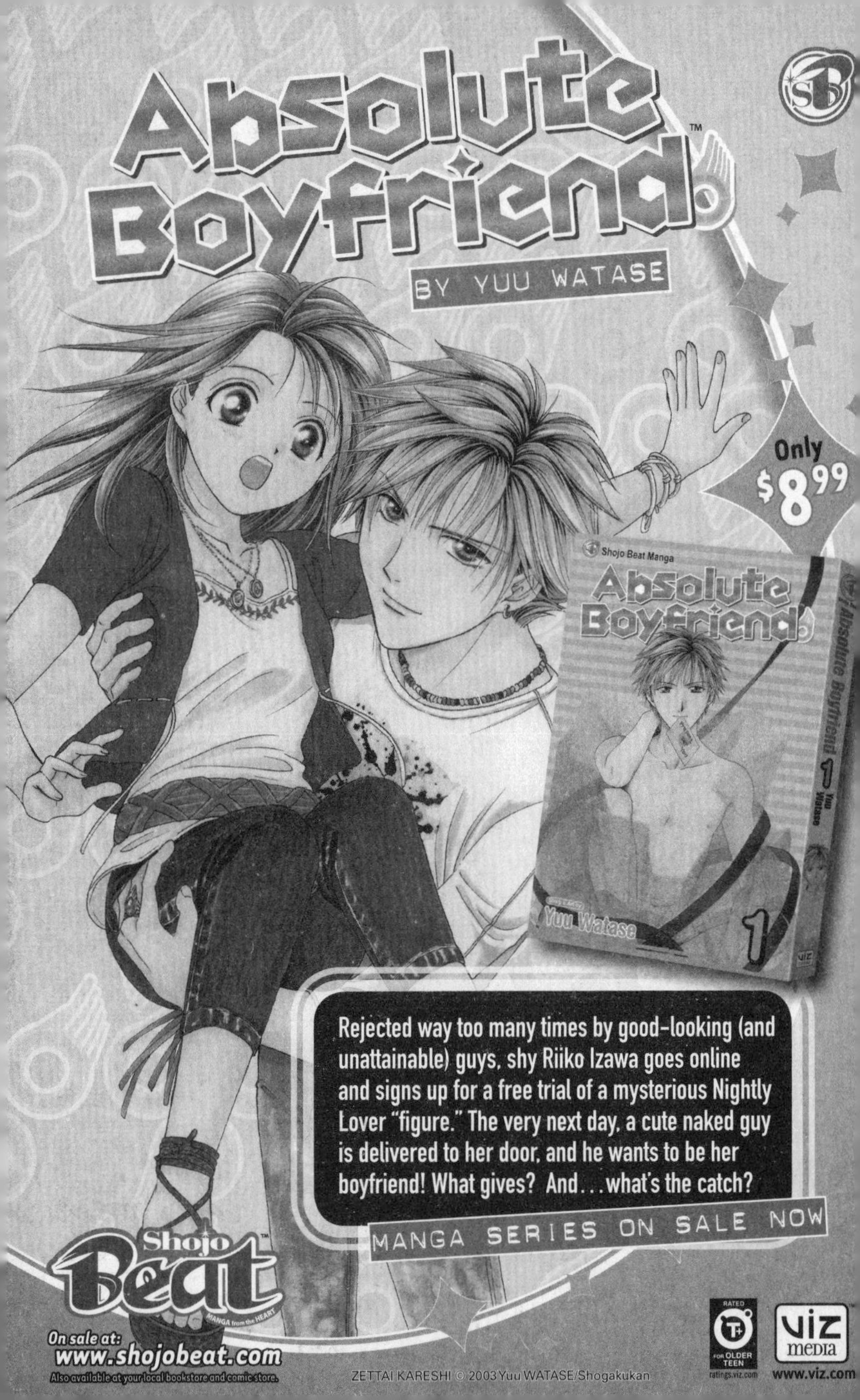
Absolute Boyfriend™
BY YUU WATASE
Only $8.99
Shojo Beat Manga
Absolute Boyfriend
Yuu Watase
1
Rejected way too many times by good-looking (and unattainable) guys, shy Riiko Izawa goes online and signs up for a free trial of a mysterious Nightly Lover "figure." The very next day, a cute naked guy is delivered to her door, and he wants to be her boyfriend! What gives? And...what's the catch?
MANGA SERIES ON SALE NOW
Shojo Beat™
MANGA from the HEART
On sale at:
www.shojobeat.com
Also available at your local bookstore and comic store.
ZETTAI KARESHI © 2003 Yuu WATASE/Shogakukan
RATED T+ FOR OLDER TEEN
ratings.viz.com
VIZ media
www.viz.com

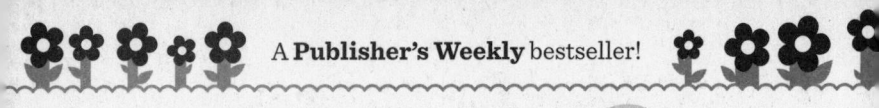